Amoureux and Steele have put together a superb collection of essays which simultaneously exhibits the coherence of a single thematic and great originality in the individual contributions. Reflections by academics confronting their own scholarship creates an honest, insightful, and arresting book. This volume provides anyone interested in the craft of good IR scholarship with an essential starting point.

Professor Anthony F. Lang, Jr, *University of St Andrews, UK*

This is an exciting book that should provoke, disturb, stimulate and resonate with scholars' thoughts and experiences in writing international relations. In thoroughly dissecting both the most obvious and the most intimate aspects of reflexivity, the authors reveal the roughness as well as the eloquence that can emanate from our attempts to grasp the meaning of our selves and our scholarship.

Professor Cecelia Lynch, *University of California, Irvine, USA*

Reflexivity and International Relations

Reflexivity has become a common term in international relations (IR) scholarship with a variety of uses and meanings. Yet, for such an important concept and referent, understandings of reflexivity have been more assumed than developed by those who use it, from realists and constructivists to feminists and post-structuralists.

This volume seeks to provide the first overview of reflexivity in international relations theory, offering students and scholars a text that:

- provides a comprehensive and systematic overview of the current reflexivity literature;
- develops important insights into how reflexivity can play a broader role in IR theory;
- pushes reflexivity in new, productive directions, and offers more nuanced and concrete specifications of reflexivity;
- moves reflexivity beyond the scholar and the scholarly field to political practice;
- formulates practices of reflexivity.

Drawing together the work of many of the key scholars in the field into one volume, this work will be essential reading for all students of international relations theory.

Jack L. Amoureux is a Teacher-Scholar Postdoctoral Fellow at Wake Forest University in Winston-Salem, North Carolina, USA. He previously taught at the American University in Washington, DC, USA.

Brent J. Steele is Francis D. Wormuth Presidential Chair and Professor of Political Science at the University of Utah, USA.

New International Relations

Edited by Richard Little, University of Bristol, Iver B. Neumann, Norwegian Institute of International Affairs (NUPI), Norway and Jutta Weldes, University of Bristol.

The field of international relations has changed dramatically in recent years. This new series will cover the major issues that have emerged and reflect the latest academic thinking in this particular dynamic area.

International Law, Rights and Politics
Developments in Eastern Europe and the CIS
Rein Mullerson

The Logic of Internationalism
Coercion and accommodation
Kjell Goldmann

Russia and the Idea of Europe
A study in identity and international relations
Iver B. Neumann

The Future of International Relations
Masters in the making?
Edited by Iver B. Neumann and Ole Wæver

Constructing the World Polity
Essays on international institutionalization
John Gerard Ruggie

Realism in International Relations and International Political Economy
The continuing story of a death foretold
Stefano Guzzini

International Relations, Political Theory and the Problem of Order
Beyond international relations theory?
N.J.Rengger

War, Peace and World Orders in European History
Edited by Anja V. Hartmann and Beatrice Heuser

European Integration and National Identity
The challenge of the Nordic states
Edited by Lene Hansen and Ole Wæver

Shadow Globalization, Ethnic Conflicts and New Wars
A political economy of intra-state war
Dietrich Jung

Contemporary Security Analysis and Copenhagen Peace Research
Edited by Stefano Guzzini and Dietrich Jung

Observing International Relations
Niklas Luhmann and world politics
Edited by Mathias Albert and Lena Hilkermeier

Reflexivity and International Relations
Positionality, critique, and practice
Jack L. Amoureux and Brent J. Steele

A Practice of Ethics for Global Politics
Ethical reflexivity
Jack L. Amoureux

Reflexivity and International Relations

Positionality, critique, and practice

Edited by
Jack L. Amoureux and Brent J. Steele

Routledge
Taylor & Francis Group

LONDON AND NEW YORK

First published 2016
by Routledge
2 Park Square, Milton Park, Abingdon, Oxon OX14 4RN

and by Routledge
711 Third Avenue, New York, NY 10017

Routledge is an imprint of the Taylor & Francis Group, an informa business

British Library Cataloguing in Publication Data
A catalogue record for this book is available from the British Library

Library of Congress Cataloging in Publication Data
Reflexivity and international relations : positionality, critique, practice / edited by Jack L. Amoureux, Brent J. Steele.
    pages cm. – (New international relations)
  1. International relations–Philosophy. 2. International relations–Moral and ethical aspects. I. Amoureux, Jack L., editor.
    JZ1305.R453 2015
    327.101–dc23
              2015014036

ISBN: 978-1-138-78920-3 (hbk)
ISBN: 978-1-315-76501-3 (ebk)

Typeset in Times New Roman
by Taylor & Francis Books

To Nick Onuf, Our Friend and Mentor

Contents

List of illustrations

Figure

Tables

List of contributors

Jack L. Amoureux is a Teacher-Scholar Postdoctoral Fellow at Wake Forest University in Winston-Salem, North Carolina, where he teaches classes in world politics and political theory. He previously taught at American University in Washington, DC. He is the author of *A Practice of Ethics for Global Politics: Ethical Reflexivity* (Routledge, 2015). His work has appeared in *Millennium* and *International Relations*. He is also Chair of the LGBTQA Caucus and a member of the Executive Committee for the International Studies Association. He received his PhD from Brown University and is from Boise, Idaho.

Huss Banai is an Assistant Professor in the Department of International Studies at the School of Global and International Studies, Indiana University and a research affiliate at the Center for International Studies at Massachusetts Institute of Technology. He is the co-author of *Becoming Enemies: US-Iran Relations and the Iran-Iraq War, 1979–1988* (Rowman & Littlefield, 2012), and has published widely on topics in diplomatic theory and practice, democratic theory, and US–Iran relations.

Ilan Zvi Baron is a Lecturer in International Political Theory in the School of Government and International Affairs, and Co-Director of the Centre for the Study of Jewish Culture, Society and Politics at Durham University. His most recent book is *Obligation in Exile: The Jewish Diaspora, Israel and Critique* (Edinburgh University Press, 2014).

Amanda Beattie is a Lecturer at Aston University, Birmingham (UK). Her research intersects with both political theory and international political thought. It engages with the idea of human vulnerability and how various aspects of moral institutional design, both historical and contemporary, address this problem in the wider theater of international politics focusing specifically on the international mobility regime. She is the author of one manuscript and two edited volumes and publishes widely in peer-reviewed journals within the field.

Mark E. Button is Associate Professor and Chair in the Department of Political Science at the University of Utah. His primary field of research is political theory, focusing on the history of political thought, ethics, and deliberative democracy. He is the author of *Contract, Culture, and Citizenship: Transformative Liberalism from Hobbes to Rawls* (Penn State University Press, 2008). His latest book, *Political Vices*, is forthcoming with Oxford University Press. His articles have appeared in *Political Theory*; *Social Theory and Practice*; *Polity*; *Law, Culture, and the Humanities*; and *The Encyclopedia of Political Thought*.

Mauro J. Caraccioli is a Visiting Instructor of International Relations in the Department of Political Science at Saint Michael's College. He received his PhD from the University of Florida in 2015. His research focuses on the intersection of empire and nature, bringing the history of political thought into conversation with environmental political theory. Additionally, Mauro is interested in narratives of human cognition, political ecology in Latin America, and the historical boundaries of international theory.

Elizabeth Dauphinee is Associate Professor in the Department of Political Science at York University in Toronto, where she teaches courses in international relations. She is interested in ethics and in narrative approaches to global politics. She is the author of *Politics of Exile* (Routledge, 2013), and *The Ethics of Researching War* (Manchester University Press, 2007), and the editor-in-chief of *Journal of Narrative Politics*. She lives in Barrie, Ontario with her husband and two young sons.

Andrea L. Dottolo is an Assistant Professor of Psychology at Rhode Island College and Resident Scholar at the Women's Studies Research Center at Brandeis University. Her scholarship explores how social identities are constructed and maintained and the ways in which they are shaped by social and political structures. She is interested in the relationships between histories, cultures, social movements, immigration, and social identities. Dottolo has a joint PhD in psychology and women's studies from the University of Michigan.

Harry Gould is an Associate Professor at Florida International University. He is the author of *The Legacy of Punishment in International Law* (Palgrave Macmillan, 2010) and is co-editor of the International Ethics volume of the *International Studies Compendium* (Wiley-Blackwell). His research addresses normative issues of international politics.

Aida A. Hozic is an Associate Professor of International Relations at the University of Florida. Her research is situated at the intersection of political economy, cultural studies, and international security. She is the author of *Hollyworld: Space, Power and Fantasy in the American Economy* (Cornell University Press, 2002), *Scandalous Economics* (with Jacqui True, Oxford University Press, forthcoming) and a number of articles in journals and edited volumes. Her work has been supported by the John D. and Katherine T. MacArthur Foundation, IREX, Fulbright, Open Society Institute and other granting institutions.

Evgenia Ilieva is an Assistant Professor of Politics at Ithaca College. Her research and writing focus is on the emergence of dialogue as a central subject of reflection in political theory, philosophy, and international relations. Her other research interests include continental political thought, hermeneutics, and postcolonial theory.

Piki Ish-Shalom is the Director of the Leonard Davis Institute for International Relations and Associate Professor in the Department of International Relations, Hebrew University of Jerusalem, Israel. He is the author of *Democratic Peace: A Political Biography* (Michigan University Press, 2013).

Daniel J. Levine is an Assistant Professor of Political Science at the University of Alabama. He is the author of *Recovering International Relations: The Promise of Sustainable Critique* (Oxford University Press, 2012).

Iver B. Neumann is Montague Burton Professor of International Relations at the London School of Economics and an affiliate of the Norwegian Institute of International Affairs.

Brent J. Steele is the Francis D. Wormuth Presidential Chair and Professor of Political Science at the University of Utah. He previously worked at the University of Kansas from 2005 to 2013. He is the author of three books, *Alternative Accountabilities in Global Politics: The Scars of Violence* (Routledge, 2013); *Defacing Power: The Aesthetics of Insecurity in Global Politics* (University of Michigan Press, 2010) and *Ontological Security in International Relations* (Routledge, 2008). He is currently working on a project investigating restraint in global politics. He is also the co-editor of three books, and has published articles in a number of international studies journals, most recently in *International Relations*, *International Politics*, the *Journal of International Political Theory*, and *Critical Studies on Security*.

Sarah M. Tillery is serving as Interim Division Dean for the Social Sciences at Portland Community College in Portland, Oregon. Her research and scholarship focuses on fatness and body size in US contemporary culture, while her teaching and instruction includes feminist theory, queer and LGBT studies, and popular and visual culture. Tillery holds a PhD in Women's Studies from the University of Maryland.

Wesley Widmaier is an Australian Research Council Future Fellow in the Griffith University Centre for Governance and Public Policy. His research interests include the sociology of knowledge and role of wars and crises as mechanisms of change. He is the author of *Constructing Crises, Fast and Slow: Crusaders, Pragmatists and Presidential Rhetoric from Wilson's Idealism to Obama's Restraint* (Routledge, 2015) and his published work has appeared in such outlets as *European Journal of International Relations*, *International Studies Quarterly*, *Review of International Political Economy*, *New Political Economy*, and *International Relations*.

Series Editors' Preface

As this thought-provoking volume makes clear, we've come a very long way since it was possible patronizingly, and grudgingly, to allow that "reflectivism" might have a few things—intersubjective meanings, say, or norms and discourse—to add to rationalism's definitive International Relations (IR) research agenda. Drawing inspiration from a range of critical traditions of analysis, this volume places "reflexivity" front and center. Instead of assuming that we know what "reflexivity" is or means and how it is or ought to be deployed, the volume questions the nature, context, practice, functions, and effects of IR's ongoing engagements with reflexivity. The volume thus asks: What can reflexivity do for the practice of scholarship and politics? Probing this question does not, of course, mean that the contributors offer a singular or a definitive answer. Instead, from a diversity of theoretical perspectives, they raise a host of insightful, puzzling, difficult, topical, sometimes uncomfortable and not always consistent questions that contribute productively to the ongoing conversation about reflexivity in IR.

As good social scientists, the editors provide a typology—a conceptual map—of approaches to "reflexivity". As signaled in the book's subtitle, these approaches highlight "positionality", "critique", and "practice". Reflexivity as positionality emphasizes the research and theoretical practices of the scholar, paying particular attention to the power relations entailed in both research and writing practices and in relations with our research subject/s. Reflexivity as critique focuses more widely on practices of intellectual communities and the political effects of knowledge production on politics. Reflexivity as practice, in turn, conceptualizes reflexivity most broadly as "a socially meaningful practice for international and/or global politics", encompassing how knowledge projects, the sciences, themselves impact upon that which they study, not least, but also not always successfully, in generating order and predictability. This typology of reflexivity is offered as provocation rather than as straitjacket: the various contributions to the volume creatively violate its categories from the outset, combining, questioning, and transcending.

The editors themselves recognize that their typologizing intervention risks disciplining scholarship on reflexivity/reflexive scholarship and they offer the countervailing hope that their contributions will both 1) demonstrate what is at stake in reflexive scholarship and how we might go beyond "its passing mention", and 2) inspire the application of reflexivity "as a socially meaningful, self-conscious, and continuous approach to ethical agency" in both the scholarship and the practice of world politics. While expressly refusing to define its "end game" in terms of promises of or routes to emancipation, this volume encourages IR scholars to be mindful of their ethical objectives, their intellectual vocation, and the intimate relations between them.

Jutta Weldes

Acknowledgments

Discussions of reflexivity in IR precede us, but since the time Brent and I began working together we have been thinking, talking, and writing about reflexivity. When we began this particular project of an edited volume we were amazed by the enthusiasm both of those who joined in this effort and of our interlocutors at various International Relations conferences and a symposium in Salt Lake City at the University of Utah. We must first thank, then, our colleagues who contributed to this volume in many productive ways, but especially the authors of these chapters. Taking this journey with them has been a thrilling academic and life experience. We have challenged and supported each other along the way and I hope that we have ultimately contributed to ongoing exchanges in the field of IR that acknowledge scholars' social and political embeddedness, that bring together those who do not usually converse, and that do a better job of seeing and hearing the reflexivity of politics.

Special thanks go to Corinne Foutz, Mark Button, Ella Myers, Tabitha Benney and Peri Schwartz-Shea for their work and guidance at the Salt Lake meeting. Earlier versions of this volume were presented at the 2014 meeting of the ISA-Northeast in Baltimore, the 2014 meeting of the ISA-West in Pasadena, and the 2015 International Studies Association and Western Political Science Association meetings. Contributors (and the editors) benefited from comments and questions posed at all of these meetings. Thanks as always go to Jon Acuff, Francois Debrix, Eric Heinze, Nick Onuf, Andrew A. G. Ross, and Molly Wallace for comments along the way. We greatly appreciate the work that Nicola Parkin, Peter Harris, Lydia de Cruz and all the editorial team at Routledge did in marshaling this book to production. We also want to thank Iver Neumann for writing the conclusion and for his guidance and mentoring as a supportive and critical voice.

Brent Steele would also like to thank the following persons: my colleagues at the University of Utah and the Francis D. Wormuth endowment for making the 2014 Reflexivity in IR symposium in Salt Lake City so worthwhile. My family—Mindy, Annabelle, Joe and our dog Chase—for putting up with my absences that this book and the meetings that went into constructing it entailed. And last but not least, I thank my friend Jack. As my contribution to this volume suggests, the graduate program where we met was not the easiest environment where one could practice reflexivity, let alone read and discuss IR scholarship on such a topic. If I didn't have Jack's mentoring and support during some of those dark days, let alone throughout the subsequent years we've known one another and worked together, I wouldn't be where I am today. He's been a model collaborator, but also the best friend any scholar or human being can have. Here's to Jack, my colleague, friend, and brother, to the past decade and a half we've known one another and to many more years of collaboration, and mutually assured self-destruction, to come.

Jack Amoureux would also like to thank: Wake Forest University for the funding that allowed me to attend meetings associated with this project, and the support of my department chair Katy Harriger and interim chair Peter Siavelis; friends and community in the many places I have lived but especially the people of Winston-Salem, North Carolina over the last few years; and my partner Angela, our oldest kid Ocean, and our twin 'babies' Theron and Jane. Finally, I want to thank Brent. I'll never forget standing next to him my first week of graduate school in Iowa City and thinking that this college golf player's arm was as big as my head. Our friendship was unlikely but fortuitous. For some time now, my many projects of self-transformation have included Brent's unruly advice, passionate advocacy, and delightful friendship. I wouldn't have it any other way.

Introduction

Jack L. Amoureux and Brent J. Steele

This volume is about reflexivity, how it has been treated by a variety of scholars and perspectives in International Relations theory, how it has functioned and been invoked, how presently "reflexive" scholars use it in their own work, and (perhaps most importantly) how scholars and students might think about using reflexivity to shape their political interests as well as their research questions, agendas, and interests going forward. The timing for a volume like this seems ripe, when one considers the evolution—jagged though it may be—of the term's uses and functions in the past three decades. In the field of International Relations (IR), beginning at least in the late 1980s and early 1990s, the terms "reflexive" and "reflexivity" began appearing with increased frequency. Yosef Lapid, in his famous "Third Debate" study (1989), noted "enhanced reflexivity" as the most significant contribution of critical restructurings of IR theory. In the following decade, Mark Neufeld (1993, 1995) likewise wrote of a "reflexive" turn in IR theory, and proposed it as one way to reconstruct International Relations as a field. After a strong set of appearances over the past decade, "reflexivity" is now a common term in IR scholarship. It is referenced often as part of the everyday language of the field of IR and there have been several in-depth efforts to articulate its importance (Dauphinee 2010; Eagleton-Pierce 2011; Guzzini 2000, 2013; Hamati-Ataya 2011, 2013; Inayatullah 2011; Levine 2012; Neufeld 1995; Sjolander and Cox 1994; Steele 2007b; Williams 2005a). Yet, for such an important concept and referent, the meaning of reflexivity has been more assumed than developed by those who use it, from realists and constructivists to feminists and post-structuralists.

This terminological ambiguity has meant that reflexivity fails to have the potency of its promise. What can reflexivity do for the practice of scholarship and politics? As if tacitly acknowledging these lacunae, both the advocates and detractors of reflexivity have shown sensitivity to the accusation of navel-gazing. For many, meta-theoretical questions in IR have become distracting, hindering important research agendas and elevating the scholar's self-importance beyond what is warranted (Elman and Elman 2002).[1] Inanna Hamati-Ataya has remarked that reflexivity is in danger of being "relegated ... to the abstract realm of meta-theory" more because of its variety of

uses than its self-referential orientation (2013, p. 671). And Elizabeth Dauphinee (2010) observes the orthodoxies of IR that would dismiss reflexive
narrative as not belonging to the proper production of IR knowledge. Thus,
the heralding of reflexivity may have marked when "the discipline of international relations found a new subject for evaluation – itself" (Cox and
Sjolander 1994, p. 3), but for many this moment has passed in favor of
"getting on" with scholarship.

Such a moment needs to be appreciated, for it comes after a period when
the "field" of International Relations appears more pluralized, but also more
fragmented into academic "sects" (Lake 2011) than ever before in its
(roughly) century of existence.[2] Whether we agree that the field has experienced such a distillation into evil "isms" or cottage "tribes" (Vertzberger
2005), International Relations has certainly experienced some impressive
growth. One crude measure of this development has been the blossoming of
the International Studies Association. Started in 1959 by a group of scholars
dissatisfied with the American Political Science Association, and with membership numbers hovering well below a hundred for its first few years of
existence,[3] the ISA now boasts over 6,000 members and includes (as of this
writing) twenty-seven distinct sections organized by issue-area and topic. This
state of affairs may explain the appearance or sense, rather than reality, of a
field in disarray, but we point to it to suggest that *any* intervention into a
conceptual referent like reflexivity (especially so, as we discuss in this introduction) comes packaged with prospects both hopeful and risky. The risk is
that any attempt at categorization let alone development is very much a
"disciplinary" move, one meant in intent or effect to cut down discussion
about what that referent—reflexivity in this case—was, is, or could be.

So why take up the question of reflexivity in this volume? What are the
hopes, in short, for this volume that may make it, on balance, worth the risks
taken? We provide further "promises" for the approaches taken here in the
penultimate section of this chapter, but for now, two broad goals animate this
collection and its contributions. *First*, we offer a conceptual basis for thinking
about and categorizing different uses of reflexivity to illustrate what is at stake
and how reflexivity might be engaged beyond its passing mention (as if simply
invoking the term "reflexivity" is doing significant work). *Second*, we want to
appeal to scholars interested and invested in reflexivity to offer innovative and
compelling applications of reflexivity to both the scholarship *and* practice of
world politics. Given the authors who appear in this volume, and several
others besides, the second task is perhaps more assured than the first by this
and other related projects (Inayatullah 2011; Schram and Caterino 2006).
Reflexivity's ambiguity as a concept is, in our view, over-stated, since it can
both be considered more simply, and more elastically, than it has been represented by some scholars. To that end we offer here a typology of the ways in
which reflexivity has been invoked and conceptualized in IR. We are mindful
that there are several possible ways to do so (e.g., Eagleton-Pierce 2011;
Hamati-Ataya 2013), and thus we offer our interpretative groupings as one

possibility. Our organization of reflexivity's uses will inevitably be inadequate as all conceptual mappings are, but it offers additional ways to think about reflexivity and to clarify for ourselves how we have and might put it to use in the past and going forward.

Those hopes will be realized (or not) in the pages that follow, but let us pre-emptively confront the risk we take in a volume meant to categorize and provoke on the topic of reflexivity. One way to respond to the variety of uses of reflexivity in IR scholarship, within (especially) an increasingly fragmentary field, is to heroically develop a "reflexivism proper". This would be, in the words of one scholar an "optimal, rather than minimal definition of what an academic turn is expected to achieve ... towards a properly new, *standalone tradition* defining an *independent* epistemic-praxical commitment for IR scholarship" (Hamati-Ataya 2013, p. 672, emphasis added). Hamati-Ataya (2011, 2012, 2013) has taken up this task by posing reflexivity as a Bourdieusian sociology of knowledge that seeks to "understand the objective structuration of IR, and reconstitute the praxical meaning that informs IR scholars' *position-takings* in relation to their position in the game and what the game and its stakes mean from *that* position" (2012, p. 633). This is an admirable purpose, but in seeking to clarify and re-organize a concept she sees in crisis, it sometimes complicates more than it clarifies. We have a strong sense that a wide variety of scholars find reflexivity important, but *why* they do and how they use it can be attributed to a variety of reasons, reasons that may be championed or castigated in any attempt to "objectivate" reflexivity as an "independent" approach.

Still, organization can be useful, so let us start with some basics regarding reflexivity. While it can be confusing to look at all of the uses of reflexivity as a term, an overview of the concept suggests that the definitional understanding of the word as a verb—to reflect (Schwartz-Shea 2014, p. 133)—is perfectly in line with not only its definition but a spirit (or attitude) that makes possible a great variety of uses. Of course, such reflection can mean a bunch of different things, but we consider it here more inclusively as a "turning back" or a "theoretical reflection" (Neufeld 1995, p. 40) on the process of knowledge production, scholars themselves, and political agents and their practices more generally.

Doing so also articulates reflexivity, with regard to IR, as an historical endeavor that "analyzes the ways in which those [historical] forces and factors are implicated in the research practices" of a field to begin with (Jackson 2011, pp. 157, 160). Its promise is that reflexivity "encourages a research practice in which the researcher understands him- or herself to be the means, the instrument used, to produce the research study" (Schwartz-Shea 2014, p. 133). Yet how researchers internalize that endeavor, let alone *which* historical forces they focus upon and which forms of theorizing they critically document—which scholarly practices they extract for examination, and how this all impacts our scholarship and our field—these are inherently subject to variation and idiosyncratic examination.

Such a concept cannot, then, be defined into existence a priori, but *instead must be utilized when it comes into contact* with the context appropriated by the researcher—a context that is both subjective (e.g., the scholar) and inter-subjective (e.g., the scholarly community). Further, we should expect this, for how will there *not* be variation in the ways through which scholars interpret their own endeavors? If one point of reflexivity is to get the scholar to reexamine their own motivations and practices, then one would think this will inevitably entail a bit of pluralism. Our point is that categorizing reflexivity and reflexive scholarship is the best we can do, because the nature of reflexivity is both so inherently varied and also (but to a lesser extent) tethered to a positivist project which still seems somewhat characteristic of the field of International Relations.

Reflexivity as a sociology of knowledge is better thought of, then, in terms of the challenge of "practising the craft of reflexivity" in the context of a field "informed by larger institutional and discursive structures of power" (Eagleton-Pierce 2011, p. 806). It is thus important to study the institutional incentives and interests of the IR field as well as our autobiographical trajectories, as Matthew Eagleton-Pierce summarizes these forms of reflexivity, but we also want to guard against reflexivity's narrowing to a particular kind of explanation. Thus, the specific categorizations we set out, organized in the table that follows, are also tied to the second purpose of the volume—to advance the claim that reflexivity as practice holds particular promise not yet realized, as a socially meaningful, self-conscious, and continuous approach to ethical agency in scholarship *and* politics. In doing so this volume's contributors draw on a wide cast of thinkers including Michel Foucault, Theodor Adorno, Anthony Giddens, Hannah Arendt, Aristotle, Judith Butler, and Edward Said. More importantly, the authors here engage various forms of reflexivity in view of how they can be pressed forward through specific tactics and in ways that are still mindful of the challenges and shortcomings of relating thought to action.

Three interpretations of reflexivity

From the starting point that reflexivity is, at the very least, the dialectic engagement of thought and action in the form of a "turning back" or reflection, we set out three broad interpretations of reflexivity in the IR literature, articulated in Table I.1. The first and most popular conception of reflexivity in IR is what Cecelia Lynch (2008) refers to as *positionality*. This is understood as a scholarly exercise that discloses the scholar's (or the scholarly field's) social/political position as (potentially) relevant for research, or as an exploration of the implications of the inseparability of subject and object for IR scholarship. Here, the object of reflexivity—that which we look back upon—is *scholarship itself and its socio-political context and impact*, as well as the *relationship* between the scholar and those whom that scholar makes objects of knowledge (Schwartz-Shea 2014, p. 133). The basic question can be

Table I.1a Reflexivity's dimensions

Site	Scholar	IR self	International politics actors (including individuals)	
Object	Research	Theorizing	Thought	Action/Policy
Process	Self-consciousness (attitude/sensibility), and its practices	Communal dialogue, discourse and criticism	Both internal (individual) and external (social) dialogue and deliberation	Tactics and practices that stimulate reflexivity (thought/action dialectic, identity/ action critique, genealogy and archaeology)

Table I.1b Reflexivity's dimensions

	Site	Object	Process	Examples*
Positionality	Scholar	Research (research design and process, writing); (Meta-) Theorizing (evaluating theories); social context and implications of research	Contextual self-awareness, documentation (journaling) of the consequences of research; narrative techniques; acts of self-transparency	Lynch; Tickner; Ackerly and True; Dauphinee; Neufeld; Cox and Sjo-lander; Ish-Shalom
Critique	IR Self; political actors	Theorizing and its influence on political action and identity	Tactics—genealogy, imaging, discourse, politics/agonism	Steele; Ashley; Der Derian; Shinko
Practice	Scholars *and* political actors	Thought, Action (of all kinds)— production of thought and action including "knowledge" and "ethics"	Ways of doing things that include processes, attitudes, tactics; internal and external debate and delibera-tion; institutionaliza-tion; methodologies	Williams; Levine; Jackson; Eagleton-Pierce

* As our discussion elaborates, some authors overlap on these categories.

rendered as, "How is scholarship (as thought) implicated in the (our) world?" IR feminists, in particular, have been concerned—for over three decades—about their relationships, as scholars, with those whom they study. Brooke Ackerly and Jacqui True ask, "How can we study power and identify ways to mitigate its abuse in the real world when we, as researchers, also participate in the projection of power through knowledge claims?" (2008, p. 693). Ann Tickner elevates knowledge that is constructed from the voices of the marginalized and unheard, and advances their agency in view of past constructions of knowledge that have been exclusionary (1997, p. 623). These considerations should extend, Lynch (2008) specifies, through decisions about research questions, methods, and findings. Reflexivity thus becomes a self-awareness of one's position as knowledge producer including one's epistemological authority endowed by the social organization of the field, the likelihood of unequal power in interactions with research subjects, and how social and political context informs research parameters, decisions, and conclusions.

Many scholars who have taken up reflexivity as positionality thus have a specific perspective on knowledge, situating reflexivity as inherent to socially and politically constructed knowledge (Cox and Sjolander 1994, Preface). To put it in terms less self-assured, reflexivity might be an ethical obligation that ensues from the impossibility of separating the object (as the "real world") from the subject (as the social scientist) (Lynch 2008; Neufeld 1995, p. 33). Invoking Anthony Giddens's concept of the "double hermeneutic" Stefano Guzzini (2000) describes scholars as interpreting an "already interpreted world" (see also Steele 2007a). To insist on the subject/object duality is to refuse responsibility for the form knowledge takes as an additional site of social construction and the impact of that knowledge on those whom we study and the wider world. Thus for Neufeld (1993), Cox and Sjolander (1994), and many others, reflexivity—as acknowledging and accounting for our role as scholar—precludes positivism. From a variety of critical approaches many IR scholars have zeroed in on the value-laden quality of facts, citing Robert Cox's famous dictum that, "Theory is always for someone and for some purpose" (1981, p. 128).

Situating reflexivity against positivism, however, has its costs and may be part of the impetus behind the desire to "move on" from meta-theoretical questions, as well as a sensitivity to being accused of languishing in this realm. An alternative framing is simply the matter of influence (influencing and being influenced), which could include an aspiration that even enthusiastic positivists could identify with—to reflect on their role as a theoretician and scholar (Steele 2010b). Influence and thus responsibility can arise out of the observation that there are at least some times when, as Piki Ish-Shalom puts it, theory "gets real" (Ish-Shalom 2011; Oren 2014) and that many have entered the political fray based on their social status as carriers of objective knowledge (Edkins 2005). If we are confident that our theorizing produces airtight conclusions then we need not worry about our well-informed recommendations, but even positivists underscore the importance of error; its possibility is, after all, an historical and conceptual basis for the scientific method (Abbinnett 2003). Thus, a perhaps more satisfactory call for reflexivity foregrounds epistemological uncertainty—the hunch that uncertainty, complexity and/or contingency confront scholars with the need for some kind of self-consciousness, self-interrogation, and even self-transformation. Any of us could be wrong about that which we see and that which we conclude, no matter the carefulness of our methods or the nuance of our interpretation. In this vein,

Daniel Levine (2012) promotes reflexivity on the related basis of reification, warning that as scholars we often mistake the concepts we have created for reality itself. Levine suggests that we maintain an awareness of this possibility and even rethink our practices of theorizing.

Nevertheless, epistemological uncertainty can only get us so far if it neglects the primacy of ethics. As Dauphinee notes, scholars possess "narrative privilege that others do not" to the extent that "scholarly writing is understood as "truth writing"", but the coherence of this quest for truth utterly falters in the face of the question, "What expert are you?", posed by those whose voices we authoritatively interpret (2010, pp. 807–808, 816; 2013). We inevitably fit these voices to our research, voices that cannot speak back. For Dauphinee, a "reflexive self-awareness" consists in acknowledging the violence of writing and pursuing ways of "conveying something that we would not otherwise have been able to hear" (2010, p. 806). Autoethnography, Dauphinee suggests, is one such possibility in that it allows us to discuss experiences in our research that are otherwise relegated to the "private" as not properly belonging to the pursuit of knowledge and the communication of research findings (2010, p. 805). These experiences include the love (or hate) scholars might have for those whom they study, as well as the doubts they may have about the limits and impossibilities of knowledge and knowledge claims.

The ethics that propel autoethnography is akin to "the political as craft" (*techne*) that is a "form of building and creating relationships" by re-centering the subject (Dauphinee 2010, p. 817). In this sense, Dauphinee's rendition of reflexivity and, we would suggest, that of Ish-Shalom (2011), bleed into the third approach to reflexivity we discuss here—that of practice—because they see the scholar as a central political actor alongside other actors and, on this basis, have prioritized *and specified* reflexivity as a kind of ethical, relational, and continuous practice. For Ish-Shalom the public has a "vested interest" in understanding the normative basis of scholarly theorizing which entails the obligation of transparency. Reciprocity, as a broader moral and social principle means that because we make others transparent in our research we have a corresponding obligation to turn the spotlight on ourselves as part of a practice of "strong reflexivity" (Ish-Shalom 2011, p. 974).

In sum, reflexivity as positionality happens at the *site* of the scholar who takes as *objects of reflexivity* the scholar's research and theorizing through *processes* of contextual self-awareness, an ethical commitment to research subjects, and documenting/writing the research process and its implications. The overriding concern is with the context and power of epistemology, though scholars can differ widely on how to respond.

A second approach, that of *critique*, involves political actors (and scholars) confronting others to stimulate self-reflexivity, oftentimes from within collective selves. Lisa Wedeen refers to its scholarly strand as an "epistemological reflexivity toward the discipline, posing questions about what bounds the discipline and normalizes its modes of inquiry" (Wedeen 2010, p. 264).

Borrowing from Michel Foucault, Brent Steele (2010b) has referred to this kind of reflexivity, to also include its political dimension, as a form of counter-power because reflexive tactics seek to critically engage aesthetic insecurities in others. "Counter-power" as an approach to reflexivity is only one step, in that it is not an "independent" form of power but rather that which hopes to turn back theorizing and its collection of assumptions upon itself. This is a modest and perhaps even mischievous form of reflexivity, one that is skeptical in that it surrenders the hope that such reflexivity can be fostered in conventional, deliberative, and reasonable ways. Instead, counter-power is a response to that which operates to silence dissidence, so here reflexivity is directed toward a targeted collective "self" and is fostered in a field of power relations through events that incite, cajole, manipulate or insecuritize actors *into* a reflexive moment. But because the response is reactionary, the quality of these reflexive moments is not guaranteed.

Such reflexive critique can be exemplified historically, with an examination of periods and cases where the transmission of theory to politics and policy led to "unexpected" outcomes, outcomes that served to create a critical space for scholars and intellectuals to consider the problematic possibilities of their work upon the world more broadly. Steele's *Defacing Power* study focused on the example of John Dewey, whose support along with that of other liberals for US participation in the First World War stemmed from his belief that such participation could lay the groundwork for international democracy going forward (Steele 2010a, pp. 122–123). The problem was that when Dewey became part of the political debates and polemics over the war and the war turned out to be more costly and less beneficial than he had envisioned at the beginning, he regretted his support even though it was based on good intentions linked to his theoretical worldview. An "ideal" result of this critique approach to reflexivity is summarized by Cai Wilkinson (2014, p. 403):

> the researcher may experience a sense of cognitive dissonance or displacement that causes her to review her understanding of her role and of her relationship to both her research and the field. While the experience may be quite uncomfortable and evoke powerful emotions, the critical sensibilities arising from such displacement can also be used strategically, to create particular opportunities for the generation of additional insights into and critiques of both the phenomenon being investigated and the *nature and politics of knowledge production*.

Post-structuralists have, in a similar way, taken aim at the IR Self, poking and prodding its self-representations. Early, realism was the main target, portrayed as posing an "anarchy problematique" that legitimates (hegemonic) states and their practices as sources of order/domestication with "reasoning man" at the center to rule and to know (Ashley 1995). Realism is also an expression of the masculinized IR Self that dichotomously excludes feminist epistemologies (Cohn 1987; Tickner 1988, 1995). Conceptual categories in IR thus offer attractive ontological anchors for securing our place in the world but in doing so they elide an "incomplete, impossible subject" with "no settled identities" (Edkins and Pin-Fat 1999, p. 1).

Post-structuralists thus pointed to IR knowledge (and thought in general) as political—working to "privilege some interpretations over others, limit discourse, discipline conduct, and produce subjective agents and the institutional structures of their experience" (Ashley 1995, p. 101). The IR Self has been constructed by a consensus—perhaps what Ole Wæver (1996) termed a "neo-neo synthesis" of neorealism and neoliberalism rooted in common texts—but its foundation, as we engaged at the beginning of this chapter, is unstable and full of cracks. In the 2000s, with its assumptions utilized by the George W. Bush administration and neoconservatives more broadly to justify the continuation of the Iraq War, liberalism's democratic peace research came under attack by a number of critical scholars such as Steele (2007a; 2010a), Ish-Shalom (2011), Hobson (2011), Oren (2014), and a variety of scholars participating in roundtables and special issues of journals (see *International Relations* 2011). Even more surprisingly, considering its supposed status as a "middle ground" theory (Adler 1997), constructivism when posed as a dominant narrative of the IR Self came under fire for neglecting its political status (Zehfuss 2002) and for "infantilizing" agency (Epstein 2012). Thus, critique can present the collective self with displeasing self-images that even prompt deep insecurities. These reflexive tactics can be strategic—to disturb and provoke the aesthetic visions that others have of themselves and the truths they hold.

The third category or interpretation of reflexivity is a *practice* approach that sees reflexivity as a socially meaningful practice for international and/or global politics. This form of reflexivity foregrounds agency as a kind of *grappling with* the world and the regimes of knowledge that influence political actors within. Such a use of reflexivity draws upon perspectives of late modernity and post-modernity for its meanings. Reflexivity here takes on a more loosened and fluid meaning, gaining its analytical significance when attached to other concepts or processes or complexes, both "in here" and "out there". For sociologists like Giddens, reflexivity is an act of self-regarding (1984), one that can occur for and by individuals, groups, states, and even the period of late modernity itself (Giddens 1991; Beck, Giddens and Lash 1994). In IR theory, this has been applied to understand a variety of processes and agents who become aware of their own capacities (Guzzini 2000), and the ways in which reflexivity is fostered, stimulated, or challenged.

Such "turning back" is both a site of, but also an effect of, reflexivity as practice. Self-awareness in late modernity can be examined (and partially generated) via discourse, words, language or what Giddens titles "[auto]biographical narratives". Self-awareness of reflexive capacity—the possibility of transformation of actions within time and space—comes through the ability of agents to place the self (including of groups and states) within an environment through a story that not only explains, but *justifies* action and orders the self within that environment on a continuous basis.

Reflexivity as practice includes the ways in which the sciences themselves impact that which they study (Steele 2007a), again to make meaning of such subjects but also to generate societal order and predictability. This comes through what Giddens calls "slippage" between the realms (1989, p. 274; see also Guzzini 2000, pp. 156–162) and what Bourdieusians (see also McCourt 2014) working on this relationship examine as forms of practice (practice-practice and science-practices) within an overall "assemblage" (Bueger and Villumsen 2007, pp. 425–427).

Yet, because such "sorting" efforts (which, again, involve the scientist or expert via classification schemes or regimes, see Foucault 1970), are *attempts* to confront immanent insecurity in the mounting chaos of a quickening pace and space of social relations in late modernity, they can fail to predict or account for the variability, the "unintended consequences", of action, for a variety of reasons. These moments of *discontinuity* reveal the insecurity of actors or agents, and propose the possibility not of order but rather the "disorder" of things in global politics. Such chaos is made possible—even facilitated—by the very attempts to fashion a routine or structure or arrangement within late modernity that, in part, seeks to deal with how unintended consequences recursively feed back into conditions for action. Thus, reflexivity as practice can be understood not only through theorists of late modernity, but also within and perhaps especially via post-structural insights. Indeed, such resources have been used, generally, to understand both how shifting grounds of late modernity in international politics are *temporarily fastened* or secured, as well as how they are unfastened or loosened through time. In this respect, IR scholars who see reflexivity as a practice of discipline or tentative control have used thinkers such as Foucault (Amoureux 2016; Der Derian 2001; Löwenheim 2007; McBride 2007; Steele 2010a), Lacan (Edkins 1999; Solomon 2013), Zizek (Debrix 2007) and Derrida (Bulley 2010), to push forward the ways in which reflexivity in global politics can be understood via *deconstruction* in addition to reconstruction and construction. Reflexivity has a polyvalent quality.

For those who have labelled post-structuralism "nihilist", then, it would perhaps be surprising (or inconvenient) to see figures such as Derrida and Butler among the first to attempt and call for an actively reflexive appraisal of post-9/11 politics and policies (Borradori 2003; Butler 2004). Derrida diagnosed the constant repetition of "9/11" as an attempt to overcome trauma by dominating it. And yet, "9/11" can be read as metaphorically symptomatic of an autoimmune disorder because what occurred on September 11, 2001 *was* foreseeable in that we can trace how it came to pass, *and* we can attempt to assess the trajectories that it might then create (Borradori 2003). For Butler (2004), this entails a reflexive responsibility for ascertaining and projecting how others, in their agency, have and might respond to our agency.

It's not necessarily the case that a reflexive undertaking such as Derrida's spotlights *the answer* to what ails us. As Dauphinee exemplifies, undecidability as the "condition of decision" is not to choose between two opposing choices "with discrete and unique consequences" (2007, pp. 82–83; also Bulley 2010). Rather, Derridean undecidability is about the impossibility of choosing—whether and how to act—without suffering (p. 83). Dauphinee draws on Derrida in noting that:

> We are urged to begin where we are; in the middle of a sentence, in the middle of the street, in the middle of a war or a trial proceeding. Beginning where we are indicates that there is no teleology of existence but only moments that are characterized by their urgency in the present.
>
> (Dauphinee 2007, pp. 83–84)

To prioritize the present, per Foucault (1984), is to mark today as different from yesterday and to present ourselves a task. This "beginning" along with similar articulations of the creative and transformative movement of reflexivity, such as Arendt's "natality" (a measure of "origin" within ourselves that exceeds what has been), point to possibilities for thinking and acting that are nevertheless in view of history and the social, and that always portend dangers (Amoureux 2016). Reflexivity as a practice involves strategies for thinking through these possibilities, with their hopeful promises and their inevitable perils.

The risks and promises of reflexivity in International Relations

If the record is any indication, we recognize that a project hoping to categorize reflexivity in IR is a tall task for IR scholars who already have theoretical and political proclivities.[4] Of course, caveats abound regarding our categories of reflexivity. We acknowledge that the categories may not capture every use of reflexivity in International Relations scholarship, and, inversely, certain uses or conceptions of reflexivity may be better understood as falling into two or more of our categories. For instance, what Steele has titled "academic-intellectual parrhesia"—truth-telling as a form of counter-power aimed at an IR Self—can be considered both a positionality approach to reflexivity as well as critique (Steele 2010a, 2010b). Autoethnography, being both subjective *and* intersubjective, is both a positioning of the scholarly self within an intellectual community as well as, many times, a critique of that community in terms of its disciplinary regimes. And in the process of demonstrating the ways in which social scientific discourses intersect with the application of politics and power (as in the contributions found in Part III of this volume), *writing* about reflexive practices is both a revelation of reflexivity as practice and its own form of reflexivity-as-critique. Our only point here is that the typology should best be considered for its ability to reveal some of the aims and means of reflexivity in IR in its theoretical and praxical instantiations.

What is not captured well in the typology is the ultimate "end game" for reflexivity. Previous understandings have linked its purpose and promise to an explicitly *emancipatory* goal. For instance, over two decades ago Neufeld (1993) outlined an account of reflexivity as central to critical theory with its emphasis on critique in order to identify immanent possibilities for transformation and change, yet Neufeld advocated that we evaluate IR theories, which already have a political perspective, according to whether they advance "human emancipation" defined as an Aristotelian project of the polis—to live the good life.[5] Yet, in the years since Neufeld's proposal, finer lines of purpose have been drawn amongst scholars otherwise considered "reflexive".

What Nicholas Rengger (2007) titled, via Oakeshott, an anti-Pelagian mindset seems to have taken hold amongst some of the critical scholars writing on reflexivity, a mindset that reveals a divide between the so-called "critical realists" of the 2000s versus the philosophical "monists". Such a mindset, Rengger notes, rather than being "nihilistic" seeks to "understand" the world "from the outside", and that while "sometimes reform will occur and that sometimes it should be welcomed" we shouldn't expect such reform to permanently alter human conduct, or even have an influence much of the time at all. Patrick Jackson, in a precursor to his magnum opus on the philosophy of science in IR, helps identify this schism between pragmatist-minded IR scholars and the critical realists as a result of "one crucial respect". For the pragmatist it is, *"not the task of scholarly analysis to engage in efforts to 'correct' the ways that actors make sense of their situations.* The effort to do so presumes a split between the mind (of the actors) and the world (in which the actors find themselves)" (Jackson 2009, p. 657, emphasis added). Such an "intervention" makes sense for critical realists, who posit what they see as "actually happening", getting closer to that happening in a way that "is not meaningful for a [monistic] pragmatist". Benjamin Herborth, too, notes that the purpose of "emancipation" that is foregrounded in the work of critical realists tends to idealize (or worse, ignore), the public realm of criticism, where discourses transform from "the ontological quest for certainty and into a problematisation of the potentially technocratic and expertocratic nature of public interventions" (2012, p. 244).

In other words, while the typology we have set up delineates various feedback loops important for, and necessitating, the turning back of reflexivity, it cannot and will not necessarily say exactly what actors should *do* with that knowledge once revealed, discovered, or articulated. For scholars, this take on their roles is inherent to a reflexive reflexivity of IR. Thus, the contributors to this volume foreground their *own political purpose* in examining their "slice" of reflexivity, suggesting (but not demanding) ways to reflect upon reflexivity in their scholarship and teaching. Further, while much of the perspectives provided by reflexivity stem from more critical constructivist and post-structural work, we think that there is a second-order benefit that can be gained for the many (more) scholars working in the neopositivist tradition of International Relations, a tradition and vocation that remains predominant in especially the United States IR field. Because it foregrounds the scholar, their practices, their evaluative "values" key to promoting careers and advancing in the field, reflexivity may in fact serve to inspire (and, one hopes, chasten) more conventional scholars re-discovering their own ethical purposes and scholarly vocations.

Plan of the book

The volume proceeds in three parts. In Part I, contributors Jack Amoureux, Brent Steele, and Elizabeth Dauphinee focus on formulating the stakes for reflexivity, and taking up its various forms which include variations across sites, objects, and processes. Amoureux draws on Hannah Arendt's writings on "thinking", "willing" and "judging" to argue in Chapter 1 that reflexivity as a form of agency for ethics takes seriously the agent's capacity to dialectically and continuously treat thought and action where each can iteratively, critically, and creatively be invoked to alter the other. Amoureux focuses on reflexivity as a practice, especially its promise as a *practice of ethics for global politics*. Such a proposal recognizes and extends reflexivity beyond scholars to the subjects they study with several advantages, but also pitfalls that should be considered. For IR scholars a political reflexivity is difficult to conceptualize and reconcile with their analytical frameworks that are applied to explain or understand the world. One advantage of looking to Arendt is that her ontology of complexity, contingency, and social construction still allows room for a reflexive agency that, Amoureux argues, can be entertained as at least some of what a practice of ethical reflexivity might entail.

In Chapter 2, Dauphinee takes stock of autoethnography's reflexive project, including its advantages for practices of knowledge, ethics and aesthetics. Dauphinee reflects upon her own work developing and practicing creative narratives in the context of reflexivity. Dauphinee assesses what narrative writing allows us to access beyond conventional approaches, and how this might impact our self-identities as scholars. Dauphinee concludes with some "heralds" of reflexivity, underscoring that reflexivity is a possibility but not an inevitability of writing or any other modality for "doing" IR.

In Chapter 3, Brent Steele engages in a detailed recent example of scholars—specifically Christopher Gelpi and Peter Feaver, whose work on US public opinion regarding war support (as a dependent variable) directly influenced the "Surge" policy which continued the US occupation of Iraq from 2007 onward. In the years following the Surge there has been little to no reflexive awareness or disclosure of their responsibilities for this late 2000s process. Owing to the expectation that *silence* is one of *the* strongest ways to resist such questioning about the responsibilities embedded with being a scholar of International Relations, Steele proposes a practice of "documentary provocation" to stimulate especially neopositivist scholars to engage in reflexivity. Scholars might first gather together in documentary form a background on the academic-intellectual, or their scholarly "field", that they are seeking to provoke, and then, second, "provoke" a response regarding the neopositivist scholars' responsibilities for *impacting that which they study* via a variety of venues and tactics from social media to conference panels and roundtables.

In Part II of the book, titled "Reflexive scholars", contributors engage exactly *how* scholars might embody a reflexive stance. The theoretical centrality of political concepts and their contestedness call for what Piki Ish-Shalom titles an epistemological and methodological strategy, developed in Chapter 4, of "Zooming in, zooming out". In this double-faceted strategy theoreticians zoom into the internal components of their theories, namely the political concepts, and at the same time, define and conceptualize them with moral sensitivity. *Zooming in* asks theoreticians to focus their theoretical rigor on better defining the concepts they use. *Zooming out* adds normativity to the commonly accepted criteria of exhaustiveness, exclusiveness, and operationalization.

In Chapter 5, Daniel Levine builds from his Adorno-inspired work on "sustainable critique" as a way to confront reification (2012), by turning to the reflexivity embodied by Edward Said, with reference to the Israel–Palestine conflict. Levine takes a close look at Said's efforts to articulate and practice an "exilic" ontology through, in part, an application of Adorno's notion of "late style". Said found that the conceptual infrastructure of his own critical thought became inevitably essentialized and reified and he confronted this tendency, Levine argues, by a chastening that could be derived from and extended to both Palestinian and Jewish exilic political traditions, on a continuous basis. Levine adds to Said's efforts with a "constellar" approach to practices of world politics that facilitates multiple interpretations and refuses easy solutions and theodicies.

In Chapter 6, Andrea Dottolo and Sarah Tillery dialogically narrate how feminist interventions in scholarly practice—methodological and political—have informed their practices of research and teaching, including the ways in which even personal identity can implicate and become implicated by others' demands of the ideal scholar. Dottolo and Tillery probe the social aspects of gender in its intersectionality in ways that both confound and empower scholarly agency. A noteworthy aspect of this chapter is the non-IR background of Dottolo and Tillery, showcasing their stories about reflexivity as scholars and administrators that are informed by feminist epistemology in other fields of study.

How does reflexivity implicate the university and not just the scholar? In Chapter 7, Mauro Caraccioli and Aida Hozic address this neglected aspect of scholarly reflexivity by uncovering the political and economic underpinnings of intellectual and pedagogical exchanges in contemporary academe through "eleven theses". In the process, Caraccioli and Hozic engage a paradox—the anxieties, performances, and insecurities that drive today's scholars to *actively participate* in the discipline of international relations yet *at the same time* reproduce the silences of international politics. Caraccioli and Hozic pose academic spaces as another fantasy in order to spur critical reflexive engagements that are multiple and micro-political. These different engagements are necessary, Caraccioli and Hozic argue, because we (as IR scholars) are not all similarly positioned in social and institutional terms.

In Chapter 8, Amanda Beattie engages autoethnographic methodology and insights to situate her own dislocating experience vis-à-vis borders that defies the scripted and easy assurances of cosmopolitanism. Bearing witness to trauma and elaborating some of its affective responses is one reflexive form of agency that can potentially struggle with reconstructing identity in the context of being exiled from that very subject position.

Part III examines reflexivity as a process and practice of world politics, one that is implicated in a variety of problematic phenomena centralized by International Relations scholars, including diasporas, neoliberal technocratic assumptions, diplomacy, and human terrain systems. In Chapter 9, Ilan Zvi Baron addresses the reflexive linkage between identity and security. Using the work of Michael Walzer and the example of diasporic identity, Baron provides a theoretical and empirical investigation regarding reflexivity and the contours and bounds of identity-based critique, including the notion of whether community membership is required for a reflexive practice of critique and what that looks like. In doing so, Baron stretches and reinterprets the tripartite typology of reflexivity we set out above.

Perhaps no other case in the past decade better represents the emotionally charged and politically problematic intersection of social science and violent power than the Human Terrain System (HTS) project carried out in Afghanistan during the late 2000s. Critics of the program worried that rather than reducing lethal operations, HTS may have enabled violence. Locating itself within the context of these debates, in Chapter 10 Evgenia Ilieva draws on Michel Foucault's late lectures on parrhesia (or truth-telling) as a framework for rethinking the controversy surrounding the Human Terrain System. Ilieva argues that the military's renewed proximity to academia as embodied by HTS presents an opportunity for the academy, and students of International Relations in particular, to rethink old questions regarding the role and responsibility of scholars, as well as the relationship between knowledge and power and between thought and action. The chapter explores the arguments put forth by the most vocal supporters and critics of the HTS program, and shows the limits of invoking "ethics" as a way of navigating the tension between utilizing scholarly expertise to protect others, and the realization that the very knowledge produced by the social sciences can be appropriated in service of less benevolent ends. Critique as truth-telling, Ilieva warns, does not render scholars free of complicity, leaving us with the unpalatable conclusion that participation may be the most viable ethico-political strategy.

Conventional accounts of diplomacy have reflected very little on the underlying ethical reasons behind its indispensable and long-standing practice. This is due to the all-too-common identification of diplomatic practice as a tool of statecraft, and hence the privileging of state interests and the ensuing power struggles among them in international society. In Chapter 11, Hussein Banai advances a critique of this amoral understanding of diplomacy, which has been particularly influential in literature on the subject in mainstream academic and policy writings. In its place, he offers a reflexive conception of diplomacy as already premised on the ideal of equal respect for state- and personhood in world politics. He argues that the institution and myriad practices of diplomacy, despite successes and tragically innumerable failures, is made possible in the first place because of the mutual recognition of sovereign rights and obligations in international society.

In Chapter 12, Wes Widmaier draws attention to how reflexivity is often naïvely proclaimed an intersubjective "fix" that can endow stability to human activity. Widmaier instead foregrounds the ways in which reflexive hubris and neoliberal technocratic confidence paradoxically induce instability, arguing that as agents engage in what behavioral psychologists term tendencies to "ambiguity aversion" they will increasingly fail to make efficient use of inter-subjective information. From this vantage, the scope for reflexive practice depends on a social psychological context and features a great deal of uncer-tainty and unpredictability. In this vein, Widmaier suggests a reflexive posi-tionality premised on ethical ambiguity to counter what can be a harmful narrowing of possibilities from ideational convergence.

By investigating certain historical elaborations that have informed our "core vocabulary and semantics of prudence", Harry Gould carefully elabo-rates prudence as one possible reflexive practice in Chapter 13. Notably, this notion of prudence as practice contrasts significantly from the "practice turn" in IR that treats rather unproblematically the role of rules and knowledge. A reflexive prudence instead is about acting, or "knowing how to go on" which requires thinking and choosing well. There is always an aspect of prudence that is instrumental because it is intention and goal-oriented, but Gould argues that prudence cannot then be reduced to instrumental reasoning. Gould concludes that to understand prudence as a reflexive practice one must draw both from Bourdieu and Wittgenstein.

Finally, Mark Button in Chapter 14 takes a more critical view of some of the conceptualizations of reflexivity presented in this volume. His primary concern is that discussions of reflexivity in IR grant too much coherency and agency to actors. Not only is it problematic to say that reflexivity might counter or correct for bias and error, Button worries that accounts of reflex-ivity also assume an unwarranted "freedom of the mind and freedom of the will" by which the subject can take hold of itself as an object of inquiry. Drawing on insights from social psychology and moral philosophy, Button warns that the failure to really search for ourselves (per Nietzsche) threatens to enact a Cartesian faith in the self's deliberative capacities rather than a pragmatic self-knowledge with public-political benefits. Button's critical appraisal may be worrisome to practically all the authors in this volume who think of themselves as taking into account the social and affective bases and dynamics of world politics and IR knowledge. Yet, Button does not ask us to abandon elaborations of reflexivity; instead, he calls for reflexivity's "psycho-logical and social refinement to serve as a meaningful form of epistemic improvement for beings like us" (p. 267). Button concludes his thoughts by gesturing toward a reflexivity that is socially and politically institutionalized with checks and balances, organized political dissent, and cultural practices that combat our "collective delusions". For Button, this is more Dewey than Descartes.

In the Conclusion, Iver Neumann reflects upon the contributions to this volume with a plea not only for complementary notions of reflexivity but for those calling for more reflexivity to not only speak, but listen as well.

Notes

1 As Elman and Elman quipped in an article that otherwise affirmed the importance of meta-theoretical concerns, "if everyone spent their time describing and assessing previous scholarship, political science would grind to a halt" (2002, pp. 232–233). For a lively discussion on whether we have reached the "end of IR theory" see the contributors to a special issue of the *European Journal of International Relations* with an introductory article by Dunne, Hansen and Wight (2013).
2 The "beginning" of International Relations as a field remains contested, but some scholars locate the field as having its beginnings with the establishment of the first department of international politics, at the University of Wales, Aberystwyth, in 1919 (see Dunne 1998).
3 www.isanet.org/ISA/AboutISA/History.aspx.
4 Michael Williams (2005a), for example, presents a compelling account of what Steele (2007b) has termed "reflexive realism", but Williams (understandably) stops short of subjecting key realist principles to the reflexive political practice he advocates.
5 Alker took a similar route by linking the hermeneutic interest to interpret ourselves and others to the emancipatory interest of "freeing individuals and collectivities from unnecessary impositions and constraints" which Alker identified as belonging to the "Aristotelian search for the 'best and most complete' 'good for man'" (1996, p. 97).

References

Abbinnett, R., 2003. *Culture and Identity: Critical Theories*. Thousand Oaks, CA: Sage.

Ackerly, B. and True, J., 2008. Reflexivity in Practice: Power and Ethics in Feminist Research on International Relations. *International Studies Review*, 10(4), 693–707.

Adler, E., 1997. Seizing the Middle Ground: Constructivism in World Politics. *European Journal of International Relations*, 3(3), 319–363.

Alker, H.R., 1996. *Rediscoveries and Reformulations: Humanistic Methodologies for International Studies*. New York: Cambridge University Press.

Amoureux, J., 2016. *A Practice of Ethics for Global Politics: Ethical Reflexivity*. New York: Routledge.

Ashley, R., 1995. The Powers of Anarchy: Theory, Sovereignty, and the Domestication of Global Life. In: J. Der Derian, ed., *International Theory: Critical Investigations*. New York: New York University Press, pp. 94–128.

Beck, U., Giddens, A., and Lash, S., 1994. *Reflexive Modernization: Politics, Tradition and Aesthetics in the Modern Social Order*. Stanford, CA: Stanford University Press.

Borradori, G., 2003. *Philosophy in a Time of Terror: Dialogues with Jürgen Habermas and Jacques Derrida*. Chicago, IL: University of Chicago Press.

Bueger, C. and Villumsen, T., 2007. Beyond the Gap: Relevance, Fields of Practice and the Securitizing Consequences of (Democratic Peace) Research. *Journal of International Relations and Development*, 10(4), 417–448

Bulley, D., 2010. The Politics of Ethical Foreign Policy: A Responsibility to Protect Whom? *European Journal of International Relations*, 16(3), 441–461.

Butler, J., 2004. *Precarious Life: The Powers of Mourning and Violence*. New York: Verso.

Cohn, C., 1987. Sex and Death in the Rational World of Defense Intellectuals. *Signs*, 12(4), 687–718.

Cox, R.W., 1981. Social Forces, States and World Orders: Beyond International Theory. *Millennium*, 10(2), 126–155.

Cox, W.S. and Sjolander, C.T., 1994. Critical Reflections on International Relations. In: C.T. Sjolander and W.S. Cox, eds, *Beyond Positivism: Critical Reflections on International Relations*. Boulder, CO: Lynne Rienner Publishers, pp. 1–11.

Dauphinee, E., 2007. *The Ethics of Researching War: Looking for Bosnia*. Manchester: Manchester University Press.

Dauphinee, E., 2010. The Ethics of Autoethnography. *Review of International Studies*, 36(3), 799–818.

Dauphinee, E., 2013. *The Politics of Exile*. London: Routledge.

Debrix, F., 2007. *Tabloid Terror: War, Culture, and Geopolitics*. New York: Routledge.

Der Derian, J., 2001. *Virtuous War: Mapping the Military-Industrial-Media-Entertainment Network*. Boulder, CO: Westview Press.

Der Derian, J., 2009. *Critical Practices in International Theory: Selected Essays*. London: Routledge.

Dunne, T., 1998. *Inventing International Society: A History of the English School*. Basingstoke: Palgrave Macmillan.

Dunne, T., Hansen, L., and Wight, C., 2013. The End of International Relations Theory? *European Journal of International Relations*, 19(3), 405–425.

Eagleton-Pierce, M., 2011. Advancing a Reflexive International Relations. *Millennium— Journal of International Studies*, 39(3), 805–823.

Edkins, J., 1999. *Poststructuralism and International Relations: Bringing the Political Back In*. Boulder, CO: Lynne Rienner.

Edkins, J., 2005. Ethics and Practices of Engagement: Intellectuals as Experts. *International Relations*, 19(1), 64–69.

Edkins, J. and Pin-Fat, V., 1999. The Subject of the Political. In: J. Edkins, N. Persram, and P.-F. Veronique, eds, *Sovereignty and Subjectivity*. Boulder, CO: Lynne Rienner.

Elman, C. and Elman, M.F., 2002. How Not to Be Lakatos Intolerant: Appraising Progress in IR Research. *International Studies Quarterly*, 46(2), 231–262.

Epstein, C., 2012. Stop Telling Us How to Behave: Socialization or Infantilization? *International Studies Perspectives*, 13(2), 135–145.

Foucault, M., 1970. *The Order of Things: An Archaeology of the Human Sciences*. New York: Vintage Books.

Foucault, M., 1984. What is Enlightenment? In: P. Rabinow, ed., *The Foucault Reader*. New York: Pantheon Books, pp. 32–50.

Giddens, A., 1984. *The Constitution of Society*. Berkeley: University of California Press.

Giddens, A., 1989. A Reply to My Critics. In: D. Held and J.B. Thompson, eds, *Social Theory of Modern Societies: Anthony Giddens and his Critics*. Cambridge: Cambridge University Press, pp. 249–301.

Giddens, A., 1991. *Modernity and Self-identity: Self and Society in the Late Modern Age*. Stanford, CA: Stanford University Press.

Guzzini, S., 2000. A Reconstruction of Constructivism in International Relations. *European Journal of International Relations*, 6(2), 147–182.

Guzzini, S., 2013. The Ends of International Relations Theory: Stages of Reflexivity and Modes of Theorizing. *European Journal of International Relations*, 19(3), 521–541.

Hamati-Ataya, I., 2011. The "Problem of Values" and International Relations Scholarship: From Applied Reflexivity to Reflexivism. *International Studies Review*, 13(2), 259–287.

Hamati-Ataya, I., 2012. IR Theory as International Practice/Agency: A Clinical-Cynical Bourdieusian Perspective. *Millennium—Journal of International Studies*, 40(3), 625–646.

Hamati-Ataya, I., 2013. Reflectivity, Reflexivity, Reflexivism: IR's "Reflexive Turn"—and Beyond. *European Journal of International Relations*, 19(4), 669–694.

Herborth, B., 2012. Theorising Theorising: Critical Realism and the Quest for Certainty. *Review of International Studies*, 38(1), 235–251.

Hobson, C., 2011. Towards a Critical Theory of Democratic Peace. *Review of International Studies*, 37(4), 1903–1922.

Inayatullah, N., ed., 2011. *Autobiographical International Relations: I, IR*. New York: Routledge.

International Relations, 2011. Roundtable: Between the Theory and Practice of Democratic Peace – Introduction. *International Relations*, 25(2), 1–4.

Ish-Shalom, P., 2011. Theoreticians' Obligation of Transparency: When Parsimony, Reflexivity, Transparency and Reciprocity Meet. *Review of International Studies*, 37(3), 973–996.

Jackson, P.T., 2009. Situated Creativity, or, the Cash Value of a Pragmatist Wager for IR. *International Studies Review*, 11, 656–659.

Jackson, P.T., 2011. *The Conduct of Inquiry in International Relations: Philosophy of Science and Its Implications for the Study of World Politics*. New York: Routledge.

Lake, D.A., 2011. Why "isms" Are Evil: Theory, Epistemology, and Academic Sects as Impediments to Understanding and Progress. *International Studies Quarterly*, 55(2), 465–480.

Lapid, Y., 1989. The Third Debate: On the Prospects of International Theory in a Post-Positivist Era. *International Studies Quarterly*, 33(3), 235–254.

Levine, D.J., 2012. *Recovering International Relations: The Promise of Sustainable Critique*. New York: Oxford University Press.

Löwenheim, O., 2007. The Responsibility to Responsibilize: Foreign Offices and the Issuing of Travel Warnings. *International Political Sociology*, 1(3), 203–221.

Lynch, C., 2008. Reflexivity in Research on Civil Society: Constructivist Perspectives. *International Studies Review*, 10(4), 708–721.

McBride, K.D., 2007. *Punishment and Political Order*. Ann Arbor: University of Michigan Press.

McCourt, D.M., 2014. Constructivism in the Academic Field: The Challenge of Reflexivity. Paper presented at the Weimar Workshop in Third Generation Constructivism, Weimar, Germany, January.

Neufeld, M., 1993. Reflexivity and International Relations Theory. *Millennium—Journal of International Studies*, 22(1), 53–76.

Neufeld, M.A., 1995. *The Restructuring of International Relations Theory*. Cambridge: Cambridge University Press.

Oren, I., 2014. Political Science as History: A Reflexive Approach. In: D. Yanow and P. Schwartz-Shea, eds, *Interpretation and Method: Empirical Research Methods and the Interpretive Turn*. Armonk: M.E. Sharpe, pp. 309–321.

Rengger, N., 2007. Realism, Tragedy and the Anti-Pelagian Imagination in International Political Thought. In: M.C. Williams, ed., *Realism Reconsidered: The Legacy of Hans Morgenthau in International Relations*. Oxford: Oxford University Press, pp. 118–136.

Schram, S. and Caterino, B., eds., 2006. *Making Political Science Matter: Debating Knowledge, Research, and Method*. New York: New York University Press.

Schwartz-Shea, P., 2014. Judging Quality: Evaluative Criteria and Epistemic Communities. In: D. Yanow and P. Schwartz-Shea, eds, *Interpretation and Method: Empirical Research Methods and the Interpretive Turn*. Armonk: M.E. Sharpe, pp. 120–146.

Shinko, R.E., 2008. Agonistic Peace: A Postmodern Reading. *Millennium—Journal of International Studies*, 36(3), 473–491.

Sjolander, C.S. and Cox, W.S., eds, 1994. *Beyond Positivism: Critical Reflections on International Relations*. Boulder, CO: Lynne Rienner.

Solomon, T., 2013. Resonances of Neoconservatism. *Cooperation and Conflict*, 48(1), 100–121.

Steele, B.J., 2007a. "Eavesdropping on Honored Ghosts": From Classical to Reflexive Realism. *Journal of International Relations and Development*, 10(3), 272–300.

Steele, B.J., 2007b. Liberal-Idealism: A Constructivist Critique. *International Studies Review*, 9(1), 23–52.

Steele, B.J., 2010a. *Defacing Power: The Aesthetics of Insecurity in Global Politics*. Ann Arbor: University of Michigan Press.

Steele, B.J., 2010b. Of "Witch's Brews" and Scholarly Communities: The Dangers and Promise of Academic Parrhesia. *Cambridge Review of International Affairs*, 23(1), 49–68.

Tickner, J.A., 1988. Hans Morgenthau's Principles of Political Realism: A Feminist Reformulation. *Millennium—Journal of International Studies*, 17(3), 429–440.

Tickner, J.A., 1995. Re-envisioning Security. In: K. Booth and S. Smith, eds, *International Relations Theory Today*. Cambridge: Polity Press, pp. 175–197.

Tickner, J.A., 1997. You Just Don't Understand: Troubled Engagements between Feminists and IR Theorists. *International Studies Quarterly*, 41(4), 611–632.

Vertzberger, Y.Y.I., 2005. The Practice and Power of Collective Memory. *International Studies Review*, 7(1), 117–121.

Wæver, O., 1996. The Rise and Fall of the Inter-Paradigm Debate. In: S. Smith, K. Booth, and M. Zalewski, eds, *International Theory: Positivism and Beyond*. Cambridge: Cambridge University Press.

Wedeen, L., 2010. Reflections on Ethnographic Work in Political Science. *Annual Review of Political Science*, 13(1), 255–272.

Wilkinson, C., 2014. On Not Just Finding What You (Thought You) Were Looking For: Reflections on Fieldwork Data and Theory. In: D. Yanow and P. Schwartz-Shea, eds, *Interpretation and Method: Empirical Research Methods and the Interpretive Turn*. Armonk: M.E. Sharpe, pp. 387–405.

Williams, M.C., 2005a. What is the National Interest? The Neoconservative Challenge in IR Theory. *European Journal of International Relations*, 11(3), 307–337.

Williams, M.C., 2005b. *The Realist Tradition and the Limits of International Relations*. Cambridge: Cambridge University Press.

Zehfuss, M., 2002. *Constructivism in International Relations: The Politics of Reality*. Cambridge: Cambridge University Press.

Part I

Formulating reflexivity for scholarship and politics

1 Promise unfulfilled?

Reflexivity as agency and ethics

Jack L. Amoureux

While Hannah Arendt is well-known for arguing that Adolf Eichmann, in his bureaucratic post in Nazi Germany, was most guilty of failing to think (of thoughtlessly following rules) rather than self-consciously advancing evil on a mass scale, Arendt was not therefore unreservedly sanguine about the merits of "thinking".[1] The philosopher, Arendt noted, may be an exemplar of thinking in its critical and dialectic form, but has a tendency to get stuck in thought and take refuge in abstractions away from the messiness of politics. Because thinking's reflexivity can get caught in the same traps of excessive abstraction and reification that Arendt and others (e.g., Levine 2012) have pointed to, Arendt also turned to and elaborated other "mental faculties" of reflexivity—such as "willing" and "judgment"—that concern generating action, judging with others (in the pluralism of politics), and judging as a "spectator".

Yet, these faculties, like "thinking", have potential disadvantages. In particular, the natality of "willing" that enables bold and courageous acts of political significance also makes possible projects of immense "political evil", such as totalitarianism. Willing also encounters the nagging prospect of being subsumed or rendered meaningless by forces and circumstances beyond the agent's control, or given too much power and autonomy by hopeful political theorizations and political projects that envision an agent unfettered by a variety of institutions, policies, actors, and strategies. Despite Arendt's perhaps undeserved reputation as an optimistic pluralist, judgment also faces steep hurdles for resolving complex and uncertain political questions. More often than not, Arendt felt a "homelessness" from the world, and thus her refusal to be "homesick" deserves more sustained attention, especially as it relates to her positive appraisal of political pluralism.

Turning to Arendt, not among the "usual suspects" in discussions of reflexivity, can add conceptual depth to extant notions of reflexivity in the literature of International Relations (IR). I argue that Arendt has presented key concepts useful for beginning to outline a practice of reflexivity. As Brent Steele and I noted in the Introduction, the "enhanced reflexivity" that Lapid attributed to IR has been cut short by calls to return to the patient and more important work of science. Yet, even among those who might favor its continued and continuous relevance, reflexivity's practice has been stymied by a great deal of ambiguity about its meaning(s) and by explications of reflexivity that move too much in the opposite direction by claiming one meaning as the right meaning. The contributors to this volume have instead organized their investigations of reflexivity along three (potentially overlapping) dimensions. In this chapter I am especially concerned with reflexivity as *practice*, conceived as an ongoing activity that is shaped by some guideposts and takes form through our capacities to narrate, fracture and critique the self, always in relation to and with others.

Reflexivity, in other words, need not be confined to a sociology of knowledge or science that "objectivates" the scholar (Hamati-Ataya 2012), or as a scholarly positionality as awareness/orientation to the situatedness and effects of research (Ackerly and True 2008; Lynch 2008). Reflexivity can instead be an approach to *grappling* with thought and action, which requires but moves beyond self-awareness. Likewise, the critical function of reflexivity need not be only performed by antagonistic others to have transformative effects. We can narrate and critique one another, as Steele (2010) elaborates through scholarly *parrhesia*, even while we seek to narrate and critique ourselves (e.g., Dauphinee 2013; Inayatullah 2011). Cultivating certain attitudes, dispositions and activities on a continuous basis might enact reflexivity as practice.

To take on this task, furthermore, is to conceptualize reflexivity as an ethics. Reflexivity's basis is found not just in the epistemological conjecture that scholars engage in hermeneutic and social acts that can impact the interpretations of the political actors they study (Anthony Giddens's commonly noted "double hermeneutic"), but in the possibility that truth is elusive, contingent, or even impossible, and that we are faced with an array of ethically complex, ambiguous, and impossible situations. To respond to such profound epistemological uncertainty is perhaps to assume Foucault's tripartite task—to take responsibility for how we constitute ourselves as subjects of power, knowledge and ethics (Foucault 1997, p. 262), rather than seeking refuge in some eternal and observable truths, norms and institutions of an international society, or cosmopolitan project. Lastly, this reflexive project (as practice) is relevant to scholars' thought and action, but also political thought and action *more broadly.* Even though the ascendant IR theory of constructivism has been billed as "reflexivist" it is troubling that we tend to be quite pessimistic about the capacities of political agents to take themselves as objects of inquiry and aesthetic self-evaluation. Instead, to the extent that we notice agency it is the power to have (international/global) structural impact and, to the extent that we entertain ethics, it is often as the normativity of social structures. While there is much to be said about the ways in which agents are socialized and participate in patterns of shared routine and ritual (Oren and Solomon 2014), it is not therefore the case that they lack the capacity to engage in reflexivity, as difficult, uncertain and troubled as that may be.

What I do not propose is that reflexivity as practice is *the answer* to global, national, local or transnational maladies of all kinds. It is instead a conceptualization of agency that seriously treats our reflexive capacities as resources for trying to get along in the world, for struggling against and yet prodding that which we feel threatened by, and for elaborating and engaging that which challenges us. We can attempt to articulate and revise political projects that are shaped by and withstand critical, dialectic, affective and relational applications. And we can begin to map some strategies and tactics that can be (at least provisionally) justified in such an effort.

Referring to the introductory typology, at what site do such reflexive practices occur? The answer, I think, is empirical and open. There may be an affective disposition, even global, to see ourselves as in struggle together (or that we should be) for some kind of justice, autonomy, recognition, or decent life chances, but it seems more likely that we feel that only some of us are in it together and we depend on and look to these communities or affective bonds in that effort. Or we feel, as perhaps Arendt did in the aftermath of her reporting on the Eichmann trial and the criticism that ensued from her Jewish community, that the world has left us almost entirely so that we are no longer intelligible to others. It is not by accident that exile and invisibility are prominent and recurrent themes in this volume on reflexivity. Moving beyond reflexivity as a general characteristic of modernity that features a disembodied recursivity, and reflexivity as a sociology or science of knowledge, I hope to instead sketch some positive possibilities for what reflexivity as practice can do for us, even in the despair and aporias of world politics, and as selves who are always problematic and social but who we still imagine and interpret with real effects.

With these considerations in mind, I move through this chapter by first noting that conceptualizations of reflexivity in IR, particularly those that draw on Anthony Giddens, have tended to downplay the role of agents in reflexivity by situating reflexivity more as a characteristic of modernity itself. Furthermore, it is the role of the "expert" more than any other roles that are empowered in these accounts. Next, I tackle a small piece of the project of elaborating reflexivity as a practice of ethics by focusing on Hannah Arendt's discussion of thinking, willing and judging as reflexive capacities, but also Michel Foucault's reflexive experimentations. In other work, I also heavily draw on Aristotle and the notion of *phronesis*, or prudence, which is attentive to the complexity and contingency of the world and thus the need for responsive judgment (Amoureux 2016; Amoureux and Steele 2014). The overall point I wish to illustrate here is how resituating reflexivity as capacities, processes, dispositions and attitudes holds some promise for theorizing reflexivity in and beyond the scholar and scholarship, as an aspect of agency. Reflexivity, then, can be an ethico-political practice, which I elaborate with some attention to affect and relationality in the final section.

From reflexive modernity to the reflexive (IR) scholar

For Arendt, the death of metaphysics that Immanuel Kant announced left a mixed legacy. On the one hand, it enabled us to "look on the past with new

eyes, unburdened and unguided by any traditions" and it spurned the possibility that reason was just for the elite few, such as philosophers (Arendt
1978a, pp. 12–13). On the other hand, a reason so unburdened and liberated
has not achieved the progress that Kant had hoped for; rather, it has ushered
in much more terror than we could have feared, as witnessed by the twentieth
century's murderous brand of totalitarianism (Arendt 1966). The extension of
social capabilities through imperialism were brought "home to roost" in the
form of technical control (and genetic manipulation) of the human species.

In a more agnostic fashion, a number of social theorists have zeroed in on
the reflexivity of modernity as knowledge production feeding back into its
very possibility and the shape of its practice. According to Anthony Giddens,
absent the repetitions of tradition that were ensured through the legitimacy of
their generational transmission, notions of "truth" and "belief" have become
experiential and contingent, and expert knowledge has assumed more legitimacy. This is an historical claim about knowledge, but one that means little
without actors who, according to Giddens (1984, p. xxii), have "the capacity
to understand what they do while they do it". This is not to say that the
unconscious or social structures are unimportant; that Giddens emphasized
the reflexive, recursive and opaque characteristics of thought and action in his
structuration theory indicated his desire to avoid a determinism/voluntarism
dualism. Our actions are informed by shared understandings and routines,
but reflexivity as a capacity allows us to potentially reflect upon why we do
what we do, and even modify our thoughts and actions on that basis. In sum,
Giddens presents reflexivity as a summary of how we have historically constituted ourselves and modernity co-constitutively and the possibility for their
re-construction, for reflexivity also means that the consequences of our
actions feed back into the very conditions we encounter in the future.

The conclusions of this literature on "reflexive modernity", however, have
been curious. Giddens (2002, 2014) and Ulrich Beck (1992) have located in
reflexivity both the rise of a risk society and the potential to mitigate its risk,
including the large-scale existential (often environmental) risks of globalization. These risks were themselves created by human societies "invading
nature" (Giddens 2002). But while our reflexive capacity promises the possibility of profound social transformation, theorists of reflexive modernity offer
no roadmap for reflexive re-constructions beyond gesturing toward them or
hoping for fortuitous events that will arrest or reverse the natural processes we
have altered and that may destroy human societies and the human itself
(Giddens 2014).

To interpret how notions of reflexivity settled more on reflexivity as a
structural (or structurational) characteristic rather than an agentic capacity,
we might turn to Giddens's larger body of work in which he identifies
routine and tacit knowledge as sustaining an "ontological security" that
basically moves us through the world. According to Giddens, we seek the safety
of routines and habits that are maintained in largely unconscious and pre-
conscious, though not necessarily unreflexive, ways: "Ordinary day-to-day

life ... involves an *ontological security* expressing an *autonomy of bodily control* within *predictable routines*" (Giddens 1984, p. 50).[2] When the reflexive link between thought and action is no longer coherent, often dramatized by others and in times of crisis (Steele 2008), a de-securitizing anxiety ensues. Giddens (1996) has argued that in a "post-traditional" society such anxieties are more pronounced and often lead to addictive behaviors. If we are driven, then, to *reflexive* but largely *unreflective* routines and their hasty and patchwork repair, it is difficult to see how reflexivity holds promise to be self-consciously taken up, particularly as a practice of ethics that may involve, as I have suggested (Amoureux 2016), careful dialectic and dialogic deliberation on a continuous basis. And, if reflexivity is not much more than a series of feedback loops between causes and effects, or constitutive processes, where modernity's institutions and practices are continuously remade through normal thoughtless social life, individual agency appears quite feeble.

The most noteworthy agents in a Giddensian account are likely those experts who can claim and wield legitimate knowledge (of the environment, technology, economies, etc.) about how risks have been induced, how they have traveled with unforeseen and unpredictable consequences, and what may be done to address them. It is this reflexivity of the (IR) expert and its implications and desirability that IR has most developed in its debates about reflexivity (Ackerly and True 2008; Eagleton-Pierce 2011; Edkins 2005; Guzzini 2013; Klotz and Lynch 2007; Levine 2012; Lynch 2008; Neufeld 1995). And it is no accident that those IR scholars who have taken up Giddens have invoked the importance of "rules", "norms" and "roles" in providing a sociological theory of international politics. Thus, Stefano Guzzini (2000, p. 162) has explained reflexive interpretation as occurring at two levels of observation, "the level of action proper and the level of observation. In both instances we interpret, at one time making sense within the life-world of the actor, and at another time making sense within the language shared by the community of observers."

Arendt, in contrast, was more concerned with the reflexive capacities of the agent. Even in a post-metaphysics age, social formations such as rules and institutions continue to offer empty promises across social and political life. Arendt (1964) put into relief just how norms and rules fail us with her study of Eichmann's trial in Jerusalem which she covered for *The New Yorker*. Eichmann's "inability to think" meant that just as he had accepted the bureaucratic rules, laws and direct orders of Nazi German officials, he also accepted the prevalent rules of the war crimes tribunal. Thus, Arendt reported of Eichmann:

> He functioned in the role of prominent war criminal just as well as he had under the Nazi regime; he had not the slightest difficulty in accepting an entirely different set of rules. He knew that what he had once considered his duty was now called a crime, and he accepted this new code of judgment as though it were nothing but another language rule.
>
> (Arendt 1984, p. 7)

Following rules enabled Eichmann to claim that he had never directly killed a Jew despite his direct participation in a system that resulted in millions of deaths, but it also demonstrated a social aptitude to adjust his identity to prevalent social standards and institutions. Perhaps one fear that animated some of the extreme negative reaction to Arendt's conclusions was that we too could orient ourselves to such a situation and thus participate in what Arendt termed "political evil". This should perhaps unnerve adherents to the view that norms and rules (whether preserved or replaced) are somehow of inherent value, particularly in managing and regulating technology and its effects in democratic fashion. Thus it is perhaps less relevant whether there are more or stronger rules than noting the effects of actors' judgments, who invoke and interpret norms and rules (and sometimes help to create them).

Arendt deemed politics as social behavior undesirable with its routines and conformist tendencies. When "behavior has replaced action as the foremost mode of human relationship" (Arendt, quoted by Buckler 2011, p. 2), we find the kind of failure to think evident in Eichmann. The negative aspects of the social as normative are compounded by technology that further distances us from the reflexive ability to judge and act. Nationalism and totalitarianism also animated modernity's instability and even created for individuals a kind of "homelessness". Arendt felt this homelessness herself, as a German Jew émigrée with no particular home. But Arendt refused to be "homesick" in her homelessness (1978b) and clung to the possibility of forging different political paths:

> Even though we have lost yardsticks by which to measure, and rules under which to subsume the particular, a being whose essence is beginning may have enough of origin within himself to understand without preconceived categories and to judge without the set of customary rules which is morality.
>
> (Arendt 1953, p. 391)

Yet, we might ask: How is this possible? With what ideational or textual resources does the agent generate different understandings, particularly as a subject who is always socially and relationally embedded?

In part, Arendt turned to dispositions and tactics that enact a type of distance for the critical and dialectic thinking of reflexivity, the task of the first volume of *The Life of the Mind*, her final work. While Arendt included the scholar in her discussions, it is also clear that political agents could and must strengthen their own ethical capacities to address complex but pervious challenges that human action contributed to bringing about. What Arendt's discussion of Eichmann highlighted was that this small slice of space and time occupied by Eichmann had its own peculiarities in terms of challenges and possibilities. His agency was contextualized but not determined by a larger discursive and institutional complex that he nonetheless acted upon, and thus he both created and sustained certain courses of action.

Reflexivity's thinking

Arendt's theorization of politics that underscores pluralism and speech in making and contesting meaning is well-covered by the secondary literature[3] including IR (Lang 2002; Lang and Williams 2005; Owens 2007). Less popular in IR is Arendt's sustained attention to "thought" and "thinking". Perhaps this aspect of Arendt is largely overlooked because thinking, in Arendt's view, shifts the time-space register to one of "non-time" and "non-space"— the gap between the past and the future of "non-politics". Yet, thinking is not therefore irrelevant to politics. Instead, thinking can be a strategy for critical distance to evaluate, engage and revise politics and the political self, as a form of reflexivity, even if thinking itself is an anti-political activity. By this, Arendt meant that self-reflexive thinking is "out of order" in a way because it requires solitude, apart from the company of others and the immediate demand to act. Yet we need not be alone to engage in thought, as captured by the figurative time-space shift indicated by the aphorism "to get lost in thought" where multiple selves can then take form. The outside world—when it makes demands on the agent to speak, listen, or act—can disrupt and crowd out reflexive thought. And to be social and to act requires the re-emergence of the singular self into the world of appearances (Arendt 1978a, p. 185). When we take shape in the world through speech we necessarily even though imperfectly, as Butler (2005) has also argued, attempt to give a coherent account of ourselves and our opinions to others.

Thinking may go together with action, but it takes shape and benefits from a turn inward. Arendt wrote, "Thoughts invariably and unavoidably accompany his acts" and thought "improves" acts, but it is "only *in thought* [that] I realize the dialogue of the two-in-one who I am" (Arendt 1990, p. 89, italics mine). Thought, as the "two-in-one" dialogue of the self (1990, p. 86), is a form of reflexivity in which one talks to oneself as though two selves (*eme emautô*). Because we are conscious of ourselves we can engage in a multiplicity of the self for the purpose of a reflective and critical dialogue:

> It is this *duality* of myself with myself that makes thinking a true activity, in which I am both the one who asks and the one who answers. Thinking can become dialectical and critical because it goes through this questioning and answering process, through the dialogue of *dialegesthai*, which actually is a "traveling with words," a *poreuesthai dia tōn logōn*, whereby we constantly raise the basic Socratic question: *What do you mean when you say ...?*
>
> (Arendt 1978a, p. 185)

Arendt sees this process as one that takes place continuously over time and as a practice that the self can improve in that the "other" within the self can become a "friend" with whom sustained exchange is possible. In sum, we are capable are splitting the self as myself for purposes of a critical, dialectic and internal conversation and for which we can entertain some markers of success.

There are, however, some corresponding dangers and drawbacks to thinking for Arendt. We may, for one, take refuge in thought and its tendency to abstraction. Like Nietzsche, Arendt was critical of German Idealists who had gone to great lengths to tiptoe across a "rainbow bridge" of concepts rather than critiquing concepts in view of interpretations of reality (made possible by our mental faculties) (Arendt 1978b, p. 157). To get too lost in thought is to engender an excessive "homelessness", to be "homesick" as so many philosophers have been. On the one hand, thought enables us to step back in wonder, to marvel at and be astonished by the world and thus enable the related capacity of imagination to dialectically engage thought and action (Arendt 1990). On the other hand, the philosopher-in-wonder might become stuck in thought with the undesirable consequences that the philosopher avoids the "messiness of the everyday world", may be "swept away by dictators" (a reference to Heidegger no doubt), or disables their own ability to make decisions (Strong 2013, citing Robinson). Arendt (1978b, 1990) instead offered Socrates as the exemplar philosopher, whose roles she likened to the "gadfly", "midwife" and "stingray"—the person who stimulates others and demands justification from them, judges the vitality of ideas, or interrupts action by insistently posing questions and objections that paralyze action, respectively. One generates perplexities that might otherwise be glossed over by the apparent homogeneities and pressures of social life.

To reject this non-worldly seclusion is to perhaps propose this question of Arendt's: "Is our ability to judge, to tell right from wrong, beautiful from ugly, dependent on our faculty of thought?" (Arendt 1984, p. 8). Is *judging* dependent on *thinking*? While thinking may draw us away from particulars it is *necessary for taking into consideration others and anything else we see in the "world of appearances"*. Arendt points out that, "In order to think about somebody he must be removed from our senses; so long as we are together with him we don't think of him—though we may gather impressions that later become food for thought" (1984, p. 14).

Hence, Arendt favored the Kantian device of "enlarged mentality" wherein we represent to ourselves the perspectives of others (Arendt 1978b) and we tell stories about the world by representing things as objects to ourselves (Arendt 1998). The internal dialogue of *self-reflexivity*, I would like to suggest, gives rise to a *political reflexivity* in Arendt's account in that there is a kind of dialectical moving back-and-forth between the work of thinking/ thought and politics/action. It also privileges the expression and representation of difference—that others have opinions that ought to have a presence in politics, through *thought and speech:* "Mental activities, invisible themselves and occupied with the invisible, become manifest only through speech" (Arendt 1978a, p. 98).

Thus, while Arendt set apart thinking as located within the self (more definitively than judgment), and thinking and judging are two different activities, the "I-with-myself" is nevertheless bound up with the I-with-others. Arendt links the dialectic and dialogic thinking of the plural self with the exchanges of a plural political world in at least two ways—in self-conscious moves away from the tyrannies of intersubjectivity and toward a multiplicity of representations and political actions, and as a device for thinking and judging the opinions of others, political and social interactions and relationships, and other things that one represents to oneself as if objects. Even those accounts that posit "understanding" as all that can potentially be achieved through dialogue (Shapcott 2001) can acknowledge that others are heard only through the filter of the self's understandings and interpreted experiences. Thinking can interact with politics, then, in a number of ways.

A substantial challenge that arises for thinking, however, is that in grappling with what has happened we engage in storytelling that endows the past with a certain amount of coherency. Arendt seems to say that we can accept contingency and know that what happened could have not happened or unfolded into the world differently, but we nevertheless try to understand and explain a "series in time" as it *did happen* (Arendt 1978b). We give an account to orient ourselves in time and space (as "memory") and to establish the basis for certain political activities such as forgiveness and promising, two strategies that Arendt identifies as coping with action's volatility. To forgive or promise (Arendt 1998) is, perhaps, to articulate what is to be forgiven and why we are making certain commitments as promises. And yet, this is not giving up on judging. Arendt maintained that judging was still important—to hold others responsible for what they do with contingent possibilities, and so here too we need a story to tell about why a person (others and the self) should be blamed or praised, even if (on a more Derridean note) we decide to forgive in order to escape a cycle of revenge or forge forgiveness as an impossible alternative in the face of impossible and unique situations (Zehfuss 2005, pp. 98–99). In view of the past (as public or spectator), we tell stories that manufacture coherency even while we generate many incoherencies when we pluralize the space within ourselves, and the space belonging to ourselves and others. Thus, we face the prospect that we mistakenly take this coherency as ontological rather than useful, biasing against the plural strands of storytelling among those who inhabit the world. To counter the tendencies to seclude oneself in thought or favor a collective interpretive coherency, we can also turn to the second and third of Arendt's mental faculties, "willing" and "judging".

Reflexivity's judgment

Both Arendt and Foucault looked to the Greeks, in addition to Kant, for inspiration in thinking about political life and judgment in light of modernity's aftershocks. For Foucault, to break with "regimes of truth" one needed to historicize subjectivities through genealogical and archaeological methods and take up specific and experimental modalities to the self, others and knowledge that one judges to be aesthetically pleasing or in care of the self (which include one's relational life). Arendt's view is more difficult to pin down because the third and final volume of her series on *The Life of the Mind* was precluded by her sudden death so that only "Thinking" and "Willing" but not "Judgment" were completed. Found in her typewriter was simply the title page with two epigraphs. Ronald Beiner (1982) suggests that Kant's view of judgment as aesthetics was to heavily inform that third volume. Substituting Kant for Arendt on judgment, however, may be too hasty given the style and critical discussions of the first two volumes of *The Life of the Mind* as well as the several references to judgment throughout Arendt's writings (including material on Aristotle and Socrates) that do not neatly align with Kant's views.

Still, the absence of this more sustained effort left Arendt susceptible to the superficial reading that her notions of political pluralism and natality are naïve and ahistorical—specifically, that a proper politics that features dialogue between equals who articulate and consider a variety of opinions to address political and policy issues seems unlikely. Yet, Arendt pragmatically engaged politics, situating her writing and reporting in view of the challenges of the day, such as automation, space travel, the rise of authoritarianism, and specific foreign policy issues such as the Vietnam War. In her political views, Arendt positively assessed political possibilities even while she always questioned political actualities from a skeptical and agonistic standpoint.

For Arendt, both judging and willing pertain to the "world of appearances" or politics. Judgment concerns the aesthetic activities of public life and the public-political benefit of considering multiple opinions. In this realm of "judgment" we encounter, take note of, and act on our historical situation with others. Whether beautiful or ugly, good or bad, judgments concern specific situations because actions and their consequences are in constant flux, dependent in part on the speech and actions of others. Arendt stressed that the realm of action is one of contingency and open-endedness. It is difficult to know how our actions will take shape in the world and even more difficult to connect them to preferred ends. When Arendt described advisers to the US president during the Vietnam War as exhibiting a "remoteness from reality" she meant their failure to consider the risks and consequences of their decisions—of their war and its diversionary tactics—preferring instead to judge success as public perception (1972, pp. 19–20).

Curiously, the very decision-makers who could have benefited from the information and conclusions of the Pentagon Papers did not seek them out or notice their availability in the media prior to Daniel Ellsberg's leak. Classification (or overclassification) served these delusions, "because they work under circumstances, and with habits of mind, that allow them neither time nor inclination to go hunting for pertinent facts" (1969, p. 30). They relinquished judgment to the overrationalization of probabilities and to suspect historical analogies; both displace the difficult work of the meaning-making of politics. What is implied, for example, by saying that a certain outcome is eighty percent probable? For the think-tank academics invested in knowledge as scientific process it meant not having to consider and grapple with the possible trajectories enabled by an outcome that had been deemed unlikely. Judgment, then, is relevant to reflexivity because it involves both taking into account how action has actually unfolded and how it might unfold under different scenarios.

Arendt advocated considering a range of details and a variety of "opinions" rather than seeking a method for arriving at some "truth" or optimal political outcome. Judging is not a matter of confidently predicting the outcomes of various alternative courses of action nor is it simply pluralism as democratic process. It is to struggle to decide in actual political situations by thinking through possible trajectories, and continuously taking notice of how action unfolds, including considering the relevance of thought from these particulars, together and as persons. Judging can also manifest by assuming the position of "spectator"—to render the acts of others according to aesthetic taste. There is some ambiguity in Arendt as to whether judgment is only a public-political activity and/or an individual activity. Beiner (1982, pp. 92–93) argues that the former is found in an "early Arendt" where judgment involves a "conception of political action as a plurality of actors acting in concert in a public space" and the latter in a "late Arendt" in which judging is "the prerogative of the solitary (though public-spirited) contemplator". On my reading, Arendt envisioned both—especially where thinking and judging are engaged in a dialectic tension by agents—but turned to the spectator in her discussion of times and places that were not as friendly to pluralist politics.

Indeed, this move to spectatorship to reveal or expose how we have been abandoned by the world, whether from its "normal" politics or its political "crises", may resonate with many of the contributors to this volume, and several others in the field of IR besides, who have challenged knowledge practices in IR as unrepresentative of their experiences and have sought other modes of scholarship. One might say there is even widespread disdain and dismissal of knowledge as, for example, writing the human experience—including the inseparability of our lives and scholarship—as we see and feel it (see in this volume Beattie Chapter 8, Dauphinee Chapter 2, and Dottolo and Tillery Chapter 6). The judgment of spectator can be a form of alienation, but as Dauphinee (Chapter 2) has suggested, she writes "the contingency, uncertainty, fear, pain, and love" of scholarship in part so that she can "be held accountable" for her "ideas and proposals".

Reflexivity's willing

Finally, reflexivity as a practice of the self needs the mental faculty of willing. More than the other reflexive capacities Arendt connects willing to natality, as the origin that each new generation and each new person asserts itself/ themselves into the world, with the desire to make a mark and forge a unique path. Moving from thinking's seclusion back to the "world of appearances" is enabled by the will's reflexivity that, *"volo me velle, cogito me cogitare"*, we only have ourselves to look to (1978b, p. 196). The will is a reflexive individuation through which we spontaneously begin a "new series in time", as Arendt (1978b, p. 158) quoted Kant. It is thus a faculty that is oriented to the future, concerned with "projects" rather than "objects". The capacity to will can also draw us out of thought and into action. Similarly, Aristotle (1984) underscored the desirability of slowing down to deliberate, but the exemplar agent also decides to act upon their judgments when it is appropriate to do so.

There is, then, a sense of optimism that arises from possibility and an open-ended temporal orientation. At the same time, the reflexive self acknowledges that the newness of our action is not *ex nihilo*, but contingent and contextual. These acknowledgments make natality possible; we cannot take on a new project if we do not first identify a certain origin within ourselves and that when we act it could have been otherwise (Arendt 1954, 1978b). We defer the need for coherency, which is to be able to narrate action as arising out of previous events and as having a basic historical continuity. And we have the ability to judge action and work with and modify various strands of thought found in speech and other texts. Through thinking, after all, we are able to resituate by refusing or deferring unity and conformity. Willing requires that the self has enough confidence in its *own interpretations and performances* even though the internal split and conversation could not have happened in the first place without some degree of uncertainty, indecision or struggle. Through thinking and willing, then, we interrupt (political) time (Arendt 1978b, p. 208). Arendt points to certain ruptures, or spurts of action or activity, such as exile and revolution, as potential incidences of natality. As a recent special issue of the *Journal of International Political Theory* attests (e.g., Hayden 2013; Steele 2013) as well as the contributions in this volume by Dauphinee (Chapter 2), Dottolo and Tillery (Chapter 6), and Levine (Chapter 5), investigations of the self as fractured and struggling with various tensions and anxieties both in the self and in the world can create key moments that alter self-understandings and the self's trajectories.

Willing also entails risk. Arendt characterized all political action as courageous, in a way, because our utterances are actions that are always open to public criticism in their visibility. In addition, the volatility of action in the world creates risk. Despite the allure of willing's visions, the future that willing holds out "never was", gone before we get there, and lost to the unpredictability and contingency of action which unfolds into the world not exactly, or at all, as we had envisioned. It is perhaps "moral luck", to borrow from Bernard Williams (1981), when our actions have felicitous outcomes. Despite the bravery Arendt noted when revolutionary Americans envisioned their possible future ending at the gallows, from the consideration of indigenous Americans, the American colonists and their "founding" were not at all fortuitous. For whatever outcomes that follow we can still be held accountable. Judgments against drunk driving, for example, are often more severe when we harm someone even though the act—driving while inebriated—occurred regardless of the harm inflicted. The Bush administration can be judged disapprovingly for its initiation and mismanagement of the War in Iraq (of 2003) but it will likely be judged more harshly, in retrospect, if the country falls apart or does not recover a semblance of stability. If we are to elaborate the reflexive capacities that might give meaning to ethical agency we need to address how actors can themselves cope with the likelihood that *their* intentions will not map onto outcomes neatly or at all. It does seem that we judge more harshly those risks that are incurred without serious attempts to try to anticipate their possible effects even if it is difficult to estimate the quality of those attempts and whether they occurred.

Affect, transformation and power

There are some remaining issues for a practice of ethical reflexivity in international/global politics that I will briefly discuss. First, it seems that an adequate account of ethical reflexivity would point to and promote the affective and relational qualities of the agent's dialectic and dialogic practice. There is a rich literature in IR and Political Theory that has sought to address the intersection of reason and affect with attention to how they are inseparable but also make unique contributions to judgment (Bleiker and Hutchison 2008; Crawford 2000; Krause 2008; Nussbaum 1994). Arendt often pointed to the excessive rationalization of political science in its efforts to quantitatively translate the social world into precise formulas for explanation and prediction. Rather than achieving better social outcomes we fail to think for ourselves and fail to cultivate a sensitivity to human relations and their effects as well as our capacity to imagine from the perspective of others and to imagine a world otherwise. The "banality of evil" lies in so many people who seemed "normal" but who could not "feel" their actions and how they struck out in the world, a "terrifying" prospect (Arendt 1964, p. 276).

Both Arendt and Foucault turn to aesthetics in a world where we must measure "without yardsticks" (Arendt 1953, p. 391)—to judge what is beautiful, ugly, good or bad, about ourselves and our actions. This self-inquiry and its techniques are not to uncover or make transparent some true self but they do imply an attitude that is open to transformation in an elusive world and in mercurial conditions, or a "critical ontology of the self" as Foucault (1984, 2007) put it. But how deep the transformation and what is its public, political or relational resonance? Foucault's (1984) exemplar was the figure of the "dandy" and the practice of "dandysme"—"searching in the night" for the beautiful and the pleasing. There is a kind of radically individualistic quality to this reflexive ethos as work on the self. The dandy "makes of his body, his behavior, his very existence, a work of art" (Foucault 1984, p. 42). To be inspired by the dandy is not to reject ethics or the idea of responsibility. Rather, it is to try to take responsibility for oneself and for who one becomes.

Foucault's figure of the dandy is also of interest because it is in tension in a way with the theoretical concepts of relationality and performativity, as might be Arendt's person-in-thought. The dandy flourishes under the cover of darkness when others are not usually around. Here, one might be freer of the social pressures and the demands and routines of everyday life. The dandy is a modality for critical distance but also for re-stylizing and producing a non-normative subjectivity that may be an exemplar of alternative ways of living. Yet, performativity as meaning-making requires a performer and an audience that understands the performance or finds it understandable enough to judge its quality. Relationality implies the centrality of social interaction, communicability, and intersubjectivity for thought and action and their critique (Arendt 1982). So what do we make of the anti-social dandy who performs for herself?

We might, for one, point to the ways in which the dandy or thinking self both returns to and emerges from the relational and political. Even while the dandy may roam the night seeking out elusive strands of beauty, these "dandysme" challenges to the socially normative do not entirely emanate from within the individual in a thorough-going way because persons often have the support of emergent communities as even loosely affiliated groups (however small), underground identities, or obscure texts and textual interpretations that provide ideational and discursive resources with which to work. Foucault also points to how our relational condition is an additional aspect of ethics in the example of gay male friendships. Such micro-political communities can issue profound challenges because they defy the dominant normativity that both heterosexuals and homosexuals have of only two "ready-made formulas"— that gay relationships must either be a "fusion of lovers' identities" or the pure sexual encounter (Foucault 1997, p. 137). They can also offer resources and support not provided by wider institutions and norms that, in a way, go around the legislating acts of others.

Noting the various ways in which Butler's (1990) seminal book *Gender Trouble* was received, Butler (2010) underscored the sense of agency that could be claimed from the concept of performativity "which involved bringing categories into being or bringing new social realities about". Butler continued:

> It seemed that if you were subjugated, there were also forms of agency available to you, and you were not just a victim, or you were not only oppressed, but oppression could become the condition of your agency. Certain kinds of unexpected results can emerge from the situation of oppression if you have the resources and if you have collective support. It's not an automatic response; it's not a necessary response. But it's possible. I think I also probably spoke to something that was already happening in the movement. I put into theoretical language what was already being impressed upon me from elsewhere. So I didn't bring it into being single-handedly. I received it from several cultural resources and put it into another language.
>
> (Butler 2010)

The point is not that to have a satisfactory ethics everyone must be non-normative and provide their own resources for judgment and action, but that reflexivity at its most thorough-going needs, at the very least, an attitude of openness to transformation of the self-as-relational that can arise out of reflexivity's hard questions. Reflexivity can benefit from, and even be made possible by, specific attitudes, dispositions and tactics, including those of smaller or dispersed communities in which perplexities *and* possibilities are multiplied.

What kinds of relationships, spaces and times might we seek out to facilitate the possibility that we can enact *thoughtful natality* in response to the challenges we face? A figure such as the dandy turns to the solitary space that Arendt's "thinking" refers to; here, one *somewhat* buffers oneself from social norms, rules and dominant narratives to explore and embellish unpopular and incipient threads of thought and visions of action. But the artist also produces, usually for public display, and challenges and finds support through and with others. She emerges in the daylight as well, potentially an exemplar of different ideas and ways of living to those not (yet) convinced. Some feminist IR literature (Särmä 2012; Sylvester 2009) has invoked "collage" as a metaphor for taking already existing everyday items and re-presenting them in ways that challenge conventional and accepted representations—normative standards within the wider community and possibly the micro-community of the "art world" as well.

Finally, we might ask how far the pluralism of politics must extend and which tactics may be deployed to realize reflexivity's political pluralism in the context of power relations. To conceptualize ethical reflexivity along the lines I suggest—as agent-centric dialectic, dialogic and affective interrogation of thought and action through both the pluralism of the self and the pluralism of self–other relations—is to also think about strategies and tactics that enact being heard and listened to. In investigating the agencies of US foreign policy and its citizens, Butler has advocated in Arendtian fashion that we seek to hear beyond what we hear. We might also seek to feel beyond what we feel and think beyond what we think, but for those who are disadvantaged in advancing and enacting reflexive engagements in politics (including many within the US), we might further inquire into relevant tactics, particularly in view of the challenges of communication and dialogue.

Perhaps we have been too loose and easy with the confidence we have placed in dialogue as that which is going to rescue us from historical inequalities and the challenges of ever-present differences (even in critical and poststructural writing). It seems unlikely that we will ever arrive at the conditions for an equal exchange of views, but it's also possible that to aim for or try to approximate such conditions is misguided in the first place. In borrowing Kant's device of enlarged mentality for thinking, Arendt noted that we represent the views of others to ourselves for the purpose of internal dialogue. Listening, however, does not unproblematically translate into understanding, as Tzvetan Todorov (1999) has illustrated with reference to European–American encounters where some conquistadors had knowledge of the language and culture but did not understand and recognize others' identities and didn't desire to do so, instead instrumentally using knowledge for religious conversion and conquest (also see Banai on empathy and diplomacy, Chapter 11 in this volume). And, premising ethics on equal communicative exchange is not the best strategy if waiting for this condition delays ethics. It may also further shore up (post-colonial) power differentials when we locate power with those who have inordinate effects on others and thus depend on *them* to listen as a prerequisite of an ethics of understanding.

In a variety of social settings, then, we might consider strategies and tactics that agents have and might take up in their attempts to equalize discursive conditions, and we should appraise their instantiation in a practice of ethics. Heckling, for example, may momentarily shrink the access gap to public dialogue, when a member of the audience interrupts to point out that which is not being said or not addressed, or who is not seen. We might see more generously, then, (in our commentary on politics and our notions of legitimate political action) some confrontational tactics. We, in the US, are only beginning to acknowledge how drones might have far-reaching psychological and social costs to individuals and communities—this could perhaps be because of political action like the heckling of American activists, and Pakistanis and Yemenis traveling to the US to confront policymakers and the media. Tactics like heckling and confrontation make us uncomfortable, but they can—even momentarily—shrink the access gap to public voice. The media may publicize the heckler's message and speakers might themselves engage rather than ignore the heckler. In theorizing ethics we, as scholars, might praise or at least not judge harshly these kinds of communicative strategies that do not conform to idealized images of democracy and dialogue. Still, even these tactics are themselves subject to reflexivity—we all can try to anticipate how they might travel and take those trajectories into account.

Conclusion

Reflexivity as a term in International Relations has been wielded and deployed in a variety of ways, some more explicitly conceptualized than others. As this edited volume attests, reflexivity is more than reflection but its purposes and modalities are many. In this chapter I have argued that reflexivity as a practice of ethics in international/global politics is possible, desirable, and in need of more sustained attention, and I have begun to sketch the capacities and self-applications that such a practice would need. This practice of reflexivity is political and relational, but it is also a form of agency in which we might seek *just enough* critical distance, as individuals, from the pressures and homogeneities of the social and the intersubjective. It is here that, per Arendt, the pluralism of the self can emerge for a critical and dialectic internal dialogue. This "non-space" and "non-time", an absence in relation to politics but a presence in relation to self-reflexivity, is not engaged to re-order the public and the political, but to participate in political life as an always relational agent who represents and critically engages what he/she hears, thinks and feels, and dialectically explores and presents perplexities of thought and action. The point is to make dominant narratives problematic but also come up with alternatives that challenge us. Thus, like Levine's contribution to this volume, I am concerned with the capacities, spaces, and temporalities of a continuous reflexivity, not to resolve questions but to formulate and act on them.

Storytelling as one reflexive modality, for example, is not meant to uncover or reveal some true self or set of events. When Dauphinee's (2013) (semi-)fictional IR professor tears up her manuscript she is unable to explain this act to herself, but it is preceded by a complex and reflexive interplay of introspection, confrontation, dialogue and even silence, within herself and between herself and others. This process is endowed with meaning and creates a new beginning as the professor sits down to try to re-write what she knows, a different truth than the one it replaced. I am skeptical, then, of Mark Button's (Chapter 14 in this volume) critique of self-reflexivity on the grounds that it cannot produce epistemically reliable judgments based on unbiased and error-free beliefs because it neglects the ways in which our judgments are affected by psychological tendencies. For me, I do not think this idealized model of rationality is possible or even desirable. As Dauphinee's (2013) characters evince (and Beattie, Chapter 8 in this volume), both scholarship and politics can be much more subjective, uncertain, affective and relational than we have allowed in our models. And, holding out democracy and shared public culture as an institutional solution for world politics has thus far had undesirable consequences. We need new and more creative ways of doing politics that do not leave out deliberation, dialogue, provocation and action (also see Gould, Chapter 13 in this volume). I think that looking inward *and* looking to each other on a much smaller scale and in less prescribed ways holds more promise than institutions and norms. Yes, the activity of politics reflects our fundamentally social condition—living with and speaking to others—but we can also note the potential downsides or dangers of politics. Its spontaneity and creativity, for one, can be crowded out and co-opted by social and institutional pressures. And when we speak of norms, rules and roles we endow them with an independence and an agency that they do not necessarily or always have (see Gould, Chapter 13 in this volume; Amoureux 2016), nor can we assume that the stability of intersubjectivity will produce "good" outcomes (see Widmaier, Chapter 12 in this volume). The power of the masses borders on murder by the masses. Legal does not amount to ethical. I would prefer, then, to rely less on institutional and cultural design in attending to reflexivity.

Nevertheless, thinking and the courage and risk of the engaged thinker can be an activity relevant to politics only if it does not fall to the opposite danger Arendt underscored—the thinker's self-seclusion in her turn to abstractions. Not just as scholars, but as political agents, we might thus elaborate and take up reflexive practices as dispositions and tactics that create and engage tensions between self and community, and between self and self. We need thinking's seclusion for critique and to try to move away from the comfort and anonymity of the intersubjective (to the extent that it is possible), but we also need willing's projects and individuation to avoid getting stuck in thought, and to participate in the intersubjective of politics by attempting to narrate and participate in the projects of the "I" and the "We". It helps to note, I think, that there is no *one* intersubjective narration of a world, a community, or self. We are always social(-ized) selves, but we have the capacity to work with and create various understandings and write/speak texts that are more or less radically different, as in Foucault's technologies of the self. And, as William Connolly has argued, to appreciate identity's contingency and commitments "is also to set up the possibility that some of these entrenchments [corporeal habits, feelings, and dispositions] might be recomposed modestly through artfully devised tactics of the self and its collective sibling, micropolitics" even though they might be "below the reach of direct intellectual self-regulation" (Connolly 2002, pp. xvi–xvii).

Because of the volatility of action, including its unforeseen consequences, we must also try to take responsibility for our actions, and judge ourselves and others for what has and will unfold. If, as Bulley (2010), Zehfuss (2005) and others have noted in Derridean fashion, it is impossible to make a "right" decision that will avoid all suffering, then ethics is about making difficult and even impossible decisions (also Dauphinee, Chapter 2 and Ilieva, Chapter 10 in this volume). I see reflexivity, not as a ready-made solution, but as offering some resources for ethics and politics by taking the self and self–other relations as something that might be provisionally articulated and always interrogated, however imperfectly. To turn to reflexivity as ethics is not to delude ourselves with visions of cooperative international and global politics in the form of robust institutions and norms or, as Charlotte Epstein (2012) has argued, to "infantilize" agency by relying too much on the concept of intersubjectivity and the norms that might displace our responsibility and the difficulties we face. This has too often been the direction of IR. It is instead to let go of these visions, trouble our favored concepts, and tackle the hard work of politics, including its agonistic projects, strategies and tactics. Though there may be other components to a practice of ethical reflexivity (Amoureux 2016), here I have focused on imagining a *fractured self* as one such device, as a place to start.

Notes

1 I wish to thank Huss Banai, Mark Button, Elizabeth Dauphinee, Harry Gould, Eric Heinze, Dan Levine, Nick Onuf and Brent Steele for helpful feedback and advice.
2 Much of our understanding is tacit, or part of what Giddens terms the "practical consciousness" which operates between the unconscious and the discursive levels (1984, p. xxiii).
3 For a sampling, see the contributors to Villa (2000).

References

Ackerly, B. and True, J., 2008. Reflexivity in Practice: Power and Ethics in Feminist Research on International Relations. *International Studies Review*, 10(4), 693–707.

Amoureux, J.L., 2016. *A Practice of Ethics for Global Politics: Ethical Reflexivity.* New York: Routledge.

Amoureux, J.L. and Steele, B.J., 2014. Competence and Just War. *International Relations*, 28(1), 67–87.

Arendt, H., 1953. Understanding and Politics. *Partisan Review*, 20(4), 377–392.

Arendt, H., 1964. *Eichmann in Jerusalem: A Report on the Banality of Evil.* New York: Viking Press.

Arendt, H., 1966. *The Origins of Totalitarianism.* New York: Harcourt, Brace and World.

Arendt, H., 1969. Lying in Politics: reflections on the Pentagon Papers. In: *Crises of the Republic.* New York: Harcourt Brace and Company.

Arendt, H., 1972. *Crises of the Republic: Lying in Politics, Civil Disobedience on Violence, Thoughts on Politics, and Revolution.* New York: Harcourt Brace Jovanovich.

Arendt, H., 1978a. *Thinking.* New York: Harcourt Brace Jovanovich.

Arendt, H., 1978b. *Willing.* New York: Harcourt Brace Jovanovich.

Arendt, H., 1982. *Lectures on Kant's Political Philosophy.* Chicago, IL: University of Chicago Press.

Arendt, H., 1984. Thinking and Moral Considerations: A Lecture. *Social Research*, 51(1/2), 7–37.

Arendt, H., 1990. Philosophy and Politics. *Social Research*, 57(1), 73–103.

Arendt, H., 1998. *The Human Condition.* Chicago, IL: University of Chicago Press.

Aristotle, 1984. *Aristotle's Nicomachean Ethics*, translated by Apostle. Des Moines, IA: Peripatetic Press.

Beck, U., 1992. *Risk Society: Towards a New Modernity.* Thousand Oaks, CA: Sage Publications.

Beiner, R., 1982. Hannah Arendt on Judging. In: H. Arendt, *Lectures on Kant's Political Philosophy.* Chicago, IL: University of Chicago Press, pp. 89–156.

Bleiker, R. and Hutchison, E., 2008. Fear No More: Emotions and World Politics. *Review of International Studies*, 34(S1), 115–135.

Buckler, S., 2011. *Hannah Arendt and Political Theory: Challenging the Tradition.* Edinburgh: Edinburgh University Press.

Bulley, D., 2010. The Politics of Ethical Foreign Policy: A Responsibility to Protect Whom? *European Journal of International Relations*, 16(3), 441–461.

Butler, J., 1990. *Gender Trouble: Feminism and the Subversion of Identity.* New York: Routledge.

Butler, J., 2005. *Giving an Account of Oneself.* New York: Fordham University Press.

Butler, J., 2010. Judith Butler: As a Jew, I was taught it was ethically imperative to speak up. Interviewed by U. Aloni. *Haaretz.* February 24. Available from: www.haaretz.com/news/judith-butler-as-a-jew-i-was-taught-it-was-ethically-imperative-to-speak-up-1.266243.

Connolly, W.E., 2002. *Neuropolitics: Thinking, Culture, Speed.* Minneapolis: University of Minnesota Press.

Crawford, N.C., 2000. The Passion of World Politics: Propositions on Emotion and Emotional Relationships. *International Security*, 24(4), 115–156.

Dauphinee, E., 2013. *The Politics of Exile.* London: Routledge.

Eagleton-Pierce, M., 2011. Advancing a Reflexive International Relations. *Millennium—Journal of International Studies*, 39(3), 805–823.

Edkins, J., 2005. Ethics and Practices of Engagement: Intellectuals as Experts. *International Relations*, 19(1), 64–69.

Epstein, C., 2012. Stop Telling Us How to Behave: Socialization or Infantilization? *International Studies Perspectives*, 13(2), 135–145.

Foucault, M., 1984. *The Foucault Reader*. New York: Pantheon Books.

Foucault, M., 1997. *Essential Works: 1954–1984. Ethics: Subjectivity and Truth*. New York: New Press.

Foucault, M., 2007. *The Politics of Truth*. Los Angeles, CA: Semiotext(e).

Giddens, A., 1984. *The Constitution of Society: Outline of the Theory of Structuration*. Berkeley and Los Angeles: University of California Press.

Giddens, A., 1996. *In Defence of Sociology: Essays, Interpretations and Rejoinders*. Cambridge: Polity Press.

Giddens, A., 2002. *Runaway World: How Globalisation is Reshaping Our Lives*. London: Profile Books.

Giddens, A., 2014. Off the Edge of History: The World in the 21st Century [online]. Available from: www.lse.ac.uk/newsAndMedia/videoAndAudio/channels/publicLecturesAndEvents/player.aspx?id=1761 [Accessed February 23, 2014].

Guzzini, S., 2000. A Reconstruction of Constructivism in International Relations. *European Journal of International Relations*, 6(2), 147–182.

Guzzini, S., 2013. The Ends of International Relations Theory: Stages of Reflexivity and Modes of Theorizing. *European Journal of International Relations*, 19(3), 521–541.

Hamati-Ataya, I., 2012. IR Theory as International Practice/Agency: A Clinical-Cynical Bourdieusian Perspective. *Millennium—Journal of International Studies*, 40(3), 625–646.

Hayden, P., 2013. Albert Camus and Rebellious Cosmopolitanism in a Divided World. *Journal of International Political Theory*, 9(2), 194–219.

Inayatullah, N., 2011. *Autobiographical International Relations: I, IR*. London: Routledge.

Klotz, A. and Lynch, C., 2007. *Strategies for Research in Constructivist International Relations*. Armonk, NY: M.E. Sharpe, Inc.

Krause, S.R., 2008. *Civil Passions: Moral Sentiment and Democratic Deliberation*. Princeton, NJ: Princeton University Press.

Lang, A.F., Jr, 2002. *Agency and Ethics: The Politics of Military Intervention*. Albany, NY: SUNY Press.

Lang, A.F., Jr and Wiliams, J., 2005. *Hannah Arendt and International Relations: Readings Across the Lines*. New York: Palgrave Macmillan.

Levine, D.J., 2012. *Recovering International Relations: The Promise of Sustainable Critique*. New York: Oxford University Press.

Lynch, C., 2008. Reflexivity in Research on Civil Society: Constructivist Perspectives. *International Studies Review*, 10(4), 708–721.

Neufeld, M.A., 1995. *The Restructuring of International Relations Theory*. Cambridge: Cambridge University Press.

Nussbaum, M.C., 1994. *The Therapy of Desire: Theory and Practice in Hellenistic Ethics*. Princeton, NJ: Princeton University Press.

Oren, I. and Solomon, T., 2014. WMD, WMD, WMD: Securitization Through Ritualized Incantation of Ambiguous Phrases. *Review of International Studies*, 41(2), 313–336.

Owens, P., 2007. *Between War and Politics: International Relations and the Thought of Hannah Arendt*. Oxford: Oxford University Press.

Särmä, S., 2012. Junk Feminism and Collages of Wanna-Be Nuclear States. Presented at the International Studies Association Annual Convention, San Diego, CA, USA.

Shapcott, R., 2001. *Justice, Community, and Dialogue in International Relations*. Cambridge: Cambridge University Press.

Steele, B.J., 2008. *Ontological Security in International Relations: Self-Identity and the IR State*. New York: Routledge.

Steele, B.J., 2010. Of "Witch's Brews" and Scholarly Communities: The Dangers and Promise of Academic Parrhesia. *Cambridge Review of International Affairs*, 23(1), 49–68.

Steele, B.J., 2013. The Politics and Limits of the Self: Kierkegaard, Neoconservatism and International Political Theory. *Journal of International Political Theory*, 2013(2), 158–177.

Strong, T.B., 2013. The Wonder That Man Endures [online]. Hannah Arendt Center for Politics and Humanities. Available from: www.hannaharendtcenter.org/?p=9751 [Accessed March 2, 2014].

Sylvester, C., 2009. *Art/Museums: International Relations Where We Least Expect It*. Boulder, CO: Paradigm Publishers.

Todorov, T., 1999. *The Conquest of America: The Question of the Other*. Norman: University of Oklahoma Press.

Villa, D.R., ed., 2000. *The Cambridge Companion to Hannah Arendt*. New York: Cambridge University Press.

Williams, B., 1981. *Moral Luck*. Cambridge: Cambridge University Press.

Zehfuss, M., 2005. Remembering to Forgive? The "War on Terror" in a "Dialogue" Between German and US Intellectuals. *International Relations*, 19(1), 91–102.

2 Narrative engagement and the creative practices of International Relations

Elizabeth Dauphinee

It is undeniable today that we are witnessing an explosion of narrative approaches to the study of International Relations (IR). Our field now has a textbook (Edkins and Zehfuss 2013) that reintroduces the subjects of IR not as traditional academic theories (realism, liberalism and critical theory, etc.), but as questions (Why do some people think they know what is good for others? How do we begin to understand the world? Why do we obey?). We have edited volumes exploring authorial identity in the crafting of our research (Inayatullah 2011), special issues or sections of prominent journals (*Review of International Studies*, 2010; *Critical Studies on Security*, 2014), single-authored narrative manuscripts (Lowenheim 2014), and novels (Dauphinee 2013; Jackson 2014a). Add to this the 2014 founding of an open-access, peer-reviewed periodical, *Journal of Narrative Politics* [1], and it is clear that narrative approaches are beginning to populate the mainstream journals and publishing houses of critical IR. And yet, there is also a thread of unease running through the warp and weft of this approach—a lack of certainty as to its merits, anxiety surrounding the lack of established criteria on which to evaluate its contributions, a fear of self-indulgence, a fear of not being sufficiently scholarly or reflexive.

At the same time, there is also a sense that we can start to move away from the constant need to justify and defend even the smallest blasphemous point with the obligatory genuflection to the dominant paradigms of *thinking IR*. I don't want to worship theory but I'm also not opposed to rigor. I'm not comfortable with big unsubstantiated claims that often populate student essays: *the United States is evil; women are nicer; we need more bombs.* Instead, I am interested in exploring the possibilities surrounding my mother's admonition to write what I know in the way that I know it, and to not ask it to be more (or less) than it can be. What it can be, in the end, will be for others to judge. So, I want to write the contingency, uncertainty, fear, pain, and love that emerges in my scholarly research experience in a way that brings the reader closer to what I consider to be the experience of the political, and which allows me to be held accountable for the ideas and proposals I put forward. I don't think that most scholars would object to that as a goal, and I don't write it as a way of suggesting that other scholars are not engaged in good work. I don't write it to stake out some unassailable ground, but rather to explore a little. What are the possibilities for relationship between narrative and reflexivity? What is enabled by understanding the reflexive capacities of narrative? And what does narrative inhibit such that we might wish to object to it in both its form and its content? How can narrative allow us to engage across different terrains and conditions? How can we respond to some of the seemingly insoluble problems that narrative evokes—its supposed "indulgence" or its extreme, potentially depoliticizing, subjectivity? How can narrative function within and across the forms of reflexivity that Amoureux and Steele identify in the Introduction to this volume—positionality, critique, and practice? There are reasons to embrace narrative, and reasons to resist it. This chapter will begin by looking at some of the critiques of narrative and getting them out of the way.

Narrative is indulgent or therapy. Naeem Inayatullah writes that the feelings of self-indulgence that dogged his 2011 *Autobiographical International Relations* project emanated from the fear of exposure—of ridicule and embarrassment, and from the possibility that our exposure reveals in us not our greatness, but the mundane ubiquity of our existence. We are frequently wrong, painfully earth-bound, and often uninteresting. Writing that does not pay close attention to form, he argues, falls into either triumphalism or self-abnegation (Inayatullah 2011, p. 8). There is a risk of self-righteousness—the mistaken belief that our lives are uniquely interesting or our observations self-evidently valid. These risks are always present in the way we express ourselves, in whatever medium, and there is no evidence that the risks are inherent in specific forms of writing. Some months ago I received a review on an article I submitted to *Security Dialogue* saying that my approach was "therapy" in its worst form and that the reviewer simply did not "agree with the approach". The reviewer did not dismiss my article, but engaged with its substance, showing how I had conflated neopositivism with all social science and that this was inaccurate on my part and should be corrected. S/he wrote that there were rich histories of thick description and that thinkers like Marx wrote with verve and life. The reviewer was right about many of the article's shortcomings and I undertook revisions. I could not, however, accept the charge that narrative writing is therapy. (In the context of the article, the reviewer was specifically challenging autoethnography, but I take Iver Neumann's point that it is problematic to talk about autoethnography as what *we* do.) I want to pull back to the broader narrative, and in some measure, the reviewer helped me to realize this. However, I challenged quite vehemently the reviewer's charge that this was therapy. This is not therapy, I wrote in my response, but an approach that allows us to explore the role of the self in the production of knowledge, something that critical theory has been presumably engaged in since its inception. Having to explain how it is not therapy after twenty years of critical theory telling us that the personal is political is frankly quite annoying, I thought. My article was published without further ado. But now, many months out from the publication of that article, I want to change my direction on this and propose that therapy *is* one of the motivations of *all* writing—insofar as writing attempts to identify and rectify the wrongs of the world. And this is so whether we are talking about realist approaches that identify fear as an inherent motivator of international life, liberal approaches that attempt to justify competing rights, the multitude of people suffering from injustice, poverty, hunger, homelessness, war, genocide, displacement, imprisonment, slavery, and so on. Inayatullah writes that we will all write from a wound that follows us. But I think it possible to imagine that all IR identifies a wound in the world and then attempts to remedy it. That the architectures of those theories do not acknowledge the role of emotion or the needs of the author/researcher should not be taken to mean that those things do not matter, nor that they do not deeply inform the motivations and the research undertaken. The identity of the reviewer for *Security Dialogue* was, of course, not revealed, but I wonder what she or he would have responded if I had been able to propose this thesis: *All IR is a form of therapy—either for the scholar, for the world the scholar identifies, or for both.*

However, I do not consider this suggestion to mean that the therapeutic aspect of IR is self-indulgent. If the discipline is self-indulgent, it is a problem that plagues all of us at some point or another and has little to do with writing per se. Staunch positivists claiming to be objective observers whose grand analyses are meaningful, transhistorical commentaries on the social and political world also need to answer to the question of indulgence. Narrative writers actually tend not to make grand, sweeping generalizations based on their experiences (indeed, they cannot realistically generalize in sweeping terms from the standpoint of personal experience), but rather attempt to connect these experiences to the social and political world in specific and grounded ways. Constant reference to the place of the self is a permanent reminder of the smallness of one's capacities and ambitions—of the inherent limitations of any "self" to erect an architecture of truth.

Standpoint epistemology: This question of positionality—of reflexivity as positionality—leads to the second critique of narrative that I want to address. That is, that it cannot be critiqued because it represents a hyper-subjective representation of a lived reality that is unique and uniquely situated within the author's cultural and political experience. How can we engage something that emerges from such a deep subjectivity? Roland Bleiker and Emily Hutchison (2008) point out that this question is not actually new, rather it is *unresolved* in the context of the analytics of social science because neopositivist methodologies cannot apprehend the emotional frames of IR and so fail to engage them in a sustained way. This suggests that there must be other ways to engage the emotional frames of IR—ways that are not necessarily more authentic, but which nevertheless provide us with purchase on a particular problem that other approaches would disallow. Personal narratives *are* political narratives and their potential for reflexivity lies in the ways they may attempt to link that relation. Where they are unable to see past themselves into the social world is where the weaknesses might occur, and where we might begin to engage critique. Where a narrative has not extended beyond the confines of the author's personal ego, Inayatullah remarks, the shortcoming is that the author has failed to see the political aspects of the text she or he is writing—not that the text is inherently apolitical. In the context of positionality, narrative must draw linkages between the writer and the world the writer inhabits and seeks to express. This has to go beyond the feelings or sentiments of the author and create the linkage—identify the position of the author vis-à-vis his or her subject matter. Writing that fails to do this— writing that hovers only on the personal without awareness of how that personal is situated in and by the political—fails. It should be remembered that some of the most powerful social theory ever produced has emerged from the political and narrative experiential writings of great thinkers like Audre Lorde, bell hooks, Cynthia Enloe, and Patricia Hill Collins, who argued that Black women's intellectual history must be recovered in novels and other creative works by Black women.

Narrative is untrustworthy: In an ironic parody, Wanda Vrasti writes:

> Rigoberta Menchu was a liar, an inventor, and a manipulator. I, Wanda Vrasti, am none of the above. I am a scientist, an academic, an expert, and a professional. I am trustworthy and exact. I am a bearer of degrees, I carry business cards, I bring evidence when I write, and I make sense when I speak. Naturally then, neither do I write well, nor do I have any captivating stories to tell.
>
> (Vrasti 2011, p. 136)

We are used to the claim that objectivity and veracity are synonymous. Insert the fragmented, subjective, or "human", and truth claims begin to dissolve like salt in water. It is interesting that critical theory has very successfully problematized the veracity of objectivity, and yet one of the lingering fears surrounding narrative is its unverifiability. But we often rely on narratives in the field, as it were. When we go "out there" and collect the stories of others (which are then mobilized into truth-making social scientific studies), there is usually no presumption that the worlds we are examining may contain untruths. Put plainly, informants lie. And yet, when faced with the stories of ourselves—I mean, our own experiential stories—a suspicion creeps in. Inanna Hamati-Ataya argues, for example, that autobiography cannot be reflexive. Her position is based on the claim that the writer is not automatically aware of the self, despite her best attempts at so being. Of course, Hamati-Ataya is right. We do not actually have privileged access to ourselves. But nor do we have privileged access to any of the worlds we write about, and the generalized abstractions required by and of theory do not help us with that access. In fact, in some instances, theory can stand in for access. This lack of substitutability is conditioned by language more generally, and it is not unique to narrative forms. In this sense, narrative does not seek to enshrine universal truths, even if it may strive toward a certain universal appeal. Narrative is a practice or ethos expressing limited and specific positionalities. These positionalities may also be critiques of the universal claims of big theory, but narratives that are grounded in the writerly experience are by definition partial and situated. This awareness of fracture and partiality is, as I have argued elsewhere, its own ethics (Dauphinee 2007).

The trace of reflexivity

Texts are living things. The test of reflexivity is not a litmus test. Like so many other features of the postmodern, its value is decided not by the author, but by the reader, and manifests in some ways as a *sensibility* rather than a scientific knowing. As Jack Amoureux notes in Chapter 1 of this volume, "[r]eflexivity can ... be an approach to *grappling* with thought and action, which requires but moves beyond self-awareness" (p. 24). This grappling is not synonymous with "success" in the way we are accustomed to marking it in our academic lives. Some subjectivities and experiences—such as those associated with trauma—are unwriteable (Edkins 2003). At the same time, there is an integrity to experience, despite its fragmented character, that cannot always be easily evaluated or qualified. It is not really controversial to propose that politics cannot be thought without emotion and subjectivity, although emotion and subjectivity can be thought without politics. What is alluded to? What is left out? What has not been problematized? Is it believable? Is it political? What are its political and ethical sensibilities? R.B.J. Walker told us some twenty years ago that all approaches to the study of IR contained an ethical orientation, irrespective of whether that ethical orientation was explicitly expressed (1993). Defense of the state is an ethics. Defense of the individual is an ethics. What remains is the question of whether these are ethics we want to live with.

Two decades ago, Mark Neufeld argued that critical IR scholars interested in reflexivity had to challenge the prevailing mode of knowledge that posited "truth as correspondence". He showed that there was a structural inhibition to reflexivity in the context of social science approaches. Their "truth as correspondence" foundations assumed a distinction between subject and object, between knower and known. A subject that does not see itself as subjectively implicated in the construction of its object is by definition not reflexive, he argued. Similarly, he argued that "paradigms are social conventions whose function is to determine what is to count as evidence" (Neufeld 1991, p. 6). Neufeld argues that "post-positivist philosophy of science affirms that all scientific inquiry ... involves interpretation of theory-laden evidence by means of incommensurable theoretical frameworks which are themselves never other than social conventions adopted by a community of investigators" (ibid., p. 7). But Neufeld also shows that the acceptance of the notion of incommensurability does not automatically result in a greater surfeit of reflexivity. The reason for this, according to Neufeld, is that incommensurability is often conflated with incompatibility. For Neufeld, if incommensurability "means that attempts at inter-paradigmatic communication are futile, and that rea-soned judgments about the relative worth of rival paradigms are impossible, then the notion of incommensurability is as much an obstacle to theoretical reflexivity as is that of 'truth as correspondence'" (ibid., p. 7). Comparability suggests that there is a common ground on which paradigms or approaches can be judged according to their proximity to some kind of natural truth or correspondence to an agreed-upon "real world".

A second option lies in the claim that paradigms or approaches are incommensurable and therefore incomparable. This is the position of stand-point epistemology, which rests on a kind of inerrant exposition of the self and its experiences as an expression of unassailable truth. The inability to identify any stable, intersubjective ground from which to critique such approaches is a common early positivist critique of post-positivist approaches. This presumed inability to share foundational space also informs the current strand of concern about narrative approaches. If we cannot critique one another, then we are reduced to the unproductive response of silence. At best, we are condemned to misunderstanding, since it is presumed that we cannot understand what we do not have direct, experiential access to. Such a position also rests on a "truth as correspondence" paradigm, but does so in a way that proposes truth as accessible only by those whose access to that truth is mediated by experiences. Any suggestion that narrative approaches are standpoint approaches is arguably inaccurate. The narrative author does not write the self into the text in order to avoid critique, but rather to access as many analytic tools as possible.[2]

Neufeld's final option—the one that he suggests offers the most prospects for reflexivity—involves acknowledgement that, even where paradigms or approaches are incommensurable, *they are still comparable.* "This stance recognizes the social nature of the standards for what constitutes "reliable knowledge". But it also affirms that these conventions can be compared and assessed by means of reasoned argument and deliberation" (Neufeld 1991, p. 11). Neufeld writes:

> The fact that no neutral, context independent standards exist to assess competing paradigms does not mean that humans cannot use their faculty of reason in a given context to articulate standards and to per-suade others, by means of argument, of the worth of those standards (even while remaining cognizant of the fact that new arguments and new contexts may result in a re-examination and revision of those standards).
>
> (ibid., p. 15)

For Neufeld, "[i]t is just this position which expresses the core of the theore-tically reflexive disposition" (ibid., p. 15). However, such a position also appeals to an Aristotelian notion of reason that all interlocutors must have access to in order to express—in convincing terms—what the shared good life might entail and for whom. Narrative and autoethnographic approaches do not share this requirement to equal access. Reason is not the basis of their claims—lived experience is.

It is possible here to consider narrative approaches in this context as reflexive critiques of the claim to universal reason, even while narrative approaches may still allow us access to something that might resemble a universal experience in the sense that it *resonates* with readers or creates tangible linkages of understanding and access. The conclusion that we can use persuasion in order to develop, amend, and reject arguments gives us a way to crack the edifice of neopositivism with the purpose of apprehending what lies outside its purview. The fact that Neufeld made this observation twenty years ago, however, and that reflexivity has come no closer to an agreed-upon definition or method since that time is not a consequence of the failure of reflexivity, but of *the failure of scholars still oriented by neopositivism to recognize in a sustained way the plural potentials of reflexivity in different kinds of texts*. Reflexivity is not systematizable. It emerges in different texts differently and it performs differently in different circumstances, as Amoureux and Steele point out in their assessment of reflexivity as critique, as positionality, and as process. Daniel Levine, Chapter 5 in this volume, refers to this space as one that "resists any single conceptual, normative, or ontological schematic" (p. 103). The multi-purposeful character of reflexivity is not unique to the form, however. For example, IR scholars of all schools have recognized in recent years that human emotions play a role in world politics. However, this has not led to a systematic theorization of emotion in the field (Bleiker and Hutchison 2008), and this should not be understood as evidence that emotion is not being widely acknowledged. The concrete emotions of fear are one of the *acknowledged* underpinnings of classical realist security and foreign policy decision-making. Additionally, behavioralist approaches recognize that emotion may underpin bureaucratic decision-making (even if this is analyzed as a regrettable deviation from rationality) (ibid.). There are essentially no methodological debates on emotion in IR, despite the recognition that "one of the most promising locations to study emotions is the manner in which they are represented and communicated" (ibid., p. 128). Emotion is only knowable through "practices of representation, through narratives, gestures, or other ways of communicating feelings and beliefs" (ibid., p. 129). Emotions require text, even where text cannot convey them adequately. So it is with reflexivity—as gesture, as position, as critique, as process. In this context, the text that conveys cannot rely on truth as correspondence. Bleiker and Hutchison argue that conveying emotion cannot take place through the mechanisms of social science, whose expansive, all-encompassing architectures are concerned with truth rather than affect. This requires attention to representation—to the multiple modes of representation—that are possible. Reflexivity is visible in the variation and nuance of texts that convey some sense of the world without seeking to totalize that sense. Nor does this leave us in the tiresome mire of nihilistic "relativity". Reflexive scholarship identifies the situatedness of the author in the political world. However, even that claimed positionality cannot be held sacrosanct. I try to express myself in a way that shows where I think I am—intellectually, but also in my physicality (of relative wellness), my materiality (of relative privilege), and in my relationality (to loved ones, to neighbors, to communities, to strangers, and so on). I might not always get this right, but the point of making the attempt is not to close off critique by encircling myself with an unassailable standpoint epistemology. The point is to *open myself to critique*—to open myself to the response of the reader. For me, reflexivity is critique, and process, and positionality. It is also an ethos through which I strive to keep my own thinking mobile and fluid. This fluidity does not guarantee a better world, and in this sense, I am mindful of Amoureux and Steele's point that there remain the many "challenges and shortcomings of relating thought to action" (p. 4).

Social science, even with its traditions of thick description, as the *Security Dialogue* reviewer rightly pointed out, still requires a broadening of analytical technique. Bleiker and Hutchison identify modes of inquiry from the humanities as potential sustained approaches (2008, p. 131). One of the strengths of narrative approaches lies precisely in the ability to connect their authors more fully with their arguments. The author cannot hide behind a theoretical architecture in which s/he is not implicated. When the author is present (even imperfectly so), the reader has the opportunity to assess his or her place in the text—his or her positions, beliefs, or commitments. Narrative approaches can democratize the subjects of concern to IR by making insights and the fruit of field research *accessible* to an invested, reading public. As Richard Jackson, founding editor of *Critical Studies on Terrorism* and author of *Confessions of a Terrorist* [3] (2014a) puts it: "As academics we're locked into communicating through peer review, journal articles, specialist research. I wanted a way to convey what I've learned about terrorism, the motivations which drive it, the reasons they do it in a way that would grab people."[4]

With similar goals, Inanna Hamati-Ataya proposes a "strong reflexivity" to confront neopositivism on its "own turf", rather than withdrawing to a marginal position in IR where it might or might not survive. She also wants to recover objectivism from the "truth as correspondence" perspectives and thereby "reclaim the cognitive, social, and ethical values of social science" (Hamati-Ataya 2014, p. 157). Strong reflexivity "entails transcending both objectivism and subjectivism by redefining, rather than abandoning ... the notion of social-scientific objectivity" (ibid.). Hamati-Ataya also remarks on the democratization of autoethnography, but for different reasons—for her the author writing the autoethnography is exercising the pluralism associated with democracy. This is an important point, but also, for me, the reader is the subject of democratization.

"By violating the established system of meanings that govern and regulate IR's academic culture, autoethnographers tell us that the road of inquiry needs to be reopened, because the lessons of the critique of objectivism have not been sufficiently translated into research practice" (ibid., pp. 158–159). But I don't see myself as engaged in something that linear. I accept that other approaches are valid. The difference here is that I (sometimes) choose to embark on an approach that allows me to say something else, to say something that is not a supplement, as Hamati-Ataya notes with respect to the impetus for the autoethnographic turn in Anthropology, but rather central to knowledge production. Not exclusive knowledge production. But knowledge production. Hamati-Ataya notes that autoethnography in IR is "still too young and too experimental to provide us with clear guidelines" and that "[i]nsofar as autoethnography includes a narrative about the self, it relies on a given ontology of the subject" (ibid., pp. 159, 161). I do not know how it is possible to employ a non-ontological subject, but I believe it is possible to embark on writing from an ontological constitution of the subject that is changing and changeable. As *Politics of Exile* showed, it is impossible to unproblematically narrate the self, and any attempts to do so should be met with suspicion. To the extent that this may fail in its purest form, as auto-ethnographers sometimes write a temporary stability of the self, well, so what? That temporary stability is a fiction, and any good writer knows it and can employ it in ways that highlight the changes undergone by the self. Patrick Thaddeus Jackson, for example, moves through these subjectivities without explicitly delineating them in his "Three Stories" (2011), particularly in his discussion of his autistic son, Quinn. The characteristics Jackson identified in himself as a child and as a young man suddenly take on a new kind of politics and a new series of interconnections in his recognition of his own autistic shadow traits in his three-year-old son. Is this a more precise discovery of Jackson's transhistorical personal qualities and affects? Are we to understand this as a move from "nerd" to "autistic"? I don't think so. In Jackson's text, *he has seen himself anew* with uncertainty, disquiet, and hope. The terms have altered. The context has changed, and has changed him. Before we have the language of autism, we have the language of quirks and idiosyncrasies, of unique and cherished modes of interacting that are also frustrating and sometimes skin-crawling. After the language of autism, we have behavioral modifications and clinical indicators. How do we arrive at these re-evaluations of qualities and connections in ways that reveal the constantly changing nature of subjectivity? Hamati-Ataya, reading Barthes and Derrida, acknowledges this inability to confess a stable self—something Jackson is clearly aware of in his "Three Stories". For Hamati-Ataya, the difficulty of unpacking the autoethnographic text is its conflation of known with knower. But just as Jackson argues that autism cannot be separated from the autistic, so the desire to separate known from knower—even analytically—is an impossible task. This means that the possibilities for response must be recalibrated. One question to pursue is whether we can consider our emotional responses—our visceral responses—as analytically valid in an *a priori* way, and then to pursue "scientific" inquiry (if we must) from that point. In this sense, reflexivity as process can highlight the contextually changing nature of self and other, and of constellations of knowledge as they change over time and space.

The everyday

Not every intervention is radical. Not every narrative is transformative. We can evaluate them on their own grounds in order to debate their relative merits. No narrative form is or can be *inherently* reflexive. In some moments it might be; in some moments it is not. That is the trouble with things that are not systematized—they can't invite nor stand up to a systematic critique. What gives narrative its potential power is its ability to mobilize a different kind of language where "truth as correspondence" experiences its worst failures: in war, famine, in utter destruction—but also in moments of elation, like love, joy, and rescue (at least, for me). This raises the question of the epistemological status of the aesthetic experience. How do we intervene at the intersection where philosophical concepts coincide with the sweat on one's skin, or with grief, or love, or fear? That encounter is a particularity. The narrative that speaks from this intersection is not a supplement to the academic text. It *is* the academic text. It does not entail writing about an experiment. Rather, the writing itself is the experiment. This does not oppose narrative to other academic forms, but neither does it relegate narrative to the status of supplement to the "real" texts of social scientific IR. In this sense, I don't share Hamati-Ataya's concern that narrative might be relegated to the margins of IR. That does not bother me. I am not seeking out the creation of a "new" paradigm to transcend or replace IR theory. I would not ask narrative approaches, for example, to replace Marxism, feminism, postcolonialism, critical disability studies, critical race theory, and so on. I believe that there is a place for plurality in our scholarship, and that this is also a manifestation of reflexivity. But the transgression of many established forms of boundary-making in IR, including in the context of its critical forms, is inherent to narrative approaches. That is, by their nature, autoethnographic and creative, narrative approaches disrupt established methodologies. This is a manifestation of narrative as critique. Good narrative will always take the form of critique. This does not make all narratives or all narrative expression unproblematically valid, nor does the question of boundaries provide us with any criteria through which to determine what narratives are better than others. However, critical theorists of all stripes have the capacity and the theoretical tools, regardless of their traditions, to ask what political and ethical work a text is doing and to thereby evaluate its merits. Not all narrative will be successful, any more than we accept that all constructivist approaches, or all positivist approaches, are successful. It is very possible to identify crude, unreflective narrative, but no form or approach to the study of IR and its subjects is immune from those risks. This, therefore, cannot be the undoing critique of narrative approaches.

It is this more than anything that I believe forms the crux of objections—the discomfort and in some cases disdain of narrative and autoethnographic approaches. Let us expand from "autoethnography", which in any event in anthropology, its mother discipline, is often critiqued for its apolitical nature.

Let us consider how narrative can facilitate a problematization of the self as a way to signal the self's instability; to maintain its critical stance and to continue to require its awareness of its own fragmentation or, as Neufeld would suggest, its incommensurability but ultimate comparability. Thoughtful people can use their powers of critique to examine these approaches for their failures, and to commend them for their successes, however particular and contextual they may be. Reflexivity means leaving room for the author and reader to *become*. It must leave room for knowledge as invention, when invention means the creation and recreation of a mobile selfhood (Shapiro 2013). I sent *Politics of Exile* to Routledge's *Interventions* series because I felt that the book came closest to what I have spent my career trying to understand: that it is possible—fearfully possible—to love people who have committed devastating crimes. And it is possible—fearfully possible—to recognize that there is no place of innocence from which to judge those crimes. This does not mean that we do not judge crimes or those who have committed them, and it does not mean that we are now flung into a relativist abyss. It means recognizing that, as Dostoevsky wrote, the one doing the judging may be just as guilty of the crime, if not more so. To me, this awareness does not necessitate any nihilistic revision of history. Rather, it attenuates me to the full promise of reflexivity: its precarious glimmer in the liminal spaces between introspection and social research. That is another, more elusive form of reflexivity, "… accessible only in its trace" (Levinas 1998, p. 64). I don't know if I can represent myself more authentically, but I am interested in what I already know about the political and social through my embeddedness within it. I am interested in exploring those connections that are seldom admitted to: the relationships between perpetrators and victims, between mimesis and torture, between ethics and research, between myself as a writer and the worlds I inhabit and that constitute me (Dauphinee 2007, 2010, 2013).

Levinas says that God is a blinking light in the darkness. So with reflexivity in this sense, its elusiveness lies in its defiance of every attempt to fully define it—its elusiveness lies in the overflow that is revealed by every attempt to firmly delineate its contours. The ineluctability of reflexivity does not mean we cannot speak of it in meaningful ways, or recognize it in the moments of its illumination in the various texts and in the textual practice of our political civilizations. It emerges in the inevitable expression of our vulnerability, intentional or unintentional. But this reflexivity also overflows the boundaries of our professional remit. It is an unsustainable posture—an emotion—a gesture toward the impossibility of truth as correspondence. Reflexivity requires awareness of the fractured mobility of the self, and of the ways in which the self attempts to hide from the exposure that writing always threatens— the revelation of its imperfection, of its weakness, of its partiality, or its *wrongness*. In the cadence of our professional journals, this weakness is denied or obscured. What narrative approaches permit is the overt explanation of this weakness in a way that allows readers to judge its role in our scholarship— how it delimits what we can say, for whom, and for what purposes. We don't have to be aware of our own limitations when we write about ourselves. The reader will see the limitations. We can trust the reader to see this. Any group of undergraduates in a seminar room who have read a text can feel its limits, even when those limits are difficult to precisely define. This, too, is a species of reflexivity—a blinking light in the darkness; the ragged edges of the wound between the sutures. It is *possibility*, not just theory. In this way, reflexivity introduces complexity—plurality—of form. It gives us a possibility of theorizing and *embracing* contingency, rather than simply acknowledging its existence and then moving on with the architecture as though we had not known it. In this sense, what narrative approaches ask is to be evaluated on their own ground, in terms of the work that each text does or does not do. Jenny Edkins (2013) says this best when she says that politics is what happens when stories confound existing categories of analysis. Insofar as this is so, reflexivity is also the process of this confounding.

Reflexivity, then, appears as a number of sensibilities—as critique, positionality, process, as vulnerability, sensuality, and uncertainty. For Amoureux, Chapter 1 in this volume, it is also a set of "resources for trying to get along in the world, for struggling against and yet prodding that which we feel threatened by, and for elaborating and engaging that which challenges us" (p. 25). There is no transhistorical architecture through which to speak of reflexivity because its sensibilities rely on a permanently fluid subjectivity—an ethos—that is nevertheless intersubjectively expressed and epistemologically plural in its interconnections, failures, and violences. Reflexivity requires an ethos of suspicion—a suspension of belief in both established theory and practice in favor of an introspective suspicion. One regards oneself with suspicion. One regards one's motives with disbelief. Patrick Thaddeus Jackson writes: "I can surprise myself by living my life, but not when I try to social-scientifically explain my academic vocation" (2011, p. 161). Reflexivity lies in the failures and promises of the Derridean notion of undecidability and in différance—the notion that one must decide under conditions where one cannot decide. There is more than a hint of the Foucauldian instructive here. If power and knowledge are inseparable, then we need to study them together. Epistemological introspection becomes politically relevant and introspection becomes "extrospection"—social research.[5] None of this negates the materiality—and the material urgency—of the everyday. None of this displaces or needs to displace other voices, even voices that speak more stridently and more violently. Ruminating on the war in Bosnia, an old man who was one of my best-loved informants once said to me: *Ne može biti ljudi isti—People can't be the same.* I know that is not a good enough ethics, but it gives a baseline for plurality in that it automatically provides the possibility of other ways of seeing the world and ourselves in it.

In this sense, motivations for writing in IR are also about wagers—practical wagers that our approaches have the capacity to make the world a different place, that we can mitigate the worst features of Westphalian politics, or at least that we are able to understand the violences that are produced by this politics and how those violences are inscribed on others. Roland Bleiker writes that "the problems that currently haunt world politics, from terrorism to poverty, are far too serious not to employ the full register of human intelligence to understand and deal with them" (2009, p. 1). And yet, rather than embrace the expansion of the modes through which we could know and write the world, we witness instead the tightening of defenses and the deeper entrenchment of ideas about what constitutes appropriate academic writing in IR. Perhaps nowhere was this more evident than in the proposal tabled by the International Studies Association (ISA) in 2014 that would prohibit the editors and editorial teams of its five scholarly journals from maintaining weblogs. While the backlash was swift and condemnatory, Harvey Starr, the University of South Carolina professor who serves as the ISA president argued for the ban as follows: "Often the sort of 'professional environment' we expect our members to promote is challenged by the nature of the presentations and exchanges that often occur on blogs", Starr wrote. "The proposed policy is one response, not to blogs *per se*, but to issues that can arise with people confusing the personal blogs of the editors of ISA journals with the editorial policies for their journals. This proposal is trying to address that possible confusion."[6] Leaving aside the obvious fact that the political proclivities and intellectual commitments of journal editors play a significant role in the sorts of things they are willing to accept and publish, the claim seems to be that editors and editorial teams should switch off their political commitments when operating in their official capacities *and that it is somehow possible for them to do so.*

This is but one example, but it highlights the question about what we want our discipline to be able to do. Rather than attempting to rest our motivations in the unassailable world of IR as social science, I am interested in recognizing IR as a part of *who we are*—or as Amoureux and Steele suggest, as part of our position in the world. I want to see why the people whose work I spend my professional life reading approach their subject matter the way they do. I want to see why they write and how they see themselves in the context of their subject matter. I do not want to see these things as an aside, a footnote, or a little human interest sliver in an acknowledgement or a footnote, but in the rich veins of their thinking and theorizing. Reflecting on her childhood self, Shiera S. el-Malik writes:

> Sabra and Shatila touched me in a space difficult to isolate with words … I learned that children with young and skinny bodies like mine were lined up against a wall and shot dead. The idea that people positioned their bodies, or were forced to physically position them, for certain death shook the chambers of my heart and made me nauseous; it still does.
>
> (el-Malik 2013, p. 361)

Reflecting on a decade of American occupation, Inayatullah writes: "I had not sensed my need for Afghanistan" (2011, p. 2). Richard Jackson writes:

Actually, I have to confess, these days when I speak in IR and security studies, I feel like a fraud. I feel as if I am speaking lies and distortions, and everyone can see it. Because I know that the numbers, labels, categories, concepts, assumptions, models, and theories we employ in our field to explain the world we study do not – and cannot – properly represent the real human beings about which we claim to speak. More often than not, there is a wide, gaping chasm between the human beings I know, and the human being I know myself to be, and the academic language used to describe and analyse them.

(Jackson 2014b, p. 225)

In these positionalities lie glimmers of reflexivity—snapshots of men and women acknowledging and grappling with the chasm between their scholarship and their lives; between their lives and the worlds they write.

Can narrative approaches be conceived as part of what Bleiker and others have called the aesthetic turn? Or the affective turn? Can we reclaim them also on the basis of their accessibility? Is there some merit in the deprofessionalizion of our field? Deprofessionalization does not equal simplification. Indeed, some of the greatest pieces of writing are great precisely because one sees something different every time one reads them. Leaving aside the mobility of the subject that revisits such texts, the texts themselves shift and change over time, across cultures and generations—texts like *The Grapes of Wrath, The Good Earth,* and *The Brothers Karamazov.* Roland Bleiker points out that the poems of Anna Akhmatova were written "in a direct and accessible way. And this was also the source of her politics" (2009, p. 144). For Bleiker, "[p]oetry alludes, rather than explains. It shows, rather than argues" (2009, p. 145. Cf. Inayatullah, 2011, p. 2). Bleiker believes that "a fictional account of an event or epoch more actively engages the gap that opens up between the event in question and its representation through language. Poetry, for instance, recognises that this inevitable gap is the place where politics and the struggle for power take place" (2009, p. 147). This struggle for power is a struggle for the ability to express what can most closely resemble experience. In Akhmatova's case, this is perhaps most powerfully expressed in her poem, "Requiem". Akhmatova is standing outside a Leningrad prison with other families waiting for word of her detained son. A woman turns to her in the freezing cold courtyard and asks:

"Can you describe this?"
And I answered: "Yes, I can."
Then something that looked like a smile passed over
what had once been her face.

(Bleiker 2009, p. 148)

Bleiker rightly points out that most social science is presented as mimetic representation. That is, social science is not presented as a form of *interpretation* (ibid., p. 27), open to revision and to the awareness of its inevitable partiality. This is one of its profound limitations with respect to reflexivity. But "knowledge and knowing are not just imbricated in social life, they *are* social life and thus they are tensed by creativity *and* apodictic determination at the same time" (Ravecca 2014). Great aesthetic writing allows us to come very close to experience in certain moments by speaking pain in an intersubjective way. Wittgenstein says that the one who cries out in pain does not choose the mouth which says it. I take this to mean that we can come very, very close to the pain of others—so close that our mouths can say something about it—can convey something about it that is part of its essence. Naeem Inayatullah understands this as a "secret belief" that at the core of ourselves we find "not world historical processes but rather an essence" (2011, p. 8).

For Inayatullah, what emerges in the context of reflexivity is the question of what the writing *writes back*. And the *unexpected* that emerges from this—the experiment—the risk—of all writing: its ability to change us; its ability to change the reader.

There are four specific features of narrative writing that I would like to highlight as possible heralds of reflexivity:

1   *Knowledge as invention*. I want to hold onto this understanding of knowledge proposed by Michael Shapiro (2013). This involves attention to the creativity of writing. And it also summons the question of vitality. "How do we create texts that are vital? That are attended to? That make a difference? One way to create those texts is to turn our attention to writing as a method of inquiry" (Richardson 1994, p. 517). She concludes that "… writing is always partial, local, and situational", inevitably relegated to a "partial presence" or a hybrid presence. In this sense, the task is not to "get it right" but to explore what other nuances and contours are possible.

2   *The power of surprise as a theoretically valuable variable.*[7] Narrative can help us rescue historical specificity and the socially situated content of everyday life. Theories of global politics do not manage surprise well. They cannot incorporate its disruptive intrusion. Narrative approaches can accommodate rupture—they can get closer to the complexities of life that elude theory. As Patrick Jackson writes, "I can surprise myself by living my life, but not by my narration of my social scientific self" (2011, p. 161). For Inayatullah, this is expressed as a meditation on what the writing writes back.

3   *The ability to embrace incompleteness in the way we see ourselves*, such that our "narratives" cannot claim to be more complete or faithful representations of the worlds they attempt to access. It is not that they are doing inherently better work (they're not, and sometimes the work they are doing is worse work), but there is a possibility of reflexivity in aesthetic writing that gets us potentially closer to experience. At the same time, there is a pressing concomitant need to maintain awareness of these

narrative limitations. Just because one writes creatively does not mean that one writes well or that one conveys something more valuable than a social scientific account might. Writing is only one way to approach the world, and different kinds of writing do different things.

4 *The use of emotion can unpack the traces of power.* Good narrative tells us something about the world that we could not know in any other way. Bleiker and Hutchison's important recognition that emotion *is* actually acknowledged across many approaches to IR should alert us to the fact that various expressions of that emotional content are already happening. I think we need to resist attempts to systematize an evaluative criteria for emotional expression. This has the double effect of leaving the possibility of closure or conclusion open, but also making the parameters of debate difficult to identify. If our goal is to take seriously the content of human emotion as a meaningful analytic, then narrative approaches are one such contribution.

***

Our apprehension of the world is always mediated by text. This is the basic claim of poststructural theory, and it is a tenet of most other critical approaches. The world is a constructed place. Few today would argue that this approach is not a valid one, even if they were not to subscribe to it themselves. The question I am interested in is how to understand and elucidate that construction, and in what that means for scholarship and writing. What are the criteria through which some people's stories are scholarship, and some people's stories are folklore or "narrative"? How can narrative contribute to the deepening of the discipline toward a posture of reflexivity in all of its possible forms?

Notes

1 *The Journal of Narrative Politics* is funded by a grant from the Social Sciences and Humanities Research Council of Canada.
2 Additionally, to what extent is the rejection of narrative on the grounds of standpoint epistemology just a reintroduction of a first-order Cartesian anxiety? After the aesthetic turn, is the fear of unverifiability still so profound?
3 Jackson's original manuscript was titled *The Interrogation of Yusef,* and his publisher, Zed Books, changed it to *Confessions of a Terrorist.* Academic publishers change titles regularly. My first book, published with Manchester University Press, was sent to the publisher under the title *Looking for Bosnia* and published as *The Ethics of Researching War.* My edited volume with Cristina Masters was sent under the title *living, dying, surviving the war on terror,* and was changed by Palgrave to *The Logics of Biopower and the War on Terror.* Ironically, only *The Politics of Exile* went to the publisher and came out again with the same title—a commentary, however anecdotal, on what else authors might retain.
4 Andrew Stone, "Terror Scholar Explores a Dark Fictional World", *New Zealand Herald,* February 22, 2014. Available from: www.nzherald.co.nz/nz/news/article.cfm?c_id=1&objectid=11207418.
5 I am grateful to Paulo Ravecca for pointing this out to me so succinctly.
6 www.insidehighered.com/news/2014/01/29/international-studies-association-proposes-bar-editors-blogging#ixzz2v0jIrOrj.
7 I am indebted to Paulo Ravecca for this specific notion of surprise as valuable to theory.

References

Bleiker, R., 2009. *Aesthetics and World Politics*. New York: Palgrave.

Bleiker, R. and Hutchison, E., 2008. Fear No More: Emotions and World Politics. *Review of International Studies*, 34(S1), 115–135.

Critical Studies on Security, 2014. A special 'Interventions' section in: *Writing In/Security*, 2(2), 224–243.

Dauphinee, E., 2007. *The Ethics of Researching War: Looking for Bosnia*. Manchester: Manchester University Press.

Dauphinee, E., 2010. The Ethics of Autoethnography. *Review of International Studies*, 36(3), 799–818.

Dauphinee, E., 2013. *The Politics of Exile*. London: Routledge.

el-Malik, S.S., 2013. Critical Pedagogy as Interrupting Thingification. *Critical Studies on Security*, 1(3), 361–364.

Edkins, J., 2003. *Trauma and the Memory of Politics*. Cambridge: Cambridge University Press.

Edkins, J., 2013. Novel Writing in International Relations: Openings for a Creative Practice. *Security Dialogue*, 44(4), 281–297.

Edkins, J. and Zehfuss, M., 2013. *Global Politics: A New Introduction*. London: Routledge, 2nd edn.

Hamati-Ataya, I., 2014. Transcending Objectivism, Subjectivism, and the Knowledge in-between: The Subject in/of Strong Reflexivity. *Review of International Studies*, 40(1), 153–175.

Inayatullah, N., ed., 2011. *Autobiographical International Relations: I, IR*. London: Routledge.

International Studies Association Proposes Ban on Blogs. *Inside Higher Education*. January 29, 2014.

Jackson, P.T., 2011. Three Stories. In: N. Inayatullah, ed., *Autobiographical International Relations: I, IR*. London: Routledge, pp. 161–172.

Jackson, R., 2014a. *Confessions of a Terrorist*. New York: Zed Books.

Jackson, R., 2014b. Writing In/security. *Critical Studies on Security*, 2(2), 224–227.

Levinas, E., 1998. *Of God Who Comes to Mind*. Stanford, CA: Stanford University Press.

Lowenheim, O., 2014. *Politics of the Trail*. Ann Arbor: University of Michigan Press.

Neufeld, M., 1991. The Reflexive Turn and International Relations Theory. *York Centre for International and Security Studies Working Paper #4*, pp. 1–22.

Ravecca, P., 2014. Personal communication.

Review of International Studies forum, 2010. Autoethnography and International Relations, *Review of International Studies*, 36(2), 777–818.

Richardson, L., 1994. Writing: A Method of Inquiry. In: N.K. Denzin and Y.S. Lincoln, eds, *Handbook of Qualitative Research*. Thousand Oaks, CA: Sage, pp. 516–529.

Shapiro, M.J., 2013. *After the Aesthetic Turn*. London: Routledge.

Stone, A., 2014. Terror Scholar Explores a Dark Fictional World. *New Zealand Herald*. February 22, 2014.

Vrasti, W., 2011. Goodbye, Nostalgia! In Memory of a Country that Never Existed as Such. In: N. Inayatullah, ed., *Autobiographical International Relations: I, IR*. London: Routledge, pp. 136–151.

Walker, R.B.J., 1993. *Inside/Outside: International Relations as Political Theory*. Cambridge: Cambridge University Press.

3 Whistle disruption

Reflexivity and documentary provocation

Brent J. Steele

The argument I put forth in this chapter depends upon disruption. Like many of the other contributions to this volume, I recognize that reflexivity has carried with it a multitude of meanings in the social sciences and specifically in the field of International Relations (IR). My purpose here is both inventory of my own work in the terms set out by the introductory chapter, but then to also situate the problem in stark, and likely uncomfortable terms. Although contentious, I assert that there is a particular irony regarding neopositivist research, one that when recognized by reflexive scholars needs to be called out. On the one hand, neopositivism assumes a distinction between subjects and objects to maintain its fidelity to "science", and yet on the other some of the most enthusiastic contributors to *policymaking itself* are neopositivist scholars, who use *their theories and hypotheses* to advocate for particular positions and policies. In other words, they embody what Giddens calls (and what Jack Amoureux and I describe further in the Introduction to this volume as) the "double hermeneutic" or "slippage" between subject and object. Yet, they need to go a step further, assessing *what* in their theories or perspectives, or, conversely, *what* in the political field that they study, made possible political outcomes—intended or otherwise—in the first place. Without such recognition, the neopositivist *political* stance towards International Relations (and international relations) presents a potentially dangerous combination. Thus, to the extent that neopositivist scholars "whistle past the graveyard" in pursuing their work, we need to think of ways to disrupt them, to force them into reflexive awareness.

The chapter begins by exploring each of the three critical reflexivity categories used to organize this volume—(1) as a critique to "stimulate" self-reflexivity; (2) As a practical-ethical approach, and (3) as a contextuality or positionality focusing on the role of the scholar. I take a somewhat self-centered (if not "auto-ethnographic") approach to this exploration—reviewing the ways in which my work has "used" and perhaps "stretched" the concept of reflexivity. Having engaged in such an attempt to connect these different uses at least in the examples from my own work, the chapter then moves to the "critique" form of critical reflexivity. Here, I assert that the productive and praxis capacities of scholarship should be considered just as, if not more important, than the "intentions" of the scholar. While all research is political, we should pay close attention, for instance, to the types of research which can be used explicitly for political purposes.

The purpose of this chapter is to push forward a practice of critical reflexivity, what I call "documentary provocation", one that attempts to hold scholars responsible for a variety of outcomes linked to their scholarship—outcomes planned, unplanned, seen, and unforeseen. While such a proposal will likely be controversial (at best), or prone to be wilfully ignored (at worst), there is the possibility that this practice can help do what Daniel Levine calls a "chastening" of perspectives and theses of their confidence, certainty, and ultimately their role in persuading policymakers (Levine 2012).

This scholarly practice of "documentary provocation" includes two main steps. First, scholars might gather together in documentary form a background on the academic-intellectual, or their scholarly "field", that they are seeking to provoke. This, as I suggest in the chapter, is not purposed by the need to collect a "dossier" of evidence on the subjected scholar (although it may appear that way and be interpreted as such), but rather as an exercise of what we might call part of the "care of the scholarly Self", and is in fact a step that can be both educational and instructive as well as generating empathy. In some ways, such documentary data is already at our disposal, as I discuss below. Second, the "provocative" step (what I title following my earlier Foucauldian-inspired studies "Cynic parrhesia") includes a variety of venues and tactics that can stimulate a response on behalf of, or even by, the scholar in question. These tactics and venues include "tweets", professional outlets or journal interviews, or even in-person (but public) questions at conferences and meetings.

Thus, I examine some existing forms, forums, spaces, and situations where scholarly documentation is either occurring or from where information can at least be collected to reveal the background of scholars, their various experiences, that may influence their scholarship and what I once titled their "vectors" of trajectory (Steele 2010a). Namely, I briefly review auto-ethnography (both in formal and subterranean forms), and critical intellectual history for their functional worth in fostering this documentation. Then, in the penultimate section, I engage in a detailed recent example of scholars whose work on US public opinion (as a dependent variable) influenced, directly, the "surge" policy of the Bush administration which continued the US occupation of Iraq from 2007 onward. I focus on the role of Christopher Gelpi and Peter Feaver who not only examined statistically and analytically, but also used (or donated, perhaps?) their thesis on "winning wars" and public opinion to influence the continuation of conflict, including especially the Iraq War. I examine how, like other neopositivist IR scholars (including Bruce Russett) before them, in the years following the Surge there has been little to no reflexive awareness or disclosure of their responsibilities for this late 2000s process. Thus, the penultimate section provides several venues for provoking a series of reflexive moments (rather than a "conversation") from scholars just like Gelpi and Feaver. Owing to the expectation that *silence* is one of *the* strongest ways to resist such questioning about the responsibilities embedded with being a scholar of International Relations, this is a modest proposal for what can be considered less a "conversation" over our role as scholars than an insurgent ethos. In other words, while dialogue following such tactics would be welcome, I am under no illusion that this may occur. At the very least, though, I am calling for disruption—we need to disrupt those whistling past the graveyards of international relations.

Reflexivity and its uses

It is typical as one advances in age to become a bit more reflective on some of the decisions, and practices, that colored one's career. So it's a bit embarrassing for me for instance when I take a look in a panoramic manner of the way in which I have traveled (Sartori 1970) and stretched (Collier and Mahon 1993) particular concepts, including "identity" and, more immediately, "reflexivity". In that sense, I am more than guilty of the kind of multiple uses of reflexive and reflexivity that Hamati-Ataya notes of the broader field of IR.[1] By my count, the term "reflexive" has appeared in at least three of my published studies (Hom and Steele 2010; Steele 2007b, 2007c), or chapters within other studies (Steele 2010b). The concepts of "reflexive" or "reflexivity" have also been foregrounded in several others, including my work on ontological security (Delehanty and Steele 2009; Steele 2005, 2008). Other work has used the term specifically in the context of the "role" of the scholar vis-à-vis her world, especially for examining the relationship between democratic peace theory and the theorist and its use in the Iraq War (Steele 2007a, 2010a).

In another study (2011), Hamati-Ataya notes that positivism's development in the 1960s through today had an impact upon especially IR scholarship. In the need to separate "facts" from "values" and to avoid the kind of "biased" interpretations that were better left to commentary and op-eds, positivism produced an "adherence to a notion of 'value-freedom'". Yet such adherence "thereby led to a generally accepted and consensual stance whereby values as both *objects of study* and as *constitutive variables* in the production of knowledge are largely disregarded" (Hamati-Ataya 2011, p. 268, emphases in original).

Indeed, this was a fairly good characterization of the graduate program where I pursued my PhD. (the University of Iowa) in the early 2000s. In those days, the key buzzword characterizing works that engaged values or ethics was "normative". And yet, also during that time there was a pronounced and stark juxtaposition between the types of "things" we were supposed to be studying, ad nauseum—like the origins and uniform variables responsible for interstate "rivalries" going back to the early 1800s, or what factors prevented democracies from fighting one another—with the way in which "values" colored the behavior of those key figures constructing policies in the wake of 9/11 and the "War on Terror". The best way to delineate the story of that decade, in my view, was to accept that ethics was a part of the processes we were studying. Thus, I found myself producing work that would define my research program for the years ahead—simultaneously in the fields of International Ethics and Security Studies—precisely because to interpret processes related to one I need to draw from processes and debates in the other (and vice-versa).

Moreover, the idea that "we" scholars could actually delineate and differentiate the "world out there" from the scholarship we produced in our ivory towers became increasingly problematic for me in the months and years following 9/11. One particular workshop organized by the neopositivist IR professors in my graduate program on Democratic Peace brought together a number of the seminal scholars in the field working on that program at that time. It was an important if also troubling experience, and not only because some scholars there joked with great humor about the "fuzzy" constructivist work that they saw as a passing fad in those days. It was also, more importantly, the distinct *lack* of any reflexive sensibility at the workshop I found so problematic, especially considering the context in which it met. Shortly before the workshop convened, then-US President George W. Bush had given his 2004 "State of the Union" address. Each passing day of that time disclosed no Weapons of Mass Destruction—one of the *casus belli*—in Iraq. In such a context, Bush invoked democratic peace theory to justify not only why the US needed to remain in Iraq, but perhaps also to provide a more legitimate reason for the invasion in the first place:

> America is a nation with a mission, and that mission comes from our most basic beliefs. We have no desire to dominate, no ambitions of empire. Our aim is a democratic peace, a peace founded upon the dignity and rights of every man and woman. America acts in this cause with friends and allies at our side, yet we understand our special calling: This great republic will lead the cause of freedom.
>
> (Bush 2004)

I remember quoting this passage, or paraphrasing it, in the only comment I issued to a participant of the workshop, the person I was told was the "one constructivist" (who turned out to be anything but). I brought it up in the context of what it meant for the workshop that an actor "out there" was using a social scientific theory to not only color, but *justify*, the continuation of violent policies. Little did I know that this was a key "whistler" of a scholar, and when I brought this observation to his attention, I was met with complete nonrecognition. Such nonrecognition—which captured succinctly the lack of any reflexive awareness on the scholar's part—also characterized that scholar's forceful work since that workshop, and especially his work conducted recently with one of the conveners of it (Harrison and

Mitchell 2014). It was this experience that compelled me to write a study distinguishing my preferred Onufian-inspired form of "constructivism" from what I termed "liberal-idealism", and democratic peace scholarship specifically (Steele 2007a).

It was the graduate school experiences, and international contexts, of that time that I hold responsible for my full-fledged fascination with reflexivity, although it was nurtured and developed with the aid of particular theoretical perspectives. First, it is obvious that my fidelity to the work of Anthony Giddens (1984, 1991) in my earliest studies, and in developing his notion of "ontological security", led to a particular understanding of reflexivity that loosely assumed a "double-hermeneutic" approach to social sciences. This was the position that "in the social sciences subjects and objects influence one another" (Steele 2007a, p. 25), and that there is "slippage" between the two realms of that which we study and we who study it (Steele 2007b, p. 275). This "epistemological" position I brought to bear on a variety of topics, including the subject-object dividing line assumed in positivist IR scholarship, and especially the democratic peace scholarship, one that was presumed but often-broken in such scholarship. Second, I had a Foucauldian "streak" which also took a more expansive, pervasive, and sometimes pernicious understanding of political power (Steele 2008, 2010a, 2010b), an understanding that extended from the academy, to the political sphere, and *especially* to the connections in-between (Steele 2010a).

This combination likely is responsible for the somewhat jumbled understandings, on my part, regarding reflexivity. Considered broadly, I understood reflexivity as a *self-awareness of position, identity, and capacity.* I focused on the practices ("reflexive discourse"; "self-interrogative imaging") that could foster a *reflection* by targeted agents (whether they be policymakers, "states", or scholars themselves) of their positions and practices in relation to whom or what they were—some kind of event or tactic or strategy to get that "turning back" upon the agent him/herself. The practices I was interested in were, in essence, ways to foster or stimulate recognition of a self-ontology. This reflection would be in light of their positions and/or capacities as agents who impact the world, the privilege of being a scholar distant from but also *impacting* through practices, discourses, methods, and arguments that which they studied. Because of my Giddensian training, I saw all of these agents (the scholar, the state agent, the fields and spheres they inhabited) connected in some way. Yet because of my Foucauldian sensibilities, I was under no illusion that scholastic endeavors could be transmitted from the scholarly "realm" to the political sphere without being implicated in political power, manifested at times in very violent and heart-wrenching forms.

Thus, my understanding of reflexivity was a blend, first, of the reflexivity of political agents that placed them within an uprooting of time and space, a characteristic of what Giddens titled "late modernity". Such reflexivity engaged this broader development that inevitably "extended into the core of the self". In the face of such upheaval, reflexivity as I appropriated it focused on how a crafting of a "new sense of self" (Giddens 1991) is intrinsically implicated in the security practices of international actors (including states). This form of reflexivity saw these actors becoming aware of how global changes impacted their self-conceptions, and their ability to act upon those, and how they could properly place themselves within a life-story or "narrative" of their selves within temporal and spatial contexts. The second part of the blend engaged the role of the theorist in such changes, as presented in and through the work also being produced during that time.[2]

Yet fostered by Foucault and other works on power I was reading at the time, I became skeptical that such reflexivity could be fostered in conventional, deliberative, and reasonable ways, ways suggested for instance in the "deliberative democracy" and "discourse ethics" literatures in both political science and International Relations (Crawford 2002; Risse 2000). Instead, I came to see reflexivity as only and sometimes solely being fostered in a field of power relations through events that incited, cajoled, manipulated, or insecuritized actors *into* a reflexive moment. In this light, when it came to the second part of the blend-understanding of reflexivity, I was interested in those periods and cases where the transmission of theory to policy led to "unexpected" outcomes, outcomes that served to create a critical space for scholars and intellectuals to consider the problematic possibilities of their work upon the world more broadly. This included an examination of John Dewey, whose support for US participation in the First World War stemmed from his belief that such participation could lay the groundwork for international democracy going forward (Steele 2010b, pp. 122–123). The problem, of course, was that when Dewey became part of the political debates and polemics over the war, and the war turned out to be more costly and less beneficial than he had envisioned at the beginning, he regretted his support for that war even if it was based on good intentions linked to his theoretical worldview. I took as a whole a less sympathetic view of scholarly "intentions", arguing that when it comes to the endorsement of organized violence the scholar needs to think about even unintended consequences that could even be plausibly linked to their theories (Steele 2010a, 2010b).

Power, scholarly intentions, and the need for documentation

In my own work, this less sympathetic view was largely centered on studies dealing with the debates in IR over the role of democratic peace theory (DPT) and the DPT theorist (like Bruce Russett), in especially developing a possible basis for the Iraq War. Sometimes, this delved into a side debate with other like-minded scholars like Piki Ish-Shalom regarding scholarly responsibility (see Steele 2010a and Ish-Shalom 2011; see also Hobson 2011a and 2011b). My point then, and now, is not that the scholar should exclude herself from policy debates, nor that we can directly connect the theorist to policy outcomes, but rather a recognition regarding the challenges of the policy-knowledge nexus when it comes to power and discipline.

Thus, what follows below may seem to be a critique of scholars acting-as-commentators, and that we should keep the two (scholarship and politics) separate. That is not my point, and of course such separations are simply absurd or highly improbable. Rather, my work until this point has led me to two general statements regarding scholarly intentions, ethics, and responsibility that relate to power.

First, if scholars wish to play some role to influence policy, *especially* when it comes to global politics where organized, even "institutionalized" violence is legal and legitimate (Lowenheim and Steele 2010), then we need to focus on ways to foster a recognition on their part of the role of *political power*, that it inevitably will transform a theory into something "else" than what it is in the laboratory or the journal forum. Some scholars—like those engaged below (Gelpi and Feaver), likely realize this anyway, even if they haven't properly grappled with the *social scientific* implications of what they do "as" political scientists. But others may not fully appreciate how the transition from one realm to another (academy to the public realm) brings with it a transformation or transmogrification of theories-as-power. Both the elites of, and the publics within, a democratic polity thus may be more receptive to particular theoretical assertions than others. Thus, proposals like Ish-Shalom's that call for the scholar to enter into the public realm as a "theoretician-citizen", are ones that "sit comfortably with the deliberative and participatory models of democracy—those models that recognize and respect the political potentiality of human reason and accordingly have high expectations of citizens' reasoning powers" (Ish-Shalom 2011, p. 181). Like most deliberative models of democracy, or even most Habermasian proposals for argumentative rationality, such proposals are highly contingent upon an enlightened public and a sphere containing an environment to maintain such enlightened reason. Such an assumption stands in rather stark contrast to the political environment one finds *during crises* where such "theoretician-citizens" are called upon to clarify their theories at the precise moments they are being "politicized" or "hijacked". That environment—one rife with hyper-emotion, exploitation, fear, and insecurity, is oftentimes corrosive and even destructive of such reason. Such environments *are* political power, and shape, constrain, and enable particular portions of the theory, and particular theories, over others.

Just as likely, such policy roles may transform the scholar, too. The theory thus in a political sphere becomes transformed from what it is in a *study* to what it does *to and for and within* a political community. If a scholar requests that their theory migrate into the policy realm, then all bets for decorum and pleas for absolution are off. This is only to suggest, contra Piki Ish-Shalom (2011, p. 181) that we definitely *can* "blame or praise [scholars] for the ramifications of their theories". One cannot advocate, as Russett did, that policymakers go around and repeat a theory to make it a self-fulfilling prophecy and then complain when this theory was "perverted" and "bushwhacked" when George W. Bush goes around repeating a thesis in like fashion. More introspection is needed (Russett 1993, 2005).

Second, to facilitate just that, I argue in this section that one function critically reflexive scholars can fulfill is to *document* faithfully and then *provoke* the scholarly-policy nexus. As mentioned in my introduction, the first step to this includes a gathering of as much information as possible that is publicly available regarding the biographical trajectories of a scholar or group of scholars pushing forward a particular theory. The provocation, detailed in the following section, will then asseses (a) how *certain* such scholars were when they said it, and (b) implicate the scholarly practices and routines and disciplinary values that may also—outside of scholarly intentions—be culpable for theories getting picked up by policymakers.

Does that mean I think such documentation will lead to more reflection? Or that it will force especially positivist scholars to recognize the way in which their own scholarly contexts place them within that which they study? I am not particularly hopeful—the aforementioned neopositivist democratic peace advocates—Harrison and Mitchell, as well as Russett himself—have never remotely acknowledged what the politicized nature of their theory means for their hard-core assumptions as "scientists" of politics.[3] Yet I think documentation is one useful function of, or position for, the reflexive scholar in a field we want to reflect more societal reflexivity. At most, it may help generate one (of many) bases for common collusion across reflexive scholarship. At the (very) least, it can serve as a snapshot of who was saying what and when, so that during more retrospective times we can narrate the particular configurations that unfolded during more urgent periods of global politics, if only to assess how such configurations come about.

Several existing types of scholarship may serve as resources for just this type of documentation. One of these is the aforementioned, and emerging, practice of auto-ethnography in International Relations, a practice that Amoureux and I defend in our Introductory chapter, and is exemplified as well by Dauphinee in Chapter 2 and Beattie in Chapter 8. Auto-ethnography's purchase can be its intersubjective insight, and the possibility of generating empathy amongst a scholarly community regarding the pressures scholars may be under. This extends even, and especially, to the neopositivist scholars I indict in this chapter whose theories, and practices, influenced violent policies that may have been more harmful than beneficial. It may provide us then a quick turn from provocation to, perhaps, forgiveness.

Following Oded Lowenheim (2010, 2014), I further aver that auto-ethnographic analyses have been practiced for ages in the field of IR (and not just there), in the form of "interviews" with scholars that we find in a variety of venues,[4] as well as the roundtables organized around a particular "scholar" and his/her works. The difference, however, is that these forms of auto-ethnography are usually conducted by "established" or "senior" or "distinguished" scholars, ones that are not only able to speak as a result of their "status", but may either not recall the past in ways that are as authentic as the more recent auto-ethnographic accounts, or may only select particular points (as all narratives do) over others to emphasize in those. Of course, the status of being senior could indeed produce the opposite—more brutal honesty than the scholar was capable of in their more junior years. Thus, one purchase for auto-ethnography is that it can "democratize" the reflexive process in ways that can be even more useful for graduate students and junior scholars seeking instruction on the purposes of our craft. But, an additional benefit is that it can provide us materiel for assessing the purposes pursued by scholars, a database of documentary evidence with which we can gather an understanding of the incentives or stakes that colored their use of research through the years.

Thus, when it comes to auto-ethnography in IR as a resource for documentation, we might recognize that such examples are broader than the explicit forms of auto-ethnographic studies. We could therefore examine the talks given by scholars at conferences (many of which proliferate on the internet via YouTube and other broadcast sites), and even conversations made in semi-private settings, as subterranean forms of auto-ethnographic disclosures that we may use to document scholarly purposes and their reflection (or lack thereof) upon the role of their theories.

A second resource for documentation comes from the field of intellectual history, studies found in a variety of journals and in books which examine the scholar as their own historical subject. In International Relations, we have seen a variety of such studies which are equal parts IR theory and intellectual history that examine not only individual scholars such as Morgenthau (Frei 2001; Williams 2007), or Schmitt (Odysseous and Petito 2007) but ones that also "biographize" entire research programs such as democratic peace (Ish-Shalom 2013).

Iraq, US public opinion, and the "surge"

> In their subsequent book, Gelpi and Feaver do acknowledge in a footnote that the numbers in the op-ed were "overly susceptible to misinterpretation" and they then rejigger their analysis of the same poll question and essentially conclude that their figure for Congo was some 6,800 percent too high. The damage, however, had already been done, this unfortunate op-ed has been widely cited, applied, and misinterpreted, particularly in military publications.
>
> (Mueller 2006, pp. 243–244)

The Iraq War had many effects, but one of the more noticeable outcomes was a re-starting of the debates over the influences upon public opinion regarding war. A variety of hypotheses have been generated to understand public opinion (measured as support for or opposition to a war) as a dependent variable. Of the many proposed over the years,[5] disagreement has centered over two competing claims: (1) that public opposition rises in reaction to rising casualties, including deaths, making the public "casualty-averse" (Mueller

2005); or (2) public opposition rises or falls in relation to the perception that a war can be "won" or "lost", making the public "losing-averse". These debates had been around in some form for decades, going back to especially Mueller's work in the months and years after US withdrawal from Vietnam (Mueller 2005). But the op-ed mentioned by Mueller above is a key moment in the debates. In their op-ed appearing in *The Washington Post* following the end of Operation Allied Force, Peter Feaver and Christopher Gelpi made the famous claim that the public would endure over 6,000 US battle deaths to bring democracy to the Congo. Referencing their survey data, the two concluded in that column:

> Collectively, these results suggest that a majority of the American people will accept combat deaths—so long as the mission has the potential to be successful. The public can distinguish between suffering defeat and suffering casualties.

> (Feaver and Gelpi 1999)

There are of course many points one could make regarding especially Feaver and Gelpi's purposes for that particular op-ed in 1999. On the face of it, they're doing the public a service by translating sometimes abstract and technical social scientific research on this topic, and issuing those translations via a widely read newspaper, all at a time when the issue of casualty-toleration was being discussed following the Kosovo intervention by NATO, one that was fought solely with airpower to minimize US battle casualties. Further, Feaver and Gelpi's op-ed is *inspiring*, in that it energizes the agency possible within war—one needn't worry about casualties influencing US public opinion if the overall "victory" is still in sight. Leaders themselves have more room to fight wars, and the public has a more open mind in supporting wars, if their thesis is correct. And if that's the case, then our judgment for foreign policy should focus upon an executive who either has the strength and will to see out a mission, or one who loses their "stomach" prematurely, as Feaver and Gelpi adjudicated in the case of the Clinton administration and Somalia (1999).[6]

It was this backdrop, along with survey results and trends throughout the two years (then) of the Iraq War, that preceded Mueller's essay on "The Iraq Syndrome", which appeared in *Foreign Affairs* (Mueller 2005). Mueller's essay came down unequivocally in support of the casualty-averse thesis, and led to a response by Gelpi regarding what Mueller titled in the 2005 essay his and Feaver's "remarkable" calculation of the US public's willingness to bear over 6,000 battle deaths for the benefit of bringing democracy to the Congo.

It should be noted that all parties involved in this debate were clearly in the neopositivist camp when it came to their views on causality, and prediction of a dependent variable. Yet in all of the back and forth, which continued well past the 2006 *Foreign Affairs* responses (see Reifler, Gelpi, and Feaver 2006), there was only Mueller's hint of an acknowledgment (noted above) of perhaps something else *besides or in addition to* social scientific "precision" at stake here. Mueller indicated that for all the clarifications made by Gelpi and Feaver regarding their Congo-democracy claim, the "damage ... had already been done". And what he means by that is fairly clear—one institution that has a stake in how it not only "games" wars but assesses them as well, the military, noticed the Gelpi and Feaver op-ed and had *used* it to influence how they would advocate for, and plan, the fighting of wars. The social scientific "data" and theory behind it had now influenced the political process it was a part of. And Mueller is indicating that this is not exactly a "hijacking" by the military of publications by Gelpi and Feaver, it was perhaps very well known by those two that their data would influence the debates over policy in this way.

Thus it should hardly be surprising that Feaver, who had worked in the National Security Council during the 1990s (a fact disclosed in the 1999 co-authored op-ed), would be an attractive voice for the George W. Bush administration to consider in late 2006, following a forceful electoral defeat by Democrats in that year's midterm elections and a study by a commission ("Baker–Hamilton") advocating an exit strategy and process from the Iraq War. There is perhaps no other moment than this one that better exemplifies, for those studying US foreign policy especially, the stakes of reflexivity when it comes to the "contamination" or slippage between subject and object. If one accepts Mueller's logic, then there is, as he noted in 2005, "very little" that an administration can do to turn the public around when it comes to their declining support for a war. But for an administration that did not want to pull troops out of Iraq even after that war had been denounced electorally in the 2006 midterms, there were other options, and social scientific theses, available to justify a continuation of policy, if not war-fighting strategy.

As detailed in Thomas Ricks's glowing and favorable account, *The Gamble,* which detailed the "surge" strategy as it was implemented in 2007 by the Bush administration, Feaver (a "cheerful son of a Lehigh University classics professor", in Ricks's words (2009, p. 41)) was a key voice advocating a change in strategy that could speak to the US public's concerns—concerns not about casualties but, according to his (and Gelpi's) logic, about "winning" (Ricks 2009, p. 13). The decision was made by Bush and his national security team (which included Peter Feaver) to implement a strategy centralizing counterinsurgency doctrine, and led by a General—David Petraeus—who had executed such a strategy earlier in his area of operations as the commanding general of the 101st Airborne Division. The strategy did coincide with an eventual decrease in disorder in Iraq, although it also coincided with other candidates for that decrease, including the Sunni Awakenings and a broader ethnic homogenization of previously "mixed" Sunni-Shia areas of Iraq (including, especially, Baghdad).

There are a number of observations I think are vitally important, and that bear upon reflexivity, to issue in this case. Two observations follow regarding specifically the content of their hypothesis. First, and even though they value criteria like "prediction" and "parsimony" in their work, the hypothesis on winning and losing depends upon less "objective" factors such as the perception of winning and losing as well as the social construction by leaders of what is "at stake" in a conflict—in other words, just what exactly is being "won" or "lost" in a conflict to begin with. Gelpi and Feaver are, in this respect, social constructivists when it comes to the contingency they place on the very abstract (and, I would argue, aesthetic) notion of "winning". Second, and this is true about Feaver especially, despite the neopositivist cliché that "correlation is not causation", you see in these scholars some rather casual and informal claims of causality.[7] Third, it should also be noted that the US public's support for the Iraq War, while a bit sensitive throughout 2007 and 2008, did indeed stay "under water" that entire time, as predicted by Mueller, where it remains even in more recent polls taken on the 10th anniversary of that conflict's commencement.[8]

Yet another set of observations should be issued regarding the reflexive role of Gelpi and Feaver in this debate, and in the strategy implemented in Iraq. Of all the opportunities both scholars have had to consider their role as social scientists in furthering the Iraq War, there has hardly been any recognition of the influence and interdependence between their assumptions, assertions, and theorizations regarding the "winning" thesis, on the one hand, and the propensity of the Bush administration to push forward with a reinforced policy of occupation in Iraq in 2007. In one notable recent article (2011), with the not-so-modest title of "The Right to be Right", Feaver simply notes (almost proudly) his "involvement" in such a strategic implementation, and that because of this he is "not an impartial observer in this debate" (2011, p.90). Such an article provides further intrigue, namely because it is produced by a scholar who advocated for a social scientific theory in a number of co-authored studies that was then used to justify the continuation of the Iraq War and US involvement in it (and, specifically, the *selling* of that continuation), and is then in the said study using the "results" of *that policy* to "test" related hypotheses regarding civil-military relations. Such a test, it should be noted, is "inconclusive" in this study. While "non-results" can be interesting, they are not usually the subject of published articles in the top journals of International Relations and political science. And yet in this case Feaver's study was published in one of the top three journals of International Relations—*International Security.*[9]

In this light, it's most remarkable, or perhaps illustrative, that while Bush's "lobbying" efforts regarding the Surge (which included the notion of "winning" as influencing public opinion) play a large role in Feaver's "analysis", of all the implications he suggests in his conclusion, none resemble a disclosure on what this implies regarding the interactions between political science (and assertions regarding what "moves" public opinion and war) and politics (which implements policy based upon the arguments of the former). This *silence* by Feaver is as common as it is disconcerting, with other scholars whose works were "politicized" (like the aforementioned democratic peace theorists in the

2000s), ignoring or obfuscating in the face of pleas regarding *their* responsibilities as scholars to the fields they are studying and influencing (Steele 2010b). It is not a coincidence, I would add, that these neopositivist scholars—while advocating a role *for* their theories in a political field of power relations—at the same time do not confront what role they may have played as theorists in justifying the continuation of violent, costly, and devastating policies.

Provocation

Let me provide a couple of caveats for what follows. First, I am not claiming that other scholars are any better (or for that matter worse) than Gelpi or Feaver at reflexively confronting their own responsibilities as scholars. But I am suggesting that it is instructive how little accountability—understood here as I've pushed for in another study as "accounting for" (Steele 2013)—there has been regarding the role of theory more generally in the production of the War on Terror policies of the 2000s. The silence, as the saying goes, is indeed deafening. And, it should be noted that silence is perhaps the most powerful, effective, and influential form of discipline one can find when it comes to reflexivity and reflexive responsibilities (Hobson 2011a; Steele 2010b). Second, I recognize that my proposals for responding to this silence, even with the somewhat diplomatic background of "documentation" coloring them, are *not* going to be easy for scholars to execute, in terms of the political, career, or social costs they entail. This is the flip side to the "power-knowledge" nexus that I claim above is an explanatory mode for the problems we are grappling with.

So, how are we to engage this silence? My suggestion for provocation builds from my, and others', previous works on "parrhesia" (truth-telling or "frank" speech) as a form of counter-power (Steele 2010a, 2010b).[10] Specifically, as a model or ethos for provocation I suggest we use (as I have before via Foucault) the "Cynic" form of parrhesia, a method for which Foucault titles the "provocative dialogue" (Foucault 2001, p. 120; Steele 2010a, p. 114), although I would avoid the latter word as what I am pushing for here is *not dialogic*. The Cynics of ancient Greece, we might recall, prided not only their purpose but behavior and lifestyle as part of a strategy to elicit truth by breaking down, overwhelming, or simply calling into question societal customs, norms, rules, and assumptions. Such conventions—we might even think of *tact* as a catch-all example—get in the way of the truth. For Foucault, if such conventions stay in place, or are lubricated or conditioned for an audience, then the speech is something else—it's rhetoric, or flattery, but not parrhesiastic truth. This was, despite (or, perhaps, because of) the transgressive tactics, an ethical purpose that was as much sacrificial for society as it was self-interested or colored with malicious drive for the Cynic.

Thus, Cynic parrhesia included three aspects relevant to this model I support for provocation today: public/publicity, spectacularity, and timing (kairos). The public nature of a provocation is at once an admission of previous failed attempts to generate reflection on the part of the targeted scholarly community (hence the jettisoning of the term "dialogue" from this provocation) *and* an attempt to stimulate, incite, or cajole a reaction in a space open to a variety of witnesses or spectators. There are no obvious options when it comes to such publicity today. But some (post)modern venues for this provocation include academic blogs where a variety of scholars with different ethical and epistemological perspectives write—like The Monkey Cage, the Duck of Minerva, Relations International, or thedisorderofthings, to name just a few.[11] A second, and perhaps even more appropriate venue would be twitter—although here there are "selection" effects if the scholarly foci of this public provocation do not have accounts. Still, (and while a systematic study is beyond the scope of this chapter), scholars who do have twitter accounts—I am thinking of for instance Patrick Thaddeus Jackson, Brent Sasley, Colin Wight, among others—tend to be extremely responsive to tweets sent their way, or regarding their work.

How can this provocation be "spectacular"? Obviously, we are speaking about both style and content, and this second element of Cynic provocation can pose difficulty. One does not want to seem *too* polemical for fear of generating the same silence that is a reason for the move to provocation in the first place. Yet, too much tact or diplomatic language can water down the punch or force of the Cynic-parrhesiastic statement. In terms of *what* we want to say to the scholar or community we are hoping to provoke, recall that we are not implicating their right to speak out to, or for, their society. We are not even questioning their role as scholars per se. However, for scholars especially who claim they are pushing forward an understanding of politics-as-science, then we can question whether some of the values they uphold are worthy of inspection and interrogation (such as parsimony in the case of democratic peace theory, or highly politicized concepts like "winning wars" in the case of Gelpi and Feaver's thesis). We further can ask whether such scholars are partially responsible for such sub-optimal outcomes (the politicization of their theories for organized violence) especially if we can demonstrate or at least strongly suggest the connections between the former and the latter. Are you, we might ask, as a scholar who also uses your theory to *advocate* policy, not part of the entire process of political power and violent outcomes and, if so, *does that not implicate the type of separation (via subjects and objects) that you assume in your analytical purpose as a social scientist? And does this not "bias" your results or position as a scholar?* Is it not, to put it another way, the very assumptions you make about social science *as a science* that are responsible for the "biasing" and thus the ability of political agents "out there" to use *your* theory to their own, sometimes drastically catastrophic, benefit? And if there is a response—and the response focuses (as the limited disclosures by folks like Russett suggest) on the *good-intentions* of the scholar's theory—then we can ask if there is not something further besides "intent" that the targeted scholar could pinpoint, and interrogate, to better assess the theory's attraction to those in power.

And what of the third component—timing? Again, although it is titled by Foucault a "provocative dialogue", Cynic parrhesia as I articulated it in *Defacing Power* is closer to a *kairotic,* disruptive, *momentary temporality* than one based on *chronos* or a "back and forth" (Hutchings 2008). The timing of instigation is important—it must be as *disruptive as possible* to be noticed. Nevertheless, if such parrhesia is issued in a one-time thrust by one scholar and one scholar only—and only via twitter or on a blog—its message may simply be ignored, isolated or quarantined as the voice of one lone, and disturbed, academic. The tactic here may be likened more to an *insurgency*—and thus scholars may consider collaborating via networks where a series of questions, connected but issued in a variety of venues towards the scholar or research community, are issued. One can envision a series of tweets issued around the same time as, or shortly after, an approaching conference where the scholar may be participating in a roundtable on that topic. Further, because the provocateur has already engaged in some documentation of the scholar or their community, they are better equipped to dialogue with the targeted individuals or groups. The provocation is based therefore in a more well-rounded understanding of the trajectory of the particular theory or hypothesis that has been politicized, and the scholar who has helped craft that theory or hypothesis as well.

Conclusions

This chapter has pursued several goals. First, it attempted to reflect on the purpose of the volume to which it is contributing. To do so, I in turn reflected on the variety of ways and directions that I used reflexivity in my own work. This included a bit of auto-ethnographic accounting, engaging how especially the work of Giddens and Foucault shaped my understanding, to date, of reflexivity and the role of the scholar in their own scholarly community as well as the fields they studied. From the starting point that reflexivity—as an assessment of scholarly values and practices that impact how theory gets imbricated in policy and politics—is mixed at best in International Relations scholarship, I then sketched a practice of "documentary provocation" to stimulate reflexive (partial or otherwise) responses from targeted scholars or research communities within International Relations.

Admittedly, there are a number of issues or limitations or dangers with documentary provocation as I have postulated it. Namely, this would be difficult and tough to pursue, especially for junior scholars who may be because of generational reasons the *most likely* and *most otherwise willing* to engage in documentary provocation of especially senior scholars and groups whose more established theoretical assertions have become part of the policy processes they (the junior scholars) find so troubling. Recall from Foucault that indeed one of the conditions of parrhesia is the *courage* to speak out against a community. Thus, I would suggest that we might consider these dangers and think about ways to support junior scholars (including especially graduate students) or, conversely, speak on their behalf when the costs are just too high for their pursuit of documentary provocation.

Yet my hunch is that this type of provocation happens, and has been happening, for a while, and it is in the generational fault-lines where we find, in my view, the greatest hope for provocation. For, I am often struck by the graduate students who, despite their vulnerability, and despite the marginal benefits in doing so, issue a pointed question to a visiting scholar (to their department), or at a conference, about their reflexive positions, or in some other more public venue. Junior scholars still require our support, but recall that one of the constitutive components of parrhesia—what in part gives it its *disruptive force*—is the "courage" to speak out. Precisely because they carry risk, those moments when the junior scholar calls out the established one can be the most influential.

More broadly, and if considered, such a documentary provocation could, ideally, lead to at least four beneficial processes. For one, and at minimum, the attempt to foster reflexivity will at least generate a public record. Should the practice "catch on", then such records could be the bases for journals, blogs, or even books devoted to the topic of which scholars respond to such critical attempts at fostering reflexivity, and how, and when, and why they responded in such a way.

Thus, a second benefit could be a sustained dialogue about the role of social science, and the social scientist, especially in regimes of violence and power. It could help color debates about the possibility—and the inherent dangers—of neopositivst research that both deny a reflexive stance but also seek out a voice in "problem-solving" via politics. Third, and conversely, if instead of a dialogue a targeted scholar overreacts with a type of rage or righteousness—a reaction just as likely considering the privileged position of the targeted scholar and the confidence with which they hold their work— then such overreactions and the contexts framing them can be documented as well, illustrating the emotional ties even analytically "objective" scholars maintain to their vocation. Fourth, this critical form of reflexivity is more versatile and flexible than a one-size-fits-all approach to "objectivating" the IR field's reflexive stance (Hamati-Ataya 2013). Individuals could approach this documentary provocation with their own sense of what is important when it comes to reflexivity—which types of "turning back" need to be fostered in their own semi-specialized research subfields of IR.

That said, I recognize the difficulties of practicing this kind of provocation. But, the difficulties to not doing so—to a status quo that institutionalizes and incentivizes a *lack* of reflexivity in International Relations—remain a threat far graver. It is, in short, time to start being disruptive.

Notes

1 In fact, in two endnotes (2–3) of Hamati-Ataya (2013), I am one of a host of individuals whose studies are criticized for the plethora of uses of this term, from "self-reflection" to "self-reflective" to "reflexive monitoring of actions". That said, there are much stronger connections between these uses than Hamati-Ataya characterizes, as Jack Amoureux and I suggest in our Introduction to this volume.

2 A very influential study in this respect for my own development was Wesley Widmaier's, that focused on the shaping of political debates by public intellectuals like John Dewey (Widmeier 2004). Precisely because intersubjectivity was "public", the intellectuals and scholars more generally played a role—in Widmaier's article this 'role' came to life even in the title—"theory as a factor and theorist as an actor".

3 In fact, Harrison and Mitchell (2014) spend plenty of space in their study engaging in self-celebration for their proposed thesis on a "clash of democracies" without ever once considering one of the many reflexive-based critiques produced over the past decade of the democratic peace program that they continue to support.

4 These have appeared in a variety of journals, but especially in *International Studies Review* through the years, along with more novel venues such as the *Theory Talks* series conducted by the ISA Theory Section.

5 John Mueller (2005) lists the less plausible (in his view) independent variables, including the notion of positive or negative events, an effective (or not) antiwar opposition, and an effective (or not) alternative strategy to the war.

6 Like a football coach trying to stimulate his team to play harder, Feaver still enjoys using this criterion of "resolve" and strength (translated as "keep bombing and fighting"), as evidenced by his judgments of the Obama administration, and Obama himself, who we are told has "many strengths but among them is *not* martial resolve in the face of wartime adversity" May 10, 2013, "Confronting Syria with the Commander-in-Chief we Have" http://shadow.foreignpolicy.com/posts/2013/05/10/confronting_syria_with_the_commander_in_chief_we_have.

7 Feaver for instance in several venues has claimed that the reasons for the instability in Syria rest on US President Obama's "rampant inaction"—"Peter Feaver Reflects on the Iraq War 10 Years Later", www.dukechronicle.com/articles/2013/03/21/peter-feaver-reflects-iraq-war-10-years-later.

8 www.gallup.com/poll/161399/10th-anniversary-iraq-war-mistake.aspx.

9 We might also note that in his acknowledgments, there is no recognition of the suggestions of any "blind reviewers" by Feaver, indicating perhaps that the article published in this top journal of International Relations was not blind-reviewed.

10 See as well Evgenia Ilieva, Chapter 10 in this volume, which focuses more broadly on parrhesia.

11 A fairly robust and contentious exchange unfolded between *European Journal of International Relations* editor Colin Wight and some commenters, regarding the selectivity and exclusiveness of the "End of IR Theory" special issues of that journal at the latter; see: http://thedisorderofthings.com/2012/08/03/the-end-of-ir-theory-as-we-know-it.

References

Bush, G.W., 2004. State of the Union Address. Available from: www.washingtonpost.com/wp-srv/politics/transcripts/bushtext_012004.html.

Collier, D. and Mahon, J., 1993. Conceptual Stretching Revisited: Adapting Categories in Comparative Analysis. *American Political Science Review*, 87(4), 845–855.

Crawford, N., 2002. *Argument and Change in World Politics: Ethics, Decolonization and Humanitarian Intervention*. Cambridge: Cambridge University Press.

Delehanty, W. and Steele, B., 2009. Engaging the Narrative in Ontological (In)Security Theory: Insights from Feminist IR. *Cambridge Review of International Affairs*, 22(3), 523–540.

Feaver, P.D., 2011. The Right to Be Right: Civil-Military Relations and the Iraq Surge Decision. *International Security*, 35(4), 87–125.

Feaver, P.D. and Gelpi, C., 1999. A Look at … Casualty Aversion. How Many Deaths Are Acceptable? A Surprising Answer. *Washington Post*, November 7. Available from: www.washingtonpost.com/wp-srv/WPcap/1999-11/07/061r-110799-idx.html.

Foucault, M., 2001. *Fearless Speech*, J. Pearson, ed. Los Angeles, CA: Semio- text(e).

Frei, C., 2001. *Hans J. Morgenthau: An Intellectual Biography*. Baton Rouge: Louisiana State University Press.

Giddens, A., 1984. *The Constitution of Society*. Berkeley: University of California Press.

Giddens, A., 1991. *Modernity and Self-Identity*. Stanford, CA: Stanford University Press.

Hamati-Ataya, I., 2011. The "Problem of Values" and International Relations scholarship: From Applied Reflexivity to Reflexivism, *International Studies Review*, 13 (2), 259–287.

Hamati-Ataya, I., 2013. Reflectivity, Reflexivity, Reflexivism: IR's "Reflexive Turn"— and Beyond. *European Journal of International Relations*, 19, 669–694.

Harrison, E. and Mitchell, S., 2014. *The Triumph of Democracy and the Eclipse of the West*. New York: Palgrave.

Hobson, C., 2011a. The Sorcerer's Apprentice. *International Relations*, 25(2), 25–31.

Hobson, C., 2011b. Towards a Critical Theory of Democratic Peace. *Review of International Studies*, 37(4), 1903–1922.

Hom, A. and Steele, B., 2010. Open Horizons: The Temporal Visions of Reflexive Realism. *International Studies Review*, 12(2), 271–300.

Hutchings, K., 2008. *Time and World Politics: Thinking the Present*. Manchester: Manchester University Press.

Ish-Shalom, P., 2011. Don't Look Back in Anger. *International Relations*, 25(2), 178–184.

Ish-Shalom, P., 2013. *Democratic Peace: A Political Biography*. Ann Arbor: University of Michigan Press.

Levine, D., 2012. *Recovering International Relations: The Promise of Sustainable Critique*. New York: Oxford University Press.

Lowenheim, O., 2010. The I in IR: An Auto-ethnographic Account. *Review of International Studies*, 36(3), 1023–1045.

Lowenheim, O., 2014. *The Politics of the Trail: Reflexive Mountain Biking along the Frontier of Jerusalem*. Ann Arbor: University of Michigan Press.

Lowenheim, O. and Steele, B.J., 2010. Institutions of Violence, Great Power Authority and the War on Terror. *International Political Science Review*, 31(1), 23–39.

Mueller, J., 2005. The Iraq Syndrome, *Foreign Affairs*, 84(1), 44–54.

Mueller, J., 2006. Response. *Foreign Affairs*, 85(1), 243–244.

Odysseous, L. and Petito, F., 2007. *The International Political Thought of Carl Schmitt*. London: Routledge.

Reifler, J., Gelpi, C., and Feaver, P., 2006. Success Matters: Casualty Sensitivity and the War in Iraq. *International Security*, 30(3), 7–46.

Reifler, J., Gelpi, C., and Feaver, P., 2007. Iraq the Vote: Retrospective and Prospective Foreign Policy Judgments on Candidate Choice and Casualty Tolerance. *Political Behavior*, 29(2), 151–174.

Ricks, T.E., 2009. *The Gamble: General David Petraeus and the American Military Adventure in Iraq, 2006–2008*. London and New York: Allen Lane.

Risse, T., 2000. "Let's Argue!" Communicative Action in World Politics. *International Organization*, 54(4), 1–40.

Russett, B., 1993. *Grasping the Democratic Peace*. Princeton, NJ: Princeton University Press.

Russett, B., 2005. Bushwhacking the Democratic Peace. *International Studies Perspectives*, 6(4), 395–408.

Sartori, G., 1970. Concept Misinformation in American Politics. *American Political Science Review*, 64(4), 1033–1053.

Steele, B., 2005. Ontological Security and the Power of Self-Identity: British Neutrality in the American Civil War. *Review of International Studies*, 31(3), 519–540.

Steele, B., 2007a. Liberal-Idealism: A Constructivist Critique. *International Studies Review*, 9(1), 23–52.

Steele, B., 2007b. "Eavesdropping on honored ghosts": From Classical to Reflexive Realism. *Journal of International Relations and Development*, 10(3), 272–300.

Steele, B., 2007c. Making Words Matter: the Asian Tsunami, Darfur, and "Reflexive Discourse" in International Politics. *International Studies Quarterly*, 51(4), 901–925.

Steele, B., 2008. *Ontological Security in International Relations*. New York: Routledge.

Steele, B., 2010a. Of "Witch's Brews" and Scholarly Communities: The Dangers and Promise of Academic Parrhesia. *Cambridge Review of International Affairs*, 23(1), 49–68.

Steele, B., 2010b. *Defacing Power: The Aesthetics of Insecurity in Global Politics*. Ann Arbor: University of Michigan Press.

Steele, B., 2013. *Alternative Accountabilities in Global Politics: The Scars of Violence*. London and New York: Routledge.

Widmaier, W., 2004. Theory as a Factor and the Theorist as an Actor: The "Pragmatic Constructivist" Lessons of John Dewey and John Kenneth Galbraith. *International Studies Review*, 6(3), 427–455.

Williams, M.C., ed., 2007. *Realism Reconsidered: The Legacy of Hans Morgenthau in International Relations*. Oxford: Oxford University Press.

Part II

Reflexive scholars

4   *Zooming In Zooming Out*
Reflexive engagements

Piki Ish-Shalom

Taking the lead from W.B. Gallie, political concepts are essentially contested (Gallie 1956; for general literature that uses Gallie in International Relations (IR), see Hobson and Kurki 2011; Kurki 2010). And having no consensual accepted definition is a constitutive and definitional feature of the conceptual phenomenon of essentially contested concept, which implies several existing meanings of a concept, at least some of which are reasonable and legitimate, and all of which are grounded within a whole normative groundwork. Stated more formally, there are three conditions for a concept to be essentially contested. First, the concept has several reasonable and legitimate meanings. Second, there are irresolvable (actual or impending) disagreements over the appropriate meaning of the concept. Third, when becoming actual the disagreements are important enough for certain interlocutors to become politicized. When these three conditions are fulfilled concepts are essentially contested.

Many concepts that we use politically and theoretically, such as democracy, power, sovereignty, equality, and freedom, are essentially contested. So is security (see for example, Buzan 1983, p. 6; Fierke 2007; Peoples and Vaughan-Williams 2010, p. 2; Smith 2005). Let me be clear on this. The dictionary definition of security is relatively straightforward. It means the absence of threats. However, that definition is good as far as it goes and it does not go far. Defining security as an absence of threats leaves us with a whole lot of unresolved fundamental questions such as: who is secured, by whom, how, and no less importantly: against what? When we talk about security these are the questions we are called on to answer, making this a comprehensive phenomenon which needs to be studied and understood in its variety of dimensions. That is, saying security is the absence of threats tells us very little if our aim is a complete understanding of the phenomenon and concept of security. And a comprehensive understanding of security involves not only the facticity of the phenomenon, but also the a priori normative groundwork with which we study the facticity, giving it meaning by defining security as a representational and theoretical concept and an analytical category of study. Thus, a comprehensive understanding of the concept of security involves nothing less than understanding and employing its essential contestedness.

And there is another crucial point for understanding the essential contestedness of the concept of security. As Michael Freeden (1996, pp. 75–91) noted, no single concept has a viable meaning in itself. Concepts gain meaning, viability, and political significance only in the context of a whole configuration of political concepts. Hence, we should not discuss security as an isolated concept, but rather as part of an assemblage of concepts. The correct level of analysis is not security in itself but the conceptualizations that together with security form a conceptual assemblage, such as international security, national security, human security, global security, social security, etc. These different conceptual assemblages lie at the heart of theories of security. And no less than theoretical apparatuses, these theories are forms of political thought, which, as defined by Freeden (1996, p. 2), are configurations of decontested political concepts which are arranged together, each conferring meaning onto the others and gaining meaning from them. Consider the conceptual relationship between security and democracy, for example, in the context of war and peace; a conceptual relationship which is fundamental to the democratic peace theories. Note that it is not only security that is essentially contested; both of the concepts are essentially contested, most notably democracy, which Gallie (1956) used as one of the paradigmatic examples in his seminal article on essentially contested concepts. Given that their internal structure consists of assemblages and configurations of political concepts, theories are referred to here as *theoretical constructions*.

The theoretical centrality of political concepts and the political centrality of theoretical concepts (the interchangeability of these two formulations will become clear below) and their contestedness call for an epistemological and methodological strategy which I call *Zooming In Zooming Out*. It is a double-faceted strategy in which theoreticians zoom into the internal components of their theories, namely the political concepts, and at the same time define and conceptualize them normatively and with moral sensitivity to their real-world ramifications.

Zooming In asks theoreticians to focus their theoretical rigor on improving their definition of the concepts they use. *Zooming Out* rejects the criteria of exhaustiveness, exclusiveness, and operationalization as inadequate when in isolation. It tasks theoreticians with morally defining their concepts, requires them to morally justify the definitions which operationalize their political concepts, and asks for their utmost effort to evaluate the real-world ramifications of their theories in moral terms. To do this theoreticians need to reflexively and critically engage with their own moral commitments; the moral commitments which inform their theoretical definitions (sometimes unconsciously).

In the Introduction to this volume, Jack Amoureux and Brent Steele suggest a typology of reflexivity based on three approaches: Positionality, Critique, and Practice. The first approach centers on scholars as individuals, the second on the scholarly community and the practices and understandings that forge them as a community, and the third approach shifts the focus of reflexivity to the practical world outside academia and the relations between academia and politics. *Zooming In Zooming Out* demands self-reflexivity, in other words the constant turning of the critical gaze upon itself, in order to address the moral commitments and normative groundwork that form the basis for scholarly theorizing. In this sense *Zooming In Zooming Out* seems to fall squarely within the Positionality approach. However, if we take the contestedness of human-made concepts and categories and the inherent fuzziness of the distinctions between those categories seriously, we reach the same conclusion as Amoureux and Steele (Introduction to this volume), "We acknowledge that the categories may not capture every use of reflexivity in International Relations scholarship, and, inversely, certain uses or conceptions of reflexivity may be better understood as falling into two or more of our categories." Indeed, even though *Zooming In Zooming Out* focuses on the individual scholar and her own moral commitments, it not only aims to improve our understanding of ourselves (and hence our theorizing), it also seeks to facilitate and encourage pluralism in the research community (in the spirit of the Critique approach), and clearer awareness of the role of academia in constructing the socio-political world (Practice approach). Positionality, Critique, and Practice feed into and spill over one into each other (see also Baron, Chapter 9 in this volume). Reflexive intervention that uses the essential contestedness of concepts as its starting point and theoretical foundation has to acknowledge this spill-over between categories. My contribution is concerned with self-reflexivity in theorizing, that is, the reflexivity of scholars as individuals, which is Positionality. Yet, it also draws on the other two approaches which facilitate and contribute to it.

The chapter is structured as follows: The first section examines the first movement of the proposed strategy, *Zooming In*. It also examines some epistemic and moral implications of the proposal, including theoreticians' responsibilities towards their societies. The second section takes a brief detour into the question of blind spots as a hindrance to self-reflexivity and how academia as a communal activity can resolve this difficulty. The third section returns the normative gaze to theoreticians as individuals, arguing that it is by *Zooming Out* that we can and must resolve the problem of blind spots and achieve self-reflexivity. The conclusion wraps up the discussion and raise the thorny issue of truth.

Zooming In

Concepts, those essentially contested political entities, are the building blocks of our theoretical constructions. The fact that they are essentially contested and essential components in theorizing is the entry point for the discussion offered here. Later, I will introduce a second entry point—the responsibilities of those residing in their so-called ivory towers to navigate themselves and their theoretical constructions within the world outside academia.

By focusing on the centrality and importance of concepts as the building blocks of theoretical constructions as well as on their morally and politically contested character, we find an epistemological and methodological strategy emerging which can help theoreticians to deal with the normative dilemmas they are facing and to discharge their responsibilities to the wider public. This strategy, which I call *Zooming In Zooming Out*, involves a two-step in which theoreticians at once zoom in on the internal components of their theoretical constructions, namely the concepts, while defining and conceptualizing them normatively with moral sensitivity and an eye to their effect on the society outside academia.

The first movement focuses on building the concepts (*Zooming In*) and by itself is not particularly novel. We are expected to take our concepts seriously, and accordingly we are trained methodologically to define them. Definitions should provide us with as precise as possible a description of the relevant concepts: a description that will enable us to clearly identify any social objects within the scope of our study, and filter out any that are not. For this purpose, a definition must be exhaustive in the sense of including all those social objects that are supposedly captured by the concept, and exclusive in the sense of ruling out all those social objects that fall outside the domain of the concept. Another fundamental criterion of theory construction is operationalization. This means ensuring the definition is testable, refutable, and, if possible, helpful for measuring the phenomenon being investigated. All together, exhaustiveness, exclusiveness, and operationalization provide us, or at least so goes the conventional wisdom, with a clear and razor-sharp scientific apparatus, with which we can proceed to develop hypotheses and test them. Moreover, as the definitions are supposedly transparent and neutral they are disposed to rational and objective concurrence among theoreticians; a concurrence that supposedly is free from any moral commitment and normative bias.

But if this depiction of the way we define our concepts is true and accurate, whence comes the contestedness of those same concepts—the same contestedness that plagues our studies, and embeds the theoretical constructions within the moral commitments and normative groundwork from which they were supposed to be free. The first step in justifying my proposed *Zooming In Zooming Out* strategy is to answer this puzzling question.

In the social world, definition involves the rounding and bounding of that which is unrounded and unbounded. In the social world, things do not fall neatly into human-made concepts. Boundaries are fuzzy at best. Social objects are connected by comparable features and set apart by distinct features. Hence, defining involves an arbitrary delineation between social objects, whether these be phenomena, processes, or otherwise. Perceptive as he so often was, Friedrich Nietzsche (1968, p. 46) made this point well, "Every concept originates through our equating what is unequal." Definition involves inflating the importance of some differences, and setting apart of some phenomena and processes (rounding). At the same time it undermines and even disregards the relevance of other differences and brings together various other phenomena and processes (bounding). Only in this way can definitions be possible in the social world. Accordingly, defining is an act of social construction of social categories: to define is to be an active participant in the social construction of social reality.

Consider war, which is one of the main phenomena examined in international relations. The well-known operationalizable figure of 1,000 deaths is an arbitrary heuristic boundary[1] differentiating events with 1,000 dead, which are identified as war, and events with a mere 999 deaths which are not considered war. As if one death can make all the difference between war and not-war. Note, however, that this arbitrary definition serves the moral purpose of studying war. The intent is to understand the causes of war and find a cure for this human malady. This research strategy follows the Weberian distinction between selecting and executing research: between morally vetting the research agenda according to considerations of pressing social problems and executing the research by objective scientific criteria (Weber 1949, pp. 21–22, 61; for International Relations writings that follow Weberian lines and recommend bridging theory and relevant policy issues see Lepgold 1998; Walt 2005). With this strategy in mind the researchers of the Correlates of War project propose the operationalizable, yet arbitrary, definition of war.

This discussion of war does not occur in a conceptual vacuum. It is tied to the discussion of the definition of security. Driven by consequentialist considerations, realists define security very narrowly—around states and their concerns. For example, Stephen Walt (1991, p. 212, emphasis in original) defines security studies as the *"study of the threat, use and control of military force"*. Walt's definition reflects the consequentialist urge to narrowly focus on military force since military force helps to stabilize or destabilize great power relations and world politics. Defining the field of security studies any other way, Walt (1991, p. 213) cautions us, "would destroy its intellectual coherence and make it more difficult to devise solutions to any of these important problems". The outcome for theory is to focus on the military considerations of states rather than the concerns of individuals who may feel threatened by non-military concerns such as pollution, disease, child abuse, or economic recession. States, rather than human beings, become the reference point for realist security studies and war becomes a clash between states and their fighting organs: their regular armies. This theoretical decision is, of course, normatively laden.

And this above theoretical focus with its normative ramifications is the target of critique for the Critical Security Studies (Aberystwyth School). Spearheaded by Ken Booth, the school's scholars embrace a different normative approach, namely Kantian-originated deontology, turning their theoretical gaze away from states. In other words, they have rejected the narrow stability-prone realist security agenda. For Booth and his coterie, the only way to secure the absence of threats—security—is to advance the Frankfurt School's inspired agenda that conceptualizes security as emancipation. Booth argues:

As a discourse of politics, emancipation seeks the securing of people from those oppressions that stop them carrying out what they would freely choose to do, compatible with the freedom of others. It provides a three-fold framework for politics: a philosophical anchorage for knowledge, a theory of progress for society, and a practice of resistance against oppression. Emancipation is the philosophy, theory, and politics of inventing humanity.

(Booth 2007, p. 112)

Security not only involves the absence of military threats, but a total trans-formation of life, political organization, and international order, so that people find themselves emancipated according to the general Kantian vision of autonomy and the Frankfurt School mode of immanent critique.

We can therefore realize that what seemed like an arbitrary definitional decision serving a heuristic necessity, is actually normatively grounded and morally laden. Hence, the unreflective pretense of arbitrariness is problematic. First, the pretense of arbitrariness obfuscates the original moral intent, discarding morality by the scientific wayside. Second, the allegedly arbitrary definition intervenes in the social world not only through the Weberian strategy of helping practitioners to formulate causes-driven solutions to the pressing social problem of war. It also intervenes in the social world more fundamentally, by delineating the category of war from other related categories, like "new war". To define "new war" is to formulate new understandings of social reality, hence actively participate in the social construction of social reality. Think of the definitional disputes in the new war literature: Is it war at all? Is there anything new about it? And while many methodological, ontological, and epistemological issues are raised when answering these two new war questions (Malesevic 2008; Newman 2004), our conception of this hellish phenomenon raises political and moral issues as well. For example, what normative importance should be attached to the requirement of wars being fought between regular armies under the accepted definition of "old war"? Is it not the consequentialist normative reasoning that drives realist security studies? Or why is it so morally important for conflicts to be (practically) symmetrical, as implicitly required by the "old war" criterion of combat between regular armies? Would it not be scornfully rebutted by Critical Security Theorists?

There is then nothing exogenously obvious about these conceptual (and sometimes measurable) boundaries, and this conclusion lends further backing to the argument defended here regarding the contestedness of political concepts. Boundaries between concepts and categories are not objective; they are embedded within normative groundwork. Defining is a moral and political act, though not necessarily a conscious or reflective one. Moreover, there is much at stake both politically and morally in definitions; for example definitions of security and war. Today, more than ever, we face moral and legal questions about just war theory and its applicability to contemporary asymmetrical conflicts. The stakes are high for those involved in contemporary conflicts: Who is eligible for protection under the war conventions? How do we calculate the proportional and necessity criteria in combat situations? Should the war conventions be revised? Who should undertake this? How? (Akkerman 2009; Gross 2010) Resolving these questions is intrinsically linked to the definitional issues of war. These concepts contain much moral and political substance, too often taken as neutral. The supposed basis for rational, objective concurrence and scientific repeatability is in fact very much contested.

Yet the contestedness of the concepts and their moral and political contents are hidden from the public eye, and by and large also from the scholarly eye, and they are hidden by, among other things, the operationalization of the definition. Operationalization entrusts research with the language of scientific objectivity. It works to hide the moral commitments and normative ground-work of the concepts that form the building blocks of theoretical construc-tions. These moral commitments are at work whenever researchers define the concepts they are working with (e.g., security and war) as they theoretically construct the social categories they later shape into rigorous research pro-grams. Operationalization, that is, obfuscates the normative underpinnings of theories.

The fact that researchers engage in defining, and actively participate in the social construction of social reality, carries several epistemic and moral implications. First, it refutes the claim of objectivity and neutrality, and does so on two fronts: objectivity and neutrality fail both the alleged value-fact distinction and the dichotomous separation between the theoretician and the subject matter theorized about. Fact and value are closely linked, and differ-ent conceptualizations of the facticity of security and war are founded on different normative groundwork (see also Frost 1996, pp. 2–23; Hamati-Ataya 2011). And this is not a contingent effect. Facts do not order themselves objectively into parsimonious theory (Guzzini 2005, p. 498; Hawkesworth 1996, pp. 90–92), hence theorizing requires an extra-theoretical mechanism to sort and filter out data and construct parsimonious theory from the complex intricacy of social reality. This extra-theoretical mechanism consists of a priori normative, ontological, and epistemological assumptions that necessa-rily precede theory. It is these a priori assumptions that enable the construc-tion of theory through "affect[ing] the process of determining which data are relevant, which are less so, and which have no relevance at all" (Ish-Shalom 2006, p. 441). In other words, there can be no theory without normative groundwork and moral commitments. Theoretical knowledge is indeed about facts, but it is about facts in a very value-laden way.

Also the alleged dichotomous separation between theoreticians and their subject matter appears fallacious. Theoreticians are not some external obser-vers of the social reality they study. By defining the concepts they use in their theories they are involved in constructing categories and participate in forming, shaping, and constructing political events and social processes.

Jürgen Habermas (1984, p. xiii) makes this point within his communicative action framework, "In the model of communicative action, social actors are themselves outfitted with the same interpretive capacities as social-scientific interpreters; thus the latter cannot claim for themselves the status of neutral, extramundane observers in their definitions of actors' situations." And Anthony Giddens (1984, p. xxxii) asserts the same with his double herme-neutics, which he defines as "a mutual interpretative interplay between social science and those whose activities compose its subject matter". Theoreticians, that is, are a part of society and they are producers of valuable knowledge; knowledge that is both value-laden and has the potentiality of being translated into actual policies.

It should be stressed that this is not just an abstract, jargonistic, theoretical argument regarding the potential of theoretical constructions to affect reality. At times, the theoretical definitions offered by the theoreticians are indeed translated into policies and thus affect social reality. This is what happened in the case of democratic peace (Büger and Villumsen 2007; Ish-Shalom 2013), and this is what happened with conceptualizations and theories of security. During the "golden era of security studies", security scholars and experts placed their expertise at the service of various states and administrations, and as Bruce Kuklick (2006) aptly phrased it, acted as blind oracles. Scholars like Bernard Brodie, Albert Wohlstetter, McGeorge Bundy, Walt Rostow, Thomas Schelling, and Henry Kissinger introduced their theoretical knowledge and abstract definitions to policy makers and policy executives, and had an immense impact on the shape of the Cold War.[2]

And to some extent this is what happened in the post-Cold War era, regarding another conceptualization of security, namely human security. Human security scholars share the Critical Theorists' normative disdain for the consequentialist normative reasoning underlying the narrow realist con-ceptualization of security. Human security scholars (aligned with develop-ment studies) were inspired by the capability approach to ethics (see also Peoples and Vaughan-Williams 2010, p. 123). That approach, developed first by Amartya Sen, reoriented distributive justice toward the ethical imperative of ensuring that people (both individuals and communities) have capabilities that enable them to function freely, as agents. As a leading human security scholar, Caroline Thomas (2001, p. 162) wrote, "human security is about the achievement of human dignity which incorporates personal autonomy, con-trol over one's life and unhindered participation in the life of the community". The operative scheme of the capability approach is to provide and ensure human and social capabilities which enable people to convert primary goods into an ability to achieve their chosen ends (Sen 2000, p. 74). In other words, it allows them to gain freedom and achieve agency. And in a circular move, Sen—whose writings provided the normative inspiration for human secur-ity—chaired the UN Commission on Human Security, whose report was submitted on May 2003, and sought to translate the normative and theore-tical approach into global policy. Theoreticians are not external observers of the social reality they study, but active agents of change in and of the world they inhabit (see also Levine, Chapter 5 in this volume).

Third, and derived from the two latter implications, theoreticians bear various responsibilities to the societies and social reality they study and which they actively participate in shaping. Once the mask of objectivity and neutrality is torn away, the ivory tower cliché will no longer shield theoreticians from their social, political, and moral responsibilities to the societies they study, theorize, and actively shape. Those who act are accountable for the results of their actions, and those who have moral commitments are accountable for those commitments. And because theoreticians both act and act with moral commitments, they are accountable for their acts, namely they bear responsibilities to their societies for their acts and the ramifications of their acts. As I have analyzed elsewhere (Ish-Shalom 2008, 2009), theoreticians have various kinds of responsibility, including social, political, and moral responsibility. Several measures ought to be taken to discharge these responsibilities, including first, being more consciously and democratically active as theoretician-citizens in the public spheres and second, conducting research in a transparent, reflexive (and self-reflexive), and communal-dialogical setting (Ish-Shalom 2011a, 2011b).

Going communal

These responsibilities are a heavy normative burden. But, besides being a heavy normative burden there are various other reasons why this set of social, political, and moral responsibilities is difficult to discharge. Here, I aim to focus on one of them, which is directly related to self-reflexivity. As explored extensively in feminist epistemology (see for example Dottolo and Tillery, Chapter 6 in this volume; Engelstad and Gerrard 2005, p. 6; Harding 1986, pp. 137–38; 1991, p. 163; 1998, p. 188; Potter 2006, p. 140; Smith 1987, p. 92), reflexivity, or strong reflexivity, requires a critical awareness of the normative assumptions and commitments that form the standpoint from which the theoretician studies and analyzes the social world and, we should add, the normative commitments that underpin the conceptualizations and definitions used when working with such essentially contested concepts as security and democracy.

But there is a problem with self-reflexivity. Though they are committed to self-reflexivity, feminist epistemologists also realize the difficulties with practicing it. As Mary Hawkesworth (1996, p. 92) argued, "The notion of transparency, the belief that the individual knower can identify all his/her prejudices and purge them in order to greet an unobstructed reality has been rendered suspect." She goes on to say that "the perspective of each knower contains blind spots, tacit presuppositions, and prejudgments of which the individual is unaware" (Hawkesworth 1996, p. 96). Despite the importance of self-reflexivity, attaining it may be impossible for theoreticians (and other individuals). This is due to blind spots that conceal the normative and ideological assumptions and social and cultural commitments that form their standpoint, and consequently, the underlying moral reasoning behind their conceptualizations and definitions. If that is indeed so, can we achieve our sought-after self-reflexivity?

One way of overcoming the blind spots obstacle is setting research communally (Ish-Shalom 2011a, 2011b). It is unquestionably difficult for individuals to identify and overcome their own blind spots and recognize the assumptions and commitments beneath their theorizing and defining. However, as a community of researchers we can overcome those obstacles. And this communal route is not that far fetched, since research is indeed communally embedded and to some extent communally conducted (Engelstad and Gerrard 2005; Weldon 2006). Not all of us conduct our research jointly, but even when we write alone we rely on the scholarly community in numerous ways: we study, are trained, and teach in an institutional setting; we share our work-in-progress with colleagues, and we look forward to their comments; when asked, we comment on their work. We peer-review articles and research proposals and in turn, we are peer-reviewed. Thus, the very concept of peers suggests a communal setting. These and other practices serve to embed our research communally. Acknowledging this communality may be helpful in overcoming those obstacles to self-reflexivity due to blind spots. Though we may be prone to blindness as to the content and specifics of our own assumptions and commitments, we can and should be aware that they exist and of their constitutive role in our thinking, and we should acknowledge their function in generating the essential contestedness of the concepts we study and use in our research. As a community we can certainly examine our colleague's blind spots and point out our colleague's normative commitments, which are so fundamental to conceptualizing, defining, and theorizing. This is a kind of communal self-reflexivity. We can argue then at least in this sense, that the social, political, and moral responsibilities ascribed to theoreticians are collective as opposed to individual.

But is the communal route enough? Is it good enough to collectivize our responsibilities? And can it be that all the steps to discharge our responsibilities are cooperative? The short answer is No. The long answer is twofold, and is concerned with the sociology and politics of knowledge production and the ethical reflections offered in this chapter. As a community, scholars are hindered by external political and economic pressures, internal power relations, academic hierarchies (see Caraccioli and Hozic, Chapter 7 in this volume), as well as epistemic norms which burden and thwart communal self-reflexivity. Scholars do not theorize in a void but in and from a social and political context. This context is not always hospitable to reflexivity. Positivists (and neopositivists) are not happy about reflexivity and often criticize reflexivity for being navel-gazing (Amoureux and Steele, Introduction to this volume; Steele, Chapter 3 in this volume; Dauphinee, Chapter 2 in this volume), and for diverting the intellectual resources away from the important task of studying the world to focus on the narcissistic task of meta-theoretical self-study of ourselves, the scholars. The funds and agencies that scholars rely on for their research may well share this attitude. It is easier to find funds for concrete IR subjects than meta-theoretical reflections and this may filter down and influence research agenda-setting in a period of shrinking internal university funding. Furthermore, reflexivity as Positionality, Critique, and Practice, might run counter to the prevailing positivistic norm of objectivity and may encounter opposition with a price tag affecting academic positioning and promotions. Mainly (though not just) young, unestablished, and non-tenured scholars may be penalized professionally for engaging in reflexivity and self-reflexivity rather than "serious IR research". The communal route may thus ultimately be limited to small groups or communities of dedicated scholars who are ready to engage in reflexivity and communal self-reflexivity. (I cannot help wondering what is the profile of the likely reader of this volume.) At least in this sense, Critique and Practice are not only conditioned by Positionality. Reflexivity as Critique (of the community of scholars as a whole) and Practice (the social and political context in which scholars theorize) are necessary to combat our communal and individual blind spots and for individual self-reflexivity (Positionality). Thus, going communal has limitations and, at best, depends on a small number of highly dedicated reflexive scholars who are willing to discharge the collective responsibilities of reflexivity and self-reflexivity.

Going communal can also charge an ethical cost of disempowering the individual researcher by absolving her of the responsibilities and obligation of self-reflexivity (on the ethical agency of the individual see also Amoureux, Chapter 1 in this volume). In other words, though on one level responsibilities are indeed collective, the individual theoretician (or at least the theoreticians who are dedicated and willing to take the above risks) is ultimately the principal agent for discharging them and as we shall see next, can try to overcome her own blind spots by *Zooming Out*.

Zooming Out

As we saw, *Zooming In Zooming Out* offers researchers an individual measure of discharging the collective social, political, and moral responsibilities. This is especially true regarding the second part of the strategy: *Zooming Out*. *Zooming Out* is the epistemological and methodological move which ensures that theoreticians will stand up to their responsibilities as individuals, affirm their own normative commitments, and convey their commitments to other members of their scholarly community and other citizens of their polity.

As we discussed, the underlying concepts of our theoretical constructions are political and contested. They have several possible meanings, which are all informed, reasoned, and justified by a different normative groundwork. Together with the normative groundwork of the concepts and of the theoretical constructions in which they are embedded, there is the set of responsibilities referred to above that theoreticians should take on board. It is these two attributes, the first relating to the concepts, and the second to the conceptualizers, which require *Zooming Out*. Notwithstanding the operationalization of the concepts and language of scientific objectivity used by theoreticians (mostly positivists), the choice of one particular meaning rather than another in fact means embracing one normative framework. Sometimes, when the theoretical discourse and its decontested concepts migrate outside academia, this choice has real-world ramifications. For this reason, *Zooming In* should be accompanied by and supplemented with *Zooming Out*. *Zooming In* calls for us to concentrate our theoretical rigor on defining the concepts we use better. *Zooming Out* affirms the inadequacy of exhaustiveness, exclusiveness, and operationalization as the sole criteria for defining. *Zooming Out* burdens theoreticians with the obligation of defining morally the concepts they employ. By doing this it asks them to be ready to justify morally the definitions they use when operationalizing the political concepts employed in their theorizing. This necessity to morally justify their definitions to both themselves and their colleagues carries an active measure for the theoreticians, one of critical engagement with the normative commitments which inform (sometimes unconsciously) their theoretical definitions. *Zooming Out* calls on theoreticians to maintain a continuous head-on confrontation with their blind spots. Thus, *Zooming Out* is a measure that necessitates and enables raising the blinds and disclosing to oneself one's own hidden spots and normative commitment. As such it is self-reflexivity par excellence. *Zooming Out* also obliges theoreticians to morally judge the possible real-world ramifications of their theoretical definitions. It is not that all possible ramifications are foreseeable (see also Widmaier, Chapter 12 in this volume), but theoreticians should do their reasonable utmost to foresee the possible real-world ramifications of their theories and evaluate them morally.

Though at first glance this strategy may seem quite modest, it carries with it some fundamental implications and outcomes for social research. One obvious outcome of the *Zooming In Zooming Out* strategy would be to better relate social and political sciences and moral and political philosophy (see also Kahn-Nisser 2011). While some social and political scientists may see this as a devastating blow to scientific integrity and the soundness of their work, moral and political philosophers won't see it that way. Keen and perceptive philosophers usually pay attention to the realities of the world, as well as to the theories that try to explain those realities (see also Chernoff 2009, p. 161; Enoch 2004, pp. 240–243). This is obviously the case with consequentialism which is supposed to judge the outcome of actions (or rules), and this cannot be done without the ability to somehow forecast those outcomes with the help of a causal mechanism that links acts (or rules) and outcomes. This causal mechanism is sought in social and political theories (see for example Singer 1972, p. 241).

The same tendency to learn real-world processes with the help of social and political science theories also exists in deontologist moral theories.

Deontologists also rely on causal mechanisms borrowed from the social and political sciences. As C.A.J. Coady (2004, p. 788) argues from the deontological standpoint, "Even those of us who think that truth, in some substantial sense, does apply to moral discourse need to acknowledge that moral truths are supported by practical reason and are dependent in complex ways on issues of practicality." Those intricate relations between moral and practical reasoning, or to put it in the terms employed here, between moral and political philosophy and social and political sciences, are relevant across the different security issues and problems dealt with by both disciplines (each with its own methodology and aims). We find it in just war theory, which relies on the security reasoning that "if there is no probability of achieving the just causes, the war's destructiveness will be to no purpose" (Hurka 2005, p. 35), and the war will be deemed unjust. We also find it in attempts to justify conscientious objection which also focus on the prospective outcomes of those acts; would they "have a devastating effect on the integrity and continued capacity for efficient functioning of the military"? (McMahan 2006, p. 387. See similar reflections by John Rawls on civil disobedience 1999, p. 328.) If they are expected to have such a devastating effect, moral judgment may sway against justifying conscientious objection. The ability to forecast those outcomes does call for a reliance and familiarity with the relevant social and political science theories.

Philosophers are well aware of the work going on in the social and political sciences. Moral and political philosophers perceptively rely on causal mechanisms to establish their justificatory schemes. In other words, they have to keep social sciences theories in mind in order to set up their moral and political theories. *Zooming In Zooming Out* calls for philosophers' awareness and reliance to be backed by a complementary awareness and reliance from social and political scientists. For this to happen, social and political scientists must be aware of the moral and analytical work conducted by moral and political philosophers. They don't need to invent the moral wheel. They just need to be able to use those moral definitions that back up their moral commitments in a self-reflexive fashion.

It should be noted that, as discussed above, theoreticians' moral commitments are operative in the acts of defining and the act of theorization that follows. Quite often, though, theoreticians are unaware of the inherent moral aspects of defining and theorizing, and hence they do not acknowledge them. Furthermore, operating in the dark and being unaware, their moral commitments are not fully developed, and at times cause internal weakness, clashing with the operationalization requirements of research as well as its epistemological attitude (see also McSweeney 1999, p. 43). This is the case, for example, with Stephen Walt and John Mearsheimer's attempt to affect American foreign policy. Using their realist theoretical insights Walt and Mearsheimer acted, as Rodger Payne (2007) puts it, as critical theorists arguing against the war in Iraq. However, as both Payne (2007) and Ido Oren (2009) pointed out, this experience with changing the reality they study runs counter to Walt and

Mearsheimer's positivism and its commitment to the separation between research and researched.

Hence, *Zooming Out* endorses the critical theory praxis and obliges a more conscious, reflexive, and acknowledged attitude regarding the workings and implications of theoreticians' normative commitments (for recent examples see Geis and Wagner 2011, p. 1577; Hobson 2011, p. 1918; Levine 2012; Steele 2010); it calls for normative commitments and their implications to be made explicit and transparent to both the theoreticians and the theorized; it calls on theoreticians to be able to morally justify the definition they choose when theorizing, and to be willing to engage critically with their own blind spots and normative commitments. Engaging critically with their own moral commitments may contribute significantly to the moral and analytical improvement and enrichment of the concepts' definitions that theoreticians employ. And using again the example of security, the different theoretical approaches explored above should explicate the role their normative ground-work plays in defining and theorizing security; explicate and use as a justifi-catory apparatus what is not merely an operationalizable method. Realists should use their consequentialism to justify conceptualizing security narrowly as militarized international security, and the same is true regarding Critical Security Studies using their critically oriented deontology to justify security as emancipation and human security studies using the capability approach to justify security as freedom from poverty.

As a result, theorizing will improve, along with its products, theoretical constructions. I will not pretend this is an easy task. It is daunting indeed, but it is doable and called for by the social, political, and moral responsibilities facing theoreticians.

Conclusions

The entry point for this chapter was the essential contestedness of the con-cepts used by theoreticians. A second entry point was the various responsi-bilities that theoreticians bear to the societies they study and are part of. To individually discharge their collective social, political, and moral responsi-bilities, theoreticians ought to be more consciously and democratically active in the public sphere as theoretician-citizens. They should also conduct their research in a transparent, reflexive, and communal-dialogical setting. The chapter argued for an epistemological and methodological strategy, *Zooming In Zooming Out*, to accompany these different measures. This strategy, which is especially apt for coping with the essential contestedness of the concepts theoreticians use, is a dual move strategy. It asks theoreticians to look into the building blocks of their theories, namely into the concepts they define and theorize with, and to apply moral sensitivity to defining those concepts: in other words, it asks them to evaluate the normative groundwork with which they approach their studies, to reflexively and consciously employ that nor-mative groundwork in defining and theorizing, and to be prepared to morally justify their definitions. *Zooming In Zooming Out* allows theoreticians to confront their blind spots and meet their responsibilities while affirming their own moral commitments.

But here arises the nagging question of truth (see also C.A.S.E. Collective 2006, p. 475). Shouldn't definitions and theories be faithful to truth? Don't they need to simply be true? Of course they should be faithful to truth, but there is nothing simple about being true. There are several theories of truth, each with its own criteria for deciding truth. They include the correspondence, coherence, pragmatic, and consensual theories of truth (see for example Booth 2007, pp. 231–232). But which theoretical criteria should we use to decide what truth is? Put differently, how do we decide which theory is valid, that is, which one is true? That is bearing in mind that these theories are theories of truth, so that we must pick one of them to be able to employ a set of criteria for deciding which theory is true and what truth is. But we must have these criteria in order to pick one of these theories. So here is the problem of truth: we need truth criteria to choose truth theory and we need truth theory to choose truth criteria. We are locked in circularity in such a way that truth remains impenetrable.

That, however, does not mean that we should abandon the notion of truth, as true and false do exist. For example, it is true, dear reader, that you are reading this sentence now. It is also true that Descartes (1988, pp. 76–77) had hands and their existence helped him to cope with radical doubt. And this is also the case with security, war, and other related concepts. Wars exist and cause suffering and insecurities. This is a true fact. Insecurities also arise for other reasons, for example hunger or lack of political freedoms. This is also a fact, as true as fact can be.[3] I do not question the reality of the phenomenon of security. Nor do I question, as did Jean Baudrillard (1995) in a post-structural fashion, the beyond-the-text reality of war. I only raise questions about the appropriate attributes of defining the concept that represents these phenomena. I ask, that is, how should theoreticians approach defining and I suggest that they should supplement their usual definitional approach with normativity. I argue that it is in the act of defining where fact and value truly join their metaphorical hands to produce truth as a living entity that ought to be treated so (Ish-Shalom 2011a, p. 839). It is in the definitions we use that value encircles fact and generates it, and where fact derives value and circumscribes it. And this is a truth we should cherish. We should cherish it not by abandoning academic rigor, but rather by joining different academic disciplines and methodologies to produce definitions that are exhaustive, exclusive, operationalizable, *and* normative. Theoreticians must strive reflexively and dialogically to explicate the normative groundwork that exists, and that exists inherently in their acts of defining the concepts they use in constructing theoretical constructions. Theoreticians must explicate the normative groundwork of their theoretical constructions, be ready to justify it truthfully, and to convey those normative commitments to other members of their scholarly community as well as to other citizens of their polity.

Notes

1 The precise, nuanced definition in the Correlates of War is: "an interstate war must have: a) sustained combat, involving b) regular armed forces on both sides and c) 1,000 battle fatalities among all of the system members involved". See Sarkees and Schafer 2000, p. 125.
2 On the nexus of theory and practice in security studies see Booth 2007, p. 4; Buzan and Hansen 2009, pp. 10, 31; McSweeney 1999, p. 148; Wibben 2011, p. 12. See also Ilieva, Chapter 10 in this volume, on the Human Terrain System project, as another instance of the nexus between academic knowledge and the power-that-be.
3 The arguments and proposal presented here are mostly relevant to social facts as they are the sort of facts that are represented by essentially contested concepts and constitute the subject matter of the social sciences.

References

Akkerman, T., 2009. New Wars, New Morality? *Acta Politica*, 44(1), 74–86.

Baudrillard, J., 1995. *The Gulf War Did Not Take Place*, translated by Paul Patton. Bloomington: Indiana University Press.

Booth, K., 2007. *Theory of World Security*. New York: Cambridge University Press.

Büger, C. and Villumsen, T., 2007. Beyond the Gap: Relevance, Fields of Practice and the Securitizing Consequences of (Democratic Peace) Research. *Journal of International Relations and Development*, 10(4), 417–448.

Buzan, B., 1983. *People, States, and Fear: The National Security Problem in International Relations*. Harlwo: Wheatsheaf Books.

Buzan, B. and Hansen, L., 2009. *The Evolution of International Security Studies*. New York: Cambridge University Press.

C.A.S.E. Collective, 2006. Critical Approaches to Security in Europe: A Networked Manifesto. *Security Dialogue*, 37(4), 443–487.

Chernoff, F., 2009. Conventionalism as an Adequate Basis for Policy-Relevant IR Theory. *European Journal of International Relations*, 15(1), 157–194.

Coady, C.A.J., 2004. Terrorism, Morality, and Supreme Emergency. *Ethics*, 114(4), 772–789.

Descartes, R., 1988. Meditations on First Philosophy. In: René Descartes, *Selected Philosophical Writings*, translated by John Cottingham, Robert Stoothoff, and Dugald Murdoch. Cambridge: Cambridge University Press.

Engelstad, E. and Gerrard, S., 2005. Challenging Situatedness. In: E. Engelstad and S. Gerrard, eds, *Challenging Situatedness: Gender, Culture and the Production of Knowledge*. Delft: Eburon, pp. 1–26.

Enoch, D., 2004. Some Arguments against Conscientious Objection and Civil Disobedience Refuted. *Israel Law Review*, 36(3), 227–252.

Fierke, K.M., 2007. *Critical Approaches to International Security*. Cambridge, UK and Malden, MA: Polity.

Freeden, M., 1996. *Ideologies and Political Theory: A Conceptual Approach*. Oxford: Clarendon Press.

Frost, M., 1996. *Ethics in International Relations*. Cambridge: Cambridge University Press.

Gallie, W.B., 1956. Essentially Contested Concepts. *Proceedings of the Aristotelian Society*, 56, 167–198.

Geis, A. and Wagner, W., 2011. How far is it from Königsberg to Kandahar? Democratic Peace and Democratic Violence in International Relations. *Review of International Studies*, 37(4), 1555–1577.

Giddens, A., 1984. *The Constitution of Society: Outline of the Theory of Structuration.* Berkeley and Los Angeles: University of California Press.

Guzzini, S., 2005. The Concept of Power: A Constructivist Analysis. *Millennium—Journal of International Studies*, 33(3), 495–521.

Gross, M.L., 2010. *Moral Dilemmas of Modern War: Torture, Assassinations, and Blackmail in an Age of Asymmetric Conflict.* New York: Cambridge University Press.

Habermas, J., 1984. *The Theory of Communicative Action, Volume 1: Reason and the Rationalization of Society*, translated by Thomas McCarthy. Boston, MA: Beacon Press.

Hamati-Ataya, I., 2011. The "Problem of Values" and International Relations Scholarship: From Applied Reflexivity to Reflexivism. *International Studies Review*, 13(2), 259–287.

Harding, S.G., 1986. *The Science Question in Feminism.* Ithaca, NY: Cornell University Press.

Harding, S.G., 1991. *Whose Science? Whose Knowledge?: Thinking from Women's Lives.* Ithaca, NY: Cornell University Press.

Harding, S.G., 1998. *Is Science Multicultural? Postcolonialisms, Feminisms, and Epistemologies.* Bloomington, IN: Indiana University Press.

Hawkesworth, M.E., 1996. Knowers, Knowing, Known: Feminist Theory and Claims of Truth. In B. Laslett, S.G. Kohlstedt, H. Longino and E. Hammonds, eds, *Gender and Scientific Authority.* Chicago, IL: University of Chicago Press, pp. 75–99.

Hobson, C., 2011. Towards a Critical Theory of Democratic Peace. *Review of International Studies*, 37(4), 1903–1922.

Hobson, C. and Kurki, K., eds, 2011. *The Conceptual Politics of Democracy Promotion.* New York: Routledge.

Hurka, T., 2005. Proportionality in the Morality of War. *Philosophy & Public Affairs*, 33(1), 34–66.

Ish-Shalom, P., 2006. The Triptych of Realism, Elitism, and Conservatism. *International Studies Review*, 8(3), 441–468.

Ish-Shalom, P., 2008. Theorization, Harm, and the Democratic Imperative: Lessons from the Politicization of the Democratic-Peace Thesis. *International Studies Review*, 10(4), 680–692.

Ish-Shalom, P., 2009. Theorizing Politics, Politicizing Theory, and the Responsibility that Runs Between. *Perspectives on Politics*, 7(2), 303–316.

Ish-Shalom, P., 2011a. Three Dialogic Imperatives in International Relations Scholarship: A Buberian Program. *Millennium: Journal of International Studies*, 39(3), 825–844.

Ish-Shalom, P., 2011b. Theoreticians' Obligation of Transparency: When Parsimony, Reflexivity, Transparency, and Reciprocity Meet. *Review of International Studies*, 37(3), 973–996.

Ish-Shalom, P., 2013. *Democratic Peace: A Political Biography.* Ann Arbor: University of Michigan Press.

Kahn-Nisser, S., 2011. Toward a Unity of Ethics and Practice: Interpreting Inclusion and Diversity. *International Studies Review*, 13(3), 387–410.

Kuklick, B., 2006. *Blind Oracles: Intellectuals and War from Kennan to Kissinger.* Princeton, NJ: Princeton University Press.

Kurki, M., 2010. Democracy and Conceptual Contestability: Reconsidering Conceptions of Democracy in Democracy Promotion. *International Studies Review*, 12(3), 362–386.

Lepgold, J., 1998. Is Anyone Listening? International Relations Theory and the Problem of Policy Relevance. *Political Science Quarterly*, 113(1), 43–62.

Levine, D., 2012. *Recovering International Relations: The Promise of Sustainable Critique.* New York: Oxford University Press.

Malesevic, S., 2008. The Sociology of New Wars? Assessing the Causes and Objectives of Contemporary Violent Conflicts. *International Political Sociology*, 2(2), 97–112.

McMahan, J., 2006. On the Moral Equality of Combatants. *Journal of Political Philosophy*, 14(4), 377–393.

McSweeney, B., 1999. *Security, Identity and Interests: A Sociology of International Relations.* Cambridge: Cambridge University Press.

Newman, E., 2004. The "New Wars" Debate: A Historical Perspective is Needed. *Security Dialogue*, 35(2), 173–189,

Nietzsche, F., 1968. On Truth and Lie in an Extra-Moral Sense. In: *The Portable Nietzsche*, edited and translated by Walter Kaufmann. New York: The Viking Press.

Oren, I., 2009. The Unrealism of Contemporary Realism: The Tension between Realist Theory and Realists' Practice. *Perspectives on Politics*, 7(2), 283–301.

Payne, R.A., 2007. Neorealists as Critical Theorists: The Purpose of Foreign Policy Debate. *Perspectives on Politics*, 5(3), 503–514.

Peoples, C. and Vaughan-Williams, N., 2010. *Critical Security Studies.* London and New York: Routledge.

Potter, E., 2006. *Feminism and Philosophy of Science: An Introduction, Understanding Feminist Philosophy.* New York: Routledge.

Rawls, J., 1999. *A Theory of Justice, Revised Edition.* Cambridge, MA: Harvard University Press.

Sarkees, M.R. and Schafer, P., 2000. The Correlates of War Data on War: An Update to 1997. *Conflict Management and Peace Science*, 18(1), 123–144.

Sen, A., 2000. *Development as Freedom.* New York: Anchor Books.

Singer, P., 1972. Famine, Affluence, and Morality. *Philosophy and Public Affairs*, 1(3), 229–243.

Smith, D.E., 1987. Women's Perspective as a Radical Critique of Sociology. In: S.G. Harding, ed., *Feminism and Methodology: Social Science Issues.* Bloomington and Milton Keynes: Indiana University Press; Open University Press, pp. 84–96.

Smith, S., 2005. The Contested Concept of Security. In: K. Booth, ed., *Critical Security Studies and World Politics.* Boulder, CO and London: Lynne Rienner Publishers, pp. 27–62.

Steele, B.J., 2010. Of "Witch's Brews" and Scholarly Communities: The Dangers and Promise of Academic Parrhesia. *Cambridge Review of International Affairs*, 23(1), 49–68.

Thomas, C., 2001. Global Governance, Development and Human Security: Exploring the Links. *Third World Quarterly*, 22(2), 159–175.

Walt, S.M., 1991. The Renaissance of Security Studies. *International Studies Quarterly*, 35(2), 211–239.

Walt, S.M., 2005. The Relationship between Theory and Policy in International Relations. *Annual Review of Political Science*, 8, 23–48.

Weber, M., 1949. *The Methodology of the Social Sciences*, edited and translated by Edward A. Shils and Henry A. Finch. Glencoe, IL: The Free Press.

Weldon, L.S., 2006. Inclusion and Understanding: A Collective Methodology for Feminist International Relations. In: B.A. Ackerly, M. Stern, and J. True, eds, *Feminist Methodologies for International Relations*. Cambridge and New York: Cambridge University Press, pp. 62–87.

Wibben, A.T.R., 2011. *Feminist Security Studies: A Narrative Approach*. London and New York: Routledge.

5 Between "late style" and sustainable critique

Said, Adorno, and the Israel–Palestine conflict

Daniel J. Levine[1]

> Could "Edward's" position ever be anything but out of place?
>
> (Said 1999, p. 19)

> The utopian trait, afraid of its own name and concept, sneaks into the figure of the man who does not quite fit in.
>
> (Adorno 1992, p. 74)

This chapter explores Edward Said's notion of "late style" in the context of his writing on the Israel–Palestine conflict, bringing it into dialogue with a reflective scholarly sensibility that I have elsewhere called *sustainable critique*. It makes three key moves. First, I unpack late style as an affective-intellectual sensibility in which a scholar's practical claims are chastened through productive equipoise with an "exilic" ontology upon which those claims are predicated, and through which they make sense. Exilic thinking, I note, had long been a means for Said to critique the unstated, but nevertheless felt and active, reified essentialisms operating in a variety of academic, disciplinary, and political contexts. Yet in the years following the publication of *Orientalism* and *Culture and Imperialism*, Said would have cause to reflect on the manner in which his own writings had themselves been so essentialized. Drawing on the work of Theodor Adorno, late style constitutes Said's response to this: to address reification and essentialism not merely as discrete historical occurrences, but as inherent to conceptual thinking, and necessitating an ongoing set of reflexive practices. Pointed critiques of such occurrences—of particular instances of "orientalist" thinking, say—would thus no longer suffice. What was needed instead was a broader chastening of thinking, one that strove to keep its own reifications present to consciousness, even as it critiqued those of others. The turn to late style, I argue, reflects that need.

In the second section, I consider how this turn to late style informs Said's critical engagement with the Israel–Palestine conflict. Said's writing on Palestinian identity, I note, had long centered on its deontological, decentered nature: "Palestinianness", on his account, constituted a hybrid form of exilic togetherness. With late style, Said would try to link that hybrid form to a Jewish exilic political tradition, suggesting this as a promising point of departure for future reconciliation between the peoples. While predicated on its own hidden foundationalisms, Said couples this call to a strong set of claims about reflection and non-identity that do much to chasten these. For students of world politics seeking to develop such practices of their own, late style may thus have much to teach.

In the concluding section, I link this brand of reflection to the negative-dialectical sensibility set up in my own *Recovering International Relations* (Levine 2012). The obligation to denounce existing forms of violence while not "smuggling in" a specter of idealist transcendence is common to both; but Said's approach remains essentially evocative. With an eye to giving students of world politics a more concrete point of methodological departure, I suggest a particular kind of multi-paradigmatism—a "constellar" approach to world politics that draws upon Adorno's use of this term.

In the context of the present volume, the argument made in the coming pages may be straightforwardly summarized. Following Amoureux and Steele's distinction in the Introduction to this volume, the move to late style reflects a transition in Said's reflexivity: from the *positional* to the *practical*. That transition can be discerned in Said's gradual re-thinking of the notion of exile, and its potential for generating a sustainably reflexive thinking space. As noted, Said's earlier work used the space of exile to problematize the routinized, "professional" conventions of both academics and public intellectuals. With late style, Said comes to realize that reflexivity is not merely positional; it requires a set of ongoing practices as well. Those practices form a kind of abductive parataxis: a back-and-forth process of interpretation and reinterpretation, in which the intuitive reworking of personal experience and "high" theoretical language serve to chasten and inform one another. For its part, sustainable critique means to develop a methodology around just that sort of parataxis. A reflexive, worldly sensibility requires the active interrogation of a complex reality, one which resolutely resists any single conceptual, normative, or ontological schematic: a *careful, willed juxtaposition* of a variety of different thinking spaces. Following Max Weber, Adorno called this willed juxtaposition a *constellation*: a carefully curated cacophony of differing and discordant voices, each negating the universal or transcendent pretensions of the others, thereby guarding against their reification and/or tendentious appropriation.

Given the particular way in which the Israel–Palestine conflict maps out ideologically in English-speaking academic circles, and the historical proximity between critical theory and the intellectual left, one proviso must be offered. No-one can reasonably deny (even if many still try) the "ruthlessly violent ethnotheological discourse[s] of alterity" present in Zionism and in the institutions and policies of the Israeli state (Makdisi 2005, p. 87). But those discourses did not emerge from nowhere. The practice of "naming and shaming", if it is not to be reduced to an endless trade in tendentious normative-political caricatures, must still be chastened by a sober understanding of the general conditions within which late modern politics unfolds, and the particular actions of individuals and groups within those conditions.

That includes the centrality of fear to late-modern Jewish political thought, and the ubiquity of such "ruthlessness" in contemporary world politics more generally. That holds, even if it is also the case that such contingencies are repeatedly appropriated in the present to conceal, distract, or to make apology for contemporary violence done to Palestinian lives and communities: both the extreme, punctuated violence of air strikes, "roof knocking", and land incursions, and the chronic, daily violence of occupation, blockade, and/or expropriation.

The wager that animates these pages is that a critical sensibility exists which can hold fast to both of these terms in the same intellectual moment. Whether that is in fact the case anywhere—and whether either late style or sustainable critique live up to that aim—may remain, for now, open questions. What can be said is that such a wager constitutes the intellectual challenge to which both late style and sustainable critique aspire, and which any critical perspective on the Israel–Palestine conflict worthy of the name would have to meet. One is reminded—with due apology, perhaps, for the presumption—of the closing sentence in the preface to Adorno's (1973, pp. xx–xxi) *Negative Dialectics:* "[t]he author is prepared for the attacks to which [this work] will expose him. He feels no rancor and does not begrudge the joy of those in either camp who will proclaim that they knew it all the time, and now he was confessing".

Said, "late style", and sustainable critique

In his final works—*Humanism and Democratic Criticism* (2004), *Freud and the Non-European* (2003), and *On Late Style* (2006)—the late Palestinian-American literary scholar and social theorist Edward W. Said developed the notion of a *late style*. The term he drew from the later compositions of Beethoven, and specifically from Adorno's musicological considerations of those compositions. On Said's account, late style involved a conscious act of turning away, or of negation: a kind of self-imposed exile from the comfortable familiarity of a particular genre or mode of literary or artistic creation. It was, he wrote:

> a moment when the artist who is fully in command of his medium nevertheless abandons communication with the established social order of which he is a part and achieves a contradictory, alienated relationship with it. His late works constitute a form of exile.
>
> (Said 2006, p. 8)[2]

A work of late style is thus several things at once. First, it is out of place, whether temporally, spatially, or aesthetically: "[l]ate style is *in,* but oddly *apart* from, the present" (Said 2002, p. 207, emphasis in original).[3] Second, works of late style have a particular kind of urgency: "a nonharmonious, nonserene tension ... a sort of deliberatively unproductive productiveness going *against*" (Said 2006, p. 7, emphasis in original). Third, such a work is cantankerous: rather than "settl[ing] down into a harmonious composure, as befits a person at the end of his life", creators working in a late style "bristle with ... new ideas and provocations", offering "episodic, fragmentary" or even "irascibly transgressive" observations and "difficult and often mystifyingly unsatisfactory conclusions" (Said 2003, p. 29). Fourth, works of late style are *irreducibly difficult*. Complex, "gnarled and eccentric" discontinuities are not smoothed into familiar, harmonious wholes, nor are they given the commodified sheen of newness or innovation (Said 2008, p. 301). Finally creators working in late style negate even themselves: their works violate the "recognizable, repeatable, preservable sign[s]" that link them and their works to their audiences; in academic settings, they violate established disciplinary or conceptual conventions (Said 1983, p. 33; Rosenthal 2010, pp. 470–472).

Somewhat paradoxically, late style thus both preserves and problematizes Said's long-standing commitment to a romantic, intellectual worldliness: the creator who resists the blandishments of professional domestication, whether in academic, disciplinary, or political contexts.[4] Conceptual, aesthetic, and academic conventions are viewed with a skepticism that verges on disdain: the "bannisters" on which professional scholastics and "company men" rely. It cultivates, and takes pleasure in, a heroic kind of *brio*: the thinker or artist who stands in the breach, denounces sameness, conformity, and mediocrity in the name of timeless truths and otherworldly vocations.[5] "On wind he walks", wrote the poet Mahmoud Darwish of Said in 2004, "and in wind he knows himself" (Darwish 2004). Or as Said told the Israeli journalist Ari Shavit, "I'm the last Jewish intellectual" (Said 2001a, p. 458).

His earlier work was, in this sense, less fraught. The power of thought to explode, decenter, or otherwise problematize reified or essentialist moments of thought—in particular when they conceal or suborn human suffering—was celebrated in more traditionally Lukácsian terms: critique was that secular vocation which insisted on the moral and ontological primacy of human beings, and from which no mystification was to be allowed to derogate.[6] Said's methods followed logically from this. Concepts were developed and placed in dialectical opposition to one another (beginnings vs. origins; orient vs. occident; filiative cultures vs. affiliative ones; traveling vs. "worlded" theory, etc.) in order to explode the particular received wisdoms on which he had trained his sights.[7]

A cultivated space of intellectual exile—a "metaphorical condition" of "productive anguish", by which theorists are pulled into new engagements and their work constantly reinvigorated—functioned as the imaginative mainspring for the production of this work (Said 1996, pp. 52–53). Exile constituted an "outside" that generated "different locales, sites, situations for theory, without facile universalism or over-general totalizing"; "a way of getting ... past the weightlessness of one theory after another, the remorseless indignations of orthodoxy, and the expressions of tired advocacy to which we are often submitted" (Said 2000, pp. 451–452).[8]

A relentless humanism underpinned this critique. Reification and essential-ism were not merely intellectual problems. They did tangible harm. "[H]uman identity"—and with it, the social and political meanings we derive from that identity—"is constructed, and occasionally even invented outright", not-withstanding "the naïve belief in the certain positivity and unchanging historicity of a culture, a self, [or] a national identity" (Said 1994, pp. 332–333). Central to that construction was the creation of "opposites" and "others" (Said 1994, p. 333). When those "naïve beliefs" were allowed to persist unchallenged—when past acts of creation were forgotten and constructed identities reified into essential, historically self-evident, or naturally given distinctions—they obscured a basic solidarity in which all human beings were presumed to share. A familiar passage from *Orientalism*—on Marx's "oriental despotism"—provides a glimpse into this humanism, and reveals both its structuring role in Said's thinking and its analytical power:

> That Marx was still able to sense some fellow feeling, to identify even a little with poor Asia, suggests that something happened before the labels took over ... It is as if the individual mind (Marx's, in this case) could find a precollective, preofficial individuality in Asia—find and give in to its pressures upon his emotions, feelings, senses—only to have to give it up when he confronted a more formidable censor in the very vocabulary he found himself forced to employ. What that censor did was to stop and then chase away the sympathy ... Those people, it said, don't suffer—they are Orientals and hence have to be treated in other ways[.]
>
> (Said 1994, p. 155)

An actual, lived moment of conceptual elision is being reprised in these lines, with its associated political and moral consequences. A suffering fellow crea-ture ceases to appear as such in Marx's mind because the *people* of Asia (whose suffering would presumably be immediately and intuitively under-standable as kindred) are forgotten: only a label ("Orientals") remains. Inter-vene to block or problematize such forgetting—banish Marx's "formidable censor"—and our instinctive compassion for one another will resume its normal flow.[9]

From dialectics to negative dialectics: the Adornian turn

The foregoing—necessarily brief—reprise of Said's exilic humanism would, in its broad outlines, be familiar to critical theory initiates in any number of humanistic-scholarly disciplines. It draws ecumenically on established western-Marxist intellectual themes and thinkers; circles within which Said would himself become a celebrated—even "talismanic"—intellectual figure (Huggan 2005, p. 125).[10] As such, Said's humanism was widely celebrated for resisting "being enclosed by any type of society", and for his "devotion to the truth of unreconciled relations" (Massad 2004, p. 8; Wood 2006, p. xvii).

Such encomia do, indeed, capture the broad aspirations of Said's critical sensibilities: to ground "a usable praxis for intellectuals and academics who want to know what they are doing, what they are committed to ... and who want also to connect these principles to the world in which they live as citizens" (Said 2004, p. 6). Yet to aspire to a mode of thinking is one thing; to have thought through its intellectual conditions of possibility is quite another. On this point, Said's thinking is not of a piece: the turn to late style comes at a particular moment, in response to a specific body of observations and experiences.

The key observation leading to late style is that "exile" comprises its own set of "social enclosures"—highly particular spaces of thinking and acting— predicated upon, and thus potentially suborning, their own distinctive reifications or received wisdoms.[11] Both the Jewish and Palestinian experiences of exile intuitively attest to this; that is why, in the 1980s, Said expressed reluctance in applying the term *diaspora,* with its particular connection to Jewish history and theology, to the post-1948 Palestinian experience.[12] Irascibly transgressive or otherwise, exilic or otherwise, thinking always takes place *somewhere.* The problem facing various brands of "exilic" critique was to account for the structuring effects of their particular "somewheres", lest they reify into their own forms of received wisdom (Said 1994, pp. 332–333). As Said, reflecting the reception accorded to *Orientalism* after its initial release, noted:

> Nevertheless *Orientalism* has been thought of rather more as a kind of testimonial to subaltern status—the wretched of the earth talking back— than a multicultural critique of power using knowledge to advance itself. Thus, as its author, I have been seen as playing an assigned role: that of a self-representing consciousness of what had formerly been suppressed and distorted ... This is an important point, and it adds to the sense of fixed identities battling across a permanent divide that my book quite specifically abjures, but which it paradoxically presupposes and depends on.
>
> (Said 1994, p. 336)[13]

In effect, Said is observing an instance of what he had earlier called "travelling theory": having "acquired the prestige and authority of age", *Orientalism*'s "explicitly anti-essentialist, radically skeptical" ontology had dissipated into "essentially an interpretive device" (Said 2000, p. 437)—an essentialist standpoint of the sort he had specifically sought to critique (Said 1994, p. 330). Stronger stuff would be needed to fend off the specter of "triumphalism and implied transcendence" on the one hand, or the tendency to fetishize "marginality and homelessness" on the other (Said 2000, p. 440, 385, respectively). "[T]he one thing intellectuals cannot do without is the full intellectual process itself"; this included "historically informed research", a clear account of alternatives, and a reflexive sensibility that takes account of "the actual participation of peoples in the making of human life" (Said 2000, p. 375).

Hence the gradual turn to a deeper mode of reflexivity, culminating in Adorno and late style. In "the more eloquent passages" of *The Critique of Pure Reason,* Adorno had written, one might discern the war between the "objective-ontological and subjective-idealist moments" of Kant's philosophy if one were sensitive enough; these emerge as "the wounds that this conflict has left within the theory" (Adorno, 1991, p. 59).[14] Read against the foregoing, the Adornian stamp on Said's late style appears in sharp relief: Adorno's "wounds" are from those "unreconciled relations" that characterize the experience of "exile". But if a particular experience of exile lies at the root of a particular intellectual sensibility, then it is to that sensibility that specific reflexive attention must be directed.

In that vein, while autobiographical asides dot all of Said's work, they take on increasing depth and seriousness in the 1990s: in lengthy reflective essays culminating in his 1999 memoir, *Out of Place* (Said 1995b, pp. 5–7, 175–99; 1986; 1999; 2001b, pp. 74–107). These, in turn, provide the grist for a more robust set of reflexive practices in the sense meant by Amoureux and Steele (Introduction to this volume): practices in which reflexivity is a double-edged sword, wielded "in here"—as a means for a theorist to take stock of herself—as well as "out there". As with Amoureux and Steele, moreover, there is a looseness and fluidity to these practices: Said's attempt to unpack the broad abstraction of exile co-evolves with the narration of his own experiences of it and in it.

Central to this effort is the attempt to map out how a particular combination of privileges and intersections—class, citizenship, religion—delimit and structure his particular experience of exile, and give him powers that others might not have.[15] The key to this style of reflexivity seems to be a kind of dialogical parataxis: a constant, repetitive movement between the high theory of "Said" (the renowned cultural theorist), and "Edward", a person whose life—as noted in the epigraphs to this chapter—could never be anything but "out of place", could never "quite fit in". The need for repetition comes from the fact that the former can never really give an account of the latter's experiences without some loss or elision: "without", as Adorno put it, "leaving a remainder" (1973, p. 5). "To understand", Pierre Bourdieu has noted in his *Sketch for a Self-Analysis* (2007, p. 4), "is first to understand the field with which and against which one has been formed". But for Said, the experience is one of constant circling: return, reformation, and repetition. The "scar" of being out of place—to borrow from Brent Steele (2013, pp. 39–40)—becomes the Kantian "thing in itself", across which literary self-representation ("Edward" in the third person) and theoretical-explanatory accounts juxtapose. One is only ever telling stories that extrapolate or extract from a body of lived experience, just as one is oneself never ultimately or definitively formed. Such stories cannot be "objectivated" once-and-for-all; only constantly retold. "One *invents* goals abductively—in the literal use of the Latin word "*inventio*", Said noted in 2004 (p. 140), "… to stress finding again, or reassembling from past performances". Each retelling becomes an instance of *chastening* one's ontological and theoretical worldview: remembering that that worldview draws on a self-understanding that is as partial, contingent, and incomplete as any other. To chasten one's understandings is to make room for others; and thus does an exilic worldview guard itself from its own forms of reified or ideological closure.

It should not therefore be too surprising that the "late stylist" sounds rather like Said himself: the master dilettante, the indefatigable *flaneur*, the gifted amateur. An "inspired, if slightly sated amateurism" informs her work, Said tells us; one buttressed by a "sense of ease and luxury", that facilitates both "a continuous familiarity with great works, great masters, and great ideas" and yet also allows a degree of critical distance from them. Where the working scholar, artist or thinker—from *Mad Men's* Don Draper to Bourdieu's (1988) *homo academicus*—must ritually genuflect in the face of these works and ideas "as subjects of professional discipline", the dilettante is free to take such genuflections or leave them: "as practices indulged in by a frequent *habitué* to a club" (Said 2006, p. 21; Bourdieu 1988, pp. 84–90).[16]

Said's late stylist is thus liable to engender the resentments of "working" artists and intellectuals, whose humble roots oblige them to bend their creativity to "the ignominy of earning money" (Adorno 2005 [1951], p. 21). "[I]n a contest between the blandishments of an intellectual Faubourg St. Honoré and those afforded by the moral equivalent of a working-class association", Said (2006, p. 21) notes, the dilettante unapologetically falls in with the former.[17] When expressed, those resentments will necessarily mix the *ad hominem* and the *prima facie* in uncomfortable ways: for one cannot separate the thinker from the thought, nor the particulars of a life, with its mix of professional, fractional, and class identities and affiliations from the intellectual horizons in which one "dwells".[18] Reflection is thus not exhausted merely by narrating one's cognitive-analytical processes—"show[ing] how one came to hold whatever opinion one does hold"—not when "money and a room of [one's] own" are necessary (if not sufficient) preconditions for them (Said 1996, pp. 33–34).[19]

Constellating the conflict: late style and Israel–Palestine

The previous section retraced the process by which late style emerged in Said's thinking: the particular tensions set up by his sense of the critical vocation on the one hand, and the limits of "positional" critique to make good on that vocation on the other. Reconciling those tensions—or rather, learning to live with their irreconcilability—would oblige new, farther-reaching reflexive practices. Late style is the term of art Said gives to those practices and to the sensibility they mean to sustain. In the present section, I trace out how late style informs Said's critique of policy efforts ostensibly intended to resolve the Israel–Palestine conflict, and his attempt to imagine alternative foundations for such efforts.

The political context in which that work unfolded bears mention. By Fall 2000, the primary framework for negotiations between Israel and the PLO—the

"Oslo process"—had profoundly foundered. As is well known, Said had long been skeptical of these negotiations: they hewed, he felt, too closely to American and Israeli interests, and devoted insufficient attention to Palestinian historical suffering, to the present needs and rights of refugees, and to the creation of durable, democratic Palestinian institutions (Said 1995a, 2005). In the wake of the second Intifada, Palestinian political prospects would grow increasingly desperate, while changes in US Middle East policy after the elections in 2000 and the attacks of September 2001 culminated in the invasion of Iraq in 2003.

There is, then, both an urgency to Said's critical reimaginings and a sense of frustration driving them. It is in these moments, perhaps, that the challenge to reflection is at its greatest: "otherworldly" thoughts take on a self-indulgent quality in the face of rapidly unfolding catastrophe, profound suffering, and even the fear that no-one is listening. Regardless of where one "comes down" on Said's particular positions, the ability to sustain the former in the midst of the latter remains an intellectual achievement of considerable note—especially for would-be students seeking to develop reflexive, politically responsive scholarship on world politics. The ability to reflect in the midst of a "madding crowd" would be central to producing such scholarship; so would a belief in the dignity and "policy relevance" of imagining alternatives—even if not in the sense that this latter term is generally used (Gallucci 2012; Avey and Desch 2014).

Said sustains this space of critical reimagination through two moves, made more-or-less in tandem. In the first, he draws on Sigmund Freud's (1967) *Moses and Monotheism* to deontologize Jewish identity. In the second, he seeks to bound that same deontological move—to guard it against its own potential for reification—through a particular "take" on Adorno's negative dialectic, which he sets up in *Humanism and Democratic Criticism* (Said 2004). Here, in an aside that appears in the book's closing pages, Said will assert the irreducibly partial nature of *all* conceptual accounts of the conflict—including, it appears, his own. The obligation of the thinker, Said concludes, is to adopt a reflexivity that challenges one's own claims to reason no less than those of others. Each of these—and their limitations—may be considered in turn.

These moves, it must be emphasized, cannot on their own produce an Israeli-Palestinian entente. Said knew this perfectly well. What they can do is demonstrate the insufficiency of all existing modes and frameworks for thinking through the present conflict: a determinate negation of the conceptual playing field as it presently exists, by revealing the insufficiency of all the "solutions" that a field seems capable of generating. If it is the case that a profound crisis attends the manner in which we think politically about Israel and Palestine, then such a negation can reveal the limits of those modes of thinking, even as it makes clear our continued dependence on them. If not a solution, that is at least an approach that considers the conflict with due respect for its depth, and for the suffering it brings.

Diasporic nationalism (or non-identitarian identity)

In *After the Last Sky* (1986), Said advances a claim about the Palestinian right to collective and individual recognition that is at once aesthetic, historical, and political. Two inter-related moves comprise this claim. The first is to deflect those who wish simply to dismiss Palestinian identity as an apologetic for either violence or anti-Semitism: "where every playground is seen as a 'breeding ground for terrorists', every pastime a 'secret plan for the destruction of Israel'" (Said 1986, p. 134). The other is to constellate a notion of Palestinianness without forcing that notion into a central, essentialized narrative. "We have no dominant theory of Palestinian culture, history, society; we cannot rely on one central image ... there is no completely coherent discourse adequate to us" (Said 1986, p. 129). Palestinian experience is "miscellaneous", "without a center", and "atonal" (Said 1986, p. 129). That quality is—somewhat paradoxically—mobilized in a manner akin to what an older generation might have called Palestinians' "national character":

> Strip off the occasional assertiveness and stridency of the Palestinian stance and you may catch sight of a much more fugitive, but ultimately quite beautifully representative and subtle, sense of identity. It speaks in languages not yet fully formed, in settings not completely constituted ... that sudden, unprepared-for depositing of a small bundle of self on the fields of the Levant after which comes the trajectory of dispossession, military and political violence, and at its most profound—the Christian incarnation and resurrection, the Ascension to heaven of the Prophet Muhammad, the Covenant of Yahweh with his people—that is knotted definitively in Jerusalem, center of the world, *locus classicus* of Palestine, Israel, and Paradise.
>
> (Said 1986, p. 36)

That exilic genius for openness thus expresses itself in a displaced, but not placeless, notion of identity: a kind of "exfoliating variation" (Said 1991, p. 99).[20] "Palestinianness" thus contrasts sharply to what Zionism had carved out of diaspora Judaism: "better our wanderings ... than the horrid clanging shutters of their return" (Said 1986, p. 150). The key insight here is that the condition of exile, as political theorist Julie Cooper (2015, p. 12) aptly put it, "[makes] insight into relational ethics available" to thinkers and to political communities. Long associated with Jewishness, such exilic openness is nevertheless a characteristic which Zionism was said to have cut away and discarded. Said wishes to claim it for Palestine.[21]

With the move to late style in the late 1990s, exilic thinking comes full circle. Through Freud's (1967) *Moses and Monotheism,* Said will try to lead his Jewish-Israeli interlocutors back to an appreciation of what Zionism took away, and then suggest a basis for reconciliation through its joint reclamation. Freud, it will be recalled, had speculatively suggested that Moses—"the greatest of [Israel's] sons"—was, in fact, an Egyptian by birth; by extension, that monotheism had entered Judaism not through a privileged set of Abrahamic or Mosaic revelations, but as a cultural borrowing from the suppressed doctrines of the heretical pharaoh Akhenaten (Freud 1967, pp. 4, 21–35).[22] The historical truth of Freud's speculative counter-history is not what interests Said, and it need not detain us; for Said, Freud's key insight is that "identity cannot be thought or worked through alone" (Butler 2012, p. 31). Every identity is mixed from the outset; identity emerges from difference:

> Freud's meditations and insistence on the non-European from a Jewish point of view provide ... an admirable sketch of what it entails, by way of refusing to resolve identity into some of the nationalist or religious herds in which so many people want so desperately to run ... even for the most definable, the most identifiable, the most stubborn communal identity— for him, this was the Jewish identity—there are inherent limits that prevent it from being fully incorporated into one, and only one, Identity.
>
> (Said 2003, pp. 53–54)

That refusal, in turn, opens up the possibility of a principled affinity between the "besieged identities" of Jews and Palestinians: an "utterly indecisive" and "deeply undetermined" history with multiple points of entry and exit, and a variety of possible points of interconnection:

> Can [such a history] aspire to the condition of a politics of diaspora life? Can it ever become the not-so-precarious foundation in the land of Jews and Palestinians of a bi-national state in which Israel and Palestine are parts, rather than antagonists of each other's history and underlying reality? I myself believe so—as much because Freud's unresolved sense of identity is so fruitful an example, as because the condition he takes such pains to elucidate is actually more general in the non-European world than he suspected.
>
> (Said 2003, p. 55)

The full measure of late style's overlapping "transgressions" may now be taken. An exiled Palestinian thinker, in the waning years of his life, draws on the work of an exiled Jewish thinker—one facing not only his own death, but the impending destruction of his kind—to light a path to a post-national Israel–Palestine.[23]

The generosity of this move bears noting, in particular given the worsening political context alluded to above. Yet this thinking does, for all that, contain its own reductive assumptions. Said's critique of Zionism focuses largely on the flawed theory of identity it ostensibly propounds: its insistence on a kind of essentialist, identitarian closure. Again following Cooper (2015, p. 82): while "Zionism may well be philosophically naïve and morally reprehensible", the demand for Jewish self-determination "rests not on a philosophical mistake about the boundaries of the self, but on a historical, political, and economic analysis of anti-Semitism". It was the persistent condition of insecurity in late-modernity that necessitated a Jewish state: the role of emergent 19th and 20th century political forms in minoritizing—to borrow Aamir Mufti's (2007) apt term—the diaspora Jewish communities of Europe.[24] Identitarian closure, on this account, is a means rather than an end; it is part of the process by which national states mobilize for the production of security. Exilic politics—binational or otherwise—can do the work Said hopes for only if it can speak practically, as well as generously, to that condition of insecurity.

In that vein, such thinking may wish to offer Israel's Jews something more than a path back to their own diaspora. It might press for reflection on the corroborating role Palestinians may have played—whether by indifference, accident, or commission—in Zionism's determination to eschew diasporism in favor of sovereign power. Many have decried—and not unfairly—the way in which the wartime activities of Haj Amin al-Husseini, the exiled "grand mufti" of Jerusalem, have been, and are, used to discredit the entirety of the Palestinian national movement.[25] But what conversation, if any, took place in Palestinian national circles in the 1930s and 1940s as to whether the looming catastrophe facing Jews obliged them—morally, politically, or pragmatically— to revise or pluralize their claims vis-à-vis Zionism? Could such a conversation— even if it was as marginal, in its way, as were comparable discussions among Zionists—provide a link to fill the present-day gap between Said's exilic binationalism and the problem to which Cooper (2015) alludes?[26] If there were no such conversations, might not some reflection by contemporary binationalists around this silence do similarly important political work? Have such conversations, perhaps, already begun? If not, what might catalyze them? If so, how can they find the attention they deserve?

Given the explosively unsettled interpretations of those events—and given the magnitude of contemporary Palestinian suffering at the hands of Israelis— such efforts at compassionate reflection may well be enormously difficult, both politically and emotionally.[27] To underscore a need for them may, as well, smack of profound impropriety.[28] But the abandonment of others to genocide—even at the hands of a third party—constitutes its own kind of political choice, not to be explained away. It was something that *was done*— or, if that point is not to be conceded, which *may have been done,* or which *was believed to have been done*—and which has contemporary political effects, regardless of the intent of particular historical individuals.[29] That holds, even if Palestinians were *themselves* unsettled—and ultimately dispossessed by—the very processes "by which the Jews became a question, both for themselves and for others" (Mufti 2007, p. 10). It holds, too, even if Palestinians bear no responsibility for the "answer" that National Socialism found for that question.

Said, it must be said, offers no such reflection.[30] The binationalism of *Freud and the Non-European* appears to be one of those "episodic, fragmentary" provocations which the late style thinker permits himself in the autumn of his life: identifying the problem, and bequeathing it to others. A graceful moment of scholarly self-erasure, of "leave taking". But without such a consideration, contemporary binationalism opens itself up to the charge of avoiding or underplaying such questions: at best naïvely, at worst cynically.

Said does, however, offer something propaedeutic to that reflection. It is here that the practice of late style—the Adornian negative dialectic—"cashes out" into a new mode of reflexive engagement. "The struggle over Palestine", Said notes in *Humanism and Democratic Criticism* (2004), belongs to that category of problem which is "not reconcilable, not transcendable, not really capable of being folded into a sort of higher, undoubtedly nobler synthesis" (Said 2004, p. 143). If the Oslo process—"a technical and ultimately janitorial rearrangement of geography allowing dispossessed Palestinians to live in about twenty percent of their land" could not produce peace given those parameters, neither "would it be morally acceptable to demand that the Israelis should retreat from the whole of former Palestine, now Israel, becoming refugees like the Palestinians all over again" (Said 2004, p. 143). What remains for Said is what remained for Adorno: a persistent negation of all simple theodicies, of all ready-made solutions that might tempt us away from the hard, daily work of reconfiguring one's political sensibilities and institutions, following from a common will not to destroy:

> Overlapping yet irreconcilable experiences demand from the intellectual the courage to say that *that* is what is before us, in almost exactly the way Adorno has throughout his work on music insisted that modern music cannot be reconciled with the society that produced it, but in its intensely and often despairingly crafted form and content ... can act as a silent witness to the inhumanity all around. [...] Only in that precarious exilic realm can one first truly grasp the difficulty of what cannot be grasped and then go forth to try anyway.
>
> (Said 2004, pp. 143–144)[31]

Concluding thoughts: from late style to sustainable critique

The determinate negation to which Said and Adorno allude is, of course, much easier to call for rhetorically than to produce. The work of translating a complex social reality into concepts, understanding how concepts reify, and identifying tactics by which to interrupt, chasten, or manage that tendency to reification requires its own kind of work: a "curatorial" sensibility in which theoretical narratives are juxtaposed to one another like paintings in a museum. They do not simply attest to that world's plurality; each narrative also chastens and dislocates the others. With so many on offer, how can any one take on the appearance of essential truth or historical necessity? So understood, it is their combined effect, and the work of "sussing out" the gaps between them, that must be attended to.

For students of world politics, that work could be likened to a set of left-right "jabs" or punches—the use of multiple theoretical narratives to keep policymakers, policy intellectuals, and the theorist herself perpetually off balance. One may hope that this experience could produce a change of affect or sensibility. That change can be described as proceeding in three phases. First, a sense of dislocation is hoped for, stemming from the realization that every theoretical narrative *both* discloses a sense of the conflict that has an immediately ideological or essentialist "upshot" within it, *and* betrays a larger reality that lies beyond its comprehension. Second, from this sense of dislocation a chastened sense of finitude or humility might follow: that while such narratives are inadequate, they are all any of us—thinkers, policymakers, human beings—have by which to make sense of the world. Third, from this sense of finitude, a sense of compassion and fellow-feeling might emerge for those bound up in the conflict, who suffer from its harms.

Elsewhere, I have both proposed a term for such a sensibility, and attempted to derive a set of theoretical practices from it (Levine 2012, pp. 51–58, 100–109). The term *animus habitandi*—"the will to dwell within, or to abide"—speaks to the sensibility; Adorno's notion of a constellation is adapted to think through the practices that would follow from it. Drawing on that earlier work, this final section will briefly delineate these terms, with an eye to suggesting links between the specific practices of students of world politics and Said's late style.

Drawn from the Latin *habitare* (to live within, inhabit, or dwell), the term *animus habitandi* takes its rhetorical cue from Hans Morgenthau's well-known *animus dominandi*: the "will to dominate", which he held to be a basic fact of political life that must be accepted *a priori*. For its part, the *animus habitandi* speaks to a particular ethos, which means to oblige theorists and policy-makers to accept their vulnerability to reification or essentialism as given. Its foundational act of faith is that the world consists of undifferentiated complexity and indeterminacy. It is precisely that complexity and indeterminacy that necessitates conceptual reduction. Yet those same reductions also obscure that world from us; we come to relate to the concepts *as though they were things in themselves,* forgetting their fullness, reducing them to objects of instrumental thinking. Accordingly, the *animus habitandi* calls on scholars to strive to abide in complexity and indeterminacy. The key move here, as with Adorno and Said, is the *animus habitandi*'s uncompromising negation of *all* transcendent, metahistorical, or providential narratives; even those that might try to appropriate negativity itself.

For its part, the constellation is an attempt to operationalize the ethos of the *animus habitandi*, in light of the account of reification offered above. Following Martin Jay, the term constellation denotes "a juxtaposed, rather than integrated cluster of changing elements that resist reduction to a common denominator, essential core, or generative first principle" (Bernstein 1991, p. 8). Reification posits that our tendency is to forget the partial nature of concepts: to conflate them—the narratives which they produce, and the ontologies to which one must stipulate for them to make sense—with the world as such (Wight 2006). In that vein, the constellation seeks *to cultivate remembering*, by "curating" our theoretical narratives against others to which they are diametrically opposed. Polyvocal and highly pluralist narratives function like snapshots, or sonar soundings: a means by which pre-existing political-social-normative sensibilities are stretched and fitted onto a complex, indeterminate, vital world. They are nothing more than fixed perspectives or worldviews derived from both consciously and unconsciously formed ontological assumptions, giving the observer a stable point of theoretical leverage over a world that resists reductive knowledge. The practice of constructing a constellation thus aims to operationalize the ethos of the *animus habitandi*.[32]

In so doing, particular narrative accounts of political conflicts are revealed within the context of the historical moment that produced them; and in that contextualization, are robbed of their implicit claim to transcendent or universal validity. Thus do they produce Adorno's negative dialectic: a form of analytical narration which documents not the *convergence* of concepts and things—Hegel's rational and real—but underscores the persistent gap between them: their non-identity.[33] The aim is not synthesis, but mutual chastening: narratives that are "linked by criticizing one another, not by compromising" or by being smoothed into reductive synthesis (Adorno 1973, p. 31). As with Said, sustainable critique does not sketch out the path to a better future on its own. What it can do is negate all short cuts to that future, by revealing what it is not: vigorously "calling out" the inadequacies, the falsehoods, the myopias, the cruelties, and the elisions—small or large—that are concealed when we trust our thinking too readily, or generalize too broadly on the basis of our desires, hopes, or historical sensibilities.

Notes

1 Thanks to Jack Amoureux, Hussein Banai, Alexander Barder, Mark Button, Bill Dixon, Simon Glezos, Waleed Hazbun, Simanti Lahiri, Utz McKnight, Daniel Monk, Ella Myers, and Brent Steele for their comments and suggestions. The usual proviso applies.
2 Also, Said 2002, pp. 196–197.
3 See also Barenboim and Said 2004, pp. 37, 41–42.
4 See, in this vein, Said 1983, pp. 4–5; Said 1996, Ch. 4; Barenboim and Said 2004, p. 63; Said 1991, pp. 15–16; Said 1995b, Chs 19 and 30; Said 2004, Ch. 5. On the tension between these two moments of thinking, see Rosenthal 2010, pp. 463–464 and 482–483.
5 "It is a spirit in opposition, rather than in accommodation, that grips me because the romance, the interest, the challenge of intellectual life is to be found in dissent against the *status quo* at a time when the struggle on behalf of the under-represented and disadvantaged groups seems so unfairly weighted against them" (Said 1996, p. xvii).
6 "Criticism in short is always situated: it is skeptical, secular, reflectively open to its own failings' (Said 1983, p. 26). For erudite complications of this position, see Asad et al. (2013) and Bennett (2010).
7 See, respectively, Said (1975, 1994 [1978], 1983, 2000).

8 See also Said (1993, pp. xxv–xxvi) and Ayyash (2010).

9 See Muppidi (2012, p. 6) for a comparable critical-affective "wager" in the context of Anglo-American IR: the effort to identify and displace the "censors" that dispel "the stench and specter of ugliness" from both the study of world politics, and its practice.

10 For useful surveys of Said's thinking in broader western-Marxist circles, see McCarthy (2013), Bayoumi (2005).

11 "Thus it will not answer to assert that diasporic communities exert the powers available to them exclusively in an *oppositional* mode ... [I]t is not clear that opposition exhausts the motivations of diasporic communities. More 'selfish' reasons – preservation of lives or identities for their own sake, without regard to any external measure of their worth – come into play equally often. [...] The powers of diaspora are not necessarily benign, whether outward or inward." Boyarin and Boyarin (2002, p. 8).

12 "I do not like to call it a Palestinian *diaspora*; there is only an apparent symmetry between our exile and theirs" (Said 1986, p. 1150); see also Said (1995b, p. 114).

13 See also Shatz (2014).

14 On the figure of the wound in Said in relation to Adorno, see Said (2000, pp. 183–4; 2003, p. 54), and Rosenthal (2010).

15 Hence, for example, his account of learning about 1948, first in *After the Last Sky* (1986) and later in *Out of Place* (1999). "My immediate family was completely insulated by wealth and the security of Cairo" (1999, p. 115). The reality of the *nakba* emerges from stories of relatives who appear there after the Deir Yassin massacre; from conversations with schoolmates; from the charity work of an aunt; and from observing the refugees themselves. It is because that war never reduces him quite so completely—he is never made a "destitute, uncomprehending waif" (1999, p. 120)—that he can relate these experiences without being rendered mute. And it is wealth and US citizenship that enables him to acquire the means and the status—an American university education, a faculty appointment—to relate that experience to others.

16 See also Biswas (2007).

17 Faubourg St. Honoré is a posh street in Paris's 8th *Arrondissement.*

18 See, in this vein, a fascinating exchange between Said and the Israeli scholar Meron Benvenisti (2000), originally published in *Ha'aretz.* Said's recollections of Jerusalem and 1948, Benvenisti argues, reflect a typical brand of upper-class Palestinian *mauvaise foi:* an elite that had abandoned Palestine sought to deflect its guilt onto Israeli Jews, who—like the *fellahin* they left behind—were left to fight tooth-and-nail for their personal and collective survival. Said's response similarly mixes the *prima facie* and the *ad hominem:* Benvenisti's myopia is generalized into a cultural phenomenon. Who gets the better of whom matters less than their *collaboration* in sustaining each other's self-conception: the aggrieved Columbia don vs. the "street-fighting" organic intellectual. In fact, Benvenisti is very much an inspired amateur in the "late style" mold. None of this was news to either scholar; yet neither "broke form". One might ask why. This exchange is archived on FOFOGNET: Palestinian Refugee Discussion List, list2.mcgill.ca/scripts/wa.exe? A0=fofognet&D=0.

19 Said is here quoting from Virginia Woolf.

20 The provenance of this term bears noting: Said uses it to characterize a particular style of Arabic music that he had known in his youth but had forgotten; he is reintroduced to it through western musicological writing. A late style "transgression", *par excellence;* much as Said will use Freud to try to "re-teach" exilic politics to Jews.

21 Notwithstanding any number of disagreements, some contemporary Jewish thinkers— myself among them—credit Said for helping to give that loss a name. "As I read

Said's words ... I found myself grateful for the understanding of Jewishness I
would not quite have arrived at without him" (Butler 2012, p. 30).

22 Freud's full argument exceeds the scope of this essay; but see Yerushalmi (1993),
Derrida (1998), Assmann (1998), and Mahfouz (2000).

23 *Moses and Monotheism*, it will be recalled, was published after Freud's flight to
Vienna in the wake of the Nazi takeover of Austria; he was then dying of cancer.

24 "Thus the greatest 'accomplishment', we might say, for nationalism as a distinctly
modern form of political and cultural identity is not that it is a great settling of
peoples ... Rather, its distinguishing mark historically has been precisely that it
makes large numbers of people eminently unsettled. More simply put, whenever a
population is *minoritized* – a process inherent in the nationalization of peoples and
cultural practices – it is also rendered potentially *movable*" (Mufti 2007, p. 13,
emphasis in original).

25 For a brief *entrée* into the historical/ideological fight surrounding Husseini's wartime activities, see Achcar (2009) and its review by Herf (2010). On the charge that
Husseini's activities have been tendentiously appropriated, see *inter alia*, Segev
(1993, p. 425), Löwenheim (2014, pp. 120–138), Pappe (2009), and Massad (2000,
pp. 52–67).

26 In this vein, Fauzi Darwish Husseini's New Palestine Party, formed in mid-1946,
bears noting; but Fauzi would be killed in November of that year, apparently for
his binationalist sentiments (Mayer 2008, p. 193; Lacqueur 1989, p. 267; Pappe
2009, pp. 328–329).

27 But see, for example: Alcalay (1993), Myers (2008), Sufian and LeVine (2007),
Bar-On and Naveh (2012), Adwan, et al. (2011); and films like *Kedma* (2002, dir.
Amos Gitai), *Divine Intervention* (2002, dir., Elia Suleiman), and *Civil Alliance*
(2012, dir. Ariella Azoulai).

28 Here recalling Said's exchange with Jonathan and Daniel Boyarin in 1989: "The
Boyarins are also unhappy with ... my acknowledgment of Jewish suffering: anti-
Semitism, they say, is only a subordinate term in my formulation. This I find
staggering in its impropriety. Can they not get it into their heads that as Palestinians, whose total dispossession and daily – I repeat, daily – torture, murder, and
mass oppression by 'the state of the Jewish people' occurs even as the Boyarins
speak, we are not always compelled to think of the former suffering of the Jewish
people. Can you imagine the brothers Boyarin standing next to the residents of
Beita as their houses were being blown up by the Israeli army, and saying to them,
'It would help you to know and remember that the Jews who are now killing you
were once cruelly and unfairly killed too'[?]" Said (1989, pp. 635–636).

29 Again, here following Steele (2013, pp. 59–60): "although we are constituted by
flesh and bone, we are also desperately contingent upon *appearance*, manifested
in our language, our aesthetics, and our pre- and re-presentations". Steele's *politics of exteriority* means to address this contingency: to consider the consequences
of our being and doing as distinct from our intentions.

30 To be clear, Said held the holocaust to be profoundly important: it obliged both
reflection and compassion, even as its horror escaped all compass. One considers
these events, he noted in 1997, "for their own sake, not for political advantage".
Nor—tendentious claims to the contrary—were those in any way new views; he
had by then held them for some two decades (Said 2001b, pp. 208–209; compare to
Said 1979, pp. 59–60). That noted, the holocaust remains in this account entirely a
matter carried out by a third party—in effect, foreclosing Said's reflections at a key
point. For while Palestinians of course played no role in the direct workings of the
Shoah, there were legal barriers to Jewish migration—even as refugees—in the
form of immigration quotas; these denied most Jews escape. Palestine's mandatory
government imposed these in part because Palestinian nationalists agitated for
them. Given the role of demographics in the conflict over Palestine, one may well

understand why they did so. Nevertheless, those efforts had consequences: more Jews in Europe were left to their fate than might otherwise have been. Of course, Palestinians were neither unique nor even atypical in their opposition to accepting Jewish refugees; nor were they sovereign in mandatory Palestine; nor does this opposition justify their subsequent dispossession and its inter-generational persistence in moral terms. But attenuated, indirect complicity still obliges reflection: both for its own sake, as Said notes, and to help contemporary Jews seeking to make common cause with Said's brand of binationalism. For it is precisely the memory of such abandonment—of being left to one's fate; of being not quite important enough to save in light of others' political interests—that resonates so acutely: both with Zionism's insistence upon Jewish sovereignty, and with the political experience of Palestinians since 1948.

31 Compare to Adorno: "The name dialectics says no more, to begin with, than that objects do not go into their concepts without leaving a remainder, that they come to contradict the traditional norm of adequacy. Contradiction is not what Hegel's absolute idealism was bound to transfigure it into ... It indicates the untruth of identity, the fact that the concept does not exhaust the thing conceived' (1973, p. 5).

32 "By themselves, constellations represent from without what the concept has cut away within: the 'more' which the concept is equally desirous and incapable of being. By gathering around the object of cognition, the concepts potentially determine the object's interior. They attain in thinking what was necessarily excised from thinking" (Adorno 1973, p. 162).

33 "That the concept is a concept even when dealing with things in being does not change the fact that on its part it is entwined with a non-conceptual whole. Its only insulation from that whole is its reification—that which establishes it as a concept ... To change this direction of conceptuality, to give it a turn toward nonidentity, is the hinge of negative dialectics" (Adorno 1973, p. 12).

References

Achcar, G., 2009. *The Arabs and the Holocaust*. New York: Picador.

Adorno, T.W., 1973. *Negative Dialectics*. New York: Seabury Press.

Adorno, T.W., 1991. The Curious Realist: On Siegfried Kracauer. *New German Critique*, 54(SI), 159–177.

Adorno, T.W., 1992. *Notes to Literature*. New York: Columbia University Press.

Adorno, T.W., 2005 [1951]. *Minima Moralia: Reflections on a Damaged Life*. London: Verso.

Adwan, S., Bar-On, D. and Naveh, E.H., 2012. *Side by Side: Parallel Histories of Israel–Palestine*. New York: The New Press.

Adwan, S., Ben-Ze'ev, E., Klein, M., Saloul, I., Sorek, T., and Yazbak, M., 2011. *Zoom In: Palestinian Refugees of 1948, Remembrances*. Dordrecht: Institute for Historical Justice and Reconciliation and Republic of Letters Publishing.

Alcalay, A., 1993. *After Jews and Arabs: Remaking Levantine Culture*. Minneapolis: University of Minnesota Press.

Asad, T., Brown, W., Butler, J., and Mahmood, S., 2013. *Is Critique Secular? Blasphemy, Injury, and Free Speech*. New York: Fordham University Press.

Assmann, J., 1998. *Moses the Egyptian: The Memory of Egypt in Western Monotheism*. Cambridge, MA: Harvard University Press.

Avey, P. and Desch, M.C., 2014. What do Policymakers Want from Us? Results of a Survey of Current and Former Senior National Security Decision Makers. *International Studies Quarterly*, 58(2), 227–246.

Ayyash, M.M., 2010. Edward Said Writing in Exile. *Comparative Studies of South Asia, Africa, and the Middle East*, 30(1), 107–118.

Barenboim, D. and Said, E.W., 2004. *Parallels and Paradoxes: Explorations in Music and Society*. New York: First Vintage Books.

Bayoumi, M., 2005. Reconciliation without Duress: Said, Adorno, and the Autonomous Intellectual. *Alif: Journal of Comparative Poetics*, 52, 46–64.

Bennett, J., 2010. *Vibrant Matter*. Durham, NC: Duke University Press.

Benvenisti, M., 2000. Meron Benvenisti Slams Edward Said: Him and Me and the Talbieh Tragedy. *Ha'aretz*, August 25. Archived: FOFOGNET—Palestinian Refugee Discussion List.

Bernstein, R.J., 1991. *The New Constellation: The Ethical-Political Horizons of Modernity/Postmodernity*. Cambridge: Polity Press.

Biswas, S., 2007. Empire and Global Public Intellectuals: Reading Edward Said as an International Relations Theorist. *Millennium—Journal of International Studies*, 36(1), 117–133.

Bourdieu, P., 1988. *Homo Academicus*. Stanford, CA: Stanford University Press.

Bourdieu, P., 2007. *Sketch for a Self-Analysis*. Cambridge: Polity.

Boyarin, J. and Boyarin, D., 2002. *Powers of Diaspora*. Minneapolis: Minnesota University Press.

Butler, J., 2012. *Parting Ways: Jewishness and the Critique of Zionism*. New York: Columbia University Press.

Cooper, J., 2015. A Diasporic Critique of Diasporism: The Question of Jewish Political Agency. *Political Theory*, 43(1), 80–110.

Darwish, M., 2004. Edward Said: A Contrapuntal Reading. *Al-Ahram Weekly Online* [online] Available from: www.alahram.org.eg/2004/710/cu4.htm [Accessed August 10, 2014].

Derrida, J., 1998. *Archive Fever: A Freudian Impression*. Chicago, IL: Chicago University Press.

Freud, S., 1967. *Moses and Monotheism*. New York: Vintage Books.

Gallucci, R., 2012. How Scholars Can Improve International Relations. *Chronicle of Higher Education*, 26 November [online]. Available from: http://chronicle.com/article/How-Scholars-Can-Improve/135898/ [Accessed October 31, 2013].

Herf, J., 2010. Not in Moderation. *New Republic*, November 1 [online]. Available from: www.newrepublic.com/book/review/not-in-moderation [Accessed August 15, 2014].

Huggan, G., 2005. (Not) Reading Orientalism. *Research in African Literatures*, 36(3), 124–136.

Lacqueur, W., 1989. *A History of Zionism: From the French Revolution to the Establishment of the State of Israel*. New York: Schocken Books.

Levine, D.J., 2012. *Recovering International Relations: The Promise of Sustainable Critique*. New York: Oxford University Press.

Löwenheim, O., 2014. *The Politics of the Trail*. Ann Arbor: University of Michigan Press.

Mahfouz, N., 2000. *Akhenaten, Dweller in Truth*. New York: Anchor Books.

Makdisi, S., 2005. Said, Palestine and the Humanism of Liberation. In: H. Babha and W.J.T. Mitchell, eds, *Edward Said: Continuing the Conversation*. Chicago, IL: Chicago University Press.

Massad, J., 2000. Palestinians and Jewish History: Recognition or Submission? *Journal of Palestine Studies*, 30(1), 52–67.

Massad, J., 2004. The Intellectual Life of Edward Said. *Journal of Palestine Studies*, 33(3), 7–22.

Mayer, A.J., 2008. *Plowshares into Swords: From Zionism to Israel*. London: Verso.

McCarthy, C., 2013. Said, Lukàcs and Gramsci: Beginnings, Geography and Insurrection. *College Literature*, 40(4), 74–104.

Mufti, A.R., 2007. *Enlightenment in the Colony*. Princeton, NJ: Princeton University Press.

Muppidi, H., 2012. *Colonial Signs of International Relations*. New York: Columbia University Press.

Myers, D.N., 2008. *Between Jew & Arab: The Lost Voice of Simon Rawidowicz*. Lebanon: Brandeis University Press.

Pappe, I., 2009. *The Rise and Fall of a Palestinian Dynasty: The Hussaynis, 1700–1948*. Berkeley: University of California Press.

Rosenthal, L., 2010. Between Humanism and Late Style. In: A. Iskander and H. Rustom, eds, *Edward Said: A Legacy of Emancipation and Representation*. Berkeley: University of California Press, pp. 462–489.

Said, E.W., 1975. *Beginnings: Intention and Method*. New York: Basic Books.

Said, E.W., 1979. *The Question of Palestine*. London: Routledge & Kegan Paul.

Said, E.W., 1983. *The World, the Text, and the Critic*. Cambridge, MA: Harvard University Press.

Said, E.W., 1986. *After the Last Sky*. New York: Pantheon Books.

Said, E.W., 1989. An Exchange on Edward Said and Difference III: Response. *Critical Inquiry*, 15(3), 634–646.

Said, E.W., 1991. *Musical Elaborations*. New York: Columbia University Press.

Said, E.W., 1993. *Culture and Imperialism*. New York: Knopf.

Said, E.W., 1994 [1978]. *Orientalism*. New York: Vintage Books.

Said, E.W., 1995a. *Peace and its Discontents*. New York: Vintage Books.

Said, E.W., 1995b. *Politics of Dispossession*. New York: Vintage Books.

Said, E.W., 1996. *Representations of the Intellectual: The 1993 Reith Lectures*. New York: Vintage Books.

Said, E.W., 1999. *Out of Place: A Memoir*. New York: Knopf.

Said, E.W., 2000. *Reflections on Exile and Other Essays*. Cambridge: Convergences.

Said, E.W., 2001a. *Power, Politics, and Culture: Interviews*. New York: Random House.

Said, E.W., 2001b. *The End of the Peace Process: Oslo and After*. New York: Pantheon Books.

Said, E.W., 2002. Adorno as Lateness Itself. In: N.C. Gibson and A. Rubin, eds, *Adorno: A Critical Reader*. Oxford: Wiley-Blackwell, pp. 193–208.

Said, E.W., 2003. *Freud and the Non-European*. London: Verso.

Said, E.W., 2004. *Humanism and Democratic Criticism*. New York: Columbia University Press.

Said, E.W., 2005. *From Oslo to Iraq and the Road Map: Essays*. New York: Vintage Books.

Said, E. W., 2006. *On Late Style: Music and Literature Against the Grain*. New York: Pantheon Books.

Said, E.W., 2008. *Music at the Limits*. London: Bloomsbury Publishing.

Segev, T., 1993. *The Seventh Million: The Israelis and the Holocaust*. New York: Henry Holt and Company.

Shatz, A., 2014. Writers and Missionaries. *The Nation*, August [online]. Available from: www.thenation.come/article/180663/writers-or-missionaries?page=0,0 [Accessed August 12, 2014].

Steele, B.J., 2013. *Alternative Accountabilities in Global Politics: The Scars of Violence.* New York: Routledge.

Sufian, S. and LeVine, M., eds, 2007. *Reapproaching Borders: New Perspectives on the Study of Israel–Palestine.* Lanham, MD: Rowman & Littlefield.

Wight, C., 2006. *Agents, Structures and International Relations.* Cambridge: Cambridge University Press.

Wood, M., 2006. Introduction. In: E.W. Said, *On Late Style: Music and Literature Against the Grain.* New York: Pantheon Books, pp. xi–xix.

Yerushalmi, Y.H., 1993. *Freud's Moses: Judaism Terminable and Interminable.* New Haven, CT: Yale University Press.

6 Reflexivity and research

Feminist interventions and their practical implications

Andrea L. Dottolo and Sarah M. Tillery

Thanks in large part to the work of feminist scholars (within international relations scholarship and beyond) such as Alvesson and Sköldberg (2000), England (1994), and Holland (1999), the use of reflexivity as a tool of investigation and engagement has gained both momentum and respect. However, despite the promise that reflexivity offers to reveal new insights, dynamics, relationships, and awareness, even the greatest proponents of its use apply its tools in what often appears to be an afterthought. This chapter has two aims. First, we explore some practical examples of how reflexive practice shapes each step of the academic research process from topic choice, framing of research questions, methodology, and interpretation and analysis. Second, we critically examine the three overarching interpretations of reflexivity (positionality, practice, and critique) in this anthology in the context of producing scholarship, teaching, and higher education administration.

To begin, we want to reflexively situate ourselves in this discussion. We approach the topic of reflexivity from our disciplinary "home" of women's studies. Through the works of Oakley (1981), Reinharz (1992), and Wasserfall (1993), each of us came to understand reflexivity as an analytical tool within the context of women's studies, while in graduate school together and as professional colleagues. We continue to employ its feminist tenets independently, and related to "reflexivity-in-relation", a topic we will address later, in our roles as researchers, teachers, and administrators. Reflexivity does not apply to only certain epistemological approaches—no approach should be immune from considering its origins, commitments, methodologies, and consequences. We have practiced and continue to practice reflexivity in moments of transition, as our professional and academic roles, authority, and identities transform and shift. This chapter will include examples from our own experiences, where we continue the many conversations about these and other topics in writing, encouraging each other to push beyond what we can see on our own, and what we even thought we might be capable of understanding. This includes reaching beyond our comfort zones by expanding our theoretical perspectives, considering alternative points of view, extending our disciplinary practices, and/or consulting marginalized methodologies (or mainstream ones, depending on how we situate ourselves). We delineate some of the benefits of each of these interpretations of reflexivity, and also model it in our explanations and illustrations.

In *Becoming a Reflexive Researcher*, Etherington (2004) outlines several different ways in which reflexivity has been defined and used. We define reflexivity as both a practice and a methodology, rooted in feminist episte- mology, that focuses on the researcher/writer reflecting upon the power rela- tionships inherent in the research (or other scholarly or political endeavor), and making those power dynamics explicit. Reflexivity is not only reflection, although some researchers and theorists have used these terms interchangeably. Other scholars such as Finlay (2002) and Woolgar (1988) have engaged in poignant debates about the differences between reflection and reflexivity. We argue that reflexivity necessitates an analysis of power, with attention to multiple epistemologies and interpretations, and extends beyond just reflec- tion, which can sometimes refer to self-awareness and internal discovery. While reflection is a necessary first step to approach reflexivity, it alone is insufficient. A more careful understanding of systems of power, institutional privilege and marginalization, and the social symbols that communicate status and hierarchy, are necessary in order to situate oneself within poli- tical structures in order to disclose one's subject position in the context of research.

Reflexivity and the academic research process

We now turn to practical examples of how reflexive practice shapes each step of academic research process from topic choice, the framing of research questions, methodology, interpretation, and analysis. Arguably individual identities, experiences, biases, institutional structures, and many other multi- ple forces always already influence research in any and all academic dis- ciplines. We believe that objectivity is a myth, that is, that there is an impartial, neutral, detached observer—is never possible. Instead, we employ a reflexive framework—a process that simply articulates and makes explicit what is already operating at all levels of research.

Because knowledge cannot be separated from its observer as DuBois (1983) states, researchers are ethically obligated to situate themselves in relation to their research so that readers and/or consumers can make an informed assessment about the knowledge that is produced. Believers of objectivity support the notion of a singular truth, a "Truth" (with a capital "T"), that is created by an omniscient observer. We argue that researchers, all of us, are telling partial truths (with a small "t") which contribute to larger, broader, bodies of scholarship. Reflexivity serves as a tool of accountability in narrat- ing the difference between many voices telling many stories, and the idea of a unique owner and supplier of information. Using this tool can help to disrupt this assumption of power of the "truth teller".

For example, when beginning a project, researchers and practitioners might consider: Why is this a topic in which I am interested? What draws me to this line of inquiry? What is it about this particular question that I want to know? What questions are not being posed? Why? What is lost by not considering these unasked questions? What theoretical perspectives are framing my research questions? Why? What theories and approaches am I choosing not to engage? How do my identities and experiences inform what I want to know? What domains of power are implicit and subsumed in these questions and in this topic? Where do I have privilege, advantage, power, and where am I marginalized, oppressed, disadvantaged? Getting clear about the answers to these questions can help shape the subsequent steps in the research process, and also has additional benefits.

For example, investigating a chosen research method can also benefit from such inquiries. Why do I think that this method is the best way to approach the answers to my research questions? How does my training influence these choices? What could be learned from considering additional or alternative methodologies? What does this method prohibit me from knowing? How does this method reflect a set of epistemological assumptions I hold? What are the political implications of choosing this method, aside from the research topic itself?

Similarly, at the point of analyses, researchers might ask: why is this tool of analysis the most appropriate for this question? This topic? This method? Where applicable, one might ask, what are the advantages and disadvantages of using this particular software (e.g. SPSS, NVivo, MPlus) over others? Am I using this program and set of tools because it is the one I happen to know? What if I ran another kind of statistical test? What if I searched for other themes, terms, or linguistic phrases? What more might I find if I examined the pauses, silences, the "ums" and "ahs" in this interview? Why am I committed to this tool of analysis?

At the level of interpretation, there are many questions to ponder, such as: What am I devoted to discovering? What do I want to avoid knowing in this study? What are the theories, perspectives, and assumptions that affect how I make meaning of this information? Am I relying on a survey or other scale to serve as an "objective" measure of attitudes, beliefs, behaviors, ideologies, identities? In an important study in feminist psychology, Landrine, Klonoff and Brown-Collins (1995) were curious about how different words may have different meanings between women of different ethnic groups. They asked white women and women of color to rate a set of adjectives as they described themselves. While there were no differences between their self-ratings, the women in the two groups understood and interpreted some of the terms to have different meanings. For example, women of color largely believed the term "passive" to mean "don't say what I really think", while white women mostly thought it meant, "am laid-back/easy-going". Women of color said that "assertive" was more likely to mean "say whatever's on my mind", and white women mostly meant "stand up for myself". This study demonstrates that while scales and measures might be validated and reliable, our assumptions about how our participants interpret the language of the items is always clouding how we make meaning of the results. In other words, if we interpret the average score on a survey item that contains the word "passive" to mean something, we miss the underlying complexities and implications, crudely assessing an importance (or lack thereof) that does not exist.

We think it is important to acknowledge that reflexivity as a process may seem foreign, complicated, and onerous to those trained in traditional social science disciplines. It takes time and practice to hone these skills, including additional reading and a reliance upon the wisdom and guidance of the multidisciplinary and interdisciplinary scholars who have successfully used these approaches before. Some traditional and/or conservative scholars may criticize reflexive methods as being "too soft", distracting, yielding information that is secondary at best and perhaps even a waste of time. While this may seem outside the scope of what IR scholars are usually concerned with, the point here is that reflexivity simply makes apparent what is always already inside the scope of what IR scholars want to know.

Moreover, international relations could use reflexivity to do what other disciplines such as anthropology, sociology, women's studies, and ethnic studies have been doing for generations—to tell a more complete story with more lenses of analysis that fashions a more responsible and informed kind of knowledge. The assumption of an objective knower precludes many different kinds of knowledge, dismissing alternative perspectives. Simply put, as scholars, we should be trying to know more, think more, ask more. Reflexivity is another mechanism or tool for thinking critically. As Ilan Baron (Chapter 9 in this volume) states, "reflexive research is normative research" and it provides "a methodological guide" for understanding, that without asking questions about our own biases and assumptions, we neglect to consider a myriad of ways of knowing and the knowledge that is tied to them.

The reflexive questions we pose here present important self-interrogations, but we do not assume that the individual alone has the ability to answer them in ways that pose challenging and transformative responses. For example, one could perhaps answer all or most of these questions without moving outside one's own pre-existing perspective. We believe that while reflexivity can certainly be attempted in a "room of one's own", a more fruitful knowledge yields from relational dialogue, to which we will speak more directly at the end of this chapter. We agree with Amoureux (Chapter 1 in this volume), that reflexivity requires a "willing".

Positionality

> *Positionality* ... is understood as a scholarly exercise that discloses the scholar's (or the scholarly field's) social/political position as (potentially) relevant for research, or as an exploration of the implications of the inseparability of subject and object for IR scholarship.
>
> (Amoureux and Steele, Introduction to this volume)

We came to understand reflexivity as feminist practice in graduate school in the late 1990s, and have found it invaluable in our scholarship. As we navigated our roles as graduate students, then faculty and administrators, we have had to continually learn the different and sometimes shifting systems of power and privilege, codes of membership and exclusion, that intersect with the "staples" of feminist reflexivity of race, class, gender, sexuality, age, body size, nationality, and physical ability (to name a few). While all firmly situated within academia, a location itself that deserves some reflexive attention as noted by Caracciolo and Hozic (Chapter 7 in this volume), each of our roles posed new challenges to ideas about how knowledge is created and sustained alongside how policies are derived and regulated. After all, "texts are living things" (Dauphinee, Chapter 2 in this volume).

Andrea

As a doctoral student in psychology and women's studies, my dissertation focused on the ways in which social identities, especially race and ethnicity, are understood and experienced by black and white men and women in the Midwest. It was a mixed method study, mostly qualitative, with 135 interviews with black men and women in their 50s and 60s. I closely examined responses to the interview question that asked: "Do you think about your own racial identity much these days? What kind of things cause you to think about it?" The framework of the study expanded the definition of race and ethnicity to include whiteness, with a specific interrogation of white racial and ethnic identities. Because race is a relational social construction, I was interested in exploring the experiences of people of color alongside the psychology of whiteness, uncovering the strategies, mechanisms, and consequences that recreate and maintain privilege while disavowing and distancing from it at the same time. One piece of this analysis by Dottolo and Stewart (2008 and 2013) explored how both blacks and whites talked about discrimination and white privilege.

Throughout the research process, I had to consider (and write about) how the analysis triggered my own interpretive concerns. I found myself increasingly uncomfortable interpreting some of the experiences of discrimination as articulated by blacks, questioning my right and the limits of my social position in doing so. As an Italian-American woman from upstate New York who came of age during the 1980s and 1990s, *who was I* to make claims about black experiences in the Midwest from those who came of age in the 1950s and 1960s? Although I am fundamentally *not* sympathetic to standpoint epistemology, suddenly I doubted what I might be able to say, especially regarding particularly painful accounts of racist cruelty expressed again and again by the participants.

For example, many black participants described being called a "nigger". I am familiar with the debate about the benefits and costs of using or repeating this word by both blacks and whites, and its resulting popular solution, "the

N-word". I have never been a proponent of censorship and do not believe that prohibiting its use promotes any kind of self-reflection or anti-racist activism. In fact, I tend to believe it does more harm than good and can further assist racist disguises in an academic context. However, after repeatedly encountering the ways that "nigger" appeared in the interviews, I began to question my role as a white researcher in repeating it. My feminist training spurred me to carefully consider my relationship to the use of the term and the effect it had on your meaning making. Kennedy's (2002) review of its usage helped to re-center my belief that it was my responsibility as a researcher in general, but even more as a white researcher interpreting black experiences to include and explore this "troublesome word" as an important element of their experiences. It seemed more important to document the ways black participants used the term "nigger" as part of their reflections and accounts, highlighting that this word became part of their responses to questions about racial identities, rather than to silence them or avoid engaging in this difficult and painful task, or replacing their language with the term "the 'N' word". Furthermore, I needed to take responsibility for the fact that the interview questions invoked these responses, calling the participants into these conversations. I reminded myself that these responses did not appear out of nowhere; these were their responses, and I knew I had a duty to try to understand them.

In contrast to my feelings of awkwardness and inadequacy in interpreting black experiences of discrimination, I was completely comfortable in "calling out" white expressions of racism, whether overt or covert. As an Italian American in the Midwest, my racial identity was constantly questioned by acquaintances, colleagues, and strangers in a way I had never experienced before, especially being from Syracuse, New York. My olive skin and dark features seemed to designate me as "Other" in a sea of blond, blue-eyed Midwesterners. In Michigan, my appearance was not read as Italian, but as various other ethnic or racial categories (including: Latina, African-American, Arab, and biracial or mixed race). For example, at a doctor's appointment on campus, a white nurse practitioner marveled at my "great Hispanic musculature", and connected this to my potential to carry children with ease (which will, of course, according to her, inevitably occur). A fellow graduate student fumbled when I clarified that my last name is Italian because there had evidently been "talk" in the department that I was Latina. Most commonly, strangers and acquaintances alike would ask, "What are you?" sometimes questioning if I could speak English. I had great difficulty finding a hair stylist, and found that salons charged extra to cut "ethnic hair". The treatment that I received in these brief moments of "raced" experiences both infuriated me, and as a result of my reflexive training, also helped me to recognize the privilege that often surrounds me, fueling my anti-racist politics.

Therefore, when analyzing narratives about white racial identities, I delighted in revealing some of the psychological mechanisms that might inform their racist tendencies. I rarely wanted to give such narratives the benefit of the doubt in their ideas about race and was more than willing to expose their privilege, probably informed by several motivations. First, as a researcher with my own marginalized identities around gender, class, and sexuality, I was sympathetic to experiences of discrimination and "angry" at its offenders. Second, this project was partially inspired by my own experiences with conditional whiteness in the Midwest, and the few glimpses of personal mistreatment based on phenotype that I had ever encountered occurred in this particular region of the United States. And I certainly wanted to distance myself from the "bad" whites, unaware, hiding, negligent in their privilege.

I am not suggesting I experienced racism in any way similar to the black participants in my study, but needless to say, particular performances of Midwestern whiteness had left me with a bad taste. For these reasons, and probably others, I was especially invested in exposing those expressions of racism. I identify as white, and believe that Italians have white privilege. I struggled to be sympathetic toward whites in the study, but nonetheless as a white woman I was familiar with the ways they talked about race. As a racial insider in a racist culture, I was privy to the discourses noted by Roediger (1991) and Guglielmo (2003) about racial hierarchies, especially those that confound race and class, often blaming race for economic inequality. I recognized the white participants' ambivalence and contradictory statements and, like many forms of covert oppression, sometimes they were the most painful to negotiate.

Engaging in the process of reflexivity positions the researcher in relation to the subject, participants, and knowledge that is created. This is always already happening with every academic endeavor, but feminist politics requires us to make these relationships to power structures explicit. For example, as a white, Italian American, working class lesbian from upstate New York, I was able to "see", understand, and interpret particular elements of these black and white racial narratives. If an African American man in his 60s from the Midwest were to read and interpret these interviews, he might "discover" other elements and themes in this study. Or, maybe not. A Vietnamese immigrant woman living in California might also approach this work from a different perspective, yielding a very different set of results. And this is not only true for qualitative research. My study also included a quantitative portion, a survey with several different kinds of items. How we might conceive of the statistical analyses and then how to interpret the results are all shaped by who we are. While it seems logical that our different experiences, identities, and cultures shape our perspectives, careful attentiveness to the multiple ways in which this occurs and its related effect on meaning making highlights why reflexivity is central to the responsible production of knowledge.

This is not to say that any one of these identities, or any set of these identities is more useful, valid, or important. It is not the case that one of these researchers has the more "accurate" findings. But making the relationship between the researcher and the researched explicit creates a space where the researcher can be conscious of their own understanding and meaning making, and allows for the reader to also be aware of these relationships, also important in situating and contextualizing the scholarship within a body of literature. There are many styles and strategies of explicating the relationship between researcher and researched, including a systematic examination of social identities, access to resources, knowledge, and institutional structures. Another type of strategy is discussed in the following section of this chapter on practice.

I am also not suggesting that these are interchangeable analytical categories or lenses of analyses. It is not that one is just as good as the next, as long as they say it. Knowledge is inherently situated at every level of its conception and construction. Furthermore, I argue that these identities or categories are *not* fixed, monolithic, or deterministic. Not all members of groups are the same, with great variation within. In other words, another researcher who is an Italian American, working class lesbian from upstate New York may very well see, interpret, and create meaning from this very same study in a completely different way than I did. This hypothetical doppelganger, for example, might be light skinned. Or she might not have interpreted this racist treatment as problematic, or may have fueled her racism instead of an anti-racist political commitment.

There are only a handful of scholars that write about whiteness, especially in psychology, but as I continue to study and critically interrogate white privilege as I did for the special issue on whiteness in *Lesbian Studies* (Dottolo 2014), I must continue to question, examine, and position my investment in my questions, methods, and the knowledge produced as result.

Sarah

My graduate school experience in women's studies in the late 1990s and early 2000s was one of discovery, question, learning, and understanding. It was also a time of incredible transition for me professionally and personally. I was entering the world of professional academia and beginning to understand myself more as a theorist and faculty member and less as only a student. I began my doctoral research exploring the social, political, and cultural representations of fat women and their bodies during a time when I, too, identified and was also marked by others as a fat woman.

My research was centered on the complexity of constructing and maintaining an identity based on being fat. For the purpose of my project, fatness was defined, not by a feeling or emotion, but by the occupation of a body that was larger than "normal", a body that was deemed unacceptable by cultural standards of beauty and typical pant sizes (anything larger than a women's size 16 or 18 is generally sold separately or not at all in typical clothing stores in the US). I was interested in knowing how fat women (and some men) understood their own bodies and self worth in a culture that consistently devalued their existence. I explored the mixed messages that fat women must contend with in their daily existence—from weight-based appearance discrimination, to plus-size fashion magazines, and the popularity of weight loss surgeries and drugs. By interrogating these messages and images in our culture, I argued that fat identity is nuanced and complex, and that women and men who identify as fat politically or socially do so against a landscape that both terrorizes their existence (in most cases) and/or validates their experiences (in rare cases).

Within my department and in certain scholarly communities, my authority to speak on the subject of fatness, fat women, and fat bodies was never questioned. In fact, it was embraced and possibly expected to some degree. The study of fatness and body size was an area of inquiry that I thought feminist theory had largely ignored. And not to say that feminist scholars were not interested in discussing women's bodies. The solipsism of thinness in US contemporary culture, and the impact of a singular, normalized, thin, and white body on various communities based on gender, race, class, and sexuality were well documented by the works of Brumberg (1988), Chapkis (1986), and Chernin (1981). The work in these areas abounded, but in my opinion and as argued in my dissertation (Tillery 2007), that left a gap where fat bodies, their representations, identities, and impact were ignored and further marginalized.

As a fat woman, my research on fat women's bodies was unquestioned by my dissertation committee and other faculty mentors. I was never asked to explain or justify why this work was important to me, or what authority I had to speak about it. Arguably, the idea that one would study something closely related to who one is is a common phenomenon in social science research. In his work, "Research to Me-Search", Christopher Avilés (2011) acknowledges that research often evolves from and into the study of the self. As researchers, we are frequently drawn to study the things that also impact and affect us as individuals. Hence the joke, "It's not research, it's me-search!" Despite the fact that one of the basic tenants of feminist research is to be reflexive about who we are in relationship to our projects, my "me-search" went relatively un-interrogated until my authority to speak was called into question.

Over the course of nine years in graduate school, my life and my body transformed rather radically. As I lost weight, the expectations about explaining myself in relation to my research project became more overt. My "privilege" to talk about the "other" (in this instance, fat women) disappeared, and suddenly I was being asked to be reflexive and acknowledge my own transitioning outsider status from the community of people to which I had once belonged. In one instance, I had a women's studies faculty member ask me in a hushed voice if I would still be researching fat women's bodies for my dissertation. This question came after I had successfully defended my proposal and completed a bulk of the work for the project. Other questions and comments were far more personal, such as "Did you lose weight on purpose?" and "How will you be able to talk about your research as a thinner woman?" Suddenly, I realized that in the eyes of others, I had lost the authority to write and research on a topic to which I felt intimately connected. My body betrayed that connection to outsiders, and it was in this transformation and revelation that I had to engage a very strategic reflexivity in my work in order to acknowledge the duplicity of my insider and outsider status to fatness.

Unlike Amanda Russell Beattie's (Chapter 8 in this volume) argument that the exiled subject is well placed to question the status quo, my own "exiled" status in relation to professional research was cause for further concern and attention to my own subjectivity in that research that had previously not been addressed. While my changing status to other faculty and colleagues became cause for question, in the end, it reinforced a kind of reflexivity to happen as author/producer of my own work. As a result, it also affected the knowledge I was able to produce. It forced a critical awareness of myself in relation to the communities of fat women, their identities, and their bodies that might have remained unchecked otherwise. As a feminist researcher, I was trained that being reflexive about my relationship to my work would be part of the process and I knew that I would need to write about my positionality along the way, but it was the shift in my own body that prompted the expectation more explicitly from others.

Although the pressure from others to explain why and how my body transformed felt invasive and unprofessional for me personally, being asked to acknowledge my increasing body size privilege (ironically as my body became smaller!) was appropriate, transparent, and critically needed. Moreover, it impacted how I asked my research questions and what knowledge I was able to produce.

Practice

> ... a *practice* approach that sees reflexivity as a socially meaningful practice for international and/or global politics. This form of reflexivity foregrounds agency as a kind of *grappling with* the world and the regimes of knowledge that influence political actors within.
>
> (Amoureux and Steele, Introduction to this volume)

Reflexivity can be described as a critical appraisal of one's own practice, considering, for example: why we frame issues or questions in particular ways, what drew us to our research questions, how we investigate and interpret, how our approaches lead us to particular kinds of knowledge and not others, and ways that our social identities (race, class, gender, sexuality, age, nationality, etc.) shape our relationships and knowledge. Reflexivity informs not only the kinds of questions we ask and how they are framed, but how those questions are operationalized, put to action, represent a shift and connection between thinking and knowing, doing and practice. The examples we provide in the following section illustrate the translation and mobilization of reflexivity as behavior—in the classroom and with colleagues in professional contexts, all the while critically reflecting upon these relationships. Andrea engages in reflective practice with her students, modeling it for them as she offers instruction in the psychology and women's studies classroom. In this way, she guides students to be reflexive themselves, which is built into the structure and design of the course from required readings to assignments. Sarah integrates her experiences as both faculty member and administrator, gathering multiple perspectives in order to problem solve, communicate, and manage in a fuller and more synthesized way.

Andrea

Here it may be helpful to offer an example of an exercise I used to teach about reflexivity with graduate students in Community and Social Psychology who were serving as interns at community practicum sites. For example, some students worked at domestic violence shelters, offices of local political leaders, schools, hospitals, and community centers. I begin by discussing reflexivity including a definition and why it is necessary in knowledge production. Students are then asked to consider ways in which their social identities influence their relationships at their practicum sites. For example:

- What (and/or who) prompted your placement in your practicum and why?
- Who do you interact with when you are there? How are your identities similar or different from the various individuals you interact with at your practicum site? In what ways do these similarities or differences shape what you can know, understand, observe?
- What is the nature of the work you do? What kinds of tasks do you do each day?
- What has been the focus of your practicum? What do you hope to accomplish for and with the people with whom you work?
- What has not been considered? Who has not been considered? What remains invisible?
- What are the intended outcomes for both you and the people at your practicum site?

Students were asked to explicate specifically how race, class, gender, sexuality, age, nationality, and ability (able-bodiedness) were at play in their experiences, and then paired up to process and analyze these insights. I encouraged students to think about how each social identity might be understood in response to each of the above questions, and then as a whole, integrating an intersectionality perspective. For example, for the question about who the student interacts with at the practicum site, I ask them to consider: How is this about race? How is the student's racial identity situated among her co-workers? Her employers? Her clients? How does her racial privilege or marginalization affect what she can know? How does she have power over others based on race? How do others have power over her based on race? How are messages about race communicated in this space? Then, the same question is asked about again, this time considering: How is this about gender? We replace "race" in the above questions with "gender". And then again, now asking questions about sexuality, and again about class, then age, and nationality, followed by able-bodiedness. I often find that this is the first time students have ever been asked to consider these identity categories in their academic work and I noticed that students react in a variety of ways, including confused, defensive, resistant, curious, relieved, and enthused. Next, I ask the students to consider what social identity or axis of power is missing from the list. Finally, we consider all of these identities together. Echoing my previous discussion, I model for them: What does it mean that I am a working class, Italian American, lesbian, able-bodied, academic from the northeast in my study on black and white middle aged men and women from the Midwest? What does it mean about what I can and cannot know in that particular classroom, at that moment, with those individual students, in that space, at that time?

Asking these questions about their experiences in their practicum sites then leads to a discussion of "helping" behaviors and professions, and the assumptions and expectations of who "helps" and who *needs* help. Students explored their host organizations/practicum and their demographic compositions, who makes decisions, who is deferred to and why, how much is explicit and what is implied. We discussed how policies at the organizations are constructed, negotiated, and implemented, how informal social functions happen (e.g. who eats lunch together and where). I encourage students to investigate the history of their organizations, who serves on the board, who is included and excluded. One student discussed that bilingual services were offered at her site, but recognized that it was only Spanish and English that were spoken, and did not adequately accommodate the many clients from across the globe. We then discussed how they will make meaning of their experiences in writing about their practicum site, who interprets and who gets interpreted.

It is important to note that this exercise may not be easily implemented at every institution or in every classroom, taking into account group dynamics, as well as the safety of the students and faculty in various campus climates. In fact, even in the most welcoming social contexts, individual and personal safety should always be considered and acknowledged, with the recognition that individuals exist at various levels of awareness and understanding of themselves and others. In addition, the exercise need not be conducted in pairs, but could be a written exercise. Of course, the questions considered in this exercise can be applied to a variety of contexts, including academic research; internships; field research; international organizing; education; medicine; service provision by non-governmental organizations; disarmament; demobilization and reintegration (DDR) processes in post-conflict environments; and virtually any domain where inquiry takes place and individuals or groups are asked to respond.

Sarah

Like Andrea, another example of practicing reflexivity comes from within my professional career as an administrator at a community college. In the last four years, I have worked for a community college in Portland, Oregon where the relationship between the faculty and academic staff with management/administration is negotiated by the American Federation of Teachers (AFT) union. In my first two years with the college, I worked as an academic staff and part-time faculty member. My position was "continuously appointed" (a status much like tenure) and, therefore, protected by our union contract. When I transitioned to a management position, my status as a union member was dissolved and I was charged with managing and supervising colleagues with whom I had once shared union membership.

Managing this professional transition effectively meant that I constantly had to invert my questions and critical framework for understanding a situation back onto my former self as a member of the union. In other words, I would call upon my own experience as a faculty member in an effort to understand and retain some perspective as a manager for my actions and decisions. It meant consciously acknowledging and taking into account my previous experience and existence in order to gain a broader understanding of any situation I found myself in with faculty and staff. One example of this came when I had to ask a faculty member to be explicit about her office hours on campus. From my position as her manager, there was a concern that she was not present on campus or fulfilling her obligations as a faculty member. As a former faculty member, however, I know that much of the work of an academic is done off campus, at home, in the coffee shop, etc., and the "production" of work is not always visible by someone's presence on campus. In talking with this faculty member about her contractual obligation to hold a certain number of office hours each week on campus, we were able to find a compromise. She understood that she needed to meet that obligation and be explicit with the department and her students about when she would be available in her office, and I was able to acknowledge that she was getting her job done in other ways that might not be seen by her colleagues or me. This kept the conversation productive and amicable. The reflexive practice in this moment, meant holding two possibly competing expectations up against one another and acknowledging them both as valuable. This type of reflexivity turned out to benefit both me and the faculty member in finding a common ground to work together, but mostly it instructed me on how to make meaning of my role in this relationship.

Similar to my dissertation project, my transitioning role from union member to manager meant both honoring and interrogating both the insider and the outsider status for the purpose of pushing beyond my present awareness and job classification. In the example above, it would have been quite easy to just dictate the contract rules to my faculty member and force her to be on campus a certain number of hours. As a manager, it would have been within my purview to handle the situation in this manner. No doubt, my power in the relationship would have allowed this to happen, but it also would have destroyed my relationship with her and potentially impacted our ability to work collaboratively together in the future. By remaining reflexive in the situation, and calling on my own previous experience, I was able to express empathy and understanding, while also clarifying my desires as her manager to see her meet the contractual obligation. Not only did this result in her coming to campus more consistently, but our relationship to one another was not compromised in the process.

Critique

> *Critique* involves actors (including scholars) confronting others (oftentimes from within collective selves) to stimulate self-reflexivity. Such critique may target identity, political action, and discourse.
> (Amoureux and Steele, Introduction to this volume)

We would like to suggest an approach to critique that we are calling "reflexivity-in-relation". This involves extending beyond the more solidary activity of reflection, to rely upon our scholarly communities, especially our trusted relationships, to mirror, interrogate, and query our positionality and connections to our research and practice.

Scholars such as Finlay (2002) and Fine (1998) have written about reflexivity as central to research, and it is often described as a process of individual critical appraisal. While this is necessary as a first step, we believe that sharing reflexive insights with others who also value the methodology is necessary. This intends to extend the processes that Steele names (Chapter 3 in this volume) of "documenting" and "provoking" to include others in that process. Perhaps informed by Andrea's psychology training, it seems we cannot really know ourselves alone, without the reflections, observations, and insights of others. We have found invaluable benefit in critiquing each other's reflexive process, both to improve the other as both scholars and administrator, and also to inform our own processes of reflexivity. For example, Sarah often observes an added layer of complexity or dimension to Andrea's scholarship that is difficult for her to see based on her perspective at the time. And, Andrea may attribute an academic exchange to gender or sexuality, when Sarah reminds her that class and race are also operating at the same time.

Andrea

As a doctoral student at the University of Michigan, I was introduced to the idea that I might not be middle class. In other words, it was the first time that I was in an environment where my class status was questioned or that I became aware that I did not have middle-class roots. As many scholars like hooks (2000) and McIntosh (2001) have explained, the class system in the

United States is predicated upon the myth of meritocracy, and unless folks are extremely wealthy or poor, most believe they are "middle class". Our class-segregated society means we are rarely exposed to individuals or communities who are not from the same (or similar) class backgrounds. It was only in Michigan where I was generally surrounded by middle-class people, and for the first time, I recognized that I was a class minority in that space.

My awareness of my class status became more acute when I engaged with another research project, analyzing interviews with graduate students in the social sciences and humanities about their experiences of academic socialization. I focused on responses to the question, "How are issues of race/ethnicity, gender and/or sexuality visible in your program?" While responses were "rich" with information, some students also mentioned social class, although they were not explicitly asked about class. As I read the transcripts I noticed these transcripts were bleeding with emotion, reflecting back to me experiences I was having at the same time. I struggled with how to make sense of this new knowledge, of how to now understand my own identity, class structure, and the intention and motivations of all those around me who were "teaching" me that I did not belong. In this confusing and intense period, I turned to my dear friend Sarah, who came to Michigan to visit on several occasions. Sarah identifies as middle class, although we never really discussed it much in the years of our friendship before then. I vividly remember how she witnessed the university community, offering her own observations and analysis to my experiences and research. Confused, I asked her then (and continue to do so) about how to make meaning of this academic culture, of the subtle messages and implications, juxtaposed against the overt assertions of my peers and advisers that something was wrong with me. That no matter how hard I tried, I would never seem to be part of this club, an experience new and strange.

Sarah validated my experiences, watching in horror and in recognition—interpreting and decoding for me, pushing me, and reflecting back to me what I told her. She helped me to see what was *not* being said, gave me tips on navigating wine and cheese mixers (talk about nothing), and how to avoid recruitment weekend (by conveniently being "out of town"). She observed and translated the many brief, seemingly non-substantive messages and exchanges in this social terrain, including the annoying niceties and unending discussions of the weather. My relationship to the research and the process of situating my interpretations would not have been possible without this "reflexivity-in-relation" experience. It also prompted Sarah to be reflexive of her own academic contexts and class position where I learned from her process—echoing, mirroring, ranting, making meaning—together.

In addition to being a gifted theorist and insightful scholar, Sarah has been an influential teacher and dear friend to me for sixteen years. We have grown together as feminists, scholars, and administrators over that time. Our notion of reflexivity-in-relation is not about being emotional companions, though we are. We are suggesting that reflexivity should not happen alone;

that it is required to advance our scholarship, as members in a community of responsible academics and practitioners. I discuss my relationship with Sarah here because we respect each other as intellectuals, and this component is one that is necessary in order to push each other toward finer and more sophisticated insights. I might gain similar kinds of understanding at a conference, in a classroom, or in a writing group, with individuals I may or may not particularly like. The point is that we try on our reflexive analyses with others, *in relation.*

Sarah

Reflexivity in relation is about knowing something differently (and arguably more thoroughly) by knowing it in comparison and in contrast to the ideas and perspectives of someone and something else. And we argue here, it is not just about acknowledging one's own position and/or identity to one's research or work (though that is an important aspect), but about understanding that position as a constantly moving target. This moving target is often identified *in relation* to other constants in our lives. Just as Andrea described knowing and understanding her own class consciousness in her transition to graduate school at the University of Michigan more explicitly by juxtaposing it to mine, I too have had similar experiences of transition where being reflexive-in-relation has moved me from one point of understanding to another. As Andrea described, we have been close colleagues and friends for more than a decade. As such, we have come to know our own experiences better because we can compare to each other's framework for understanding, thus leading us to question, validate, and reinforce what we know and what we think we know.

One of my first professional positions after graduate school was a job I took in student affairs at a very small, exclusive private liberal arts college on the west coast. Although I was raised in an environment that was solidly middle class and I had all the privilege and support that a middle-class upbringing afforded me, I had zero experience with this type of college environment. My own education had been completed at the community college and the large public regional universities in my area, but my class privilege never allowed me to question whether I would "fit" or successfully transition to this new college environment. Until one day, I was walking through campus in mid-October, and I noticed that all the flowerbeds on campus had been overturned and new flowers were being put in their place. This struck me as particularly funny since I thought the "old" flowers looked perfectly nice. Later that evening, Andrea and I were catching up over the phone and I benignly mentioned this business about the flowers and how I did not understand what was going on. Immediately, she commented that the school was likely preparing for a parent's weekend given the time of year and instantly, I knew she was right. Andrea explained that her first year of college took place at a school very similar to my institution and she distinctly remembered (the feeling of shock and confusion) when the campus suddenly became "prettier" for all the parents upon their return that fall.

This shared experience of reflexivity-in-relation is notable for two reasons. One, my own class privilege protected me from feeling ignorant in not understanding the situation to its full capacity. And therefore, my ability to be self-reflexive in the situation (from the perspective of middle-class white woman) didn't serve me. Two, it was only in relation to Andrea's life experience that I was able to grasp a fuller picture of a very routine campus practice and make more meaning out of it. In this way, we can see how reflexivity is a process with components that can be used separately and together. By acknowledging our positionality to the situation or the research, we provide the information needed to understand where/how our perspective is generated. By practicing reflexivity, we attempt to make meaning from what we study or from the questions we ask. And finally, by doing reflexivity-in-relation we expand the meaning we are able to make to include new perspectives and new practices.

Conclusion

In the following passage, Fine (1998) questions the relationship between researcher and researched, interrogating, or "working the hyphen" between self and other in the context of qualitative methods:

> By working the hyphen I mean to suggest that researchers probe how we are in relation with the contexts we study and with our informants, understanding that we are all multiple in those relations. I mean to invite researchers to see how these "relations between" get us "better" data, limit what we feel free to say, expand our minds and constrict our mouths, engage us in intimacy and seduce us into complicity, make us quick to interpret and hesitant to write. Working the hyphen means creating occasions for researchers and informants to discuss what is, and is not, "happening between," within the negotiated relations of whose story is being told, why, to whom, with what interpretation, and whose story is being shadowed, why, for whom, and with what consequence.
>
> (Fine 1998, p. 135)

While Fine is referring specifically to qualitative research, the questions she poses can be applied to all methodologies in all disciplines, urging us to consider these multiple layers of reflexivity. In this chapter, we have demonstrated ways in which reflexivity can foster understandings that are enhanced in a variety of scholarly and professional academic environments. In this way, the potential of reflexivity to have both theoretical and practical benefits is compelling. While we have emphasized psychology and women's studies, reflexivity is not disciplinarily bound, with its benefits extending to all levels and roles in academia, including students, faculty, and administrators.

In her description of "working the hyphen", Fine (1998) also refers to the three interpretations of reflexivity discussed here, including positionality, practice, and critique in her discussion of reflection, behavior, and relationships, respectively. While some scholars may continue to need justifiable reasons for adopting a reflexive approach in their next project or class session, it is our mutual hope that reflexivity become integrated into the academic work of IR scholars in such a way that even the smallest pause for consideration of some of the tools we outline here might offer a more authentic and transparent scholarship, offering possibilities to enrich, extend, and deepen the production of knowledge.

References

Alvesson, M. and Sköldberg, K., 2000. *Reflexive Methodology: New Vistas for Qualitative Research*. London: Sage Publications.

Avilés, C., 2011. Research to Me-search. *Critical Praxis Research: Explorations of Educational Purpose*, 10, 219–231.

Brumberg, J.J., 1988. *Fasting Girls: The History of Anorexia Nervosa*. New York: Penguin Books.

Chapkis, W., 1986. *Beauty Secrets: Women and the Politics of Appearance*. Boston, MA: South End Press.

Chernin, K., 1981. *The Obsession: Reflections on the Tyranny of Slenderness*. New York: Harper Perennial.

Dottolo, A.L., ed., 2014. Special issue: Lesbians and White Privilege. *Journal of Lesbian Studies*, 18(2).

Dottolo, A.L. and Stewart, A.J., 2008. "Don't Ever Forget Now, You're a Black Man in America": Intersections of Race, Class and Gender in Encounters with the Police. *Sex Roles*, 59, 350–364.

Dottolo, A.L. and Stewart, A.J., 2013. "I Never Think About My Race": Psychological Features of White Racial Identities. *Qualitative Research in Psychology*, 10, 102–117.

DuBois, B., 1983. Passionate Scholarship: Notes on Values, Knowing, and Method in Feminist Social Science. In: R.D. Klein and G. Bowles, eds, *Theories of Women's Studies*. Boston, MA: Routledge & Kegan Paul, pp. 105–116.

England, K.V.L., 1994. Getting Personal: Reflexivity, Positionality, and Feminist Research. *The Professional Geographer*, 46(1), 80–89.

Etherington, K., 2004. *Becoming a Reflexive Researcher: Using Our Selves in Research*. London: Jessica Kingsley Publishers.

Fine, M., 1998. Working the Hyphens: Reinventing Self and Other in Qualitative Research. In: N. Denizenand Y. Lincoln, eds, *The Landscape of Qualitative Research: Theories and Issues*. Thousand Oaks, CA: Sage.

Finlay, L., 2002. Negotiating the Swamp: The Opportunity and Challenge of Reflexivity in Research Practice. *Qualitative Research*, 2, 209–230.

Guglielmo, T.A., 2003. *White on Arrival: Italians, Race, Color and Power in Chicago, 1890–1945*. New York: Oxford University Press.

Holland, R., 1999. Reflexivity. *Human Relations*, 52, 463–483.

hooks, b., 2000. *Where We Stand: Class Matters*. New York: Routledge.

Kennedy, R., 2002. *Nigger: The Strange Career of a Troublesome Word.* New York: Vintage.

Landrine, H., Klonoff, E.A., and Brown-Collins, A., 1995. Cultural Diversity and Methodology in Feminist Psychology: Critique, Proposal, Empirical Example. In: H. Landrine, ed., *Bringing Cultural Diversity to Feminist Psychology: Theory, Research and Practice.* Washington, DC: American Psychological Association.

McIntosh, P., 2001. White Privilege and Male Privilege: A Personal Account of Coming to See Correspondences through Work in Women's Studies. In: L. Richardson, V. Taylor, and N. Whittier, eds, *Feminist Frontiers V.* Boston, MA: McGraw Hill.

Oakley, A., 1981. Interviewing Women: A Contradiction in Terms. In H. Roberts, ed., *Doing Feminist Research.* London: Routledge and Kegan Paul.

Reinharz, S., 1992. *Feminist Methods in Social Science Research.* New York: Oxford University Press.

Roediger, D.R., 1991. *The Wages of Whiteness: Race and the Making of the American Working Class.* New York: Verso.

Tillery, S., 2007. *Performing Fatness and the Cultural Negotiations of Body Size.* (Unpublished doctoral dissertation). University of Maryland: College Park, MD.

Wasserfall, R., 1993. Reflexivity, Feminism and Difference. *Qualitative Sociology,* 16(1), 23–41.

Woolgar, S., ed., 1988. *Knowledge and Reflexivity.* London: Sage Publications.

7 Reflexivity@Disney-U

Eleven theses on living in IR

Mauro J. Caraccioli and Aida A. Hozic

Figure 7.1 Timeless Waltz at the Plaza
Photo by Marijka Willis of Seward Johnson's *Whispering Close* on the University of Florida campus in 2011. (Available from: https://flic.kr/p/ajcbvZ and published thanks to Creative Commons: https://creativecommons.org/licenses/by-nc-sa/2.0/)

Thesis #1: The Janus face of the American academe

We shall start with two images: *reflections*, indeed.

Several years ago, as we toured the Social Sciences building of the University of Buenos Aires, a Latin American colleague said: "You, North Americans, teach at Disneyland. What with your glorious campuses, manicured lawns, beautiful libraries, large offices, computers, databases, all that technology ..." The Social Sciences building in Buenos Aires was plastered with political posters, fliers calling to meetings, and banners denouncing Argentine and global injustices. There were at least five different Trotskyite groups advertising their meetings within a few steps of each other while a homeless man, who looked like Lenin, roamed the corridors, just as he had done for the last 20 years. A librarian, who had dedicated his life to the task of preserving knowledge, showed us a small but well-selected book collection. And our colleague, a distinguished professor who also taught at two other institutions outside of Buenos Aires in order to make a living, explained that he was teaching his classes at night, in a long hallway, since none of the classrooms could accommodate the number of students interested in his course.

That same summer of 2011, and in the middle of the worst budget cuts to US public education in decades, our own University of Florida (UF) was hosting an exhibit of 25 sculptures by Seward Johnson, a "Band-Aid" heir to the Johnson & Johnson family fortunes. The sculptures were supersized and hyper-realistic figures of people, inspired by iconic art works and photographs—from Grant Wood's *American Gothic* (here entitled *God Bless America*) to Alfred Eisenstaedt's *The Kissing Sailor* in Times Square at the end of World War II (here entitled *Unconditional Surrender*). The largest sculpture, placed on the centrally located Plaza of the Americas, depicted a dancing couple. Called *Whispering Close*, it was supposedly inspired by Pierre-Auguste Renoir's painting *Dance in the City*. But on our Southern campus, the grotesquely large dancing figures looked much more like a scene from *Gone with the Wind*—with all its political texts and subtexts. That September, UF's chapter of Students for a Democratic Society put a large yellow price tag on the couple protesting a tuition increase. And a year later, an LGBT-straight alliance staged a queer dance under the sculpture questioning the public affirmation of hetero-normativity. But, for the most part, and despite—or, perhaps, because of—its 927 student organizations, the campus remained politically quiet, much as it had been throughout its history.

And so we start our own version of a *documentary provocation* (Steele, Chapter 3 in this volume) by acknowledging the Janus face of the American academe—as "the envy of the world" and "one of the country's most valuable resources" (Gilpin Faust 2009)—but also as a Disneyesque arena of privileges and complacencies, rarely recognized even at times when they are fiercely defended. Even more importantly, we wish to draw attention to the practices upon which this Disney look-alike space thrives these days: increasing inequalities, suspect labor relations, uneven opportunities, and mystifying institutional hierarchies.

The discipline of international relations (IR), we would argue, cannot be disentangled from the fantasy-filled academic world in which it dwells. If the layout of a disciplinary neighborhood matters, especially when gentrified (Schulman 2012; Weber 2014a)—then so does the materiality of the buildings in which the discipline resides. Any analysis of reflexivity—as a "turning back" or a "theoretical reflection" (Neufeld 1995, p. 40) "on the process of knowledge production, scholars themselves ... and their practices more generally" (Amoureux and Steele, Introduction to this volume)—presupposes the question of its location. How can we speak of *positionality* without investigating the place where scholarship is being produced? How can we engage in a *critique* without mentioning the vectors determining the inside and outside of our assumed community of scholars? How can we think of *practices* if they only relate to the supposed object of our study—world politics—but do not address the micro-political: the uses and abuses of power on our campuses or in our conference hotels—from odd silences to instances of micro-aggression to harassment (sexual and otherwise)?

Thesis #2: The promise and failure of reflexivity

There was, we should say, a promise in the turn to reflexivity in international relations that such academic fantasies would be tackled and unmasked. The Third Debate intended to promote "a more reflexive intellectual environment in which debate, criticism, and novelty can freely circulate" (Lapid 1989). The meta-theoretical calling of post-positivism was supposed to trickle down and—following Giddens (1979)—"systematically reconstruct" the field of international relations, generating diversity and a plurality of theoretical positions. The quest for reflexivity was also meant to be a corrective to the power/knowledge nexus in world politics and it was supposed to unveil the complicity of a researcher/scholar in the reproduction of existing power relations (Neufeld 1993; Oren 2002; Ackerly and True 2008; Steele 2010; Ish-Shalom 2011). At the heart of these discussions about reflexivity in international relations—regardless of disagreements over its definition—was "the problem of values", whose explicit treatment—both through meta-theory and through the analysis of IR's socio-political context—could have made way for the emergence of a truly *Reflexivist IR* (Hamati-Ataya 2011).

Put to practice, reflexive IR has brought us different historiographies (and geographies) of the discipline (Oren 2002, 2006; Long and Schmidt 2005; Tickner and Blaney 2012; Levine 2012; Guzzini 2013), which recognized its long-standing racial blindness, preoccupation with US dominance, servitude to Washington, devotion to market economies, politically problematic acceptance of positivist epistemology, and reductionist understandings of power. A variety of critical or dissident approaches have now become "a part of the pluralist disciplinary fabric of the discipline" (Lapid 2014). But, as Cindy

Weber (2014a) has recently argued, responding to Lapid's disciplinary optimism, this pluralism has come at a cost: "the hard, troubling, political edges of critical IR were substituted with softer, more soothing critiques of upscale IR that left critical politics behind". Two decades into this introspective disciplinary exercise, conducted amidst perpetual wars and deeply disturbing exercises of authority in the name of democracy, international relations—at least in the American academe—still follows the signals of positivist political science (Oren 2014; Wibben 2014) and its meta-theoretical insights have not assuaged the world's violent nightmares. Thus, we too share the sentiment of scholars who believe that reflexivity—enhanced or otherwise—might not have delivered on its promises.

Thesis #3: Depoliticization of international relations

The first, and the most obvious, sign of these unrealized hopes is the continued depoliticization of IR as a discipline, which cannot be simply subsumed under the rubrics of the lack of relevance or public engagement. In the US context, throwing such charges at academics seems to be a recurring motif. They are raised by scholars or journalists with proximity to Washington's policy circles (see, for the latest round, FP Staff 2014; Kristoff 2014) and tend to be equally dismissive of positivist/quantitative and critical/post-structuralist works in IR. But, although there is always an element of truth in critiques of the Ivory Tower's insularity, those who engage in such criticism often have little or no knowledge of the incentive structures in the academic world (Campbell and Desch 2013; Walt 2013; Robin 2014) and/or seem to be totally unaware of the many ways in which IR scholars communicate with the public (blogs, films, poetry, narratives, public lectures, museum exhibits) *despite* such incentives.

More importantly, however, the question of relevance begs another question: relevant to whom? The underlying assumption of discussions about relevance in the United States is that political scientists and IR scholars owe something to the world and that the world is invariably synonymous with the United States (Diamond 2002). If, at times, scholars acknowledge their misguided subservience to the state in an address to their peers—the community of scholars—their confessions are likely to incur significant social costs (Steele 2010). The situation is apparently not much different in other parts of the world (Tickner and Blaney 2012), underscoring Weber's (2014b, p. 3) point that disciplinary IR maintains its pledge to Martin Wight's idea that "for international theorizing to succeed, it must accumulate knowledge about interstate relations". There is, therefore, an unquestioned bond of IR to the state and to the presumed community of scholars (whose inner boundaries of belonging are rarely examined) that individual gestures of *parrhesia* cannot easily dislodge.

Thus, the depoliticization that we have in mind is substantive and intrinsic to the discipline. It comes closer to Jenny Edkins's (1999) claim that political has been reduced to calculable, and echoes Barder and Levine's (2012) assessment that the move away from the political has been aided *via media* constructivism and its nominal nods to reflexivity. Challenges to the (positivist/rationalist) epistemology and (materialist) ontology of the neo-neo IR synthesis have not necessarily led to a more (or differently) politically engaged discipline. Rather, as mentioned above, the critical edge of IR has been dulled (Weber 2014a, 2014b). The political has been reduced to the problem of global administration and management for the betterment of mankind (witness, for instance, the hard work of some IR scholars on R2P), where the notion of betterment has been left "singularly unproblematized, resting in part on Western liberal notions of the 'good life'" (Barder and Levine 2012).

Thesis #4: The perils of self-love

And then—and this would be the second symptom of a reflexive malaise—there is this endless pre-occupation with the self of the discipline, which seems to have been additionally nourished rather than questioned by the reflexive turn in IR. It has fostered a renewed sense of self-love and belief in self-importance, as evident in the most recent cycles of debates about the end of IR theory or its "isms." Yet—as, Marysia Zalewski (1996) warned many moons ago—"the bodies just keep piling up". Perhaps it is the underlying anxiety about a discipline that has never quite managed to find its distinctiveness vis-à-vis political science; or, perhaps it is the perpetual fear of being run over by events—another Iraq, another Congo, another Ukraine—always a step behind the course of history, which the discipline attempts to shape. Either way, IR is often so self-referential that one has to wonder if it has not become its own favorite object of study. Even in this respect, it is much like Hollywood, which has always, in moments of its decline, loved to make and celebrate movies about itself.

There is, therefore, a narcissism here at work quite different from the one that the authors working on autobiographical IR have felt compelled to address (Dauphinee 2010, and Chapter 2 in this volume; Inayatullah 2011). This is the narcissism embedded in the real or imagined entitlements of the discipline (the presumption of its necessity/mission) and reconstituted through the quest for meta-theoretical reflexivity itself. If anything, we would contend, autobiographical IR is one avenue where the pursuit of reflexivity has actually been productive—opening wounds of scholarship, creating space for narratives about complicity in the micro- and macro-aggressions of knowledge production, lifting hopes that "living in international relations" can redraw the violent lines of difference. It is precisely upon this opening towards the micro-political, created by an autobiographical IR, that we build these theses as well.

Thesis #5: Bringing the micro-politics back in

Yes, one of the explanations for the unintended consequences of reflexivity—envisioned, lest we forget, as a deeply critical, political intervention into

IR—is that engagements with the micro-politics of the discipline are still so rare. How often do we openly confront academic privileges, career expectations, institutional constraints and incentives that dominate educational structures and make IR possible? How often do we relate our daily worries, complaints, conflicts at work to the theoretical or political positions we take vis-à-vis analysis of world affairs? Not often enough. For, despite—or, perhaps, along with—the reflexive turn, we have continued to assume that we all have paychecks, that merit guides academic careers and publishing, that we can all freely travel to conferences and exchange ideas in public fora, that universities foster critical and creative thinking. In other words, we have left unexamined the space of the discipline imagined as an open space and a leveled field, a more real than real "marketplace of ideas".

At the moment of a *great transformation* in higher education, it no longer seems possible to ignore the links between the micro- and macro-politics of disciplinary IR. With the shrinking number of tenure-track positions in the American academy, the costs of dissent are bound to rise. Conformism, always a tendency in American IR scholarship (Hoffmann 1977), is now a recommended strategy of survival in the difficult job market. Anonymous contributions to various different job rumor mills reveal the level of vitriol towards difference (sexual, political, racial) that parallels America's right-wing radio. But the most pernicious are, perhaps, the most normalized comments—those that we have heard so many times from our own colleagues and graduate students. As one of the respondents to an (anonymous) discussion about queer IR theory said: "You can study it, but you will never get a job with it" (Mackenzie 2014). This is a market-driven form of the preemptive censorship of knowledge that keeps eating the Academy from within—and aligning it with the irrelevance that the political world wants to ascribe.

Yes, it is time to bring the micro-political back in.

Thesis #6: Disney as a spatial metaphor for American academe

Perhaps now the comparison with Disney may seem more apt. As we have already alluded in Thesis #1, Disney can serve as a useful spatial metaphor for the current situation in the American academe. Disney's signature theme parks produce and reproduce fantasies through spatial and temporal zoning: time and memory are erased in Disney's parks while an "architecture of reassurance" (Marling 1998) replaces the dangerous and chaotic world off its property. The practice of temporal and spatial zoning is seemingly intent on separating fantasy from the real world. In fact, Disney operates precisely at the boundary between these two worlds, maintaining the right to be the ultimate arbiter of their delicate borders. By doing so, it affirms the relevance of its own symbolic—but also political and economic—order (Hozic 2002).

Universities too are redesigned as safe spaces for those who can afford them. They distinguish themselves from communities which house them—and compete among themselves—by investing heavily in their beautiful land-scaping, student activity buildings, high-tech facilities, and, most importantly, recreational centers and athletic fields. *Allegedly* offering protection from real-life problems (sexism, racism, poverty, violence), while ignoring suicides and rapes on their campuses, colleges and universities market themselves as prep-steps to the 1%. They have data to support it. As a recent Pew (2014) report claims, even in this time of recurring economic crises, college graduates in the US are outperforming their peers with less education "on virtually every measure of economic attainment—from personal earnings to job satisfaction to the share employed full time." Indeed, the gap between Millennial gradu-ates and those with less education is now at its historic high. Never mind the fact that the path to Millennials' satisfaction is paved by ballooning student debt and disposable faculty: the architecture obviously works for those who are willing to pay.

And then there is the issue of knowledge production itself. The analogue to Disney's fantasies in higher education—and then especially in the social sci-ences and humanities—is the trust that students in the American academy (as opposed to most other countries in the world) acquire critical thinking skills. Yet, raising truly critical issues, the ones that could cause discomfort or offend student sensitivities, is becoming more and more difficult in American class-rooms. The art of teaching—particularly in large, public universities—revolves around discipline and marketable skills, the ones that will help our students get jobs, go to better schools, build careers, be good alumni. Thus, our classrooms are places where discipline is installed through an entertaining pursuit of knowledge ("edutainment"), where future productive members of the society are taught to obey deadlines, show up at work on time, package and market themselves properly, act as professionals, and fundraise/network/ lobby for their individual interests. Nonetheless, the fantasy of knowledge as a form of critical reflection tends to be carefully maintained by university administrators (course assessment tools always include "critical thinking") but also—and primarily—by faculty themselves. Believing that "we are making a difference" in the classroom makes a lonely, and increasingly difficult to attain, academic career bearable. It is also a way to distinguish university/ college level teaching from high school (where teachers are forced to "teach to the test", because their evaluations depend on their students' performance) and from the mushrooming world of Wikipedia knowledge outside of the academy. Guarding of these distinctions accounts, at least in part, for the increasingly stringent criteria in academic hiring and promotion. The other reason for the narrowing of academic gates rests, of course, in the shifting political economy of higher education (La Capra 1998; Dersiewicz 2011; Frank 2014), which manifests itself in obsessions with measurable outcomes, quantification of teaching and research performance, departmental and uni-versity rankings, and the most elusive of academic feeds—anxieties about prestige and self-importance.

Thesis #7: Bringing disruptive innovation home

It is not just Disneyland's landscaping that universities emulate, but Disney's corporate vision as well. With its modernist emphasis on safety and control, Disney's corporate universe turns technology (from rides to animation) into the key agent of history. Nature, on the other hand, including humans themselves, is often viewed as an obstacle on an otherwise clear path to a better future (Hozic 2002). Current enchantment with on-line education in American universities follows a similar line of thought. Technology is viewed as a panacea for all the troubles currently haunting higher education: rising costs, predicted to drive a number of colleges to bankruptcy; greater access, especially for workers seeking competency or retraining; even projections of American power abroad through education of eager learners in developing countries (*The Economist* 2014a, 2014b). The guiding principle behind the new wave of technological transformation—particularly "Massive Open On-Line Courses" (MOOCS)—is the idea of "disruptive innovation," coined by Harvard Business School Professor Clayton Christensen (Barlow 2014). Author of nine books, including the best-selling *Innovative University: Changing the DNA of Higher Education Inside and Out* (Jossey-Bass 2011), Christensen has devoted his life to the study of economic failures: industries which, through no fault of their own, collapse under pressure of new market arrivals—"cheaper, simpler, smaller, and more convenient to use" products. These "disruptive innovations", which often start "at a lower price and relatively poor level of performance" quickly attract new customers and new producers, shattering the dominance of existing industrial giants (Lambert 2014). Christensen views the relatively cheap on-line courses as such "disruptive innovators" and colleges and universities as the dying dinosaurs of higher learning.

However, behind Christensen and his celebrated low-cost start-ups stand some big and powerful interests: state legislators interested in slashing budgets for public education; Silicon Valley innovators, venture capitalists, and high-tech giants like Microsoft and Apple; textbook publishing behemoths such as Pearson, McGraw-Hill, and Houghton Mifflin Harcourt, as well as other do-gooders interested in lowering the cost of education; and brand-name politicians like Jeb Bush and his Foundation for Excellence in Education. Their reach is most felt in states that have the power to shape the textbook adoption market—California, Florida and Texas—and, because of the concentrated lobbying efforts, their influence goes far beyond K-12 education. Thus, in 2013, our own University of Florida was pushed by state legislators to trade its hard-fought pre-eminence status for a commitment to establish an Online Institute, a series of low-cost and strictly on-line baccalaureate programs (O'Neil 2014). As the icing on the cake, the legislature mandated that the Advisory Board for UF Online also include one member with "expertise in disruptive innovation, appointed by the Speaker of the House of Representatives" in Florida. The lawmakers then promised to contribute US$35 million over three years towards the cost of the new programs. The University, allegedly forced into a corner by pressing deadlines, contracted with Embanet, an Orlando-Florida based subsidiary of Pearson, to help with the creation of the new on-line majors and student recruitment (Newfeld 2014). If all goes well, and according to the business plan, the contract would allow Pearson-Embanet to earn as much as $186 million over ten years from the UF Online Institute (Schweers 2014). Not surprisingly, the contract has raised legitimate concerns that online education is first and foremost "a means for private firms to access public funding".

Christensen's vision of history, wrote Jill Lepore (2014) in a *New Yorker* article about disruptive innovation, "is atavistic. It's a theory of history founded on a profound anxiety about financial collapse, an apocalyptic fear of global devastation, and shaky evidence". Much like the disaster economy and its accompanying shock therapy cures, so well-described by Naomi Klein (2008), Christensen's worldview promotes complacency towards those same measures that will create further destruction. Applied to universities, "disruptive innovation" preys upon a population of students and parents, who are strapped by debt and uncertain about their—or America's—future in the world. To them, the theory holds out "a hope of salvation against the very damnation it describes: disrupt, and you will be saved" (Lepore 2014). And in the narrative about the rising costs and declining quality of education in the United States, it is usually the teachers who are portrayed as the villains blocking such change: to reform means to replace them, especially if they are unionized. The result thus far has not been open access education for all but the rise of the faculty precariat—adjuncts, lecturers, and overworked graduate students whose own prospects in the academic market appear quite grim.

Thesis #8: The yellow brick road of graduate education

At stake therefore in our exercise of reflexive scholarship is the alter-world of graduate education. Post-graduate instruction in the United States has long been tied to regimes of competitive funding, time-to-degree evaluations, and exercises in academic "professionalization". Yet the increasingly erratic budget crises affecting the American academy over the last decade have greatly exacerbated already stressful norms of scholarly worth and conduct, particularly for students outside of the "charmed circle" of the top-ranked programs (Cassuto 2013). Though there is a growing awareness surrounding the economic conditions of graduate students—overworked and underpaid— no discussion has begun on how many feel trapped by their own fantasies and expectations. Missing from the conversation is the extent to which the commitment to a "yellow brick road" of scholarly professionalization is both ideological and material.

As the Research I University model of "scholarly excellence" becomes the desired norm across American academia, many departments have sought to improve their rankings by producing highly specialized—and therefore "competitive"—PhD candidates. The expected norms of collegiality, however, vary from department to department as the lack of a brand or name recognition begets the establishment of appropriate metrics for productivity and scholarly "impact" that all members must meet. More worrisome than the evaluation of faculty by these standards, though, is that graduate students are now expected to do more with less. As funding packages and research subsidies shrink, the demands on technical proficiency (both quantitative and qualitative) grow larger. Each passing year in these new "results-oriented" programs is accompanied by directives to publish, engage in field-work, attend Summer schools centered on technical training, and write up grants for ever greater amounts of extracurricular funding. Not doing so entails the threat of "falling-behind" your timeline (i.e., the threat of running out of funding), but also "falling-behind" your cohort (i.e., the threat of social alienation). That only a few graduate programs in the country can provide their students with a living wage, as well as the opportunity to develop their "academic capital" in creative ways, does not dissuade lower-ranked programs from accepting higher numbers of candidates.

Many of the students in today's graduate programs represent an indispensable part of the university's workforce through teaching, mentoring, and even administrative assistance. Greater levels of personal and financial resilience are demanded from them every year, particularly as "successful" graduate students are expected to model the kind of lifestyle they wish to have, with only a fraction of the resources to pay for it. (Who amongst us hasn't been encouraged to attend the right receptions and discuss the virtues of a nice wine—but only with someone above his/her own rank?) Behind this process of socialization lie the demands to become an appropriate member of the American middle class, an experience that is highly alienating for anyone born outside of these privileges. Thus the precarious material conditions under which academia's scholarly norms are developing adds another layer of cognitive dissonance for young scholars. As graduate students are "encouraged" to develop "safe" research programs and attend only the most "useful" venues for their employability, they are also expected to attend conferences at high-end hotels, in cities with their own indifference to economic inequality, and socialize with the well-established (and well-protected) members of the discipline. Many often forget the reasons they wanted to join the professoriate to begin with.

The most flagrant sin of omission might be in the failure to address the employment conditions at the other end of a degree program—that there are few jobs waiting for anyone at the end of a PhD, not at least without a fair amount of uncertainty, mobility, and capacity for re-invention. This is a taboo topic in most departments, but its effects are not a secret. Far worse, conscious of the uncertain costs, many graduate students remain in academia as a result of the reassuring claims (often from mentors) that they'll "be fine"; no acknowledgment is ever made of the fantasy through which many are inspired to join the system and therefore keep the machine running. A majority of tenured professors send their mentees into a job market that is radically different from what they experienced. Mentors are often ignorant of, or oblivious to, the multiple obstacles and instances of disillusion surrounding today's graduate experience. They have difficulties envisioning any other future for their mentees than the one prescribed by and for R1 scholarship since their own reputations and promotions are deeply entangled with it. And so it is because of the silences that surround this changing landscape of graduate education—not least because of its shifting material and intellectual repercussions—that we consider it as a prime space where reflexivity should be exercised.

This is not to suggest that graduate students have no agency; many of them across North America actively challenge the working conditions of their peers through strikes, sit-ins, unionization drives, and denouncing the ever-growing exploitation of adjunct labor (Loriggio 2009; Patton 2013). Yet theirs is certainly not regarded as an example to emulate, let alone to discuss in polite conversation. As Brent Steele's own experience as a graduate student illustrates (Steele, Chapter 3 in this volume), as long as you are locked into a "value-free" definition of results-oriented and "relevant" scholarship, there is little room to localize and articulate the collective injuries faced in the cycles of graduate training. In a neopositivist world—one where scholars "delineate and differentiate the 'world out there' from the scholarship we produced in our ivory towers" (Steele, Chapter 3 in this volume)—a precarious economic standing more often inhibits what students say, rather than enabling them to have a political voice. It doesn't mean that graduate students shouldn't speak out (many of us do); as essential members of higher education's reproduction no one else can tell this story better. But we must acknowledge that precarity is a powerful silencer.

Thesis #9: Broken "circles of niceness"[1]

Despite the greater consciousness of mental health issues emerging within contemporary academia, there is an overwhelming tendency to lament the personal politics of "knowledge-production", with most of these laments failing to question the material positionality of scholarly work. Though earnest challenges to the structures against which IR scholars operate have emerged from the position of "reflective scholar", "critical theory", or through the elusive deployment of "frank-speech", even in this respect the academy continues to operate as a fantasy land (Smith 2004; Cox 2008; Steele 2010). No one wants to change the structure because we all want to be part of it. We begrudge the micro-aggressions and pettiness, but we do not question the enterprise because the role of a gate-keeper, up-and-coming scholar, or faculty superstar is still much too desired.

Many of the emerging confessions of physical and mental strain on graduate students, adjuncts, and itinerant faculty require that scholars begin advocating for the inversion of the adverse material conditions under which academic production recurs. Otherwise, we all risk succumbing to further individualization of suffering which currently shapes our craft. Potential for change will be determined by the degree to which graduate education is taken as an opportunity to resist the constraints of fantasy production, or, as just another instance of "professionalization" where the body and mind are disciplined to look and feel the right way. What is missing, therefore, is addressing the perversion of contemporary graduate education: as an ostensibly crucial part of creating new scholars, graduate education in the US is helping to support the business of the university through cheap labor. Yet how should the ethical question of graduate education be revived if the university's mission is increasingly fulfilled through the scantest of resources? By conceding that the separation of scholars from their material conditions only buttresses the divorce between academia's fantasies and its realities.

In our times, it is no secret that the "business of education" entails a new model in which universities seek to compete with corporations for the best administrative and scholarly talent. Yet the exposés, confessions, and revelations that surround the shifting interests behind the education-industrial complex are downright shocking. There is a mountain of dangerous liaisons between consulting firms, venture capitalist groups, and corporate education agencies far too massive for us to address here, but which nevertheless triggers the issues we are concerned with. One answer to this flood of dilemmas has been unionization. Still, even this imperfect solution proves costly for many, as union involvement—certainly at the junior faculty level, but especially at the graduate student level—is treated ambiguously at best and aggressively at worst, by administrators and faculty alike. The very idea of union organization and campus involvement runs against the ideological push towards productivity, impact, and scholarly "creativity" or even "genius", highlighting the issue we began with: we don't know how bad some have it since no one talks to each other.

Thesis #10: Towards a political economy of reflexivity

Though profoundly imbricated, the changing roles of "graduate student" and "faculty" have so far failed to elicit a serious conversation over the future of academic production. In writing this chapter, our own lack of institutional hierarchy—that there is no *dissertation chair–doctoral candidate* dynamic ruling over us—has helped us recognize the power imbalances behind many of the relationships in graduate education. Our power relation—should there be one—is modified away from something that we may owe each other (a dissertation progress outline, or, a letter of recommendation) towards the common goal of speaking out against the silence over our complicity in the business of higher ed., To employ a reflexive attitude towards the presumed authority of the mentor–mentee relation demands taking the political economy of academic production more seriously (Schmidt 2001). A fruitful dynamic need not be based on mimesis, exploitation, or fulfilling a placement agenda alien to a student's experiences. A collegial mentoring becomes far less pernicious when "marketability" is not the prime objective. A community of scholars can in fact thrive when we don't shy away from exploring opportunities for mutual learning that challenge an instrumental notion of higher education.

The academic hierarchies that stifle a more reflexive graduate education are not as prevalent in the humanities and social sciences as they are in disciplines where a student's funding is often tied to grants, labs, or a faculty member's prestige. Yet the shifting economic bases of contemporary academic authority are nevertheless becoming obstacles for young scholars. Indeed, one always wants the blessing of their academic godparent; it is still dissertation chairs (presumably) that bear the final responsibility of guiding a doctoral candidate through the socialization and market process. Why then, as participants, should we ignore the ways in which these charges are strained in an exploitative economic environment? Only rarely have the lines of academic reproduction been dispelled or made evident. And where they have, concrete challenges to the process are never regarded as legitimate alternatives.

In our own case, had we been bound by such hierarchy, this chapter might have looked quite different. The lack of a formalized relationship offers us an opportunity to upset the symbolic and material conditions under which graduate education develops. There is no protocol for interaction, no mantra of employability, and to put it bluntly, no material or symbolic power for either of us to lose. Perhaps we presume too much about our powers to resist the nature and development of intellectual power. Perhaps we give too much credit to the capacity to divorce ourselves from those aspects of the academy we despise, and embrace those we see as enriching. But if critical thought— indeed, the kind we've learned from a material exposure to Critical IR and its sources of inspiration—has taught us anything, it is that academia and university life are not exempt from the material conditions and politics of a globalized capitalist world.

Perhaps we need not go so far. There is a sense that maybe we have been too optimistic as to what academia holds for its members. Victims of our own fantasies, we may just be exiles from a post-war boom that only briefly existed. It may be true that academia has never been an egalitarian space, inside or outside of the Ivory Tower. Nevertheless, in the midst of greater calls for scholarly "relevance", as support for public universities becomes more precarious, we concur with critics that there is an internal problem within higher education that in fact does begin with its most well-endowed and protected members. That problem, however, is not an unwillingness to see social and political problems for what they are. Perhaps, more scandalously, it is an unwillingness to accept that we may not be so special and different from the rest of society. That our world too suffers from the same collusions that plague modern life.

Thesis #11: A solution more puzzling than the riddle?

In this spirit, we feel a constrained, or dare we say gentrified, sense of reflexivity may do more harm than good. This is particularly true as the emphasis on reflexivity as theory—or meta-theory, rather than praxis—draws attention away from ongoing and evolving sites of injury where our labor and existence takes place. A return to one of Adam Smith's classic adages seems in order now more than ever: "Sympathy ... does not arise so much from the view of the passion, as from that of the situation which excites it" (Smith 1982, p. 12). If reflexivity as a practice is to exhibit the potential its proponents once professed, scholars need to begin with the locality and conditions of those around them that make their scholarship, in large part, possible. This is the great scandal of the Research University in America today—we continue to create more and more doctoral programs, without a responsible sense of how to sustain them.

A reflexivity—indeed, a *sustainable critique* (Levine 2012)—that is far more sensitive to the material context in which these affronts, doubts, and fantasies operate would go a long way in opening the field of debate towards action, not just criticism. A precedent is already being set by the rise of an "alt-academy" movement. Veterans, rejects, and all-around misfits of the academic establishment have begun to promote alternative routes for PhDs who find themselves over-worked and/or under-employed. Some advocate greater politicization against the market forces that universities have aligned themselves with (Lewin 2013). Others sell their services as mentors and advisors for new market conditions, soliciting doctoral students who may otherwise have no other recourse.[2] While responses vary across the board, the point, it seems to us, is that the tenured center of the academic establishment can no longer pretend they have no role to play in the ongoing market failure that is shaping higher education. Moreover, they have no more room to evade their own responsibility in failing to speak out against unfair labor practices surrounding graduate, adjunct, and even assistant professor socialization. Although in limited and self-interested ways, "alt-academic" movements have put theory to practice in an effort to no longer remain indifferent. Tenured faculty should now do the same.

Not only has the number of students who find tenure-track positions decreased, but the number of disillusioned and disenfranchised professionals has by extension also risen. Is the lack of a discussion of alternatives to academic jobs—and moreover, the non-existence of alternatives—a result of an incentive structure that keeps academics from contributing to finding and creating these alternatives? As star power is measured at the level of self-perpetuation and reproduction, the educational system perpetuates entrapment. This feeds back into the implicit and dangerous narcissism that we had already mentioned: you endure the heartache because you are special, you have a mission, and you will be even more special when you come out. This is, indeed, a suspect narrative. Just as the inimitable Walt Disney is quoted as saying in the 2013 production of *Saving Mr. Banks*: "That's what we do, we storytellers. We restore order with imagination. We instill hope, again and again and again." The language we use creates our reality and IR scholars know how this works on a global scale just as well as Hollywood producers. It is high time to turn that narrative in on itself. Let us use that language to make a different order. Let us stop performing the critique and seek change instead.

Notes

1 With the title of this thesis we wish to salute the author of the academic blog The Thesis Whisperer (http://thesiswhisperer.com/2013/02/13/academic-assholes/) and Annick Wibben who organized a very successful and moving panel entitled "Creating Circles of Niceness in the Academy" at ISA 2014.
2 See Karen Kelsky's now trending blog, "The Professor Is In": http://theprofessor isin.com/.

References

Ackerly, B. and True, J., 2008. Reflexivity in Practice: Power and Ethics in Feminist Research on International Relations. *International Studies Review*, 10(4), 693–707.
Barder, A.D. and Levine, D.J., 2012. "The World is Too Much With Us": Reification and the Depoliticising of Via Media Constructivist IR. *Millennium*, 40(3), 585–604.
Barlow, A., 2014. Disruptive Innovation in Education. *Academe Blog*, June 17. Available from: http://academeblog.org/2014/06/17/8156/ [Accessed July 30, 2014].
Campbell, P. and Desch, M.C., 2013. Rank Irrelevance: How Academia Lost Its Way. *Foreign Affairs*, September 15. Available from: www.foreignaffairs.com/articles/139925/peter-campbell-and-michael-c-desch/rank-irrelevance [Accessed July 30, 2014].
Cassuto, L., 2013. What Are Low-Ranked Graduate Programs Good For? *Chronicle of Higher Education*, January 28. Available from: http://chronicle.com/article/What-Are-Low-Ranked-Graduate/136823/ [Accessed July 30, 2014].
Cox, R.W., 2008. The Point Is Not Just to Explain the World But to Change It. In: C. Reus-Smit and D. Snidal, eds, *Oxford Handbook of International Relations*. New York: Oxford University Press, pp. 84–93.
Dauphinee, E., 2010. The Ethics of Autoethnography. *Review of International Studies*, 36(3), 799–818.
Dersiewicz, W., 2011. Faulty Towers: The Crisis in Higher Education. *The Nation*. May 4. Available from: www.thenation.com/article/160410/faulty-towers-crisis-higher-education# [Accessed July 30, 2014].
Diamond, L., 2002. What Political Science Owes the World. *PS: Political Science & Politics*. Available from: apsanet3b.inetu.net/imgtest/PSOnlineDiamond911.pdf [Accessed July 30, 2014].
Economist (The), 2014a. Creative Destruction. *The Economist*, June 28. Available from: www.economist.com/news/leaders/21605906-cost-crisis-changing-labour-markets-and-new-technology-will-turn-old-institution-its [Accessed July 30, 2014].
Economist (The), 2014b. The Digital Degree. *The Economist*, June 28. Available from: www.economist.com/news/briefing/21605899-staid-higher-education-business-about-experience-welcome-earthquake-digital?frsc=dg%7Cc [Accessed July 30, 2014].

Edkins, J., 1999. *Poststructuralism and International Relations: Bringing the Political Back In*. Boulder, CO: Lynne Rienner Publishers.

FP Staff, 2014. Does the Academe Matter?: Do Policymakers Listen? Should You Get a Ph.D.? And Where Are All the Women? *Foreign Policy*, March 14. Available from: www.foreignpolicy.com/articles/2014/03/14/does_the_academy_matter_do_policymakers _listen_should_you_get_a_phd_and_where_ar [Accessed July 30, 2014].

Frank, T., 2014. Colleges are Full of It: Behind the Three Decade Scheme to Raise Tuition, Bankrupt Generations, and Hypnotize the Media. *Salon*, June 8. Available from: www.salon.com/2014/06/08/colleges_are_full_of_it_behind_the_three_decade_ scheme_to_raise_tuition_bankrupt_generations_and_hypnotize_the_media/ [Accessed July 30, 2014].

Giddens, A., 1979. *Central Problems in Social Theory*. London: Macmillan.

Gilpin Faust, D., 2009. The University's Crisis of Purpose. *The New York Times*, September 1. Available from: www.nytimes.com/2009/09/06/books/review/Faust-t. html?pagewanted=all [Accessed July 30, 2014].

Guzzini, S., 2013. The Ends of International Relations Theory: Stages of Reflexivity and Modes of Theorizing. *European Journal of International Relations*, 19(3), 521–541.

Hamati-Ataya, I., 2011. The "Problem of Values" and International Relations Scholarship: From Applied Reflexivity to Reflexivism. *International Studies Review* 13(2), 259–287.

Hoffmann, S., 1977. An American Social Science: International Relations. *Daedalus*, 106(3), 41–60.

Hozic, A., 2002. Zoning or How to Govern (Cultural) Violence. *Cultural Values*, 6(1), 183–195.

Inayatullah, N., 2011. *Autobiographical International Relations: I, IR*. Abingdon: Routledge.

Ish-Shalom, P., 2011. Theoreticians' Obligation of Transparency: When Parsimony, Reflexivity, Transparency and Reciprocity Meet. *Review of International Studies*, 37(3), 973–996.

Klein, N., 2008. *The Shock Doctrine: The Rise of Disaster Capitalism*. London: Picador.

Kristoff, N., 2014. Professors, We Need You! *The New York Times*, February 15. Available from: www.nytimes.com/2014/02/16/opinion/sunday/kristof-professors-we-need-you.html?_r=0 [Accessed July 30, 2014].

La Capra, D., 1998. The University in Ruins? *Critical Inquiry* 25(1), 32–55.

Lambert, C., 2014. Disruptive Genius. *Harvard Magazine*, July–August. Available from: http://harvardmagazine.com/2014/07/disruptive-genius [Accessed July 30, 2014].

Lapid, Y., 1989. The Third Debate: On the Prospects of International Theory in a Post-Positivist Era. *International Studies Quarterly*, 33(3), 235–254.

Lapid, Y., 2014. 25 Years After the Third Debate: Two (Pianissimo) Bravos for IR Theory. *International Studies Quarterly Blog*. Posted on March 20. Available from: www.isanet.org/Publications/ISQ/Posts/ID/304/25-Years-after-The-Third-Debate-Two-pi anissimo-bravos-for-IR-Theory [Accessed July 30, 2014].

Lepore, J., 2014. The Disruption Machine. *The New Yorker*, June 23. Available from: www.newyorker.com/magazine/2014/06/23/the-disruption-machine [Accessed July 30, 2014].

Levine, D.J., 2012. *Recovering International Relations: The Promise of Sustainable Critique*. New York: Oxford University Press.

Lewin, T., 2013. More College Adjuncts See Strength in Union Numbers. *The New York Times*, December 3. Available from: www.nytimes.com/2013/12/04/us/more-colle ge-adjuncts-see-strength-in-union-numbers.html?pagewanted=all&_r=0   [Accessed July 30, 2014].

Long, D. and Schmidt, B., eds, 2005. *Imperialism and Internationalism in the Discipline of International Relations*. Albany, NY: SUNY Press.

Loriggio, P., 2009. 5,000 York U. Students Return, Feeling Torn. *The Star*, January 27. Available   from: www.thestar.com/news/gta/2009/01/27/5000_york_u_students_ return_feeling_torn.html [Accessed July 30, 2014].

Mackenzie, M., 2014. You Make My Work (im)Possible: Reflections on Professional Conduct in the Discipline of International Relations. *The Duck of Minerva* Blog. Posted on April 9. Available from: www.whiteoliphaunt.com/duckofminerva/2014/ 04/you-make-my-work-impossible-reflections-on-professional-conduct-in-the-discip line-of-international-relations.html [Accessed July 30, 2014].

Marling, K.A., 1998. *Designing Disney's Theme Parks: The Architecture of Reassurance*. London: Flammarion.

Neufeld, M., 1993. Reflexivity and International Relations Theory. *Millennium— Journal of International Studies*, 22(1), 53–76.

Neufeld, M., 1995. *The Restructuring of International Relations Theory*. Cambridge: Cambridge University Press.

Newfeld, C., 2014. University Week: Virgin Air, UF Online, The Price of Privatization (Updated). *Remaking The University Blog*. Posted on Sunday, March 30. Available from: http://utotherescue.blogspot.com/2014/03/university-week-virgin-air-uf-on line.html [Accessed July 30, 2014].

O'Neil, M., 2014. Pushed by Lawmakers, U. of Florida Dives into Online Education. *Chronicle of Higher Education*, May 23. Available from: http://chronicle.com/article/ Pushed-by-Lawmakers-U-of/146767/?keepThis=true&TB_iframe=true&height=650& width=850&caption=The+Chronicle+of+Higher+Education+%7C+News   [Accessed July 30, 2014].

Oren, I., 2002. *Our Enemies and US: America's Rivalries and the Making of Political Science*. Ithaca, NY: Cornell University Press.

Oren, I., 2006. Political Science as History: A Reflexive Approach. In: D. Yanow and P. Schwartz-Shea, eds, *Interpretation and Method: Empirical Research Methods and the Interpretive Turn*. Armonk, NY: M.E. Sharpe, Inc.

Oren, I., 2014. A Sociological Analysis of the Decline of American IR Theory. Paper presented at ISA Annual Convention in Toronto, March 26–29.

Patton, S., 2013. Pay Delay Puts a Pinch on Scores of Graduate Assistants at U. of Florida. *Chronicle of Higher Education*, September 11. Available from: http:// chronicle.com/article/Pay-Delay-Puts-a-Pinch-on/141547/ [Accessed July 30, 2014].

Pew Research Center. 2014. The Rising Cost of Not Going to College. February 11, 2014. Available from: www.pewsocialtrends.org/2014/02/11/the-rising-cost-of-not-going-to-college [Accessed July 30, 2014].

Robin, C., 2014. Look Who Nick Kristof's Saving Now. *Corey Robin Blog*, February 16. Available from: http://coreyrobin.com/2014/02/16/look-who-nick-kristofs-saving-now/ [Accessed July 30, 2014].

Schmidt, J., 2001. *Disciplined Minds: A Critical Look at Salaried Professionals and the Soul-Battering System that Shapes Their Lives*. Lanham, MD: Rowman & Littlefield Publishers, Inc.

Schulman, S., 2012. *The Gentrification of the Mind.* Berkeley, CA: University of California Press.

Schweers, J., 2014. Firm Will Get About $186 Million to Manage UF Online. *The Gainesville Sun*, March 27. Available from: www.gainesville.com/article/20140327/a rticles/140329618?p=3&tc=pg&tc=ar [Accessed July 30, 2014].

Smith, A., 1982. *The Theory of Moral Sentiments.* Indianapolis, IN: Liberty Classics.

Smith, S., 2004. Singing Our World into Existence: International Relations Theory and September 11. *International Studies Quarterly* 48(3), 499–515.

Steele, B.J., 2010. Of "Witch's Brews" and Scholarly Communities: The Dangers and Promise of Academic Parrhesia. *Cambridge Review of International Affairs*, 23(1), 49–68.

Tickner, A. and Blaney, D.L., 2012. *Thinking International Relations Differently (Worlding Beyond the West).* London: Routledge.

Walt, S., 2013. Breaking Ranks in Academia. *Foreign Policy*, September 18. Available at www.foreignpolicy.com/posts/2013/09/18/grading_academia [Accessed July 30, 2014].

Weber, C., 2014a. The Gentrification of International Theory. *International Studies Quarterly Blog.* Posted on March 25. Available from: www.isanet.org/Publications/ ISQ/Posts/ID/313/The-Gentrification-of-International-Theory [Accessed July 30, 2014].

Weber, C., 2014b. Why is There No Queer International Theory? *European Journal of International Relations.* Published on-line April 3.

Wibben, A.T.R., 2014. Look Who's Talking. *International Studies Quarterly Blog.* Posted on March 27. Available from: www.isanet.org/Publications/ISQ/Posts/ID/ 316/Look-Whos-Talking [Accessed July 30, 2014].

Zalewski, M., 1996. "All These Theories yet Bodies Keep Piling Up": Theories, Theorists, Theorising. In: S. Smith, K. Booth and M. Zalewski, eds, *International Theory: Positivism and Beyond.* Cambridge: Cambridge University Press, pp. 340–353.

8 Exile as reflexive engagement

IR as everyday practice

Amanda Beattie

In April 2013 I was ordered deported from the United Kingdom (UK). As a Canadian citizen living in the UK I was stripped of my mobility rights, denied government representation, and struggled to find an effective mode of agency to navigate this experience. As a scholar of International Relations (IR) this proved a double blow as the experiences I was subject to did not align with the assumptions, theories and practices I examined on a daily basis.[1] In order to make sense of it all, a task which I must admit is by no means complete; I turned to the ideas of trauma, suffering and exile.

This chapter is an exploration of this process. I employ these themes and draw on autobiographical memories in order to make four inter-related claims; first, reflexive practices of IR attend to the harm that emerges from within applied assumptions of certainty and predictability as evidenced in discussions of order, security and institutional design.[2] I interrogate the intersection of mobility rights and state security to defend this assertion. Second I contend that a personal, emotional engagement with security delivery can soften the intermingling of disorder and uncertainty within the international. I draw on the newly applied approaches of autobiography and autoethnography in IR to do so (see for example Brigg and Bleiker 2008, 2010; Dauphinee 2010). Third I contend that the practices and outcomes of both IR and ir are not ethereal concepts that stand one degree removed from the everyday lives of ordinary people. Rather, I show that IR and ir have an impact, positive and negative alike, on the quotidian. Finally I propose that the quest for certainty, for scripted narratives of IR, can situate portions of the global population outside the status quo. In order to make sense of this phenomenon I turn to the philosophical engagements with exile. Exile, as an idea and experience, fosters reflection and creation prompting alternative renderings of the international.

Exile is incisive as it is interdisciplinary in nature and provides a contrapuntal narrative to mainstream discourses of IR. By mainstream, I am gesturing towards, but not unpacking what Roland Bleiker (2001) has labelled the mimetic practices of IR. Such practices reify a particular subset of being human drawing on technical reason in the ever elusive quest for certainty and stability. The exiled individual stands outside such renderings. I argue that the exile exists simply because they do not fit within the status quo of the international. Drawing on Judith Shklar's article, "Obligation, Loyalty, Exile" (1993, p. 187) I understand an exile as "someone who voluntarily leaves the country of which he or she is a citizen". Exile, she goes on to say can be an internal or external experience that may, or may not be, attached to a territorial space and has much to say about individual conscience, obligation and loyalty. There is, on this interpretation, a significant and important linkage to the ideas of exile promoted by Edward Said.

Like Shklar, Said (2000) notes that exile reflects displacement, yet he reveals in his essay "Reflections on Exile" that it is a highly scripted, human creation that denies one's dignity and demands a thoroughgoing interrogation of one's subjectivity. In fact, such an interrogation asks of the individual, as an agent, to think creatively both within and throughout the institutional structures that define the exile in order to "cross borders, break barriers of thought and experience". His account of the exile is both personal, as described by Levine (Chapter 5 in this volume), as well as a thoroughgoing engagement with reflexive practice. He demands that the exile cultivate a "scrupulous (not indulgent or sulky) subjectivity" in order to attend to the very indignity exile fosters.

In this chapter I want to probe the possibilities of reflexive practice of the exile. The exilic subject is informed by both a notion of "the tragic" but also "the traumatic" and I use both of these dialogues to interrogate my own disillusion with the discipline and its practices. By this I mean to say that while a tragic understanding of human motivations, decisions and actions may offer solace in one's experience, it is only when we turn to the narrative of trauma and an ensuing account of therapy that we begin to truly work through the impacts and influences of such harmful events. In developing an understanding of exile this chapter attends to the experience of harm.

Trauma, I must acknowledge, does not express itself at the point of experience, nor is the expression of traumatic experience easily aligned with everyday experiences of IR. In fact, in her description of trauma time Jenny Edkins (2003) argues forcefully that trauma is non-linear. It challenges both our understanding of and the unfolding of history. To wit, as Kate Schick (2011) has shown, it also wreaks havoc with liberal emancipatory attempts at redressing and in turn addressing harm and suffering. While I do not propose to navigate this particular problematic what I do attempt, albeit within the limitations of a single chapter, is to reflect upon the creative possibilities of the exiled traumatized subject.

As the chapter unfolds it will become clear that exile stands as a counterpoint to certainty and predictability. It reflects an attempt to circumnavigate the problems that irregularity, uncertainty and misidentification pose to the status quo of institutional design in IR. It makes this claim by assessing two inter-related ideas; namely, that the experience of exile is akin to "hitting rock bottom". Living with the label of amoral beings, without a community to establish both identity and personality, the exiled subject lacks a voice. I imagine the possibilities of reclaiming a voice, drawing on the methods of autobiography and story-telling, arguing that reflexive practice can embrace such practices. In this way the chapter heeds the call of Amoureux and Steele, who argue in the Introduction to this volume that reflexivity highlights "what is at stake" for not just scholars, but those who live with the outcomes of international relations in their daily lives. In so doing I hope to demonstrate, and attend to the importance of, reflexive practice. In other words I am heeding their call to offer "innovative and compelling applications of reflexivity to both the scholarship and practice of world politics".

An account of exile, interwoven with the underlying ideas of reflexivity, does not offer a scripted future for international politics. It does not proscribe standard operating procedures, nor does it begin its travails with a particular set-out end. There is no blueprint. It reveals a deep-seated vulnerability that is eschewed among the dominant narratives of IR and in so doing paves the way for a more personal, emotional engagement with the discipline.

One

I was sitting in my kitchen, a galley kitchen, trying to build a toddler bicycle. It was a decadent type of morning. My eight month old (I was on maternity leave) was having a rather long morning nap. I decided not to shower, to stay in my pjs, and put together a bicycle for my two year old, at nursery for the day. As I struggled to insert the wire connecting the tire to the front hand brake, I really did wonder if there was any language more difficult to discern, than the instruction manuals that come with children's toys. At that moment in time, I was certain; nothing could possibly be more challenging.

I was wrong.

The doorbell rang. I flew to open the door, worried I would miss the post. February 3rd, ten weeks ago, I had sent my passport and supporting documents to renew my work permit in the UK. I have lived in the UK for some twelve years now. I first arrived in St Andrews, Scotland to study terrorism and political violence in 2002 only to stay on for five more years as I traversed the ups and downs of a PhD in international political thought (IPT). During this time I met my now husband who with me, moved to Birmingham in 2008 as I began a career as a lecturer in Politics and International Relations. I lecture on the History of Political Thought, Ethics and International Politics and Contemporary Political Theory. During this time I have had a Student Visa, A Fresh Talent Scotland Visa, a Highly Skilled Worker Visa, and now, after a year-long struggle with the United Kingdom Border Agency (UKBA), I am a permanent resident of the UK. But before this, I was told to leave the country.

I was being deported.

On April 18th I was expecting the return of my passport and a work permit which would allow me to keep my job, remain with my family and return to life as normal. By normal, I mean, travel outside of the UK, as the UKBA had my passport and had limited my mobility rights. I was free to travel within the UK but was not to pass its borders. However, when I opened the door, signed for a recorded delivery and hastily opened the letter as soon as I bid the postman goodbye I learned life as normal would not be resuming. Reading the letter as I walked down the hallway to the unfinished toddler bicycle I read, with absolute shock, that my work permit was denied and that I had seven days to appeal the decision or 28 days to leave the country.

I was numb.

The confusion I was wrestling with as I read through the bicycle manual was quickly replaced by the indecipherable language employed by the UKBA as they simultaneously told me I could not, but also could, appeal their decision to deport me. The first paragraph informed me of my imminent deportation and right of appeal. The second paragraph confirmed the application for a work permit had failed and there was no recourse to appeal. A third paragraph indicated I could appeal owing to the European Declaration of Human Rights. Needless to say, in the absence of specialist law/immigration knowledge, I did not know what to do. What ensued was seven days of hastily locating a solicitor and many sleeplessness nights as I wondered if I would be separated from my family, friends, community; the life I was building in Birmingham.

We did challenge the decision. In a rather bizarre turn of events, interpreted to us by our solicitor, I was protected by the European Code of Human Rights. The work permit, it transpires, was denied owing to clerical errors within Human Resources. On that front, we could not challenge the ruling. Aston University had to live up to certain sponsoring obligations and they had not done so. On the other hand, as a resident of England I was entitled to a family and a private life. Therefore, those confusing three paragraphs that outlined both a right to and not to appeal were simply telling me I could appeal on alternate grounds. Owing to the fact that I was a mother, and my youngest child was so dependent on me, I had the right to appeal. It was on this ground that we built our case.

The entire process lasted just under one year. During this time our entire life was interrogated not only by the civil service but also by various legal institutions. My husband and I had to prove that our marriage was genuine. Rather bizarrely, having two children, of British Nationality, was not sufficient proof. It was at that time that seemingly innocuous decisions of our past turned out to be rather significant and proved problematic. For example, we met in 2004 and moved in together in 2005. But we both lived and worked in a university hall of residence. The address to this building, because it was university accommodation, was not recognized by Royal Mail, a legitimate government institution. Therefore it was hard to show how our relationship had started, generating doubt if we were in fact genuine. More doubt was generated simply because we had decided some years prior to this deportation ordeal to get married in Canada and not England. The decision was economical. It would have cost us over 500 British Pounds to gain the required documentation to prove at that time, our relationship was legitimate. Instead, we could pay a small fee of 30 Canadian Dollars to have a marriage certificate issued the week of our wedding. But this led to further queries on the part of the UKBA. In essence, what seemed, at the time like simple decisions had a significant impact on the ability to challenge the deportation. It could be interpreted that this economical decision was in fact an indication that we did not have a history, a marriage if you will, we simply had a wedding.

It was easy to speak through the technical details of our marriage. It was with deep anger and resentment that we had to do it; however, the legal jargon and historical fact remained a language that I could use during this ordeal. It was not personal nor was it emotional. It was simply, "the facts". I still could not, at that time express the emotions I felt that the entire experience was happening. The attendant harm could not be expressed with any of the tools I had developed both as a scholar or member of a family and community. I could not make sense of it all. There was, to be sure, a deep sense of mistrust and disbelief that this was happening to me. I had trusted trained individuals to ensure that the appropriate forms were filled out. Similarly, I had behaved as the appropriate democratic citizen ought to. Not only that, I taught students about being good democratic citizens. Part of the message I put forward in any classroom is that we all have an agentic capacity to do good, to improve the world around us. Yet this experience revealed to me that on some occasions, traditional modes of agency, moral or otherwise, simply will not suffice.

All the while one thing kept going through my mind: if my mobility rights could so easily be stripped in a democratic nation, is anyone truly secure and, to wit, is there really any truth to the notion of a global citizen?

In the end I was allowed to stay in the UK. I applied for a Visa in February 2013 and the outcome of my appeal was handed down on December 17, 2013. But what I have come to realize is this: there is no title that appropriately describes my condition during this experience. I was not stateless, although Canadian institutions would not come to my aid. Although I did pay taxes to the central UK government, they were keen on my eventual removal. I did have the help of our local MP, who suggested in the end that we hire a solicitor, which we did. My own voice in this process was rather abruptly silenced for fear of saying and/or doing the wrong thing. I could not leave the UK either because any venturing across, or beyond, UK borders, was understood as complicit acceptance of the removal order. I was, in essence, exiled within the borders of the UK.

I have arrived at the label of exile only after a long, drawn-out, interrogation of my experiences. I now understand that what unfolded over a series of months was not only one of exile; it was also akin to trauma. I believe that there exists a large segment of the global population that experience what I now label migration trauma. In short, such trauma ensues when one's mobility rights are curtailed. The limitation of mobility denies personal relationships that facilitate access to the goods necessary for personal development.

While social justice narratives explain that individuals are entitled to travel the world, the assumption, excavated in the third section of this chapter reveals an underlying assumption of human stasis that challenges this normative proscription (see for example Benhabib and Resnik 2009; Lenard and Straehle 2012; Carens 2013). Mobility rights, I argue, will be curtailed when the security of the domestic community is called into question. Individuals who traverse borders are thus vulnerable to this plight and, in the face of insecurity, are set outside the state. In effect a cordon sanitaire is erected in order to preserve the scripted narrative of state security. In essence those that challenge the status quo are exiled, set outside the everyday, in the quest for security.

By adopting a traumatic framework I can reflect upon this state of exile and understand that this experience simultaneously ruptured not only my personal life, but my professional life as well. Not only was I a citizen internally exiled within the United Kingdom, I lost my voice as a scholar/ lecturer as well. I have reflected on this experience both personally and professionally. I had, until recently, subscribed to the cosmopolitan worldview— or a variation of it. I wholeheartedly believed, as the cosmopolitan project argues, in a shared human vulnerability, a need for "the social" and the ability of individuals to act as moral agents working together for a moral and enlightened global world (see Beitz 1979; Waldron 1991; O'Neill 1996; Lu 2000; Erskine 2008).

This experience shattered that understanding—I will admit I lost faith in it and am, to this day, hard pressed to support, and give credence to, a moral global community of citizens. I am skeptical of this worldview in light of the dominance of territorial borders that define "safe spaces" (Walters 2006); I am troubled with accounts of order that seek universal stability (Buchanan and Keohane 2004; Williams 2007; Ikenberry 2009) and fail to acknowledge the inherent, and I believe natural, mobility and nomadism of the human people. I also harbor deep misgivings about the role and authority of government in delivering security to its citizens in traditional ways that build on these two assumptions. I believe that government and institutional design do not attend to the troubles and misgivings I hold and, to wit, foreclose discussion that can engage with these challenges.

Two

It is, I believe, in the writings of Martha Nussbaum (2001), and in particular *The Fragility of Goodness*, that the idea of a cosmopolitan ethos comes about. She draws on Aristotle, and *inter alia*, Plato to attend to the idea of being human. She locates a central role for practical reason, and this particular skill modifies human agency and personality. Two central ideas flow from all of this—we can as moral beings embark on a particular course of action with the hopes of making the world a better place. It is a call to attend to the particularities of human cruelty in the face of a savage and brutal world. This brutality is all the more marked when we understand the role that moral luck plays in the mediating accounts and encounters with human happiness. Happiness, for Nussbaum, is a genuine human good that can be identified within the community, developed and allowed to thrive, for the most part. Its fragility is evidenced in the lack of control that individuals face in the various worlds they are a part of. Her account of cosmopolitanism identifies a shared human vulnerability in the social and political worlds. This vulnerability is the product of our social nature—the need we have as human beings, as social beings, to live in a community and our inability to control the world around us. And it is this lack of control that intermingles with happiness. Life is thus, bitter sweet.

This is not to say that human agency cannot also be the product of cruelty and harm—there remain in the world far too many instances of intentional human cruelty. Reflecting on the fact that I was ordered deported paints a stark picture on how the need to securitize the state, render people static beings, and foreclose any presumption about our own natural vulnerability reveals just how easy it is for humanities' creations to invoke and perpetuate harm. But what is distinct and welcome in the accounts offered by Nussbaum is that there is interwoven in her notion of vulnerability an account of the uncontrollable—that ethereal component of being human that stands outside universality, stability and order and reflects the reality of being human in common; namely that life is messy, unpredictable and simultaneously exhilarating and challenging. Nussbaum's cosmopolitanism is steeped in an Aristotelian tradition that stands in sharp contrast to the liberal and Kantian invigorations of cosmopolitan ethics as it relates to International Relations. Indeed, we must recall that, above all else, Nussbaum is by trade a philosopher who dabbles heavily in ethical debates of IR and this, I believe, is a significant difference.

The significance of Nussbaum's work is that it eschews universal claims and instead acknowledges the particularities of being human. Such cosmopolitanism invites emotions and personal stories as a way of enhancing humanity. Humanity may be rendered more vulnerable because of this but the ensuing potential for tragedy reifies what it is to be a social and moral being. It suggests life as a creative, but at times tragic, endeavor.

I will acknowledge that prior to facing my deportation I believed one could pass seamlessly from Nussbaum's cosmopolitanism to the cosmopolitanism discussed by Charles Beitz (1979), Onora O'Neill (1996), Catherine Lu (2000) and even Toni Erskine (2008). Their work is elegantly and convincingly written. But, underscoring all of these interpretations is an assumed empowered agent—the agent that for better or worse, (*pace* the Kantian assumptions of O'Neill) embodies the universality of the human rights project. Having had to rely on others to listen to me, to act on my behalf, to do so with both compassion and humility, I began to wonder, could cosmopolitanism adopt the necessary quiet needed to listen, to empathize and acknowledge what it is to be vulnerable without recourse to agency?

I am not alone in this concern. Writing on the theme of the vulnerable subject in IR, Kim Hutchings (2012) queries the role of the global ethicist. Are such agents, positioned as they are in a global world actively engaged in the ends of global social justice and human rights, properly able to reflect upon their position in the world? Can they attend to the potential for harm when they speak for those without a voice in a globalized environment? She proposes to the reader that a cosmopolitan agent cannot speak to the harm faced by those less fortunate, that they are so steeped in a worldview of universalisms, of stability and conformity that the plight of the other is marginalized. But this is not to say that the agent is not capable, rather, it is to argue that they do not have the space, theoretical or actual, to be actively reflective. Because of this, I too, remain skeptical of this project—it requires others to be quiet. And, I wonder, is this possible? The noise and furor surrounding the cosmopolitan project does not tend to accommodate the quiet, the space in between the empowered and powerful and the disenfranchised. We need this element of calm, of serenity if you will, if individuals (whoever they are) seek to move beyond the emotional promptings of sympathy, compassion and empathy, and engage.

How do I know there is so much noise within the cosmopolitan project? I was that scholar. I was trained as a political scientist to disavow the personal. To write, and teach, in the third person and to seek, in my research theoretically sound outcomes that were verifiable, reproducible and could withstand the rigor of academic peer review. Truth be told, looking from afar into the critical discourse communities of IR I saw anger, deep-seated unhappiness and an unsettled series of emotions that I could not understand as I sat comfortably in this proscribed worldview. I wondered, prior to facing my own vulnerability in the political world, how such anger could be productive and never sought out such communities for dialogue. I have gained much insight into my interpretations of the critical community. Theirs is/was not a community of anger. I now understand that it was their challenge to my surprisingly tenacious hold on a global universal morality that tinted my view of their aims, ends, and most importantly, interrogations. It forced me, although I could not admit it, to question my own assumptions. Their anger was, in reality, my insecurity.

Yet, it is that same arrogance, nay insecurity that allowed me the necessary blinders to navigate the disciplines of philosophy, politics and international relations with ease. And while I believed that my embracing Nussbaum's writings meant I could abandon the much-taught undergraduate mantra of the three Ss of realism; namely, statehood, survival and security, I was wrong. The same single-minded focus that attends to the simplicity of the realist message that I was taught likewise sustained my own arrogance when I believed I could take a highly nuanced understanding of being human and transpose it into the domain of International Relations, albeit in an overtly normative frame. This assumption, combined with a deportation order, was my undoing.

To be fair, cosmopolitan international relations is a varied and nuanced discourse. Yet it does assume, on some level an institutional design that is democratic (see for example, Archibugi 1995; Held 1995; Benhabib 2007; Cabrera 2014). It strives for universally democratic institutions that can facilitate such an aim. Moreover, it believes that all individuals are valuable and worthy of such institutions. I have yet to come across a cosmopolitan scholar, however, that challenges the territorial, spatial and cartographical representations of the international. I am mindful of Jeremy Waldron's (2000) interrogation of the cosmopolitan ethic which, upon close reading, is about communities intersecting, engaging with each other, but always keeping their inner structure intact. Cosmopolitans may eschew harm, they may envision a hospitable and compassionate world, but they do so all the while accepting the centrality of states and the borders that define them. A cosmopolitan institutional design inherently assumes internal order and external disorder, mediated by a desire for a democratically guided international. So, while I, as a scholar of IR wholeheartedly adopted the cosmopolitan ethos, the global nature of human vulnerability *cum* morality, I was simultaneously being asked, rather unceremoniously to leave the UK. Despite the best democratic intentions, I was not wanted.

I could not reconcile on a personal level, or an academic one, how I could champion universal morality and a global common humanity all the while I was stripped of my passport and rendered voiceless. My mobility rights, part and parcel of what it is to be a member of a democratic polity, were stripped. This was the paradox that I wanted to write about but to do so meant that I had to disavow the impersonal and begin to speak in an emotive voice. I had been taught this would be detrimental to my scholarly abilities, nay reputation; however, I had to give a voice to the contradictions that my situation revealed. How could a universal cosmopolitan framework eschewing harm and acknowledging vulnerable beings simultaneously silence the exile? This personal insight caused me to pause and question the various worlds I was a part of. But, I had no training on how to give voice to an experience rooted in the personal motivated by the emotional. In order to realize this goal I had to "unlearn" what I had been taught.

It was at this point that I happened upon the writings of Elizabeth Dauphinee (2013) and *The Politics of Exile*. In her recounting of her discussions, shall I say relationship, with Stojan Sokolovic, I recognized a similar challenge. The wider message of *The Politics of Exile* asks how one can reconcile loving someone who has done terrible things. In this query I recognized much of what Nussbaum (2001) was speaking to when she highlighted the tragic nature of our existence, the decisions of Hecuba, as a mother and tragic heroine lamenting the decisions that rendered her daughters victims, but also Menelaus, the father, the military leader, the man trying to be moral but condemned by fate to irrevocably harm the communal good.

Dauphinee repeatedly turns to Levinas to work through the idea that people are rendered guilty because they must choose between two irreconcilably difficult, if not inherent, hard choices. There is, like Nussbaum, a tragic element in this particular unfolding plot line. In their introduction Amoureux and Steele point to such renderings. They highlight the anti-Pelagian framework proposed by Rengger (2005) drawing on Oakshott, and *inter alia*, Augustine. But a tragic motif while offering solace in understanding, only tells part of the story. It might explain the circumstances informing individual choice but it does not attend to the harmful outcomes inflicted, at times, on others. Tragedy is an enhanced moral casuistry. It does not, however, allow for a working through the outcomes of agency and the impact that outcomes, intended or otherwise, might have on the person, the exile.

Three

Jenny Edkins (2002, p. 245) writes that trauma "involves an exposure to an event so shocking that our everyday expectations of how the world works are severely disrupted". It can reflect a sense of betrayal, a loss of trust and a challenge to one's worldview. It ruptures the status quo that can render the experience incommunicable. For Edkins, trauma time stands outside the linearity of history. It is not experienced in the moment in which it occurs. It is only recognized as trauma at a future date, and it is at that point when agents begin to work through the events. But paradoxically, it is always with us. Trauma, as Edkins reminds us, focuses sharply on the mortal nature of our being, i.e. our vulnerability. It reminds individuals of the finite, the inescapable inability to overcome nature, to draw on our ingenuity and creativity to erect the safe spaces within which the quotidian can unfold. At the site of trauma, individuals must not only face their mortality, but re-focus how they engage as trusting beings with the people around them, the institutions of everyday life and the larger structures that inform the political. And how they do this reflects the worldview they adopt and their position therein.

Kate Schick (2011) likewise understands the rupturing associated with traumatic events. She draws on the works of Gillian Rose in order to attend to the real-time unfolding of trauma (Schick 2012). She points to an Hegelian Speculative reason to navigate what Rose terms "the broken middle" seeking out a more hopeful future. While Edkins situates trauma outside of the linear interpretation of history, Schick demands that trauma be centrally located within both the social and historical context of everyday so that those affected by trauma can work through the experience thereby achieving the emancipatory ends associated with a critical theoretical approach to IR. The idiosyncrasies of this particular approach provide a mediated worldview whereby suffering is understood as an experience to be worked through; an episode within the political that attends to the particular while remaining aware of the universal.

Schick's (2009, pp. 147–148) interpretation of Adorno, and its relation to human suffering is personal. It locates, in Adorno's understanding of the dark side of enlightenment the silent suffering other. "The concrete other, passed over in the pursuit of universal guidelines for living, is often the individual experiencing the negative aspects of progress and is precisely the one who suffers in silence", she writes. "Although a desire to emancipate humankind from suffering provides the motivation for mainstream international ethics, this suffering is too quickly passed over in the attempt to delineate universal norms, and the influence of present emotion or past traumas on present capability for political interaction is all but ignored." Shick's work identifies a key problem with accepted ethical encounters with suffering. Trauma is unaccommodating to its assumed temporality. It defies time, space and history. Perhaps even more problematic is that in eschewing harm and acknowledging vulnerability the liberal cosmopolitan endorses a particular encounter with humanitarian aid which further silences the lived experience of the suffering other, the exile.

In her exploration of exile Lisa Malkki (1996) reveals such a silencing. Her ethnographic work of exiled communities in the Rwanda/Burundi region of Africa details how the specifics of the exile, either within a community or as a single person, occur. She realizes early on in her field-work not only that her experiences do not align with status quo interpretations. To wit, she witnesses at the level of discourse an inexplicable trend that pigeonholes knowledge within a pre-existing paradigm; namely, the liberal rights discourse. This, she demonstrates to the reader, is the image that frames humanitarian engagements with displaced peoples, statelessness and wider humanitarian appeals. She demonstrates that this image is flawed and does not accurately portray both the plight of the displaced person, nor the particularities that render them human. In a bid to ensure that top-down, universal procedures of humanitarianism can function appropriately, the particularities of being human are set aside. This is a process that she labels "corporeal anonymity". It facilitates the delivery of a particular type of aid while ensuring that the realities of being displaced, for whatever reason, are left unsaid.

Perhaps even more problematic is the narrative that fills the void of the personal, which renders specificity silent. In lieu of the moral, globally democratic, cosmopolitan citizen there is, in the wider literature that reflects upon refugees, displaced persons and asylum seekers, i.e. the exiles, an inherent assumption of amorality. Instead of the universal moral *cum* vulnerable global citizen there is an image of the individual who willingly eschews the comfort and stability of home to seek out alternative territorial spaces within which their lives might unfold. In the absence of a homeland, a motherland, the citizen is unable to suitably cultivate the requisite knowledge of appropriate citizen or moral agent. Malkki (2008, p. 280) writes the following: "The point to be underscored here is that these refugees' loss of bodily connection to their national homelands came to be treated as a loss of moral bearings. Rootless, they were no longer trustworthy as 'honest citizens'." They become the other and, as Malkki argues, are portrayed as pathologically ill, unable, and arguably, undeserving of treatment. Transplantation, the last resort of medical intervention, is not an option here. To be uprooted is to stand outside the margins of healing. The possibility of cultivating new roots pre-emptively curtailed.

Rendered voiceless, unable to communicate their own experiences, exiled peoples can experience trauma. Gemignani's (2011) work with Kosovo Refugees identifies how violent conflict not only shatters a collective notion of the European identity, likewise identified in Dauphinee's *The Politics of Exile*, he also reveals how fleeing conflict, and rebuilding a life in the United States has a profound impact on the identity and personality of such people. There is, for such refugees, a clear break in their lives; a life prior to and a life after the experience of war, displacement and resettlement. Gemignani adopts a narrative methodology when he rehearses their stories. Twinned with his psychoanalytical approach he identifies two coping methods within the survivor stories he hears. While some refugees draw a line and do not engage in what they believe is a futile exercise of past memories, other refugees navigate the present while constantly reflecting on the experiences of the past, if only to educate their children on the possibilities of a now lost life. In rehearsing their stories refugees begin to engage with the traumatic experience. This therapeutic engagement does not seek to re-insert the refugee in their previously held worldview. It seeks to help the refugee negotiate the present with much-needed strength and support.

While trauma may defy temporal and spatial assumptions of a liberal worldview, the moment of the traumatic experience is explicit. As Crossely (2000) reminds us for the traumatized person there is life before, and after, the traumatic experience. If we think of this particular moment as a "knock" or a crisis, the writings of Carolyn Ellis (2004) become rather important. She explains how crisis inspires her own research outputs. "I tend to write about experiences that knock me for a loop and challenge the construction of meaning I have put together for myself", she writes. "I write when my world falls apart or the meaning I have constructed for myself is in danger of doing so" (p. 33). I suggest that crisis, or knock, is a central theme of this edited volume permeating many of the included chapters (Dauphinee, Chapter 2, and Steele, Chapter 3, in this volume) and I suggest that such de-centering is both a powerful and valuable experience to the IR scholar and part of the reflexive process. Rendered exiled I began to question many personal and professional assumptions that supported an exceptionally privileged worldview. This worldview, I now admit, was highly problematic, inherently arrogant, and admittedly, shameful.

As Ackerly and True (2008, p. 697) point out in their writings on a feminist research ethic in IR, the process of becoming shaky, of losing faith, reveals the way in which research marginalizes, excludes, and silences the experiences and ideas that do not align with status quo research assumptions. They turn to the exemplary work of Sterne (2005, 2006) and D'Costa (2003, 2006) to reveal the impact of reflection on both research design and practice. In their recounting of this process Ackerly and True inform the reader that both Sterne and D'Costa faced a similar situation. The information they acquired during the research process did not align with the research design, nor the assumed ends of the project itself. In light of this situation both authors faced a decision. They could either exclude the information or redesign the original research framework thereby accommodating the unexpected outcome.

I suggest that this process is similarly revealed in the experiences of Mallki. Her conclusion, the idea of corporeal anonymity, showcases the self-same reflexive practice as described by Ackerly and True. Similarly, it parallels the experience of Ellis when seemingly strong impermeable boundaries are rendered tenuous and fragile. There was, for Mallki, a need to probe this particular problem. Her demonstrated reflexivity revealed the problematics of a liberal aid discourse as it relates to the particularities of being human. More importantly, it gestures to the need for a more personal rendering of the exile. To live in exile is to be without the relationships that sustain our very natures. Not only does the exile live in the absence of a community, they can find themselves separated from friends, family and various institutions that help them navigate their daily lives. They are labelled pathological and amoral owing to the challenge they pose to modern institutional design. Consequently, the traumatic experiences of the exile unfold in isolation. The exile is isolated because they exist outside of the political. This marginalization not only renders the exile silent, it marginalizes the possibility of agency.

Conclusion

Exile reflects a way of dealing with those that do not align with a scripted account of politics. It manages the extraordinary, the rootlessness of mobility. Nomads are set outside the political because their contingency and dynamic lifestyle challenges the stasis of international institutional design. Exiles are rendered silent thereby foreclosing any potential threats to the status quo. Render the stateless amoral and it is considered acceptable to situate them outside the remit of a democratic polity, international or domestic. In the absence of a voice the exile cannot be independently creative. They must rely on the goodwill of others. Their very existence challenges the status quo but their agency must function outside the sovereign assumptions of time, space and territory.

My experience of exile, I acknowledge, was borne out in a high level of comfort, especially when compared to those forced migrants fleeing war, persecution and violent conflict. I chose to remain in the UK and challenge the directives of the UKBA. Forced migrants do not have such agentic capacities. When I write my story it is not to take away from their trauma, or marginalize their voice. I write my own experience of exile in order to focus on the voice of a story and prompt reflection, aware of the very particular and idiosyncratic nature of trauma in and of itself. The comfort of my trauma does not, I believe, make it any less relevant to the discussions of IR, but remaining aware of such differences, and carrying the insecurity of a traumatic experience with me, does help inform the ethical and normative discussions herein. Moreover, it suggests some interesting and poignant parallels within discussions of exile and trauma as they challenge a universal unfolding account of ethics and IR.

A traumatic intervention into the status quo of the exile allows the wounds of migration trauma to be probed. It speaks to a more personal rendering of the stateless and imagines not solutions, but negotiations. It opens up a space to listen and reflect and offers a more humane face to those who stand outside the remit of the state simply because they challenge the status quo. Reflexive practices have a central role to play in this process. To be reflexive is many things, as Amoureux and Steele (Introduction to this volume) point out. Drawing on their proposed threefold typology my story reveals the possibilities of both an agentic and political account of reflexive practice. I am, however, mindful of a caution offered by Finlay (2002a). Reflexivity, she reminds us, should not be "an opportunity to wallow in subjectivity nor permission to engage in legitimized emoting". Rather, as she further writes (2002b), such introspection must be a springboard for interpretations and more general insight. I describe my experience in order to instigate such reflections.

Autobiography, or autoethnography, as a source of reflexive engagement provides some exceptional surprises. Reading Ruth Behar's work *The Vulnerable Observer* I am reminded that outside Academia autobiography as methodology is both accepted and enthralling:

> No one objects to autobiography, as such, as a genre in its own right. What bothers critics is the insertion of personal stories into what we have been taught to think of as the analysis of impersonal social facts. Throughout most of the twentieth century, in scholarly fields ranging from literary criticism to anthropology to law, the reigning paradigms have traditionally called for distance, objectivity, and abstraction. The worst sin was to be "too personal".
>
> (Behar 1996, pp. 12–13)

This is a sentiment shared by Inayatullah in his writing on autobiography and IR. Our revelations are more than the personal experiences that define our singularity. He forcefully argues that our stories actually deepen the relational nature of our very being:

> Fear of autobiographical writing may be calmed when we entertain the possibility that rather than being indulgent, we are actually not indulgent enough. The deeper secret we hide from ourselves is that, in the end, there is little to our claim of uniqueness or our presumed self-indulgence. Excavate the self and what do we find? Not ontologized and essentialized indulgence, but the differentiated dynamism of the whole worlds.
>
> (Inayatullah 2011, p. 8)

Autobiographical revelations are personal. They are also emotional. They reveal a shared vulnerable nature. They do not recognize one pre-eminent story but rather highlight the importance of diversity and difference in understanding the various worlds we are a part of.

In light of my disillusion with the cosmopolitan worldview I suggest that story-telling, one component of reflexive practice, can begin to rebuild the ties that bind. Stories render us vulnerable. They reveal commonalities that can transcend isolation. Such therapeutic processes can instigate the re-creating of relationships and communities. As Geminani's work in psychotherapy reveals, story-telling or narrative psychoanalysis can help the displaced, nay exiled, re-imagine their place within the political. In this way this chapter is sympathetic to the ends outlined by Dauphinee (Chapter 2 in this volume). She probes the relationship of narrative and reflexivity. I humbly suggest one (but not the only) coming together of these two approaches lies in the ability to render the outcomes of international relations, forced migration in particular, more personal, less ethereal and altogether more humane as individuals negotiate the experiences of trauma therein.

Notes

1 Throughout this chapter I use "IR" to indicate the discipline of International Relations and "ir" to refer to the events of international politics.
2 When addressing the idea of institutional design I am referring to the works of Robert E. Goodin, in particular, *Theory of Institutional Design* (1998).

References

Ackerly, B. and True, J., 2008. Reflexivity in Practice: Power and Ethics in Feminist Research on International Relations. *International Studies Review*, 10(4), 693–707.

Archibugi, D., 1995. From the United Nations to Cosmopolitan Democracy. In: D. Archibugi and D. Held, eds, *Cosmopolitan Democracy: An Agenda for a New World Order*. Oxford and Cambridge, MA: Polity Press, pp. 473–502.

Behar, R., 1996. *The Vulnerable Observer: Anthropology that Breaks your Heart*. Boston, MA: Beacon Press.

Beitz, C., 1979. *Political Theory and International Relations*. Princeton, NJ: Princeton University Press.

Benhabib, S., 2007. Democratic Exclusions and Democratic Iterations: Dilemmas of "Just Membership" and Prospects of Cosmopolitan Federalism. *European Journal of Political Theory*, 6(4), 445–462.

Benhabib, S. and Resnik, J., 2009. *Migrations and Motilities: Gender, Borders and Citizenship*. New York: NYU Press.

Bleiker, R., 2001. The Aesthetic Turn in International Political Theory. *Millennium—Journal of International Studies*, 30, 509–533.

Brigg, M. and Bleiker, R., 2008. Expanding Ethnographic Insights into Global Politics. *International Political Sociology*, 2(1), 89–90.

Brigg, M. and Bleiker, R., 2010. Autoethnographic International Relations: Exploring the Self as a Source of Knowledge. *Review of International Studies*, 36(3), 779–798.

Buchanan, A. and Keohane, R.O., 2004. The Preventive Use of Force: A Cosmopolitan Institutional Proposal. *Ethics and International Affairs*, 18(1), 1–22.

Cabrera, L., 2014. Individual Rights and the Democratic Boundary Problem. *International Theory*, 6(2), 224–254.

Carens, J., 2013. *The Ethics of Immigration*. Oxford: Oxford Political Theory.

Crossley, M.I., 2000. Narrative psychology, trauma and the study of self/identity. *Theory & Psychology*, 10(4), 527–546.

D'Costa, D.B., 2003. *The Gendered Construction of Nationalism: From Partition to Creation*. Canberra: Australian National University.

D'Costa, D.B., 2006. Marginalized Identity: New Frontiers of Research for IR? In: B.A. Ackerly, M. Stern and J. True, eds, *Feminist Methodologies for International Relations*, Manchester: Manchester University Press, pp. 129–152.

Dauphinee, E., 2010. The Ethics of Autoethnography. *Review of International Studies*, 36(3), 799–818.

Dauphinee, E., 2013. *The Politics of Exile*. New York: Routledge.

Edkins, J., 2002. Forget Trauma? Responses to September 11. *International Relations*, 16(2), 243–256.

Edkins, J., 2003. *Trauma and the Memory of Politics*. Cambridge: Cambridge University Press.

Ellis, C., 2004. *The Ethnographic I: A Methodological Novel about Autoethnography*. Lanham, MD: Altamira.

Erskine, T., 2008. *Embedded Cosmopolitanism: Duties to Strangers and Enemies in a World of "Dislocated Communities"*. Oxford: Oxford University Press.

Finlay, L., 2002a. "Outing" the Researcher: The Provenance, Principles and Practice of Reflexivity. *Qualitative Health Research*, 12(4): 531–545.

Finlay, L., 2002b. Negotiating the Swamp: The Opportunity and Challenge of Reflexivity in Research Practice. *Qualitative Research*, 2(2), 209–230.

Gemignani, M., 2011. The Past if Past: The Use of Memories and Self-healing Narratives in Refugees from the Former Yugoslavia. *Journal of Refugee Studies*, 24(1), 132–156.

Goodin, R.E., 1998. *The Theory of Institutional Design*. Cambridge: Cambridge University Press.

Held, D., 1995., *Democracy and the Global Order: From Modern State to Cosmopolitan Governance*. Cambridge: Polity Press.

Hutchings, K., 2012. A Place of Greater Safety? Securing Judgement in International Ethics. In: A. Beattie and K. Schick, eds, *The Vulnerable Subject: Beyond Rationalism in International Relations*. New York: Palgrave Macmillan, pp. 25–42.

Ikenberry, G.J., 2009. *After Victory: Institutions, Strategic Restraint, and the Rebuilding of Order after Major Wars*. Princeton, NJ: Princeton University Press.

Inayatullah, N., 2011. *Autobiographical International Relations: I, IR*. Abingdon: Routledge.

Lenard, P.T. and Straehle, C., 2012. Temporary Labour Migration Global Redistribution and Democratic Justice. *Politics, Philosophy and Economics*, 11(2), 206–230.

Lu, C., 2000. The One and Many Faces of Cosmopolitanism. *Journal of Political Philosophy*, 8(2), 244–267.

Malkki, L.H., 1996. Speechless Emissaries: Refugees, Humanitarianism, and Dehistoricization. *Cultural Anthropology*, 11(3), 377–404.

Malkki, L.H., 2008. National Geographic: The Rooting of Peoples and the Territorialization of National Identity among Scholars and Refugees. In: T.S. Oakes and P.L. Price, eds, *The Cultural Geography Reader*. Abingdon: Routledge, pp. 275–282.

Nussbaum, M.C., 2001. *The Fragility of Goodness: Luck and Ethics in Greek Tragedy and Philosophy*. Cambridge: Cambridge University Press.

O'Neill, O., 1996. *Towards Justice and Virtue: A Constructive Account of Practical Reasoning*. Cambridge: Cambridge University Press.

Rengger, N., 2005. Tragedy or Skepticism? Defending the Anti-Pelagian Mind in World Politics. *International Relations*, 19(3), 321–328.

Said, E., 2000. *Reflections on Exile: And Other Literary and Cultural Essays*. Cambridge: Convergences.

Schick, K., 2009. "To Lend a Voice to Suffering is a Condition for all Truth": Adorno and International Political Thought. *Journal of International Political Theory*, 5(2), 138–160.

Schick, K., 2011. Acting Out and Working Through: Trauma and (In)security. *Review of International Studies*, 37(4), 1837–1855.

Schick, K., 2012. *Gillian Rose: A Good Enough Justice*. Edinburgh: Edinburgh University Press.

Shklar, J.N., 1993. Obligation, Loyalty, Exile. *Political Theory*, 21, 181–197.

Stern, M., 2005. *Naming Security–Constructing Identity: "Mayan-women" in Guatemala on the eve of "peace"*. Manchester: Manchester University Press.

Stern, M., 2006. Racism, Sexism, Classism and Much More: Reading Security-identity in Marginalized Sites. In: B.A. Ackerly, M. Stern and J. True, eds, *Feminist Methodologies for International Relations*, Manchester: Manchester University Press, pp. 174–198.

Waldron, J., 1991. Minority Cultures and the Cosmopolitan Alternative. *University of Michigan Journal of Law Reform*, 25(3&4), 751–793.

Waldron, J., 2000. What is Cosmopolitan? *Journal of Political Philosophy*, 8(2), 227–243.

Walters, W., 2006. Border/Control. *European Journal of Social Theory*, 9(2), 187–203.

Williams, A., 2007. *Failed Imagination?: The Anglo-American New World Order from Wilson to Bush*, Second Edition. Manchester: Manchester University Press.

Part III

Reflexivity and world politics

9   Reflexivity, critique, and the Jewish Diaspora

Ilan Zvi Baron

In the Introduction to this volume, Jack Amoureux and Brent Steele outline the multiple influences and methodological positions behind different forms of reflexivity. They write that what unites reflexive research across these differences is an acknowledgement that it involves, "the dialectic engagement of thought and action in the form of a 'turning back' or reflection". If, however, research is a reflexive process of self-awareness and self-introspection, of turning back, is it reasonable to assume that anyone other than the author would be interested in the research project?

Usually, explaining, or rather, justifying how one's research is a contribution to knowledge by contextualizing it via a literature review is how most of us avoid this problem. As scholars, we can then claim that our research matters for someone other than the author, and any potential accusations of reflexive navel-gazing can be avoided. Yet the literature review, what the sociologist Manuel Castells (2010, p. 12) has dismissively called "bibliographic commentary", is not by itself a methodological engagement with reflexivity. The methodological aspects of reflexivity, some of which feature importantly in what Anthony Giddens (1976) has described as the double hermeneutic, can be difficult to apply. Reflexivity may be increasingly common in IR research, but it often remains a murky reference to various forms of autobiographical influence on the research process. At issue are two inter-related problems. The first is a meta-theoretical debate focusing on methodological issues of what is meant by reflexivity, and a second is how to actually conduct reflexive research. Texts that focus on the former are philosophically rich but not always clear on empirical guidance. Texts that focus on the latter can all too easily be read as self-indulgent, overly descriptive, and not analytical enough.

As a methodology, reflexivity finds its origins in Anthropology[1] (Davies 2008). Within that discipline there exists extensive debate about the methodological, political and ethical issues involved in reflexive research. The debate that has had the widest impact outside of Anthropology concerns Clifford Geertz's (2000 [1973]) distinction between thick and thin descriptions. Part of this debate has been an engagement with writing and the role of the author; hence, the edited volume *Writing Culture* (Clifford and Marcus 2010).

In IR, however, there is little related debate about writing and authorship. When writing is addressed, it is done so in a very different sense than James Clifford (Clifford and Marcus 2010) does. For anthropologists, writing is a performative process contained within ethnographic practice, and, consequently, there is an ethical responsibility that accompanies the role of being an author. For IR scholars, writing is less about what the researcher pens to paper, and is more often a reference to the ongoing social construction of the world. Both *Writing Security* (Campbell 1998) and *International/Intertextual Relations* (Der Derian and Shapiro 1989) treat writing in this way. The challenge for IR, consequently, is to explore reflexivity in ways that move beyond variations of post-structuralism, critical realism and/or social constructivism. As reflexivity becomes increasingly accepted to be important, IR should have its own version of *Writing Culture* where the writing is not about social constructions of the world, but instead pertains to a kind of hermeneutic identity-affirming process and the impact that this process has for research.

In their Introduction, Amoureux and Steele helpfully categorize reflexivity into three forms or types. The first is positionality, the second critique and the third practice. As is often the case with classification schemes, and as they recognize, the dividing lines are not perfectly clear. There is overlap. In the case of reflexivity, however, it is not just that the boundaries can be blurred. The three forms of reflexivity can be understood to function as a continuum. Positionality is necessary for a reflexive inspired critique. Critique is needed for practice, and practice in turn influences positionality.

While reflexivity begins with the positionality of the scholar, of the writer, once this step is taken reflexive research can become critique, the second of the three types. At this point reflexive research can become the third form, that of practice, with the subsequent political and ethical implications for the relevant community. Reflexive practice in turn, contributes to shaping the positionality of the scholar. In this continuum, reflexivity becomes much more than navel-gazing, as it is sometimes derisively described, but a significant contribution to social and political research offering unique insights as well as methodological guidance. Not all scholars will want to position their research as reflexive. Nevertheless, for those engaged in explicitly normative work, this reflexive continuum is an important methodological guide.

Reflexive research is normative research, and normative research can take many forms. However, the kind that I am interested in is what Michael Walzer calls social criticism. As Walzer (1987) argues, the social critic and the practice of social criticism necessarily require an engagement with reflexivity. Through an examination of social criticism, focusing on Jewish Diaspora critiques that are either about Israel or are related to events going on in Israel, I aim to reveal how the three forms of reflexivity function as a continuum, and demonstrate how the question of critique itself is potentially the most challenging and problematic aspect in the Diaspora's relationship with Israel. Understanding reflexivity in this way, as a continuum, is useful because it helps reveal the multiple ways in which normative research can function as both social criticism and as a kind of performative identity-constructing practice.

Positionality and autobiography

In his famous essay *Methodology of the Social Sciences*, Max Weber (2011 [1949]) emphasized the importance of positionality, of acknowledging the personal elements in how research is approached and topics selected, even if he also sought to limit such personal or subjective influences in research methods. Be that as it may, it is not uncommon to find in the introductions or forewords of academic books positional autobiographical commentary locating the author's intellectual interests and sometimes the author's personal journey behind the writing of the text. This kind of commentary is consistent with a reflexive methodology, and can be found across a range of scholars occupying different methodological positions. In IR, James Der Derian (2001) provides such an autobiography at the beginning of *Virtuous War*. Kenneth Waltz (2001) provides various autobiographical insights about how he ended up writing some of his classic texts.[2] In a chapter on security, Ken Booth (1997) offers an autobiographical account of his intellectual journey away from realism.

In Jewish Studies, David Biale (2011) uses autobiography to introduce his classic work on the historical process of what has come to be understood as secularization among Jews. Warren Rosenberg (2001) also uses an autobiographical introduction in his fascinating exploration of Jewish masculinity and violence. In addition, a couple of recent historical works about generally forgotten figures in the history of Jewish critiques about Israel and Zionism begin with autobiographical statements, both of which refer to the need to revisit the past so as to seek out alternative narratives in order to challenge the present, and perhaps write a better future (Myers 2008; Pianko 2010).

What such autobiographical commentaries reveal is how research stems from something more than intellectual curiosity, but from one's personal history, and thus one's self-understanding. Autobiography can also feature as a critical methodology in the social sciences, as Kathryn Church's (1995) work in medical anthropology demonstrates. In a related vein, Naeem Inayatullah's (2011) edited book, *Autobiographical International Relations*, demonstrates how autobiography can provide the context for and of the study of international relations. That autobiography informs research is well acknowledged, even if it is not widely agreed on how to translate this background into social scientific knowledge production. Nevertheless, research begins not with the subject of study, but with the researcher, not with them but with I.

My own research about the Jewish Diaspora and Israel was not a random choice. One of my interviewees even stated as much. As he said, "It is not by chance that you are writing [this] book ... It is in the psyche" (Anonymous 2013). My research on this topic did stem from autobiography and is indeed in my psyche. The pressure to embark on this research project thus stemmed in part from a personal experience of how Diaspora Jewry relates with Israel and how non-Jews understand Diaspora Jewish identity and Diaspora Jewish commitments insofar as Israel is concerned. In this way, my autobiography has led me to care about some issues over others.

One's life journey will shape the selection of research topics, but that on its own is not sufficient as a reflexive methodology. My research about the Diaspora/Israel relationship and how Israel features in the construction of Diaspora Jewish identity (Baron 2014a, 2014b, 2015) is about contributing to critique, and opening up uncomfortable insights in order to stimulate debate. In opening up debate my research is also about exploring the role of debate in the Diaspora/Israel relationship, in the hopes that I have something to contribute that will matter and might even have some influence. My own research thus crosses the dividing lines between reflexivity as positionality, as critique and as practice. My research about the Jewish Diaspora is a type of social criticism in large part because it is reflexive, and it is reflexive because it is a type of social criticism.

Toward social criticism: the Diaspora, Zionism and Israel

One of the more controversial Jewish critics of Zionism and Israel, and a leading gender theorist, Judith Butler (2012), has suggested that a problem framing the Diaspora/Israel relationship is the assumption that being Jewish necessarily involves supporting Israel. She writes that, "It continues to surprise me that many people believe that to claim one's Jewishness is to claim Zionism or believe that every person who attends a synagogue is necessarily a Zionist" (Butler 2012, p. 3). The correlation between being Jewish and being a Zionist, while problematic, is, however, not especially surprising. Butler is correct in identifying that this assumption needs to be challenged, but she is mistaken in presuming that it should be unexpected. Indeed, Stephen J. Whitfield (2002, p. 414) writes, in the final chapter to David Biale's edited three-volume work, *Cultures of the Jews*, that "After the Six Day War of 1967 support for Israel became the *sine qua non* of [American] Jewish communal affairs and leadership, so that an agnostic or even an atheist became more acceptable as an attribute of, say, a synagogue president than an anti-Zionist."

It may seem hard to accept that it is more important for a synagogue president to believe in Israel than in God, but it is plausible, even though it is disturbing as it suggests a kind of idolatry where Israel displaces God in the traditional sacred order of God, Torah, Israel. Whitfield is, nevertheless, correct to identify just how important Israel has become for Diaspora Jews. As such, Butler's surprise can be understood as a consequence of forgetting the deeply political history that has made Whitfield's comment plausible, and in forgetting that for many Diaspora Jews, supporting Israel or at least having a positive relationship with Israel is crucial for their Jewish identity, and for sustaining a sense of Jewish peoplehood and Jewish continuity. How we have come to this point is, thus, worth going over.

Historically, the very idea of being a Zionist Jew in the Diaspora was an oxymoron. Certainly for political Zionists like Ben-Gurion and Golda Meir, to be a Zionist meant to live in Israel. Anything else was nonsense, or "pseudo-Zionism" (Eisen 1986, pp. 118–119). However, Zionism came to include Diaspora Jews who supported at first the idea of the Jewish State in Palestine, and then Israel, but who were not prepared to uproot their lives and move there. Indeed, it was not the aim of all Zionist thinkers for all of Diaspora Jewry to move to Israel. Ahad Ha'Am, for one, saw Israel as the spiritual home of the Jews and was a place that Diaspora Jews could turn toward for their spiritual and cultural needs. They need not move there. Yet, with the creation of the State of Israel and the successes of political Zionism, to be a Zionist seemed to logically require that one live in Israel. This view posed a problem for Diaspora Jews.

In North America, which was home to the largest Jewish population after the Second World War, the development of Diaspora Zionism goes back to before the First World War and was firmly established at the 1942 Biltmore Conference (when American Zionist Jews agreed to support the policy of Palestine as a national commonwealth). Diaspora Zionism that did not require immigration was articulated by a variety of Jewish leaders, of whom Louis Brandeis (1856–1941) was one of the most famous (Laqueur 2003). What Brandeis did was to equate being Jewish with being a Zionist (Urofsky 1975). According to Brandeis (1997 [1915]), to be a good Jew and a good American, one should become a Zionist. As he argued, "loyalty to America demands … that each American Jew become a Zionist" (Eisen 1986, p. 157). He claimed that American Jews had a home, and did not need a new one, but many Jews did not and for them there was Israel.

Another important American Zionist was Solomon Schechter (1847–1915). Schechter saw Zionism as an important factor in preventing assimilation because it helped to maintain a sense of Jewish identity in the Diaspora (Eisen 1986; Schechter 1959). As he saw it, the role of Israel as a cultural and spiritual center would help support Jewish identity in the Diaspora. This Ahad Ha'Am style of Zionism also influenced Mordecai Kaplan (1881–1983). Kaplan's Zionism also accepted the importance of the Diaspora as opposed to its negation. For him, American Jews should not embark for Palestine (and later Israel). They needed to remain home in the United States and continue to develop Judaism there. As he argued, long-distance Zionism was as important for the success of Israel as immigration. In, *A New Zionism* he wrote that, "Zionism has to be redefined so as to assure a permanent place for Diaspora Judaism" (Kaplan 1959, p. 40).

These thinkers helped pave the way for how Diaspora Jewish identity came to require a connection with Israel. The Jewish establishment in the Diaspora has for years continued to develop this line of argument that associates a strong Jewish identity and a deep connection to the Jewish people with having a positive relationship with Israel (Podhoretz 1974).

To return to Butler, what is surprising is not that there is the expectation that being Jewish means supporting Israel—from before the First World War there has been an ongoing effort to develop precisely this connection—but that it has become controversial to either offer contrasting accounts of how this relationship ought to be understood and acted upon, or to suggest alternative avenues for strengthening Jewish identity in the Diaspora. As usual, the devil is in the details, for what is understood by supporting Israel will vary considerably.

In other words, it is not that Jews are expected to have a relationship with Israel that is the problem, because it is fair to argue that for many Diaspora Jews Israel does play an important role in their lives. Rather, the problem is that there have been increasing limits on how this relationship is to be manifested and understood. It is this point that Butler is ultimately concerned with. At issue in the Diaspora/Israel relationship is what kind of political relationship Diaspora Jews are expected to have toward the Jewish State (Karpf et al. 2008; Rose 2005).

While religion can clearly inform this relationship, the decision of how to react to Israeli government policy is ultimately not a matter of spiritual belief or religiosity but of politics. Moreover, often it is the politics of security that matter. For at stake in most debates surrounding the Diaspora/Israel relationship are matters that pertain to Israeli policy in the West Bank and Gaza, its domestic policies relevant to Arab minority rights, its security policies in regard to terrorist violence, and its foreign policy toward the Arab world.[3] The views held by Diaspora Jews cover the full range from extreme right to extreme left and can include the support Israel at all costs position, or the opposite path that, following in the footsteps of the French Jewish sociologist Maxime Rodinson (1973), emphasizes human rights, Zionist colonial policies, and international law above ostensibly parochial claims to Jewish peoplehood. This range is both reflected and reflective of how emotional the discourse is surrounding this relationship. The intense emotions also explain why David Twersky, who, when he was the international affairs director of the American Jewish Congress, told me in 2008 that when it comes to Israel, "We tend to get hysterical in the Jewish community" (Twersky 2008).

The location, consequently, for an examination into Diaspora Jewish identity and its relationship with Israel is not an easy place to be: it is marred by conflict, hysteria, significant political and historical pressures to toe the party line by becoming a Zionist, and conversely equal pressure to stand up for human rights and not just Jewish rights (as if either Manichean viewpoint is unproblematic). It is, consequently, no surprise that many younger Jews, at least in the United States, are turning away from centralizing Israel in their understanding of Jewish identity (Pew 2013). To do otherwise is to engage in a deeply divisive debate that does not appear to have an easy resolution (Beinart 2010, 2012; Kahn-Harris 2014), if indeed a resolution even exists.

This split between Diaspora Jewry and Israel is not new (Vital 1990). It has been and remains an important point of debate within the Jewish community. Similarly, the divisions within the Jewish Diaspora over Israel are also not new (Selzer 1970; Shatz 2004). Zionism may have succeeded insofar as Israel exists as the Jewish State, but it has created new problems that traditional political Zionism seems unable to resolve (Baron 2014b). Moreover, and paradoxically, as Israel has become stronger militarily and thus ostensibly more secure, debate in the Diaspora about Israeli security and the policies of Israel have increased. In a sense, the more secure Israel becomes the less secure it is understood to be.

The vast majority of texts about Diaspora/Israel relations or about the security challenges Israel faces function as a form of social criticism. They instruct, advise, comment and suggest. However, they also function as a commentary about what it means to be a Diaspora Jew. For example, focusing on insecurity is, thus, consistent with the historical consciousness of Jewish victimhood (Rose 2005), and social criticisms about Israel that emphasize security above all else contribute to writing a sense of Jewish identity that is familiar, albeit perversely comforting, in its self-understanding of victimhood.

A different writing of security

Yossi Shain is one of the foremost scholars on the international relations of Diasporas. He clearly identifies the importance of identity for security but in his constructivist writings identity is treated as a variable. As such, Shain maintains the kind of reification that Daniel Levine (2012) identifies as inhibiting a reflexive inspired critique. In this regard, the security discourses in the international politics of Diaspora/homeland relations are only partly addressed by Shain (1994–1995, 2007). What is missed in the relevant literature about the Jewish Diaspora and Israel is that there is little on how the debates about this relationship influence Diaspora Jewish identity. Shain does not explore the construction of the identity-group itself because he views identity as informing security, not as part of a reciprocal process whereby security also informs identity.

This double orientation in the security/identity nexus is emphasized in David Campbell's (1998) book, *Writing Security*, where he writes about the relationship that exists between how the construction of America's identity influences its foreign policy and how its foreign policy in turn informs the construction of American national identity. Identity informs security, in this case the security aspects of foreign policy that reflect American interests, and security informs identity, of how foreign policy contributes to reflecting and shaping American senses of self. Brent Steele (2010) addresses a similar dynamic in his discussion about aesthetic power and counterpower. However, even in Campbell's reflexively informed critique, there is an additional dimension to this double orientation that is missed.

Part of the point in bringing reflexivity into IR is to encourage awareness of how research is an important part of critique and carries consequences for political action. In other words, as the other contributors to this volume address, reflexivity involves understanding the implications for how IR research is understood, conducted and acted upon. The positionality that reflexivity encourages is not just a critique directed against those who side with facts instead of values, as if the two can be distinguished and separated. It is also about acknowledging the normative position of the author as a social critic. In this sense, the move toward reflexivity is a further shift in the direction of a post-positivist research agenda within IR (Hamati-Ataya 2013; Neufeld 1993) that includes a wide range of scholars influenced by continental philosophy,[4] but is generally consistent with the anti-positivist writings of the Critical Theory scholars, Theodor Adorno and Max Horkheimer (Adorno and Horkheimer 1986; Horkheimer 1974 [1947]).

It is not by accident that some of the major critics of positivist methodology were European Jews. They saw within positivist scientific philosophy a dangerous instrumental reason that underpinned select aspects of European civilization, which in their lifetime had contributed to two world wars, and the Holocaust (Stirk 2000). It is, then, with some irony that arguments for supporting or critiquing Israel are often made in a positivist-influenced style that assumes that what is being argued for cannot be objectively dismissed.[5] Consequently, the turn toward a reflexive Critical Theory makes sense as a remedy to a methodologically one-sided debate about Diaspora Jewish identity and Israel, where the role of critique is not addressed as a positive force, but is viewed as a potentially negative reaction against Jewish peoplehood.

It is in this vein that we need to understand the debate that surrounded Hannah Arendt's (1994) reporting of the Eichmann trial that was originally for the *New Yorker* but was published as a book as well. Gershom Scholem accused Arendt of being heartless and of having no love of the Jewish people. As he wrote to her, "In the Jewish tradition there is a concept, hard to define and yet concrete enough, which we know as *Ahabath Israel*: 'Love of the Jewish People ...' In you, dear Hannah, as in so many intellectuals who came from the German Left, I find little trace of this" (Arendt 1978, p. 241). The view that associates being Jewish with seemingly unconditional support of Israel is a continuation of this debate between Scholem and Arendt, with the mainstream major Jewish Diaspora organizations siding closer to Scholem than with Arendt. Scholem's attack is personal precisely because he believes that her critique is the greatest of all betrayals. For him, her critique challenges the very idea of Jewish identity and Jewish continuity.

In a sense, one of Scholem's lessons from this debate is that critiques of Jewish political matters by Jews need to accept a love of the Jewish People as a starting position. Although love need not be devoid of uncomfortable critiques or harsh criticism—indeed, it is often those closest to us that are best able to reveal the most pressing criticisms—the underlying claim by Scholem is that somehow Arendt went too far. Anything less than starting with a love of the Jewish people is a betrayal of the Jewish people, and as such could prove threatening to Jewish continuity. While his debate with Arendt was focused on her reporting of the Eichmann trial in Jerusalem, which she described as a show trial (Arendt 1994), his argument also speaks to contemporary critiques of Diaspora/Israel relations. To the extent that Israel is recognized as the Jewish State, it plays a crucial role in contributing to Jewish peoplehood and the development of Jewish life and culture. Love of the Jewish people thus seems to require also a love of Israel, as if the two cannot be separated. The security of the Jewish People and of Israel thereby become tightly linked. This connection is precisely what Judith Butler is uncomfortable with and one that Jacqueline Rose (2005) has placed under psychoanalytic analysis. It is also a connection that Arendt was never comfortable with. In her reply to Scholem, she said how she did not understand what it meant to love a people or a collective, writing that, "the only love I know of and believe in is the love of persons" (Arendt 1978, p. 246).

Butler and Rose's concerns notwithstanding, in the Diaspora's relationship with Israel, security is present, and in a myriad of ways. These can range from concerns over Israel's security against terrorism or war, to Israel becoming a global target of anti-Semitic inspired condemnation, to how Israeli policy can impact Diaspora Jewish life, to how Israeli security policy could be linked to increased attacks against Jews in the Diaspora, to increased fears of anti-Semitism globally, to concerns about human rights violations and international law, to economic, religious, environmental, social and political factors. The relationship is complex, and the connection between identity and security rests in this complexity. The methodological knee-jerk reaction of social scientists to simplify, which is always necessary in some form, increases the risks of misunderstanding and/or mischaracterizing the relationship.

Yet, one necessary component of social science research is to simplify. Indeed, I recall attending an IR summer school taught by Professor Stephen Walt, where he defined a good theory as one that simplifies. It is, of course, not possible to take into account every contributing factor, even if all of them could be identified, for any given phenomenon. There is necessarily a discriminatory process of emphasising some factors and marginalizing others. Whether or not this process is apolitical (it is not) or scientifically sound is not the point. The point is that if the simplicity is too great, the research findings are compromised. However, if they are too complex, the research may be impenetrable. This is not to suggest that we need to find a middle ground. Instead of a *via media* it is possible to recognize the complexity instead of trying to modify it. Thus, in the Jewish Diaspora's relationship with Israel, it is the multiple ways in which security informs this relationship that is significant, and not how each security discourse can be explained individually.

As the British Jewish sociologist Keith Kahn-Harris (2014) points out, and as is explored in the award-winning novel, *The Finkler Question* (Jacobson 2010), critiques of Israel matter for many Jews in a unique way. They are not empty social criticisms but deeply personal ones as the critiques speak to how

Diaspora Jews are expected to feel about Israel. As written texts, however, social criticism of Israel necessarily focuses on specific points, such as particular policies or events and in the process they simplify. In simplifying, however, these critiques gloss over how Israel and how debate about Israel contributes to the construction of Diaspora Jewish identity. In this sense Ahad Ha'Am was correct. Israel does serve as a centre for, if not all, a lot of Diaspora Jews by strengthening their Jewish identity, and as such to offer critical judgment about Israel is to explore the place of Israel in the construction of Diaspora Jewish identity.

Writing as a Diaspora Jew about the Diaspora's relationship with Israel is to write about myself. To cut myself out of the equation would be to limit my own understanding of the relationship. It is noteworthy that Butler's and Rose's Jewish identity also features as a methodological backing in their relevant writings. As Rose (2005, p. xvi) writes, "I came to this topic having been preoccupied for many years as a Jewish woman with Israel–Palestine. Having felt, most of the time, repeatedly appalled at what the Israeli nation perpetrated in my name." Their Jewishness is not used to give their voices authority—as if to shut out other voices—but to contextualize their concerns. The security issues that they feel concerned about are thus a product not only of their moral views as human beings, but their moral views as Diaspora Jews as well. The security issues are thus both internal to their own sense of feeling secure in their moral relationships as Jews to other Jews vis-à-vis Israeli discourse, and external insofar as at issue is Israel's own security policies as well as how these policies are felt by Diaspora Jews and, of course, Palestinians.

The flurry of Diaspora commentaries in response to the July 2014 Gaza War reveals the extent to which Diaspora Jews can identify with Israel, with Israeli security needs, and how Israeli and Diaspora Jewish security are linked. Three articles in the *Forward*, one of the most important of the North American Jewish news periodicals dating back to 1897, help make the point. The first, by the writer Tova Ross (2014), is an admission that she was wrong to disagree with her hawkish father about Israel being "all the Jews have" and that the world "is not kind to the Jews" and consequently:

> Just as I'm finding that anti-Zionism and anti-Semitism are too closely intertwined for comfort, I'm also finding that it's becoming increasingly difficult to separate my identity as an American Jew and as a Jew who needs a homeland where I will always be welcomed solely because I am Jewish.

The second is by Menachem Creditor (2013), a self-defined progressive rabbi of a congregation in Berkeley, California. He writes:

> Having watched in this last week anti-Semitic "die-ins" in Boston, violent assaults against Jews in Los Angeles and Antwerp, and an almost pogrom at a synagogue in Paris, I'm done mincing my own words.

We will do what we must to protect our people. We have that right. We are not less deserving of life and quiet than anyone else.

No more apologies.

The third is by Sigal Samuel (2014), writer, editor and playwright. She writes:

Dear Diaspora Jews, I'm sorry to break it to you, but you can't have it both ways. You can't insist that every Jew is intrinsically part of the Israeli state and that Jews are also intrinsically separate from, and therefore not responsible for, the actions of the Israeli state. You can't support or attend a Birthright trip, the basic premise of which—just look at the name—is that a Jew has only to be born to win the "right" to romp all over Israel, and then act all surprised when these things are conflated. You can't applaud Israeli Prime Minister Benjamin Netanyahu when he goes around calling himself "the leader of the Jewish people," and then get all huffy when Arabic-speakers use a single word to denote "Zionists" and "Israelis" and "Jews."

These three voices highlight how Diaspora Jews understand the security elements that feature in their relationship with Israel. Underlying their comments are individually, collectively and historically informed relations that reveal the complexity in how security features in this relationship. Each of these examples reveals a different manifestation of how Diaspora Jews understand the security dynamics that connect them to Israel.

With Israeli security policy often playing a pivotal role in Diaspora debate about Israel, it makes sense to assume that an important security focus has to do with foreign policy. Israeli policy is clearly relevant here, and Jewish organizations certainly lobby for specific foreign policies (Goldberg 1996). Yet, to focus on Israeli security policy, on what Israel does or does not do, which is what most critiques about Israel address, misses something important. The identity/security relationship is shaped by how Diaspora Jews understand the role that Israel has for Diaspora Jews, and critiques about Israel play directly into this relationship.

To engage in any debate or commentary on the Diaspora/Israel relationship—to critique—is to contribute to a debate about the construction of the Diasporic Jewish self, as is evident in David Vital's (1990) book *The Future of the Jews*. To provide social criticism, to debate and critique Israel as a Diaspora Jew is necessarily a reflexive process that speaks to one's own self-construction.

The reflexive continuum in social criticism

All writing is necessarily a reflexive process. This reflexivity pertains to how the author becomes or is made self-aware as an author trying to convey a message. Max Weber (2011 [1949]) seemed to acknowledge as much even while it worried him as a potential factor undermining objective research.

However, whereas his focus was on how the social scientists' position can influence research, my focus is on how the research informs the researcher, especially in regard to normative research and normative writing. The reflexive continuum starts with the positionality of the researcher, but it must pass through the back-and-forth relationship that exists between the researcher as an author and the written words that the author creates. Daniel Levine's exploration in this volume of Edward Said's *late style* provides one way to make sense of this relationship, but another is to focus on the act of writing social criticism.

The Critical Theorists, the original source of Said's *late style*, were often social critics (Adorno and Horkheimer 1986; Horkheimer 1974 [1947]) but they also offered methodological critiques that have had a wide-ranging influence. In his short book, *Interpretation and Social Criticism*, the philosopher Michael Walzer (1987) provides a theoretical and methodological exploration of writing social criticism. Walzer's position is influenced by Critical Theory, although Antonio Gramsci's words appear more often, but Walzer states that he wants to argue his case in his own way, without too many references.

The point of his short book is to provide a brief outline of what social critics do and how they do it. He aims to set out a "theoretical preamble" that argues for social criticism to be best understood as a form of critical interpretation (Walzer 1987, p. vii). *Interpretation and Social Criticism* is ultimately a methodological text that reveals different vantage points from which positionality and reflexivity are addressed, acted upon and/or rejected. This focus is evident in that a central problem facing social criticism (by which he means political criticism or political commentary, that is to say normative work on matters of a socio-political character) is objectivity and distance. The question is whether or not distance is required to be a successful social critic, and if so, how much?

The book is a rejoinder to his critics who argue that moral philosophy, and thus any normative social and political commentary, must have distance and start with neutral positions that could be applied to anyone and that provide a basis for moral judgment if it is to have any chance of challenging current injustices. He identifies three ideal selves, each one representing a different positionality. The first is the subjective and angry critic who speaks directly from experience. The second is the detached observer, standing from a neutral position that enables objective moral judgement. The third, which follows from the second, is when self two is able to look back on self one but through the eyes of another. He writes:

> Criticism requires distance. But what does that mean? In the conventional view, critical distance divides the self; when we step back (mentally), we create a double. Self one is still involved, committed, parochial, angry; self two is detached, dispassionate, impartial, quietly watching self one. The claim is that self two is superior to self one, at least in this sense, that

his social criticism is more reliable and objective, more likely to tell us the moral truth about the world in which the critic and the rest of us live. Self three would be better still. This view is plausible, at least for self two, because we have all had the experience of remembering with embarrassment, chagrin, or regret occasions on which we behaved badly. We form a certain picture of ourselves (from a distance), and the picture is painful. But this is most often a picture of ourselves as we are seen, or think we are seen by people whose opinion we value. We do not look at ourselves from nowhere in particular, but through the eyes of particular other people—a morally but not an epistemologically privileged position. We apply standards that we share with the others to ourselves. Social criticism works differently: we apply standards that we share with the others *to the others*, our fellow citizens, friends and enemies. We do not remember with embarrassment; we look around with anger.

(Walzer, 1987, pp. 49–50)

This passage begins to reveal how the reflexive continuum works. Whereas I have in the past found myself critiquing Walzer (Baron 2009, 2015), I am here arguing with him.

As Walzer suggests, for the social critic there is always a process of reflexivity, of turning back not just onto oneself, but also onto the standards that are shared with others. Walzer's position is interesting for a few reasons. First, he suggests that a social critic necessarily requires a reflexive self-awareness, and only by having this awareness does social criticism become possible. Second, Walzer argues against the abstract objective positions that characterize much Anglo-American moral philosophy. This is the position represented by self two, the objective observer with the tools to apply moral truths as a standard for judgement. Third, Walzer, however, wants to claim that a social critic needs to be a member of the community that is the target of the social criticism. He argues against the view that if criticism is a form of interpretation by members of the community, it is necessarily conservative in that it "binds us irrevocably to the status quo—since we can only interpret what already exists—and so undercuts the very possibility of social criticism" (Walzer, 1987, p. 3). For Walzer, the opposite is the case. Social criticism involves reflexive interpretation. For him, self two cannot be a successful social critic and any success for self three is contingent on placing reflexivity centrally and in acknowledging the personal and emotional reasons for social criticism. Indeed, self three can only become a social critic once the individual positionality is reframed into one of membership and shared values. The reflexivity in this case is a step further than looking back onto oneself, and is also about looking back onto the shared values of the community that one belongs and contributes to. His point is that social criticism requires not just an acknowledgement of the positionality of the writer, but that this positionality is itself crucial for social criticism and that the conventional view requiring the social critic to have distance is flawed.

The requirement of distance is of course well known, and is similar to a naturalist methodological position that seeks to replicate the objective researcher who observes an independent object of study. I cannot think of any social science research text that makes this correlation between the role of being a social critic, a public intellectual who offers normative commentary on political and social matters, and that of a writer of normative social science, although the two are obviously related. Walzer's text is a challenge to the idea that distance is required to pursue social criticism, and by inference normative political commentary or normative social science more generally. In challenging the centrality of distance he is in effect arguing for the centrality of reflexivity. In identifying how reflexivity is a crucial piece of even ostensibly objective social criticism (as represented by selves two and three) Walzer is able to suggest that there is value in the social critic having an attachment to the society that he or she critiques. It is not just that Walzer cannot imagine a social critic totally removed (and thus imagined to be entirely objective and fair) from the society in which the criticism is directed. Rather, it is also that in the act of social criticism there is a personal investment.

The critic ultimately "wants things to go well ... He is not a detached observer, even when he looks at the society he inhabits with a sceptical eye" (Walzer 1987, p. 61). It is, consequently, not by accident that one of the models of the critic that "is one of us" (Walzer 1987, p. 39) is Ahad Ha'Am. The father of spiritual Zionism, Ahad Ha'Am called for a radical self-reflective Zionism by which the purpose of the Zionist project was not sovereignty or national-self determination in the model of the European nation-state, but a process of self-actualization by which Diaspora Jewry and world Jewry would become stronger and more connected to their Jewish identity. Ahad Ha'Am represents the style of the critic that has no pretensions of emotional detachment or of being an outsider. The social critic, in this view, is always an insider, a member of the community. "The outsider", writes Walzer (1987, p. 39), "can become a *social* critic only if he manages to get himself inside, enters imaginatively into the local practices and arrangements".

This position is controversial, as it suggests that only members can be effective social critics. Indeed, according to this position much of Walzer's work on just war should be irrelevant to those who fight wars. Walzer is not a member of the military community even though his normative writings on ethics and war are relevant for this community. Presumably, Walzer's citizenship in the country that is sending people into war is enough. Whatever the case may be, with the word "imaginatively" Walzer is saying that it is not membership as such that is the point, but instead the possibility that those to whom the social criticism is directed are able to listen to the criticism.

A successful social critic is able to articulate criticism in such a manner that those to whom it is relevant will not only hear the criticism but will listen to it. To offer social criticism ultimately brings one into contact with a community, and it is this contact that matters. What is required is a deep understanding of the community that is the recipient (or target) of the social critique, and that does not proceed from a presumed place of superiority. It is not membership but understanding and engagement with the community, and an acknowledgement of how both shape the author's own viewpoints and writing that matter for writing effective social criticism. The point is to jettison the pretext of neutral outsider status (and its presumed claims to methodological superiority and thus better knowledge production) through, at minimum, imagining how the social criticism will be understood and listened to, although not necessarily agreed with. The social critic needs to understand the community for whom the critique is directed and be respected by the community.

Indeed, a similar view was articulated to me by the retired Israeli general, one-time Director of the Strategic Planning Division in the Israeli Defence Forces and current research associate at the Institute for National Security Studies at Tel Aviv University, Shlomo Brom. As he said:

> How do you decide who to listen to? Well, as a human being obviously I will listen to those that are closer to my own thoughts. But let's remove this variable. Who do I listen more to? To people that I respect because I acknowledge their contribution to the common Zionist goal, to the common Jewish goal (they are the same for me, although others will not think so).
>
> ...
>
> Residency does matter in how seriously I will take involvement. But I apply the same criteria to Israelis as to Diaspora Jews. If you are deeply involved, know a lot about it, etc. I will take them seriously.
>
> (Brom 2013)

Some voices will take precedence, but he ends by saying that he will hear what almost anybody has to say about the Israeli–Palestinian conflict, although this does not mean he will take what they say seriously. They do not need to be Israelis, Diaspora Jews or Palestinians, but they do need to have a significant understanding that respects the views one would have as a well-informed and thoughtful member of the community. Indeed, it is not residency or even crude forms of membership that ultimately matter. Being well informed is what matters, hence why he would seriously listen to both Martin Indyk and Dennis Ross over Israeli taxi drivers who, as anyone who has ever travelled in an Israeli taxi will know, are self-proclaimed experts in all things, especially politics.

For the social critic, membership may enable empirical knowledge that outsiders might not have, but this does not mean that membership is necessarily required to be a social critic. By saying that the successful social critic is a member of the society, Walzer is making a democratic defence of social criticism insofar as the critic does not function as an outside expert who claims superior knowledge by virtue of a presumed claim to objectivity and distance. This discussion about membership brings us back to the question of critique and the Jewish Diaspora. Diaspora Jews are both insiders and outsiders insofar as Israel is concerned. By definition, Diaspora Jews are not Israelis and do not live in Israel. Yet as Jews they ostensibly have vested interests in wanting things to go well in Israel. Nevertheless, Israel is one of the greatest flashpoints of debate among world Jewry and in some ways is tearing the Jewish people apart (Kahn-Harris 2014). How to respond to Israel and what it means to support Israel are becoming increasingly contested subjects. However, Diaspora Jews have limited influence on Israeli government policy and Israeli public opinion. Certainly there is a disproportionate relationship between how important Israel is in the construction of contemporary Jewish identity and in the ability of Diaspora Jews to contribute to Israeli society and politics. Nevertheless, in words and in public criticism, in being a social critic, Diaspora Jewry can do something.

This influence is partly because of the logical connection that if Israel is the Jewish homeland and the State for all the Jews, then Jews in the Diaspora carry significant weight when it comes to questioning Israeli policy. In this way, Diaspora Jewish criticism is written by those who are invested in the outcome. More importantly is that in the process of critique, which as Walzer points out as a form of interpretation is necessarily reflexive and involves self-criticism, a kind of autobiographical normative commentary takes place. This is the second form of reflexivity, that of critique, but which is only possible after the first form, that of positionality, is taken. Reflexivity as critique is practised in public social criticism about Israel insofar as it is about theorizing the relationship that Diaspora Jews have or ought to have with Israel and about uncovering potential contradictions that inform this relationship. However, in making such a critique, Diaspora Jews participate in a reflexive autobiography whereby the process of critique both represents a self-awareness by the critic of his or her identity and related values, but also poses a challenge for others who share in this identity-based value. Hence Rabbi Creditor's (2013) piece about his refusal to continue apologizing for what Israel does or does not do. He wants other progressive Diaspora Jews to feel confident in not apologizing also.

Creditor, Ross and Samuel are all wanting to influence Diaspora Jewish thought about Israel and public debate about Israel, just as Butler argues for both a change in thinking and a change in what Jews say and do in regard to Israel. They all have different arguments, but on this topic they are all engaging in reflexive positionality, critique and action. In the process they also help shape their own identity as Diaspora Jews.

Creditor's "no apology" position is not unique, but it is interesting in that it is reflexive and critical, but the conclusion seems to close off further avenues for any kind of reflexivity. He does represent a reflexive response insofar as the argument is based on appreciating the role that Israel plays in the construction of Diaspora Jewry. The "no apology" is because of the associational view that connects Diaspora Jewry with Israel. Previously, he felt the need to apologize for the actions of the Israeli state. Now, he no longer does. His identity as a progressive rabbi was regularly being questioned by his support of Israel, but, finally, he had enough. In his view, Israel does all that can be reasonably expected of it and more while Hamas stockpiles weapons in mosques and transports them in ambulances. It was no longer tenable for him to apologize as a Jew when Jews are being attacked because of what Israel is doing in Gaza, and Hamas is not deserving of any moral respect that would accompany an apology. Moreover, his argument is clearly meant to provoke a reaction. It is a piece of social criticism by someone who is not embarrassed but angry. His critique is a contribution to debate about what Diaspora Jews should do. He is not just asking that his readers think and perhaps change their mind. He is also suggesting that they modify their conduct for the same reasons that he is. The feelings animating both paths are indicative of a reflexive connection between Creditor's sense of his Jewish self with what Israel does in the name of self-defence. It is also a reflexive and critical argument insofar as it is seeks to challenge other Jews to question their own moral commitments vis-à-vis Israel. Yet, in another sense it is decidedly uncritical. Israeli violence against the Palestinians is not beyond reproach simply because Hamas may do despicable things.

His example raises a difficult question: If all social criticism and normative research is reflexive, what about arguments that conclude in ways that refuse further self-critique and do not acknowledge let alone question the consequences of one's argument? Creditor seems to be guilty of both. His "no apologies" position closes off avenues for self-criticism and minimizes the responsibility of those who defend the use of violence. Yet, it is precisely on these issues that rest the most challenging questions for Diaspora Jews in regard to Israel. The controversy that often follows critiques of Israel, constructive or otherwise, follows from the characteristics of reflexive critique, even if the conclusions may appear to be un-critical. The act of social criticism about Israel is a flashpoint for controversy because it is a tipping point for how Jews in the Diaspora understand their identity, their sense of self as a Diaspora Jew. To engage in social and political criticism about Israel as a Diaspora Jew is to contribute to one's own sense of Jewish identity and how other Jews will understand the critic's identity as a Diaspora Jew. Attempts like Rabbi Creditor's to close down debate and limit self-critique paradoxically have the opposite effect by encouraging collective self-critique about how Diaspora Jews ought to relate to Israel.

However, what Creditor's position also reveals is that self-critique cannot go on indefinitely because at some point positionality will stop it. Positionality is not a never-ending abstract starting position or standing. It rests on a position, or perhaps multiple positions, and to self-critique indefinitely would be to regularly call oneself into question and lose any positionality in the process. An indefinite reflexive self-critique would eventually lead to such complete transparency of self that no positionality could be possible. None of this is to say that once a normative position is arrived at it cannot be changed. It is also possible to locate positionality by being dislocated. Positionality does not require a firm foundation, as Edward Said (1999) demonstrates in his autobiography *Out of Place*. Rather, the point is that the reflexive continuum itself is unstable, much like our individual and collective selves are in ongoing processes of self-discovery and self-creation.[6]

Conclusion

I have adopted a fairly broad account of reflexivity insofar as all normative research is reflexive. By reflexivity I mean a continuum of positionality, critique and practice. What I mean by this continuum is that reflexivity as a process involves not only the self-awareness that comes with positionality, but that it also requires intellectual confrontations that seek to stimulate reflection about one's own intellectual and political positions, that it involves a commitment to appreciating how one's research contributes to the subject of study and to the identity of the author, and that these three reflexive processes inform each other. The different categories of reflexivity (positionality, critique and practice) focus primarily on how reflexivity matters for the subject matter, for the research, and for the implications of research. What can be easily missed is how reflexivity also matters for the author, that in writing normative research the researcher engages in a process of reflexivity that is not only one of critique or practice, but also one of authorship. The process of reflexivity as a continuum helps reveal how reflexivity matters in the construction of the author's identity, how this identity in turn both shapes and is shaped by normative research, and that in being a normative researcher, a social critic, the author must recognize the ethics involved in claiming authority to speak out on behalf of an issue and for a community.

This understanding of reflexivity may not apply in all cases, but it is consistent with my own experiences as a researcher studying the Jewish Diaspora's relationship with Israel. This definition also reflects how debate about Israel within the Diaspora is important for defining individual and collective Jews' sense of self, and why debate about Israel is so contentious among Diaspora Jewish communities (Baron 2015).

Twenty years ago, the Canadian novelist Mordecai Richler (1994) provided his own reflexive auto-ethnographic work about his relationship with Israel. *This Year in Jerusalem* involves critique, introspection and reflexive commentary, historical research and sociological reporting. His book clearly reveals the reflexive experiences involved in Diaspora Jews thinking about Israel just as much as it is about his own journey growing up in Montreal, learning about Zionism, dreaming of moving to Israel, and of exploring Israel later in life. The book is about both Israel and the author as a Diaspora Jew.

Reflexive research brings a humanity to the writing process by realizing that in the process of writing one is not reporting but creating, and that in the process of creating the author also changes. It is precisely this uncertainty, of not knowing what the change will be and what it may lead to, that renders the role of critique so powerful. For in expressing an argument of social criticism, the author is creating a viewpoint that reflects back onto the writer as a revealing process in identity-affirmation and identity-creation. The social critic writes something because he or she cares. To care is, however, emotional, and thus opens up a potential vulnerability that is otherwise hidden in social science research. It is, for all of these reasons, that when Israel comes up as a matter of debate the topic is so controversial, because in the process of critique, a challenge is being made about the contemporary construction of Jewish identity.

In the process of exploring, analysing and critiquing Israel, Jewish identity and a lengthy history of what it means to be a Jew in the Diaspora in the age of Israel becomes questioned. This process can be challenging. It can remake Jewish identity and lay out question marks on topics that otherwise have been taken for granted. It can be frightening, which may be why the Jewish community has trouble knowing how to provide open spaces for critical voices to speak (Nemes 2014). It is also a reflexive process of writing security, of writing culture, and of writing identity.

Notes

1 Anthropological research in Israel Studies involve first-person reflections that explore identity and Israel, but also are examples of a reflexive methodology. See Jasmin Habib (2004) and Julianan Ochs (2011).
2 One example is in his nearly hour-long interview with Harry Kreisler as part of the "Conversations with History" series in 2008 (Waltz 2008).
3 This is not to discount the extensive religious debates that exist, but they are not my focus here and function in a different fashion than those with which I am concerned.
4 Just how wide the range of influences is, is evident in Emanuel Adler (2002).
5 This is especially true of Norman Finkelstein's work (Finkelstein 2005, 2012).
6 See for example the edited collection by Elliot (2011). Charles Taylor (1989), Anthony Giddens (1991) and Donna Haraway (1997) all provide significantly different accounts of the making and remaking of identity in different contexts. Michel Foucault (1990 [1978]) provides, arguably, an account of the unmaking and remaking of identity. Nevertheless, what they all share is the recognition that identity is never static and is constructed in a variety of different ways that are all too often open-ended. At issue here, however, is the extent to which identity-creation is self-driven through a process of reflexive authorship. This focus is influenced by Clifford and Marcus (1986) but it does not preclude the importance of others and of representation in identity formation.

References

Adler, E., 2002. Constructivism and International Relations. In: W. Carlsnaes, T. Risse and B.A. Simmons, eds, *Handbook of International Relations*. London: Sage, pp. 95–118.
Adorno, T.W. and Horkheimer, M., 1986. *Dialectic of Enlightenment*, 2nd edn. New York: Verso.
Anonymous, April 11, 2013, Interview in Tel Aviv.

Arendt, H., 1978. *The Jew as Pariah*. New York: Grove Press.

Arendt, H., 1994. *Eichmann in Jerusalem: A Report on the Banality of Evil*, revised and expanded edn. New York, London: Penguin Books.

Baron, I.Z., 2009. *Justifying the Obligation to Die: War, Ethics and Political Obligation, with Illustrations from Zionism*. Lanham, MD: Lexington Books.

Baron, I.Z., 2014a. Diasporic Security and Jewish Identity. *Modern Jewish Studies*, 13(2), 292–309.

Baron, I.Z., 2014b. The Jewish Question in the 21st Century: An Unanswered Question? Exploring the Jewish Question in Literature and Politics. *Jewish Journal of Sociology*, 56(1), 5–28.

Baron, I.Z., 2015. *Obligation in Exile: The Jewish Diaspora, Israel and Critique*. Edinburgh: Edinburgh University Press.

Beinart, P., 2010. The Failure of the American Jewish Establishment. *The New York Review of Books*, June 10.

Beinart, P., 2012. *The Crisis of Zionism*. New York: Times Books.

Biale, D., 2011. *Not in the Heavens: The Tradition of Jewish Secular Thought*. Princeton, NJ: Princeton University Press.

Booth, K., 1997. Security and Self: Reflections of a Fallen Realist. In: K. Krause and M.C. Williams, eds, *Critical Security Studies: Concepts and Cases*. London and New York: Routledge, pp. 83–120.

Brandeis, L.D., 1997 [1915]. The Jewish Problem and How to Solve It. In: A. Herzberg, ed., *The Zionist Idea: A Historical Analysis and Reader*. Westport, CT: Greenwood Press, pp. 517–523.

Brom, S., 2013. Interview in Tel Aviv, April 10 by Ilan Zvi Baron

Butler, J., 2012. *Parting Ways: Jewishness and the Critique of Zionism*. New York: Columbia University Press.

Campbell, D., 1998. *Writing Security: United States Foreign Policy and the Politics of Identity*, revised edn. Manchester: Manchester University Press.

Castells, M., 2010. *The Power of Identity*, 2nd edn. Oxford: Wiley-Blackwell.

Church, K., 1995. *Forbidden Narratives: Critical Autobiography as Social Science*. Philadelphia, PA: Gordon and Breach.

Clifford, J. and Marcus, G.E., 1986. *Writing Culture: The Poetics and Politics of Ethnography*. Berkeley, CA: University of California Press.

Creditor, M., 2013. I'm Done Apologizing, *The Jewish Daily Forward*, July 23. Available from: http://blogs.forward.com/forward-thinking/202924/when-anti-israel-looks-li ke-anti-semitism/?utm_source=Sailthruandutm_medium=emailandutm_term=Opiniona ndutm_campaign=Opinion [Accessed July 28, 2014].

Davies, C.A., 2008. *Reflexive Ethnography: A Guide to Researching Selves and Others*, 2nd edn. London: Routledge.

Der Derian, J., 2001. *Virtuous War: Mapping the Military-Industrial-Media-Entertainment Network*. Boulder, CO and Oxford: Westview Press.

Der Derian, J. and Shapiro, M.J., eds, 1989. *International/Intertextual Relations: Postmodern Readings of World Politics*. New York: Lexington Books.

Eisen, A., 1986. *Galut: Modern Jewish Reflection on Homelessness and Homecoming*. Indianapolis: Indiana University Press.

Elliot, A., ed., 2011. *Routledge Handbook of Identity Studies*. London, New York: Routledge.

Finkelstein, N.G., 2005. *Beyond Chutzpah: On the Misuse of Anti-semitism and the Abuse of History*. Berkeley, CA: University of California Press.

Finkelstein, N.G., 2012. *Knowing Too Much: Why the American Jewish Romance with Israel is Coming to an End*. New York and London: OR Books.

Foucault, M., 1990 [1978]. *The History of Sexuality: Volume 1: An Introduction*. New York: Vintage.

Geertz, C., 2000 [1973]. *The Interpretation of Cultures: Selected Essays*. New York: Basic Books.

Giddens, A., 1976. *New Rules of Sociological Method: A Positive Critique of Interpretive Sociologies*. New York: Basic Books.

Giddens, A., 1991. *Modernity and Self-Identity: Self and Society in the Late Modern Age*. Cambridge: Polity.

Goldberg, J.J., 1996. *Jewish Power: Inside the American Jewish Establishment*. Reading, MA and Harlow: Addison-Wesley.

Habib, J., 2004. *Israel, Diaspora and the Routes of National Belonging*. Toronto, ON: University of Toronto Press.

Hamati-Ataya, I., 2013. Reflectivity, Reflexivity, Reflexivism: IR's "Reflexive Turn" and Beyond. *European Journal of International Relations*, 19(4), 669–694.

Haraway, D.J., 1997. *Modest_Witness@Second_Millennium.FemaleMan©_Meets_Onco-Mours^{TM}: Feminism and Technoscience*. New York and London: Routledge.

Horkheimer, M., 1974 [1947]. *Eclipse of Reason*. London: Bloomsbury.

Inayatullah, N., ed., 2011. *Autobiographical International Relations: I, IR*. London: Routledge.

Jacobson, H., 2010. *The Finkler Question*. London: Bloomsbury.

Kahn-Harris, K. (2014). *Uncivil War: The Israel Conflict in the Jewish Community*. London: David Paul Books.

Kaplan, M.M., 1959. *A New Zionism*, 2nd enlarged edn. New York: The Herzl Press and the Jewish Reconstructionist Press.

Karpf, A., Klug, B., Rose, J., and Rosenbaum, B., eds, 2008. *A Time to Speak Out: Independent Jewish Voices on Israel, Zionism and Jewish Identity*. London: Verso.

Laqueur, W., 2003. *The History of Zionism*, 3rd edn. London and New York: I.B. Tauris and Co. Ltd.

Levine, D.J., 2012. *Recovering International Relations: The Promise of Sustainable Critique*. New York: Oxford University Press.

Myers, D.N., 2008. *Between Jew and Arab: The Lost Voice of Simon Rawidowicz*. Waltham, MA: Brandeis University Press.

Nemes, H., 2014. Feud Over Israel Erupts at Jewish Institutions, *The Jewish Daily Forward*, February 26. Available from: http://forward.com/articles/193400/feud-over-israel-erupts-at-jewish-institutions/?p=all [Accessed July 28, 2014].

Neufeld, M., 1993. Reflexivity and International Relations Theory. *Millennium—Journal of International Studies*, 22(1), 53–76.

Ochs, J., 2011. *Security and Suspicion: An Ethnography of Everyday Life in Israel*. Philadelphia: University of Pennsylvania Press.

Pew, 2013. A Portrait of Jewish Americans. *Pew-Templeton Global Religious Futures Project*, Washington, DC: Pew Research Centre.

Pianko, N., 2010. *Zionism and the Roads Not Taken: Rawidowicz, Kaplan, Kohn*. Bloomington, IN: Indiana University Press.

Podhoretz, N., 1974. Now, Instant Zionism, *New York Times*, February 3. Available from: www.nytimes.com/books/99/02/21/specials/podhoretz-zion.html [Accessed July 28, 2014].

Richler, M., 1994. *This Year in Jerusalem*. Toronto: Knopf.

Rodinson, M., 1973. *Israel: A Colonial-Settler State?* Translated by D. Thorstad. London: Pathfinder Press.

Rose, J., 2005. *The Question of Zion.* Princeton, NJ and Woodstock: Princeton University Press.

Rosenberg, W., 2001. *Legacy of Rage: Jewish Masculinity, Violence and Culture.* Amherst, MA: University of Massachusetts Press.

Ross, T., 2014. Gaza War Proves My Pro-Israel Dad Was Right. *The Jewish Daily Forward*, July 23. Available from: http://blogs.forward.com/forward-thinking/202669/gaza-war-proves-my-pro-israel-dad-was-right/?utm_source=Sailthruandutm_medium=emailandutm_term=Opinionandutm_campaign=Opinion [Accessed July 28, 2014].

Said, E., 1999. *Out of Place: A Memoir.* New York: Knopf.

Samuel, S., 2014. When "Anti-Israel" Looks Like "Anti-Semitism", *The Jewish Daily Forward*, July 28. Available from: http://blogs.forward.com/forward-thinking/202924/when-anti-israel-looks-like-anti-semitism/?utm_source=Sailthruandutm_medium=emailandutm_term=Opinionandutm_campaign=Opinion [Accessed July 28, 2014].

Schechter, S., 1959. Zionism: A Statement. *Seminary Addresses and Other Papers.* New York: Burning Bush Press.

Selzer, M., ed., 1970. *Zionism Reconsidered: The Rejection of Jewish Normalcy.* New York: The Macmillan Company.

Shain, Y., 1994–1995. Ethnic Diasporas and U.S. Foreign Policy. *Political Science Quarterly*, 811–841.

Shain, Y., 2007. *Kinship and Diasporas in International Affairs.* Ann Arbor: University of Michigan Press.

Shatz, A., ed., 2004. *Prophets/Outcast: A Century of Dissident Jewish Writing About Zionism.* New York: Nation Books.

Steele, B.J., 2010. *Defacing Power: The Aesthetics of Insecurity in Global Politics.* Ann Arbor: The University of Michigan Press.

Stirk, P.M.R., 2000. *Critical Theory, Politics and Society.* London: Continuum.

Taylor, C., 1989. *Sources of the Self: The Making of the Modern Identity.* Cambridge: Cambridge University Press.

Twersky, D., 2008. Interview by I.Z. Baron.

Urofsky, M.I., 1975. *American Zionism from Herzl to the Holocaust.* New York: Anchor Press/Doubleday.

Vital, D., 1990. *The Future of the Jews: A People at the Crossroads?* Cambridge, MA: Harvard University Press.

Waltz, K.N., 2001. *Man, the State, and War: a Theoretical Analysis*, revised edn. New York: Columbia University Press.

Waltz, K.N., 2008. *Theory, International Politics, Kenneth N. Waltz (Conversations with History).* Interview with Harry Kreisler. University California Berkeley. Available from: www.uctv.tv/shows/Theory-International-Politics-Kenneth-N-Waltz-Conversations-with-History-7386 [Accessed July 28, 2014].

Walzer, M., 1987. *Interpretation and Social Criticism.* Cambridge, MA: Harvard University Press.

Weber, M., 2011 [1949]. *The Methodology of the Social Sciences.* London: Transaction Publishers.

Whitfield, S.J., 2002. Declarations of Independence: American Jewish Culture in the Twentieth Century. In: D. Biale, ed., *Cultures of the Jews: Modern Encounters Vol. 3.* New York: Schocken Books, pp. 377–424.

10 Human Terrain Systems and reflexivity

Evgenia Ilieva

When the US Army launched the Human Terrain System (HTS) in late 2006, at first only as an experimental program, Afghanistan and Iraq were enveloped in the flames of a brutal insurgency. In Iraq alone, Oliver Belcher reminds us, "a wholesale distribution of death was underway", with hundreds of thousands of civilian casualties from Coalition and insurgent forces (2012, p. 259). Meanwhile, in the Afghan countryside, US and NATO warplanes were contributing to the steady rise in the number of razed villages and flattened homes. To stem the escalating violence, which was increasingly linked to the American military's inability to understand the "human terrain", a group of self-described scholar-warriors came together to revive the dead spirit of counterinsurgency (COIN)—a doctrine that had last been implemented with disastrous results in Vietnam (Belcher 2012, p. 258). The outcome of their collaboration was the Counterinsurgency Field Manual (FM 3–24), "a work of extraordinary influence, discussed on television and in newspapers and bought in quantities normally reserved for airport thrillers" (Burke 2011, p. 265).

Written to promote population-centric counterinsurgency as America's 21st century strategy in the global "war on terror", the manual makes a number of "radical" moves that have been deemed nothing short of progressive. Most notably, it advocates a shift from the Weinberger–Powell doctrine of overwhelming force towards the adoption of a non-kinetic, "soft power" approach that urges military personnel to make protecting the civilian their top priority. Adamant that damaging civilians' property as well as humiliating, killing, and otherwise harming the local population are actions that only serve to bolster the insurgency, the new doctrine places a premium on understanding and respecting the culture of the occupied territories as a way of winning over the population and preventing blowback. To this end, the manual directs US forces to live among the "host" nation's civilian population and engage in nation-building efforts that effectively expand the military's authority to encompass the diplomatic, political, economic, and humanitarian sides of warfare.

The rationale behind what has been dubbed a more "humane" and "culture-friendly" approach to war and imperial policing stems from a number of

Pentagon studies which revealed that it was a series of cultural faux pas and general cultural misunderstandings that had fueled the insurgencies in Afghanistan and Iraq (see Porter 2009). As a result, it seemed only natural that cultural knowledge, cultural awareness, and greater sensitivity towards non-Western worldviews and ways of life would come to be touted as essential for reducing the number of civilian casualties, defeating the insurgencies, and restoring peace. Enter the Human Terrain System program.

Designed to work in tandem with the US counterinsurgency campaigns in Iraq and Afghanistan, HTS was created to fill the perceived void of understanding facing the US armed forces. The centerpiece of the program are five-member Human Terrain Teams (HTTs) composed of social scientists, cultural anthropologists, and area studies experts who embed with combat forces in the two countries. Their purpose is to serve as cultural analysts and advisors to the military, helping brigade commanders "understand and deal with the 'human terrain'—the social, ethnographic, cultural, economic, and political elements of the people among whom a force is operating" (Kipp et al. 2006, p. 9). As Andrew Rubin notes, from the very outset the goal of HTS was to create an archive of knowledge about Afghan and Iraqi culture, which could then be used to supply military commanders with more effective ways to administer and manage the local populations (2012, p. 5). Its aim, in short, is to increase the effectiveness and success of COIN operations and prevent the kind of cultural mishaps (such as the "accidental" burnings of the Qur'an by American soldiers in Afghanistan) that might otherwise lead to violent backlash (Lucas 2012).

Together with the Field Manual's celebration of cultural difference, HTS received overwhelmingly positive coverage in the media and was heavily promoted as a program that saves lives. But due to its use of embedded scholars, the program very quickly became a subject of intense criticism, with questions being raised about the morality and professional appropriateness of academics collaborating with the military. While supporters of the program claimed that the use of embedded social scientists has helped reduce violent interactions between the military and the occupied populations, its harshest critics worried that HTS was nothing more than an intelligence gathering program, and that rather than reducing lethal operations the work of HTTs may in fact enable lethal targeting. Although there has been little empirical evidence to support claims made by parties on either side of the debate, it is instructive that much of the ensuing controversy surrounding HTS was framed around the perceived lethality of the program, its effectiveness or utility, and its capacity to "do good" for the local populations. Even more telling is that while the program employs social scientists from a variety of academic disciplines (including political scientists, sociologists, anthropologists, and area studies experts), it is members of the academic anthropological community who have been the most vocal participants in the debate and the most outspoken critics of HTS. This despite the fact that of the 417 HTS employees, only six possessed a PhD and another five an MA in anthropology whereas a substantial number of HTS recruits held degrees in political science and its various subfields (CEAUSSIC 2009, pp. 13, 60–61). It is somewhat surprising, therefore, that with a few exceptions, political scientists (and IR scholars in particular) have been notably absent from these debates.

This chapter revisits the controversy surrounding the Human Terrain program with the aim of reflecting on the theme of this edited volume. While the US military identified the discipline of anthropology as a main resource for its shift in policy towards COIN, it would be incorrect to portray the HTS debates as being solely "about" anthropology and anthropologists' attempts to defend the integrity of their discipline. Even a cursory look at the HTS scandal, its portrayal in the media, and the variety of emotionally charged responses it engendered reveals that the importance of these developments extends far beyond their ethical implications for anthropology. The HTS debates bring to the foreground important questions regarding the relationship between theory and practice, between academic knowledge and power, and the possibility of critical thought in times of war. In various ways, these questions bear upon the three dimensions of reflexivity explored in this volume: positionality, critique, and practice (Amoureux and Steele, Introduction to this volume). In a world where academic knowledge is frequently derided for being out of touch with "reality" and therefore "useless", HTS not only speaks to academics' desire to make their knowledge relevant and useful, but also to their aspirations to change the world for the better. Wanda Vrasti captures this nicely when she writes that HTS both "plays upon academics' greatest hopes" and simultaneously threatens to realize "their greatest fears" (Vrasti 2010, p. 88). Indeed, the tension between utilizing scholarly expertise in order to "save lives" and the possibility that this very knowledge can be appropriated in service of unintended, less benevolent ends assumes its maximal form in the Human Terrain System.

Aligning itself most closely with the approach to reflexivity that views it as a form and practice of critique—as a critical turning back "on the process of knowledge production, scholars themselves, and political agents and their practices" (Amoureux and Steele, Introduction to this volume)—this chapter uses the case of HTS as a way of reflecting on the meaning and possibility of critical thought in times of war, especially when critical thought itself has been shown to be complicit in and easily compatible with the spirit of war (Ansorge 2010). Drawing on Michel Foucault's late lectures on parrhesia (or truth-telling), the first part of the chapter revisits the controversy surrounding the Human Terrain System. A return to the debates engendered by the creation of this program presents an opportunity for the academy, and students of International Relations in particular, to rethink old questions regarding the role and responsibility of scholars, as well as the relationship between knowledge and power. Rather than look for modern-day counterparts of the ancient "parrhesiastes" and identify individual gestures of scholarly parrhesia,[1] the second part of this chapter draws on Foucault's lectures in order to highlight the way in which he grappled with and reconceived the relationship between philosophy and politics (or thought and action).[2] My broader aim is to show that the separation of ethics from politics that underpinned much of the HTS debates resulted from a prior, unacknowledged separation of theory from practice. This separation, in turn, served to occlude the central anxiety that lies at the heart of the academic enterprise and which is articulated so concisely by Vrasti. The chapter concludes by advancing the modest claim that instead of seeking to suppress and forget this constitutive anxiety we would be better served by remembering it, for it is this anxiety that keeps us in touch with our complicity in the structures of oppression we condemn.

Culturally sensitive war and its critics

If cultural awareness and counterinsurgency were not part of the Pentagon's vocabulary during the invasions of Afghanistan and Iraq, by 2007 they had not only become watchwords among members of the defense establishment but, in the words of one political scientist, they were now "part of the zeitgeist" (Kahl 2007). Some of the conditions that occasioned this demand for cultural knowledge have already been sketched in the introduction. In this section, I highlight the arguments that sought to make the case for the importance of culture in understanding conflict, as well as to bring to light the various critiques that emerged in the wake of the military's embrace of culture and its creation of HTS.

The case for HTS

One of the first statements announcing the shift from network-centric to culture-centric warfare can be traced to retired Major General Robert Scales. Speaking in front of the House Armed Services Committee in July 2004, Scales admitted that the "conflict [in Iraq] was fought brilliantly at the technological level but inadequately at the human level" (2004). He argued that the nature of contemporary war had changed, and that soldiers and Marines now found themselves "immersed in an alien culture, unable to differentiate friend from foe" (Scales 2004). In situations of asymmetric conflict where the enemy "adapts and finds ways to obviate the advantages of net-centric warfare", cultural awareness and knowledge of the adversary's motivations—or the "psycho-cultural" factors in war—become just as important as combat operations (Scales 2004).

To meet the cultural knowledge deficit, Scales called for a "cadre of global scouts, well educated, with a penchant for languages and a comfort with strange and distant places" (2004, p. 4), but deplored the lack of funds and institutional resources within the US military that could provide adequate cultural awareness training. In an article that appeared two years later, Scales went further by suggesting that success in the current wars could come only if the military enlisted the help of the social and human sciences. If the military's failures in Afghanistan and Iraq were human rather than technological, then the single most important objective in this new era of war is "to make better soldiers, more effective humans" (Scales 2006). To this end, Scales argued, "understanding and empathy will be important weapons of war". Given that traditional methods of warfighting had proved inadequate, Scales argued that social science could help the military identify and nurture those soldiers who possess an intuitive and innate ability to connect with other cultures. He would not have to wait long.

Where Scales laid out the argument for the shift towards culture-centric warfare in its broadest terms, it is Montgomery McFate who forcefully put forth the case for anthropological engagement with the military and gave some specificity to Scales's more vague pronouncements about the military's need for reform. McFate, who received a PhD in anthropology and would later become the public face of HTS, gained recognition amongst military circles for making it her "evangelical mission" to convince the Department of Defense that cultural knowledge of the adversary should be considered a national security priority (Packer 2006). McFate identified the discipline of anthropology as the untapped resource that could address the military's cultural knowledge needs, but was especially critical of anthropology's unwillingness to consider the merits of collaborating with the military. She argued that the cause for the cultural knowledge gap was "the almost total absence of anthropology within the national-security establishment" (McFate 2005b, p. 24).

To correct for this, she insisted that the national security apparatus needed to be infused with "anthropology across the board" (McFate 2005a, p. 47) because anthropology, on McFate's account, "is the only academic discipline that explicitly seeks to understand foreign cultures and societies" (2005b, p. 28). In an effort to mobilize her field in service of the US military, McFate called on anthropologists to set aside their colonial guilt and urged them to reclaim the historical role of their discipline as "an intellectual tool to consolidate imperial power at the margins of empire" (2005b, p. 28). McFate deplored the anthropological community's retreat to the Ivory tower after the Vietnam War and lampooned their turn towards postmodernism and the study of the "exotic and useless" (2005b, p. 28). Instead, she implored anthropologists to emerge out of their self-imposed isolationism, abandon their tendency towards "self-flagellation" over the discipline's shameful past as the "hand-maiden of colonialism", and urged them to step boldly out into the world, become publicly engaged, and use their knowledge to inform policymaking. If successful counterinsurgency depends on attaining a "holistic, total understanding of local culture", McFate reasoned, it was precisely anthropological expertise that could provide an understanding of the culture of the occupied societies. The best way to go about this would be to embed anthropologists with army units. The program created to facilitate this endeavor was the Human Terrain System. Largely motivated by an attempt to correct the strategic failures of the US military in Iraq and Afghanistan, the logic and rationale behind the program would come under attack almost immediately.

Critiques of HST

While the idea of using embedded anthropologists and other social scientists seemed to make sense and resonated quite well with some members of the military establishment, the anthropological community received it with outrage. Indeed, criticisms from anthropologists have been numerous and diverse. Soon after the first Human Terrain Team deployed to Afghanistan in February 2007, a group of anthropologists formed an ad-hoc association called Network of Concerned Anthropologists (NCA) that launched a searing critique of the Human Terrain System. Seeking to promote an ethical anthropology, the NCA vehemently opposed participation in counterinsurgency work and what they perceived as the dangerous militarization of anthropology. By late October of the same year, the executive board of the American Anthropological Association (AAA) issued a preliminary statement denouncing the HTS project as an "unacceptable application of anthropological expertise". Two years later, the Association's ad hoc Commission on the Engagement of Anthropology with the US Security and Intelligence Communities (CEAUSSIC) produced a lengthy final report that unequivocally condemned HTS, specifically on ethical grounds. The report expressed concern that deploying anthropologists to war zones to collect information for the military violates four core principles of AAA's code of ethics: the directive to do no harm, the requirement of obtaining voluntary informed consent, the obligation to other anthropologists, and the requirement of openness and full disclosure to the human subjects anthropologists study (CEAUSSIC 2009, pp. 70–71).

In a statement delivered before the US House of Representatives and signed by over 700 anthropologists, in 2010 the anthropological community, spearheaded by NCA, reiterated its charge that HTS constitutes an "inappropriate and ineffective use of anthropological and other social science expertise".[3] The statement called on Congress to halt government support for HTS and cancel plans for the program's expansion. In addition to condemning HTS as a program that betrays the fundamental principles of anthropological ethics, the anthropologists listed three additional reasons in support of their rejection of the HTS project: lack of evidence that HTS saves lives; the program is dangerous; and it wastes taxpayer money. The death of three social scientists[4] while on assignment with HTS adds another layer of complexity to the debate over the program and was put forth as an additional reason for anthropology's rejection of HTS. Citing these fatalities, anthropologists condemned the program as "dangerous and reckless". Not only did it place academics in harm's way, complaints from field commanders revealed a concern that protecting HTT members puts the lives of soldiers at risk.

As this admittedly brief survey illustrates, the bulk of the criticisms leveled at HTS have been framed around the program's failure to follow AAA's professional ethics code. Interestingly, and perhaps unintentionally, these critiques revealed more about the anxieties of anthropologists than about the

Human Terrain System itself. David Price, one of the founding members of NCA, argued that HTS and "culturally informed counterinsurgency" more generally "present three types of problems for anthropology: ethical, political, and theoretical" (Price 2011, p. 179). While he acknowledged the importance of critiquing HTS on ethical grounds, Price noted that the framing of the HTS debates almost exclusively as a matter of professional ethics meant that the political issues involved in conducting anthropological research for a nation engaged in "global military expansion" remained largely unaddressed (2011, p. 31). Price urged anthropologists to "resist limiting their critiques to issues of ethics and bring the political issues of domination to the fore of their critiques" (Price 2011, p. 31). For Price, it is misleading to view the Human Terrain System as a "neutral humanitarian project" (2011, p. 96). Rather, he insists that HTS is nothing other than "an arm of the US military and is part of the military's mission to occupy and destroy opposition to US goals and objectives" (Price 2011, p. 96). Price sees HTS as a program aimed at facilitating "a gentler form of military domination" and argues that it would be dishonest to view it as anything other than an agent of conquest (2011, p. 96).

Maximilian Forte and Hugh Gusterson have likewise pointed to the limits of confining the HTS debates solely within the realm of ethics. Gusterson in particular argues that while the ethical critique of the program resonated quite powerfully within anthropology, it failed to have an impact outside the discipline where it only "mystifie[d] liberals who oppose the war but are drawn to the rhetoric of cross-cultural understanding and harm reduction that shrouds HTS" (Gusterson 2011, p. 16), and was altogether dismissed in military circles (Gusterson 2011). Along the same lines, Forte (2013) observes that ethical critiques of HTS often boiled down to the "minutiae of research procedures: were identities of informants kept confidential, where did the information go once it left the hands of the civilian researcher, was informed consent possible in a war zone, etc.". As Forte (2013) points out, the focus on these kinds of issues left out some very important questions. For example, if HTS could be shown to be ethical on all of these fronts, would that mean that scholars should support the program or at the very least, suspend their criticism of it?

Although Forte notes that the focus on ethics and on defending the integrity of anthropology had succeeded in diverting attention away from some fundamental transformations occurring in academia (such as the overproduction of PhDs, the rise of part-time adjunct positions and the attendant erosion of job security), he nevertheless leaves this avenue of inquiry open for others to explore. Like Price, Forte similarly suggests that the separation of ethics from politics that structured the HTS debates ultimately resulted in a lack of critiques of imperialism. Forte captures this when he observes that "the critique of HTS was tied to a critique of militarism, which was itself conceptually and theoretically divorced from critiques of imperialism" (2013). As someone who has commented on the HTS controversy almost from the beginning, Forte concluded one of his last articles on the subject by reflecting that the debate around HTS had largely been a diversion, that its real purpose was to domesticate academics, and interpreted the end of debate against HTS as an end of critiques of empire. Had scholars pursued the critique of empire, Forte suggests, they would have easily seen that rejecting HTS on the basis of its perceived lethality would do little to discredit the program. Imperialism functions quite well and is at its best, Forte reminds us, precisely when it does not kill (2013).

If the bulk of the objections to HTS centered on the program's potential lethality, other critics took the opposite stance and sought to show that HTS is a feeble, ineffective program that could never do any real harm even if it wanted to. These critics observed that, contrary to its claims and the way it has been portrayed in the media, the HTS program is incompetently staffed and deploys individuals with little to no prior regional or cultural knowledge of Iraq and Afghanistan, nor with the necessary linguistic skills to communicate with the local populations. Critics have used this argument to undermine the program's claims to its effectiveness in smoothing relations between the invading army and the occupied populations, and to call into question its potential to reshape the struggle between the US forces and the insurgency. Precisely for these reasons, Hugh Gusterson has argued that the modus operandi of HTS (in its current incarnation) is such that it makes "good applied anthropology all but impossible" (2011). For Gusterson, the difference between an independent anthropologist and a social scientist embedded with HTS amounts to "the difference between anthropology and a form of glorified tourism". According to Gusterson, the knowledge and understanding produced by HTTs amounts to nothing more than "data scraped off the surface of daily life". As such, it can never be as rich and nuanced as that produced by a bona fide anthropologist.

Gusterson's argument, which can be read as clear defense of anthropology and anthropological knowledge, relies on an implicit separation of knowledge into "good" and "bad" varieties. In this respect, Gusterson's remarks can be interpreted, in line with many of his colleagues' critiques, as an attempt to protect the discipline of anthropology (and the knowledge it produces) from its abuse by power for the purposes of war. If the problem for the Network of Concerned Anthropologists was how to resist the Department of Defense's appropriation of anthropological knowledge, the solution was to frame their response to this challenge through a defense of anthropology's research methods and a concomitant critique of HTS's research practices. In this context, Barkawi and Ansorge (2011) have argued that by showing that HTS fails to follow the code of ethics, that it does not abide by accepted standards of research, and that HTS research lacks academic integrity, anthropologists in effect produced a bifurcation knowledge, splitting it into "pure" and "fallen" knowledge. They argue that such splitting is the product of a type of thinking that sees "truth" (which can only be derived from the application of correct "method") as allied with peace, and that to militarize anthropological knowledge is necessarily to corrupt it (Barkawi and Ansorge 2011, p. 6).

In a recent article examining the military's appropriation of academic knowledge and the operationalizing of this knowledge in the form of smart cards and field manuals, Barkawi and Ansorge are right to point out that critiquing HTS and the military on the basis of their failure to be proper anthropologists and social scientists misses the mark, and only marginalizes the academy leaving "the field to politicized think tanks and 'mercenary social scientists'" (Ansorge and Barkawi 2014, p. 22). The implication of such critiques is that if the military did "good research" everything would be different. As the authors show, however, this is not the case. They conclude on a somber note, arguing that the rise of contemporary information technology disables the kind of content-based critique that has been the dominant form of criticism of the cultural turn in the war on terror. The authors raise the question of what would constitute effective critique of the wartime use of academic knowledge, and suggest that one could start by studying the operations of power, i.e. how power puts academic knowledge to use in times of war and imperialism (Ansorge and Barkawi 2014, p. 22).

In a recent engagement with the HTS controversy, Maja Zehfuss (2012) draws attention to an important point of convergence between critics and supporters of HTS. Zehfuss is correct when she observes that what unites both proponents and critics of the program is a shared belief in what she calls the "fantasy of protection". HTS was sold to the public as a program that saves lives. This was part of its seductive appeal. As Zehfuss notes, some of the program's critics recognized "the powerfully seductive logic of the claim that cultural knowledge may reduce levels of violence" (2012, p. 183), but few have been willing to examine this logic in depth. Instead, critics of the program rushed to foreclose this line of inquiry by suggesting that this seduction is illusory and is entirely unsupported by evidence. While this may have been the case, such criticisms obfuscate the fact that both opponents and supporters of HTS construct their arguments on the basis of the conviction that they can save lives. HTS bids scholars to join the program and help save lives. Critics of HTS enjoin scholars to refuse participation in the program as such participation may endanger lives. Both subscribe to what Zehfuss calls "an extra-political ethics rooted in our obligation and—by implication—capacity to protect others" (2012, p. 187). Reduced to its simplest terms, the HTS controversy presented academics with the following dilemma: to participate, or not to participate? These are the questions.

Zehfuss moves us towards a more nuanced understanding of the HTS debate when she suggests that the conflict between proponents and critics of the program reproduces the bifurcation of thinking on the ethics of war that pitches just war scholars against pacifists: "The former are at their most disturbing when they are most well intentioned, failing to appreciate how construing certain uses of political violence as morally required facilitates war, while the latter aim to stand apart from war in order not to facilitate it" (Zehfuss 2012, p. 186). Zehfuss demonstrates very well how the anthropological reliance on a generalized ethics hides from view the way in which such an ethics can help legitimize the use of force in the first place (2012, p. 187). She also reminds us to be wary of the temptation to equate non-participation in larger structures of oppression with the absence of complicity in maintaining such oppression. Instead, she wishes to see us inhabit the space of tension that opens up once we acknowledge that our actions "confront the terrible possibility of causing harm to others; yet, they also hold the promise of creating something positive with them" (Zehfuss 2012, p. 186).

Zehfuss's insightful discussion not only helps us see the limits of invoking ethics to negotiate this tension, it also helps us become aware of another bifurcation that has organized and sustained the HTS debates. Taking a cue from the work of Zehfuss, I suggest that we can begin to understand the bifurcation of knowledge that structures the anthropologists' critique, and the separation of ethics from politics that undergirds their rejection of HTS, as the result of a prior, implicit and unexamined separation of theory from practice that underpins much of these arguments. The upshot of a renewed focus on the relationship between theory and practice can help bring about the "day of reckoning" for anthropology and the social sciences more generally that Maximilian Forte hoped for. He writes that instead of reexamining their own built-in conventions that support the status quo or at least that facilitate the continued functioning of some of its parts, the social sciences externalized and deflected these debates (Forte 2013). In other words, Forte observes, critique of the HTS program was externalized whereas it could have, and should have, been directed internally as well. Against this context, a reexamination of the relationship between theory and practice helps us return to the question posed by Zehfuss, namely, why benignly intentioned social scientists might be drawn in by the promise of improving war, despite the evident danger of playing 'into the worst tradition of social science as a "handmaiden of colonialism"' (2012, p. 184). While Zehfuss suggests that such decisions remain unintelligible, the late work of Michel Foucault examined in the next section points us to a different answer, one that highlights the constitutive anxiety that binds the benignly intentioned scholar to the state.

Theory, practice, and critique

In what were to become the last two lecture courses of his life, *The Government of Self and Others* and *The Courage of the Truth*, Foucault returns to ancient Greece to explore the historical development of parrhesia or the activity of speaking truth to power. In tracing the genealogy of this term, Foucault's broader project is to recover and reactivate a spirit of critique as the enduring task of philosophy. Foucault accomplishes this via an original reinterpretation of the relationship between philosophy and politics (or thought and action).[5] Through a rich and insightful analysis of letters traditionally ascribed to Plato, Foucault challenges the accepted understanding of philosophy as *logos* (discourse) and argues that philosophy must also be understood as *ergon* (action).

The most important part of Foucault's discussion of Plato is dedicated to Letter VII as this letter reveals to us "the other side of political thought", namely, "political thought as advice for political action, political thought as the rationalization of political action, much more than as the foundation of right or as the foundation of the organization of the city" (2010, p. 215). From the perspective of this chapter, Foucault's analysis of the letter is also significant because it reveals to us a Plato who, much like the contemporary academic, is tormented by the desire to be more than just "hollow words", more than just someone engaged in detached and disinterested contemplation of the world. Structured around the anxiety that philosophy (and the philosopher) should not be confined solely to the realm of *logos*, Letter VII articulates the central tension that resides at the heart of the academic enterprise.

Letter VII comprises three important elements. In it Plato offers readers an account of his attempt to become *ergon* as embodied in his failed mission in service of Dionysius II—the tyrant of Syracuse—and seeks to justify his decision to advise a despot; he offers readers a sort of political autobiography in which he describes his two great disappointments with Athenian politics; and finally, he provides an explanation of what it means for him to give advice and act as counselor to a prince (Foucault 2010, pp. 223–224). Foucault isolates a number of passages in Letter VII for close consideration in order to offer a fuller sketch of philosophy's relation to politics. Reflecting on the conditions that need to obtain for philosophy to realize itself in action, Foucault identifies three circumstances that are absolutely essential if philosophy and the philosopher are to be more than just *logos*. First, Foucault suggests that philosophy should not be addressed to everyone, but only to those who wish to listen and follow it (2010, p. 230). A philosophical discourse that only "protests, challenges, shouts, and rages against power and tyranny" would not be philosophy (Foucault 2010, p. 235). Here we can already discern that for Plato the relationship between philosophy and politics should be one of "intersection, pedagogy, and identification of the philosophizing subject and the subject exercising power", rather than of violence and direct confrontation (Foucault 2010, p. 287).

Second, philosophy will only realize itself in action if "it is accompanied, sustained, and exercised as a practice and through a set of practices" (Foucault 2010, p. 245). Philosophy, Foucault suggests, comes into being through the constant and difficult work of the self on itself. As such, it is best understood as a series of practices "through which the subject has a relationship to itself, elaborates itself, and works on itself" (Foucault 2010, p. 242). Third, for philosophy to find its reality it must engage in a "permanent practice of knowledge" (Foucault 2010, p. 255), but this is a knowledge which cannot be learned and passed on through *mathemata*, i.e., through the books or formulae by which ready-made knowledge is transmitted from a teacher to a disciple. The implications of this claim for the role of the philosopher are instructive: "if ... philosophy cannot be practiced and learned in the form of mathemata, then a philosopher's role will never be that of a lawgiver, it will never be present as a system of laws to which the citizens must submit for the city to be governed properly" (Foucault 2010, pp. 252–253). To acquire philosophical knowledge one must choose to live with philosophy and this, in turn, entails a continuous work of the self on itself.

Although these conditions were absent in Syracuse, Foucault's analysis of Plato's letters allows him to formulate an alternative relationship between politics and philosophy. As he writes, "the relations between philosophy and politics are not to be sought in the possible ability of philosophy to tell the truth about the best ways to exercise power … But philosophy has to tell the truth […] not about power, but in relation to power, in contact with it, in a sort of vis-à-vis or intersection with power" (Foucault 2010, p. 286). On Foucault's understanding, "philosophy must not define for politics what it has to do; [rather,] it has to define for the governor, the politician, *what he has to be*" (2010, p. 295; my emphasis). What is at stake here, then, is nothing less than the very mode of being of the political agent. As such, we can begin to see that the task of the philosophical parrhesiast consists in showing the sovereign that he must first be able to govern himself (to master himself) before trying to govern others (Foucault 2010, p. 303).

While Foucault's analysis of Plato's letters allows him to reconceptualize the relationship between thought and action, it is important to keep in mind that Plato's mission to Syracuse is ultimately an example of the breakdown of parrhesia and illustrates Plato's failed attempt to serve as advisor to a tyrant (and to cultivate a potential philosopher king). Regardless of the philosopher's failed confrontation with politics, the central theme that Foucault extracts from Plato's letters is that philosophy (as parrhesia) and political practice must exist in a correlation, but they must never coincide (2010, p. 289). Just as philosophy should not tell politics what to do, politics should not look to philosophy for its own justification. Rather, philosophy must confront politics in order to find its reality for itself in that confrontation. As Foucault concludes, philosophy has to exist as a "permanent and restive exteriority with regard to politics" (2010, p. 354). What this means is that the task of philosophy (and philosophical parrhesia) is not simply to reveal the "conditions of possibility of present political problems", but to challenge, confront, and problematize political life (Koopman 2013, p. 28). On this view, we can easily see the overlap between reflexivity and the type of critical thought associated with parrhesia.

Remembering philosophy's anxiety

The brief reconstruction of Plato's excursion to Syracuse undertaken in the previous section had as its goal a twofold task: to highlight Foucault's attempt to grapple with the relationship between thought and action; and to show readers, via Foucault's help, a Plato deeply disturbed by the prospect of being just "vain *theoria*" (Bourgault 2011). As an account of the failure of the transformative promise of parrhesia, Letter VII throws into doubt the possibility of an effective critique of power. At the same time, however, it succeeds in bringing to light an important element that is often forgotten in discussions regarding the role and responsibility of scholars. Structured around Plato's, and by extension philosophy's, anxiety that it should be more than just "mere words", Letter VII reminds us that a similar anxiety lies at the heart of the contemporary academic enterprise. It is this anxiety that helps us understand why, in the words of Maja Zehfuss, "benignly intentioned social scientists" might be seduced by the promise of improving a war, despite being aware of all the dangers that attend such an endeavor. Whereas Zehfuss (2012) suggests that such decisions remain unintelligible, Foucault's late work allows us to formulate a different answer by pointing to the constitutive anxiety that binds the benignly intentioned academic to existing forms of power.

Foucault's discussion of Letter VII and his concern to redefine the link between *logos* and *ergon* helps us understand the nature of the HTS debates in yet another way. Whereas supporters of the program (such as McFate) took the side of *ergon* by encouraging scholars to take part in a program that promised to save lives, opponents of HTS, through their condemnation, rejection, and refusal to participate in HTS, took a stance on the side of *logos*. The severing of the connection between *logos* and *ergon*, I argue, is one of the main factors that not only rendered most critiques of the program ineffectual, but also prevented opponents of the program from examining their own complicity in reproducing structures of oppression and injustice. Indeed, the anthropologists' refusal to join HTS did not bring the program to a halt as HTS was able to find recruits from other academic disciplines. Nor did the refusal to participate put an end to empire.

Following Judith Butler's (2001) reflections on the meaning of critique, we may understand the outright rejection and condemnation of HTS as a "withdrawal from praxis". In an essay titled "What is Critique? Reflections on Foucault's Virtue", Butler sets up a distinction between criticism and critique. Where the former limits itself to "fault-finding", the latter is best understood as a suspension of the rush to "judgment". Butler suggests that we can understand Foucault's notion of critique along similar lines. The point of critique, writes Butler, is not to evaluate whether the object of critique is good or bad, but rather to ask how knowledge and power work together to preclude us from asking certain questions and prevent us from "thinking otherwise." In the rush to judgment, Butler argues, we are prevented from exposing the "constellations of power" and interrogating our investment and complicity in them. Referencing the work of Theodore Adorno, Butler explains that "the very operation of judgment serves to separate the critic from the social world ... a move which deratifies the results of its own operation, constituting a 'withdrawal from praxis'" (Butler 2001). Where judgment leads to closure, Butler (and Foucault) advocate a suspension of judgment so as to prevent such closure.

If the separation of *logos* from *ergon* produced a closure of debates about HTS, we might speculate that restoring the previously severed linkage between the two would lead, if not to a more effective critique of power, then at the very least to a more nuanced understanding of phenomena such as HTS. But even with the recovery of the connection between *logos* and *ergon*, we are tempted to suspect that the outcome, as Plato's failed mission to Syracuse attests, might still produce closure. If, as Joseph Ansorge has shown, "power inoculates itself against critique by appropriating critical intellectual resources" (2010, p. 376), it becomes difficult to articulate a critical standpoint that does not draw on those very practices that it is subjecting to critique. An alternative option may be to try a different starting point. Ansorge and Barkawi (2014) pursue this path when, rather than launching a direct critique of power, they instead attempt to study the operations of power in the context of the military's cultural turn by showing how "power puts knowledge to use in times of war and imperialism" through the production and dissemination of smartcards and field manuals (2014, p. 22).

In a similar vein, Brent Steele suggests that the main purpose of academics is not so much to oppose power through parrhesia (or a discourse of counterpower) as it is "to tell the story" of the developments that "unfold in front of us and collectively analyze the testimony of that which happens before us … to document and faithfully capture both history's events and context" (2010a, p. 131). Such an approach is also exemplified in *Human Terrain*, a film by James Der Derian, Michael Udris and David Udris. The documentary rejects the easy "for" or "against" binary that characterizes the stances of proponents and opponents of HTS. As Der Derian explains in a recent interview, by allowing different voices on all sides of the debate to speak, the film aimed to expose viewers to the complexity of the issues involved with the hope that the audience could decide on their own how to respond to the vexing problem regarding the appropriateness of academic collaboration with the military (Stavrianakis and Selby 2012a).

And yet such approaches that reject the separation of knowledge and power, and refuse the stance of detached external observers, may still leave us wanting as they seem to leave power undisturbed. The film *Human Terrain* has been criticized for leaving out a range of criticism (such as poor management, incompetence, sexual harassment allegations) in its portrayal of the HTS debates. While the film exposes viewers to a variety of perspectives on the HTS program—from its harshest critics to its most adamant supporters— in the end it leaves viewers at a loss as to the filmmakers' take regarding the appropriateness of academic collaboration with the military. Der Derian has defended the film's approach by stating:

> I am … opposed to making an authorial statement that would pretend to trump or exhaust all other meanings that an audience might attach to the film. That goes against all my post-structuralist beliefs about the role of the author or director. I've been asked this question many times and try to remain agnostic on the political aspects of it. I obviously have a viewpoint that comes out in other ways, in my other writings; but I don't want

people going into the film thinking they're going to get a pat answer to this question. We allow everyone to speak, including the most vocal opponents from the Network of Concerned Anthropologists as well as the founders of HTS. I'm not ducking the question; I'd rather leave it for the audience to decide on their own.

(Stavrianakis and Selby 2012b, p. 63)

Although I am somewhat sympathetic to this response, I worry that it leaves its own authorial stance unexamined. I also worry that the continuous work of exposing the functioning and organization of power as exemplified by the work briefly mentioned above not only runs the risk of leaving us without much guidance and direction, it also keeps in place the very institutions it seeks to critique. If critique as suspension of judgment is what might allow us to avoid blanket categorizations of programs like HTS as either "good" or "bad", the lingering question is whether a return to some form of evaluative judgment after suspension is possible and necessary. This question takes us back to our original starting point: philosophy's, and by extension, academics' anxiety.

If we turn to Foucault's attempt to redefine the relationship between philosophy and politics via his study of Plato's letters we may be led towards the conclusion that academics, if they are not to be merely *logos* but also *ergon* should participate in programs such as HTS. While this is not a conclusion that I am willing to defend, this seems to be the position that is left open to us if we agree, with Zehfuss, that we cannot simply stay out of things, that our actions are capable of effecting political reality and that every time we act we "confront the terrible possibility of causing harm to others". And yet, as Zehfuss reminds us, our actions "also hold the promise of creating something positive with them" (2012, p. 187). I cannot resolve the aporia that opens up once we accept that we are *of* the world and not simply detached spectators of it, and once we withstand the temptation to condemn HTS on the basis of professional ethics. Nevertheless, I would like to suggest that if there is any value to Foucault's re-articulation of the relationship between philosophy and politics, it lies in the fact that it urges us to remember the central anxiety that resides at the heart of the academic enterprise: the obligation to be not merely *logos* but also *ergon*. Perhaps it is only by remembering this anxiety and the aporias it produces that we can keep in touch with our complicity in the very injustices we condemn.

But rather than conclude that *logos* and *ergon* necessarily come together as participation in HTS, why not suggest, instead, that academics should simply engage in these debates? If the general disengagement from the HTS controversy on the part of IR scholars points to the broader depoliticization of the discipline, it is not immediately clear that a recommendation to take HTS more seriously would do much to change the contours of the debate, put an end to the program (or others like it), and significantly alter the course of American imperialism. My concern is that such a recommendation, paradoxically, would do more to conceal our affiliation with the structures of power we bow down to, desire to be part of, and that enable our work. In the context of the brazen militarization of academic knowledge, where military manuals make nods towards cultural relativism, plagiarize from critical social theorists, and the military's "cultural turn" itself enacts the very same reflexivity that was welcomed as a breath of fresh air promising to "assuage the world's violent nightmares" (Caraccioli and Hozic, Chapter 7 in this volume), I share the sentiment of scholars who believe that it is no longer sufficient to quote some critical theorist in order to make a politically meaningful statement or intervention (Ansorge 2010). In this context, contemporary critique, no matter how self-reflexive, seems to be quite compatible with the very power it seeks to chasten and subvert.

What, then, are the implications of this chapter for the broader project undertaken in this volume? Why revisit the HTS debates when there is such little hope for change? What, if any, is the value added of using Foucault in attempting to think about the promises and dangers of reflexivity? In so far as reflexivity can be understood as "an approach to grappling with thought and action, which requires but moves beyond self-awareness" (Amoureux, Chapter 1 in this volume), Foucault's analysis of the relationship between *logos* and *ergon* illustrates such a reflexive stance and performs a twofold task. It urges us to remember the central anxiety that resides at the heart of the academic enterprise, and it shows us that, despite our best intentions, our interventions (be they practical or theoretical) in world politics can do little to prevent political disasters. Does this mean, then, that reflexivity is a false promise? While I hesitate to conclude on a pessimistic note, I do worry that the so-called "reflexive turn" in IR is performing the same function for IR as the critique of HTS did for anthropology—it is simply a way of safeguarding the integrity of the discipline and of concealing the myriad ways in which reflexivity works to legitimize power.

We live in a world created by the violent entanglements of imperialism, colonialism, and the numerous institutions that work to destroy human life. Perhaps our task as students of international relations can only be to recall the sadness of history, expose the wounds of IR, and acknowledge that we can do little more than provide the justifications for existing power structures even as we work to expose our complicities in them. Only in doing so may we hope to catch glimpses of that beauty and resilience that, like Tolstoy's thistle in *Hadji Murat*, still adorn the earth amidst all the destructiveness and cruelty of man (Tolstoy 2009). It is to this end that I have sought to revisit the HTS debates in this chapter.

Notes

1 For such an account, see Brent Steele's work (2010a, 2010b).
2 In its attempt to grapple with the relationship between theory and practice, and the real-world ramifications of the theories we use, the chapter overlaps with a number

of contributions to this volume (see Amoureux (Chapter 1), Steele (Chapter 3), Ish-Shalom (Chapter 4), and Levine (Chapter 5)).
3 See www.ncanthros.org.
4 Michael Bhatia, Paula Lloyd, and Nicole Suveges.
5 For the sake of avoiding repetition, I treat the conceptual pairs "philosophy and politics", "theory and practice", "thought and action" as interchangeable.

References

Ansorge, J.T., 2010. The Spirits of War: A Field Manual. *International Political Sociology*, 4, 362–379.

Ansorge, J. and Barkawi, T., 2014. Utile Forms: Power and Knowledge in Small War. *Review of International Studies*, 40(1), 3–24.

Barkawi, T. and Ansorge, J., 2011. Monographs, Manuals and Smart Cards: Power, Knowledge and Form in "Small Wars". Paper presented at the ISA Annual Convention, Montreal, Quebec, Canada, March 16–19.

Belcher, O., 2012. The Best Laid Schemes: Postcolonialism, Military Social Science, and the Making of U.S. Counterinsurgency Doctrine, 1947–2009. *Antipode*, 44(1), 258–263.

Bourgault, S., 2011. Putting Bullshit on Trial: The Closing Chapter of Michel Foucault's Voyage to Antiquity. *Theory & Event*, 14(1).

Burke, J., 2011. *The 9/11 Wars*. London: Allen Lane.

Butler, J., 2001. What is Critique? An Essay on Foucault's Virtue. Available from: http://eipcp.net/transversal/0806/butler/en [Accessed August 9, 2014].

CEAUSSIC, 2009. *Final Report on the Army's Human Terrain System Proof of Concept Program*. Available from: www.aaanet.org/cmtes/commissions/CEAUSSIC/upload/CEAUSSIC_HTS_Final_Report.pdf [Accessed August 9, 2014].

Forte, M., 2013. The End of Debates About the Human Terrain System? February 17. Available from: http://zeroanthropology.net/2013/02/17/the-end-of-debates-about-the-human-terrain-system [Accessed August 9, 2014].

Foucault, M., 2010. *The Government of Self and Others: Lectures at the Collège de France 1982–1983*, translated by G. Burchell. London: Palgrave Macmillan.

Gusterson, H., 2011. Human Terrain Teams and the Militarization of Anthropological Conscience: A Meditation on the Futility of Ethical Discourse. Paper presented at the ISA Annual Convention, Montreal, Quebec, Canada, March 16–19.

Kahl, C., 2007. COIN of the Realm. *Foreign Affairs*, November/December. Available from: www.foreignaffairs.com/articles/63035/colin-h-kahl/coin-of-the-realm [Accessed August 9, 2014].

Kipp, J. et al., 2006. The Human Terrain System: A CORDS for the 21st Century. *Military Review*, September–October, 8–15.

Koopman, C., 2013. *Genealogy as Critique: Foucault and the Problem of Modernity*. Bloomington, IN: Indiana University Press.

Lucas, G.R., 2012. Military Ethics and Cultural Knowledge, March 20. Available from: www.e-ir.info/2012/03/20/military-ethics-and-cultural-knowledge/ [Accessed August 9, 2014].

McFate, M., 2005a. The Military Utility of Understanding Adversary Culture. *JFQ: Joint Force Quarterly*, 38 (Summer), 42–48.

McFate, M., 2005b. Anthropology and Global Counterinsurgency: The Strange Story of their Curious Relationship. *Military Review*, March–April, 24–38.

Packer, G., 2006. Knowing the Enemy. *The New Yorker*, December 18. Available from: www.newyorker.com/magazine/2006/12/18/knowing-the-enemy [Accessed August 9, 2014].

Porter, P., 2009. *Military Orientalism: Eastern War Through Western Eyes*. New York: Columbia University Press.

Price, D., 2011. *Weaponizing Anthropology: Social Science in Service of the Militarized State*. Petrolia and Oakland, CA: Counter Punch and AK Press.

Rubin, A., 2012. *Archives of Authority: Empire, Culture, and the Cold War*. Princeton, NJ: Princeton University Press.

Scales, R.H., 2004. Statement of Major General Robert Scales, USA (ret.). Testifying before the House Armed Services Committee on July 15, 2004. Available from: www.au.af.mil/au/awc/awcgate/congress/04-07-15scales.pdf [Accessed August 9, 2014].

Scales, R.H., 2006. Clausewitz and World War IV. *Armed Forces Journal*, July. Available from: www.armedforcesjournal.com/clausewitz-and-world-war-iv [Accessed August 9, 2014].

Stavrianakis, A. and Selby, J., 2012a. *Militarism and International Relations: Political Economy, Security, Theory*. New York: Routledge.

Stavrianakis, A. and Selby, J., 2012b. War Becomes Academic: Human Terrain, Virtuous War, and Contemporary Militarism. An Interview with James Der Derian. In: A. Stavrianakis and J. Selby, eds, *Militarism and International Relations: Political Economy, Security, Theory*. New York: Routledge.

Steele, B., 2010a. *Defacing Power: The Aesthetics of Insecurity in Global Politics*. Ann Arbor: University of Michigan Press.

Steele, B., 2010b. Of "Witch's Brews" and Scholarly Communities: The Dangers and Promises of Academic Parrhesia. *Cambridge Review of International Affairs*, 23(1), 49–68.

Tolstoy, L., 2009. *The Death of Ivan Ilyich & Other Stories*, trans. Pevear and Volokhonsky. London: Vintage.

Vrasti, W., 2010. Dr. Strangelove, or How I Learned to Stop Worrying about Methodology and Love Writing. *Millennium—Journal of International Studies*, 39 (1), 79–88.

Zehfuss, M., 2012. Culturally Sensitive War? The Human Terrain System and the Seduction of Ethics. *Security Dialogue*, 43(2), 175–190.

11 Reflexive diplomacy

Huss Banai

At first glance, diplomacy may seem constitutionally averse to reflexivity.[1] Premised as it is, in conventional terms, on the representation of sovereign interests in international society, diplomacy's realm appears to begin where internal dialogue and reflection end. This is due to the commonplace identification of diplomatic practice as a political tool of statecraft, and hence the privileging of state interests and the ensuing power struggles among them in international society. As famously stated by the American diplomat, George Kennan, "Government is an agent, not a principal. Its primary obligation is to the *interests* of the national society it represents, not to the moral impulses that individual elements of that society may experience" (1985, p. 206, emphasis in the original).[2]

Indeed, to demand much else of diplomacy above its basic commitments to the advancement of sovereign interests would be, as countless diplomats since at least the advent of early modern European international society have routinely proclaimed,[3] to confuse life among fellow citizens with that of cohabitation with strangers. In the foundational works in diplomatic studies, diplomacy has thus been conceived of as a political mechanism for managing relations—whether artfully or not—between interest-bearing collectives through official representatives (Nicolson 1939; Satow 1979 [1917]). This begs a rather obvious question, then: how could a practice so implicated in the seemingly impersonal imperatives of survival and power politics ever be expected to account for its own actions and reflect on their consequences?

Mercifully, the actual practice of diplomacy has always been at variance with this rather rigid conception. More than just a means for the exertion of sovereign interests, diplomacy is in essence a testament to the desire for reconciliation between competing interests, values, and identities in international politics. For there would be no need for representation, negotiation, forging of compromise, and dialogue—i.e. the essential functions of diplomacy—if the sole purpose of diplomacy was the projection of sovereign interests (in the latter case, power would simply sweep all that obstructs its path toward total domination). It is more accurate, therefore, to conceive of diplomacy as a practice concerned with determining the terms of coexistence between a range of actors, stakeholders, and audiences in international society, whose interests, values, and identities are as varied in their orientations as they are in their consequences. As Costas Constantinou puts it in simple terms, "If politics is about *the organization of life in common*, diplomacy is about *how we can live together in difference*" (2013, p. 142, emphasis in the original). This conception not only takes account of the underlying pluralism of international life in all its sound and fury, but more importantly it also distinguishes diplomacy as a particularly *moral* intervention and practice in relations among peoples—as both individuals and collectives—in world politics.[4] It is through diplomatic reciprocity and dialogue that "conditions of separateness" (Sharp 2009) and sources of myriad "estrangements" (Der Derian 1987) are first identified and further elaborated on. Diplomacy facilitates these exchanges by recognizing the equal standing of individuals and collectives as sovereign participants.

This deeper and more expansive conception of diplomacy, however, further compounds the relationship between diplomacy and reflexivity. The recognition that the domain of diplomacy includes ever-expanding categories of interests, belief systems, and modes of life, makes it that much harder to devise an inclusive framework for how the diplomatic method might account for the efficacy of its interventions across a wide range of issue areas that involve a multitude of actors. To be sure, the referent object of diplomacy will always vary from one domain (inter-state, intra-state, global, inter-cultural, inter-personal, etc.) to another; but this reality need not detain us. For the diplomatic method in each case is premised on the same *understanding* of the world. This, as Paul Sharp explains:

> is an understanding that privileges the plural character of human experience, the plural character of the ideas and arguments by which people make sense of their lives both to themselves and to others, and it treats as axiomatic the proposition that relations between groups are different from those within them.
>
> (Sharp 2009, p. 10)

Any attempt at self-examination by either diplomats or students of diplomacy must begin by engaging with these essential characteristics of diplomatic understanding. Moreover, it is precisely because so much pain, suffering, and exclusion can be inflicted in the name of diplomacy that reflexivity has a significant role to play as a check against abuses of power and privilege in world politics. In this sense, reflexivity in the practice of diplomacy consists of examining and shortening the distance between the core principles of diplomatic understanding and the purported imperatives of *raison d'état, raison de système, raison de souverain,* or *raison de peuple*. At the core of this exercise is of course the relationship between morality and politics in international society.

The purpose of this chapter is to hazard an explanation as to what reflexivity in diplomatic practice would entail. It does so by offering a substantive account of the moral basis of diplomacy in contrast to purely political accounts of diplomacy predominant in positivist approaches in both International Relations (IR) theory and Foreign Policy Analysis (FPA). I argue that diplomacy is made possible in the first place because of *the recognition of equal standing* and the *moral imperative of coexistence* among sovereign entities. Far from disavowing the political functions and practical concerns of diplomacy, I wish to substantiate them by revealing the underlying moral reasons that impel sovereign entities to engage in diplomatic relations with each other. Simply put, diplomacy is a political mechanism grounded in the moral principles of equal respect for sovereignty and coexistence in international society. Much has been written on and speculated about the political functions of diplomacy, but the moral grounds on which diplomacy stands have merely been hinted at in a select few works within the school of thought most directly concerned with the systematic study of diplomacy, namely the English School of IR. My basic aim in this chapter is to change the subliminal status of such discussions, and to elaborate on a more substantive approach to the study of diplomacy.

This chapter proceeds in three parts. In the first part, I demonstrate how the tendency to view diplomacy as especially resistant to ethical considerations is due to a singularly political conception that underlies most conventional accounts of diplomacy in the IR literature. The second part of the chapter offers a moral basis for the political functions of diplomacy with reference to key neglected works in the diplomatic studies canon, most notably works by English School theorists. Here I will argue that the moral basis of diplomacy provides diplomats and students of diplomacy with sufficient resources for self-examination of both diplomatic discourse and practice. The last part explores the implications of this substantive account for the relationship between reflexivity and diplomacy. The aim of this section is to elaborate on the intricate linkages between diplomacy and other institutions of international society such as war, the great powers, international law, balance of power, and sovereignty, as per the English School's conceptual framework.

Purely political conceptions of diplomacy

"Manipulative, and hence secret", observed one-time American diplomat and political scientist, Paul S. Reinsch, during the interwar period, "diplomacy is in fact the most complete expression of the purely political factor in human affairs" (1922, p. 15). Meant as an antidote to the excessively cheerful outlook of Woodrow Wilson's "Fourteen Points"—which, among other moralistic proclamations, first and foremost called for diplomacy among the great powers to "proceed always frankly and in the public view"—Reinsch's pithy, if not also dramatic, rejoinder aimed to recast diplomacy as the logical extension of human nature, which, to him, was at its core "purely political". Indeed, even a cursory look at the historical development of modern diplomacy among states seems to support this view. Established as it was in the early Renaissance environment of seemingly perpetual warfare among the Italian city-states, diplomacy, as Garrett Mattingly wrote, was born out of "a series of maneuvers for political advantage". As both the human and material costs of war rose, "Success depended less upon the brutal shock of massed force than upon vigilant and agile politics. The diplomat was needed to supplement the soldier" (Mattingly 1955, p. 62).

This emphasis on prudence in the exercise of *raison d'état* was first articulated in the writings of Niccolò Machiavelli, chiefly in *The Prince* (1998a [1532]) and *Discourses on the First Ten Books of Titus Livy* (most commonly known as *The Discourses*) (1998b [1531]). In Machiavelli's terms, since the fortunes of any polity are contingent upon a set of circumstances beyond the control and designs of any one person or group of persons, the interests and hence actions of the state are mainly driven by the principle of "necessity" (1998b, I.6, p. 23). Under these conditions, states do what they must in order to preserve their interests and ensure their survival, however expansionist or isolationist their dispositions. The prudent management of an array of domestic and foreign relations, carried out by the prince and other authorized agents of the state, therefore, constitutes the idea of diplomacy in Machiavelli's formulation. Diplomacy is the means by which the *political* implications of "necessity" are handled. It is not undertaken out of concern for the interests of others and their sovereign prerogatives, but rather necessitated by the double imperatives of self-preservation and advancement in the ever-turbulent domain of international politics.

Indeed, if war, as Clausewitz famously observed, was the continuation of politics by other means, then the European practices of early modern diplomacy were but variations on the tactics and strategies employed by the commanders on the battlefield. For it was in this period when diplomats began to gain a reputation as essentially ruthless and deceitful executors of raison d'état. As Machiavelli advised the prince, "A prudent lord ... cannot observe faith, nor should he, when such observance turns against him, and the causes that made him promise have been eliminated" (1998a, p. 69). Prudence, he insisted, required a realistic appreciation of the imperfections of human nature: "And if all men were good, this teaching would not be good; but because they are wicked and do not observe faith with you, you also do not have to observe it with them" (Machiavelli 1998a, p. 69).

According to Harold Nicolson, this advice was on the whole regrettable, especially in terms of its corrupting implications for the behavior of Renaissance-era diplomats:

> The diplomatists of the sixteenth and seventeenth centuries often provided ground for the suspicion from which their successors have unjustifiably suffered. They bribed courtiers; they stimulated and financed rebellions; they encouraged opposition parties; they intervened in the most subversive ways in the internal affairs of the countries to which they were accredited; they lied, they spied, they stole. An ambassador in those

days regarded himself as "an honorable spy". He was sincerely convinced that private morality was a thing apart from public morality. Many of them imagined that "the official lie" bore out slight relation to individual mendacity.

(Nicolson 1960, pp. 43–44)

Nicolson's critical take has, in turn, rightly been ridiculed by some scholars as too sweeping and selective a reading of Machiavelli's prescriptions. For instance, as G.R. Berridge has argued, whether born out of a desire "for a reputation for integrity" or the necessity to demonstrate "good faith" in negotiations with other states, Machiavelli's observation that "international obligations only endure as long as the conditions that generated them ... was a condition of diplomacy and, for that matter, of the emerging international law itself" (2001, pp. 546–548). In this regard, the prudent pursuit of sovereign interests has been, and can also be, politically efficacious.

But gleaning the essence or chief characteristics of human nature is necessarily a speculative endeavor, since for every instance of political calculation or a self-serving pattern there are innumerable corresponding instances of self-sacrifice and good will. Indeed, it was precisely this point that many interwar period (and later) theorists and historians of diplomacy were insisting upon. The aims of this particular line of criticism were twofold. First, to redeem the image of the diplomat in the public imagination as a dutiful servant of power and a fundamentally mendacious agent. Neither depictions were true since the practice of diplomacy was now carried out by professionals of impressive "intelligence and tact" whose ultimate responsibility was to ensure peace and stability (Satow 1957). The second and more important purpose behind the reaction to the Machiavellian line of argument was to demonstrate how, through the proliferation of legal norms and commercial contacts among nations, diplomacy could be put at the service of moral aims (Nicolson 1960, pp. 48–49). Far from grounding diplomacy in morality, however, the point here is that when combined with "common sense" and exercised prudently, diplomacy can serve moral ends as well. As Nicolson pointed out, "Diplomacy is not a system of moral philosophy ... Thus it is not religion which has been the main formative influence in diplomatic theory; it is common sense" (1960, p. 50).

Moving forward and beyond the postwar period, accounts of the nature and functions of diplomacy in the latter half of the twentieth century, while drawing attention to the social construction of diplomatic norms and practices, have nonetheless retained the political conception of its foundations. Thus, writing in the classical English School tradition, Hedley Bull conceived of diplomacy as a primary institution of international society with five important political functions: (1) "facilitate[ing] communication between political leaders of states and other entities in world politics"; (2) "negotiation of agreements"; (3) "the gathering of intelligence or information about foreign countries"; (4) "minimization of the effects of friction in international relations"; and (5) "symbolizing the existence of the society of states" (Bull 1977, pp. 163–166). For Bull and other adherents of the classical English School view, the central dilemma at the core of the institution of diplomacy was the rather glaring gap between the political imperatives of security in the society of states and the moral aims of justice and equality in world society of humankind. As Herbert Butterfield observed with palpable trepidation:

> Recent Years have seen an important development of the role of what might be called the "moral factor" in international relations; and it is strange that in this period, when armaments have become formidable beyond all precedent, actual weapons have lost some of their relevance and power, and an imponderable factor has acquired unusual importance. It is this which is altering (or which ought to alter) the character of twentieth-century diplomacy more than anything else.
>
> (Butterfield 1966, p. 190)

Of course, Butterfield's observation about the increasing weight of the "moral factor" in international politics has proven to have been prescient, as advances in international humanitarian law and the greater emphasis on human security have redefined the sources of international legitimacy and served to restrain arbitrary exercises of state power. But this too was less a result of the recognition of the moral basis of diplomacy than merely an astute observation about the evolution of international society itself.

As the preceding reflections show, the lack of inquiry into the moral sources of diplomacy is generally due to a misunderstanding concerning the distinction between the moral conduct of foreign policy and the moral basis of diplomacy. Mainstream accounts of diplomacy eschew any discussions of morality because at bottom they regard any interactions between states to be conditioned by national interests and power political considerations. Therefore, any injection of moral principles into the conduct of foreign policy is at best naïve and at worst a recipe for utopian thinking and hence messianic behavior in international society. Diplomacy in this telling, then, represents fundamentally political sets of practices that are premised on the preservation and advancement of sovereign interests in world politics. This view, exercised in moderation, may indeed be correct, and at any rate represents the predominant view among contemporary statesmen and diplomacy's practitioners. But appreciating what necessitates the practice of diplomacy is an entirely different matter altogether, which touches very significantly upon the moral status and privileges of sovereignty in international politics.

Post-positivist ambiguities

Post-positivist approaches to international relations, on the other hand, have been more conscious of this distinction, and on the whole more cognizant of its significance for the study and conduct of diplomacy. Key among the works by interpretivist and post-classical scholars that I wish to highlight (though by no means the following exhaust the list) are Adam Watson's historical account, *Diplomacy: The Dialogue Between the States* (1983), James Der Derian's genealogical study, *On Diplomacy* (1987), and Costas Constantinou's ideationist account, *On the Way to Diplomacy* (1996). My aim in examining this representative sampling is to demonstrate how while post-classical approaches self-consciously begin with a distinction between the conduct of diplomacy and the conditions that necessitate its practice, they too nevertheless neglect the moral sources behind diplomacy. The reasons for this are different in each case, as I will attempt to show below, but the implications are roughly the same across cases: diplomacy is born out of and regenerated through its key function, mediation.

For Watson, diplomacy was necessitated by the mere fact of the "plurality" of nation-states in international society: "It arises out of the coexistence of a multitude of independent states in an inter-dependent world' (1983, p. 15). Since states' welfare and sense of identity relied a great deal on the welfare and sense of identity of other states in international society, according to Watson, it was necessary to devise a method for communication between states. Thus: "This dialogue between independent states—the machinery by which their governments conduct it, and the networks of promises, contracts, institutions and codes of conduct which develop out of it—is the substance of diplomacy" (Watson 1983, p. 14).

Watson's conception, with its emphasis on "plurality", "coexistence", and "inter-dependence", signals a major shift away from the classical view that accorded priority to the dictates of power and hence conceived of diplomacy as a linear practice. This is not to say that his account overlooks the importance of power imbalances in international society; rather, that it takes seriously the power of persuasion in the dialogue among nations to achieve coexistence. The underlying condition of pluralism in international society, Watson therefore concluded, makes diplomacy "a sensitive instrument, designed to register and work on the smallest shifts in the attitudes of states to one another, and ... well equipped to detect the attempt to use its mechanisms to intensify rather than mitigate conflicts of interest" (1983, p. 66). This conception certainly touches on the important moral principles (i.e. autonomy and reciprocity) at play in interstate relations, but Watson is careful not to label them as such. The hesitation is perhaps understandable given the aforementioned conflation of morality and foreign policy, which had been the norm at the time of his writing. But it is perhaps more accurately the reflection of Watson's hard separation between the diplomat's realm of "private morality" and a given state's "public interests" (1983, p. 153).

Der Derian's post-classical approach, however, is resolutely clear about any such distinctions. Offering a "genealogical" conception, he defines diplomacy "as a mediation between estranged individuals, groups or entities" in world politics (Der Derian 1987, p. 6). Estrangement is a key descriptor here, for it speaks to the underlying condition of "alienation" from which states and non-state entities seek to emancipate themselves "through systems of thought, law, and power" (Der Derian 1987, p. 7). Mediating estrangement, in other words, draws upon a variety of sources, political as well as moral, precisely because it operates at different levels of analysis and with varying layers of human relations. As such, diplomacy is practiced differently across time and space since it speaks to the prevailing norms, rules, and relations of power that govern societies large and small. We cannot speak of diplomacy as a singular practice, therefore, but must conceive of it as a "cultural" phenomenon (Der Derian 1996). In this sense, diplomacy is very much implicated in the moral and political orders of the day itself. It is not a freestanding conception that only exists to facilitate communication and resolve needless frictions, but rather a representation of the (un)equal conditions of coexistence in international and world society. For these reasons, diplomacy can be both emancipatory and alienating at the same time. If carried out by the great powers that are endowed with the political and economic capacities to shape other entities' preferences, diplomacy can be deeply alienating. But when it is exercised for the purposes of reflective understanding and solidarity, it has the potential to emancipate estranged peoples.

Der Derian's reworking of the classical conception of diplomacy offers a novel opening for an inquiry into the moral foundations of diplomacy. Unburdened by positivist presuppositions about the nature of international society, it shifts the focus from the official interests and policies of states to the identities of human collectivities with political standing and claims to morality in world politics. Indeed, this is the same framework that also enables Constantinou's (1996) conception of diplomacy as simply the effort to negotiate new identities and shape new meanings in international society. Diplomacy, in other words, is as much conditioned by the prevailing values and norms of international politics, as it is an intervention designed to reconstitute those norms and values. Together, these views seek to draw attention to the very subjective character of human relations in world politics. But given their respective recognition of mediation and negotiation as the essential modes of diplomatic interventions, it is unclear why the principles enabling the practice of diplomacy would be anything but objective. Diplomacy is indeed practiced and experienced differently depending on the prevailing power structure and value systems inside which it operates, but this does not mean that the exercise itself—i.e. the very act of recognition, dialogue, and negotiation—is not constituted by a separate set of principles and values that are precisely meant to function independently of the prevailing interests and value structures in international society.

To sum up: while the strict separation between morality and politics has been much disputed by a variety of positivist and post-positivist perspectives in the discipline of IR,[5] the realist inheritance on the political foundations of diplomacy has received far less scrutiny. In fact, even as the scope of inquiry into the theories, methods, and practices of diplomacy has expanded (Jönsson and Langhorne 2004), almost no direct attention has been paid to the moral considerations that necessitate its practice in the first place. To be sure, there have been illuminating exceptions along the way in works by critical and English School scholars (Watson 1983; Der Derian 1987; Constantinou 1996, 2013; Sharp 1999, 2009; Neumann 2005, 2012; Bjola 2013); but here, too, the chief concern has been to expand the scope of inquiry into the subject matter of diplomacy as a political mechanism, not its moral antecedents.

This rather hard separation between politics and morality, however, rests largely on a mistaken understanding of morality that confuses it with utopian moralism. To observe that diplomacy is based on a set of moral principles is not to endorse diplomatic moralism. The former simply refers to moral principles (e.g. mutual respect and dialogue) on which the political institutions and practices of diplomacy are based, whereas the latter notion signifies the pursuit of moral ends (e.g. spreading democracy, ensuring human rights, eradicating inequality, etc.) through diplomacy. This distinction is an important one, for the confusion about the sources of diplomatic legitimacy has obscured judgments about the nature, scope, functions, and effectiveness of diplomacy. The net result of these tendencies has been a noticeable decline in both the normative coherence of diplomacy as a subjective enterprise (Constantinou 2013) and the explanatory power of diplomatic theories of international politics (Bjola 2013). As the proliferation of so-called "hyphenated diplomacies" (Sharp 2009, p. 75) amply demonstrates, diplomacy has become a catch-all term signifying any and all non-violent human interaction. Understanding the moral sources of diplomacy would help to establish a firm basis not only for grasping what renders a given action or set of interactions "diplomatic", but also for envisioning possible pathways and obstacles in the way of reflexivity in the practice of diplomacy.

The moral conception of diplomacy

As the preceding discussion makes clear, the plural condition of international politics provides the impetus for accounts of diplomacy to shed their purely political presumptions about the sources of diplomatic representation and dialogue between sovereign entities. Diplomacy's political functions, I should like to argue, are a manifestation of much deeper moral considerations regarding the normative aim of coexistence and cooperation in international society. The moral basis of diplomacy in international society, then, rests on the principle of *respect for sovereignty*. What makes diplomacy possible in the first place is the awareness on the part of sovereign entities that recognition of their sovereign interests, rights, and prerogatives is premised on their reciprocal acknowledgement of other sovereign entities' interests, rights, and prerogatives, however disagreeable or burdensome they may be. This is not to suggest that a "harmony of interests" is achievable in every case; to be sure, some interests and claims are inherently irreconcilable and may lead to conflict. But such differences and disputes are secondary questions to be resolved by diplomacy itself, and therefore not a challenge to the claim about its moral foundations. In short, my argument here is that the practice of diplomacy is necessitated by the moral recognition of respect for sovereignty as a basis for coexistence in international society.

Respect for sovereignty, it is important to note from the outset, is not limited to nation-states—it includes all entities with sovereign status in international society (i.e. states and non-state actors endowed with rights and prerogatives before international law). Sovereignty, of course, has a double meaning as both an organizing principle of international politics and a highly contingent social construction of norms in international society (Krasner 1999). The moral conception of diplomacy is particularly useful because it demonstrates why and how interaction between sovereign entities in international society is never delimited by the arbitrary political dictates of state sovereignty. States and non-state actors are always compelled to understand and explain one another, and it is this recognition, more than any other principle, that speaks to the moral underpinnings of diplomacy. Alas, this point is lost on most observers of modern diplomacy. A laudable exception has been Sharp's much-needed theoretical intervention, *Diplomatic Theory of International Relations* (2009). His is a major contribution, not least because it lays out clearly the normative and moral bases of diplomacy that amount to what he calls a "diplomatic understanding" of world politics:

> Those whom we regard as diplomats occupy positions between human communities that make possible a specifically *diplomatic understanding* of the world. It is an understanding that privileges the plural character of human existence, the plural character of the ideas and arguments by which people make sense of their lives both to themselves and to others, and it treats as axiomatic the proposition that relations between groups are different from those within them ... *Thinking diplomatically*, therefore, privileges the maintenance of relations—peaceful relations at that—over whatever those relations are purportedly about.
>
> (Sharp 2009, p. 10, emphasis in the original)

Diplomacy seeks to resolve the irreducible variety of estrangements, misunderstandings, and conflicts that the "plural character of human existence" stands precisely as a testament to. In other words, it is the recognition of pluralism (of values, interests, and identities, which may clash or complement each other) that gives diplomacy its moral character. Simply put, in the absence of such recognition there would be no need, no purpose, no possible benefit to diplomacy. This is not to say that all values, interests, or identities are of equal weight—again, the merits of such claims are themselves subjects of discussion through diplomacy—but rather that their mere existence is cause for further reflection and dialogue. In this regard, "thinking diplomatically" is really a reference to the moral imperative of reflective thought and dialogue that are the essential characteristics of diplomacy.

Why does recognition of pluralism amount to an essentially moral, as opposed to a purely political, conception of diplomacy? My argument, derived from highly influential tracts in moral and political philosophy (Hampshire 1984; Rawls 1996; Larmore 2008), is the acknowledgement of the irreducible difference in values, interests, and identities in international society. This is tantamount to the Kantian recognition of human beings as ends in themselves, and not as means to certain political aims or ideals. Diplomacy stands as a symbol of the moral recognition of sovereign agency, whether the resolution of differences in values, interests, and identities would eventually be to the satisfaction of all involved or not. Diplomacy, then, to paraphrase Larmore, engages directly the "distinctive capacity" of participants in a dispute as sovereign agents.

Now, it may well be objected to that this moral conception overlooks the outsized role of power in determining the preconditions leading to, and the outcomes of, diplomacy. This is not an insignificant objection. The history of international society can certainly be viewed in terms of the ebbs and flows of powerful currents propelled by sheer material and even ideational advantage. But such a view does not in fact undermine the argument about the moral basis of diplomacy, for the recognition of difference in international society is not the same as the recognition of the *equal validity or worth* of claims arising from such difference. Indeed, an elegant elaboration of this point can be found in Watson's (1983) much overlooked meditation on the subject:

> Conflicts of interests are a major subject of diplomacy, which can func-
> tion effectively only when the necessary level of understanding exists
> between the parties to the dialogue about the maintenance of the system
> as a whole and about the rules for the promotion of their separate inter-
> ests within the system. The diplomatic dialogue is thus the instrument of
> international society: a civilized process based on awareness and respect
> for other people's points of view; and a civilizing one also because the
> continuous exchange of ideas, and the attempts to find mutually accep-
> table solutions to conflicts of interest, increase that awareness and
> respect. This civilizing tendency visibly does not prevent diplomacy from
> being perverted and misused—its methods lend themselves to duplicity.
> But the bias towards understanding other points of view and other needs,
> towards a search for common ground and a resolution of differences, is
> unmistakably there.

> (Watson 1983, pp. 20–21)

Unlike the moral principle of equal respect for persons in democratic theory and practice, the principle of respect for sovereignty that underlies diplomacy merely attests to the fact that difference begets understanding, which in turn begets dialogue in the form of diplomacy. It is this moral precept, more than anything else, which accounts for the imperative of contact and dialogue between sovereign entities in international politics. To the extent that attempts at understanding fail to impress themselves upon the cold and often profligate aims of politics, moreover, does not diminish their moral quality—in fact, it attests to the complex relationship between morality and politics.

Appreciating the moral basis of diplomacy is important because it enables us to become aware of the seemingly unbridgeable distance between the moral impulse to understand and the political temptation to exploit the knowledge gained through understanding for the purpose of fortifying sovereign interests. This awareness, in turn, compels us to reconfigure the functions of diplomacy in such a way so as to minimize the possibilities for exploitation and alienation between the powerful and the weak. In other words, the central challenge of diplomacy is to construct a sustainable framework for understanding and dialogue that is immune from the temptations of power politics (Constantinou and Der Derian 2010). The moral conception of diplomacy provides a critical framework for reflexive interventions into the study and practice of diplomacy in international society, and to an elaboration of which I turn next.

Reflexivity and diplomacy

As I argued in the introductory portion of this chapter, the capacity for self-examination is not alien to the study and practice of diplomacy, especially if the concept of diplomacy is disabused of its purely political articulations. I hope that the preceding sections have made it clear that a moral account of the foundations of diplomacy allows for a more substantive and accurate understanding of its myriad concerns and interventions in international society. Chief among the concerns is the capacity of diplomacy to not only examine its own methods and means of mediating differences between states, peoples, and institutions, but also to act as a reflexive enterprise in the process of generating and representing knowledge between sovereign entities. The aim of this section is to lay out in simple terms what self-examination in diplomatic practice amounts to, and to offer an overview of a reflexive approach to international diplomacy involving both scholars and practitioners. I refer to the Critical Oral History (COH) methodology, which was first pioneered by James G. Blight, Janet M. Lang, and David A. Welch (1993) and subsequently used to explore alternative pathways to constructive engagement and peace in the Cuban Missile Crisis, the war in Vietnam, US–USSR relations in the Cold War, and US–Iran relations since the Iranian Revolution in 1979.

Any reflexive approach to the study and practice of diplomacy must begin with the problem of representation, which is one of the core functions of diplomacy. *Whose interests, values, and identities are being represented by whom, on account of what authorization, for what purpose, and to what effect?* As far as interstate affairs are concerned, it is often taken for granted that diplomats serve at the pleasure of persons, political parties, or institutions whose mandate has been secured through either democratic elections or arbitrary exercise of power. In either case, it is often assumed that diplomatic representation consists of articulating and implementing the relevant stake-holders' political agendas in any given situation. These assumptions are of course derived from purely political conceptions of diplomacy, which conceive of diplomacy as little more than a mechanism for the revelation of elite preferences. But if, as I have argued, the moral conception of diplomacy elevates above these assumptions the imperative of coexistence and mutual respect for sovereignty, then the representation of interests, values, and identities must first and foremost be reconciled with those moral precepts. In this sense, reflexive diplomatic representation must be fundamentally premised on the necessity of reflecting the diversity of interests, values, and identities—i.e. the plural condition of international life. Furthermore, it must engage in a critical dialogue with those approaches that seek to either deny or obscure this underlying diversity in order to account for the presence of marginalized voices and agencies.

Of course, these principles are easier to invoke in abstract terms than they are to achieve in everyday practice. Such reflexive practices, however, are in fact routinely undertaken by transnational advocacy networks, non-governmental organizations, and even governmental agencies in international society (Keck and Sikkink 1998; Risse-Kappen, Ropp and Sikkink 1999). What renders these efforts "diplomatic" is their core function in mediating the conditions of separateness and alienation by facilitating reflective understanding of core interests, values, and identities that are in dispute. The diplomat, in other words, not only acts as a representative of stable and already recognized values, interests, and identities, but more importantly has the capacity to articulate into existence hitherto neglected and overlooked minority interests, values, and identities. This is an exceedingly important function, for as Cornelius Bjola aptly states, "Denial of equal treatment and legal protection of one's moral integrity and dignity prompts feelings of humiliation, shame and anger, which have been a major source of grievance, tension and international conflict" (2013, p. 12). Reflexivity in diplomatic representation, therefore, belongs to the third category of interpretation—that of practice—which the editors of this volume identify in the Introduction. According to this interpretation, "reflexivity foregrounds agency as a kind of *grappling with* the world and the regimes of knowledge that influence political actors within" (emphasis in the original). Reflexive diplomacy, as an ethical practice, entails "grappling with" the terms of coexistence in light of the moral imperative of respect for sovereignty. In other words, it involves the practice of self- and collective-examination of the methods and reasons employed to assert one's interests, values, and identities in encounters with other sovereign agents (i.e. all rights-bearing beings and states) in international society.

Reflexive diplomacy must also come to grips with the relationship between diplomatic knowledge and political power. Constantinou sums up the issue in the following manner: "How information is secured and appropriated, who has an input in the production of diplomatic knowledge, what regimes of truth does it support or challenge, ought to be matters of political concern"

(2013, p. 144). Of course, as an ethical issue, it ought to be a matter of utmost moral concern as well. Given the predominance of state prerogatives—over those of non-state actors—in diplomatic terms, it is hardly surprising that the constellation of protocols, rules, vocabularies, and accreditations—i.e. the knowledge base of diplomacy (Vienna Convention on Diplomatic Relations and Optional Protocols 1961)—conditioning the behavior and thought of diplomats is so highly influenced by great power interests, values, and identities. Devising a reflexive remedy to this problem, according to Constantinou, requires the reincorporation of the "humanist legacy of diplomacy":

> specifically as a "usable praxis", whereby thinkers and practitioners "who want to know what they are doing, what they are committed to" (Said, 2004: 6), familiarize themselves with a wide spectrum of human relations, escape the dominant perspective, and thus connect to diplomacy not merely as passive observers or public servants but as active humans. In other words, they try to look critically and self-critically at diplomatic action on all fronts. They engage in introspective or human diplomacy, practice "homo-diplomacy"—that is negotiating identity borders, one's own interests, and needs—not just strategic "hetero-diplomacy", that is concerned with persuading or controlling others by way of implementing given policy.
>
> (Constantinou 2013, p. 144)[6]

The "usable praxis" cited by Constantinou offers diplomats and those who study diplomacy a useful mechanism with which to continually examine the commensurability of policy prescriptions with the moral basis of diplomacy. In other words, as users and producers of diplomatic knowledge, diplomatic agents must constantly strive to reconcile their interventions into micro and macro issues in world politics with the imperative of coexistence and mutual respect for sovereignty.

Indeed, this mode of practice—reflexivity through empathy—has always been a central preoccupation of scholars of diplomacy. For example, as Ernest Satow noted in *A Guide to Diplomatic Practice* (1917), "A good diplomatist will always endeavor to put himself in the position of the person with whom he is treating, and try to imagine what he would wish, do and say, under those circumstances" (1979 [1917], pp. 133–134). Empathetic understanding of other diplomats' and leaders' predicaments and aspirations enables the diplomatist to reconsider the normative and material bases of one's own objectives in any given diplomatic exchange. This shift in perspective in turn infuses the process of negotiation itself with good faith, which is a necessary precondition for any breakthrough, especially when interests and values are seemingly irreconcilable. Empathy paves the path toward self-examination by transforming the basis of diplomatic exchange from game-theoretic advantage seeking to one based firmly on mutual gains. Examples of such exercises in self-examination, although rare, exist in international politics. The most famous and perhaps significant is of course the Cuban missile crisis, which nearly resulted in nuclear Armageddon (Kennedy 1999; Blight, Welch and Bundy 1989). In that particular crisis, recent scholarship has revealed that the absence of empathy in President John F. Kennedy's approach to the discovery of nuclear-armed missiles in Cuba combined with the reexamination of short-term strategic goals of the United States and the Soviet Union vis-à-vis Fidel Castro, were critical in the diffusion of the conflict (Blight and Lang 2012).

Given the subjective nature of each crisis, however, there is no single template for how empathy might be operationalized in service of reflexivity. As Blight and Lang insightfully demonstrate in their study of Kennedy's decision-making before, during, and after the Cuban missile crisis, personal psychology, political considerations, and the costs and benefits of alternative decisions combine in unique and indeterminate ways in every leader's personality and behavior (Blight, Lang, and Welch 2009). Still, far from being a quixotic project, such a pathway toward greater reflexivity already exists in the form of the Critical Oral History (COH) methodology, which Blight, Lang, and Welch pioneered as a means of gleaning lessons and missed opportunities during and after the Cold War. The COH method requires the simultaneous interaction, in a conference setting, of three elements: former diplomats and officials, declassified documents, and scholars of the events and issues under scrutiny. Former diplomats are presented with critical accounts of their actions as official representatives of the state, and are then asked to reflect on them in conversation with their counterparts from a formerly hostile (or per-ceived of as) state. These critical interventions are meant to provoke rethinking and deliberation about the nature of decision-making, the sources of beliefs about Self and Other, the range and plausibility of alternative courses of action, and the consequences of chosen actions.

As an organizing member of COH workshops on US–Iran relations since the advent of the Islamic Republic in 1979, I have observed firsthand the merits behind the method.[7] As a thoroughly reflexive exercise in the study and practice of international politics, COH holds officials accountable for their past actions by cross-checking their oral testimony with documentary evi-dence, and vice-versa. Moreover, by bringing together former and current adversaries, it forces the officials to come to terms with the feasibility, validity, and wisdom of their interpretations of one another's aims, prerogatives, and claims. Most significant, the method helps to elucidate the *meaning* of decision-making and past actions. As we note in the prefatory note in the volume on US–Iran relations:

> Each participant typically moves into, and withdraws from, a figurative "time machine" many times during the exchanges, as the discussion moves back and forth from retrospective immersion *in* the forward movement of the historical events (this *happened*), to the retrospective

analytical interpretation *of* those events (this is the *meaning* of what happened).

(Blight et al. 2012, p. 14)

This approach has yielded some rather impressive revisions of otherwise trenchant perspectives from diplomats and policymakers in Cuba, Iran, the former Soviet Union, Vietnam, the United Kingdom, and the United States, not to mention practitioners from a host of international and non-governmental organizations.

As a reflexive intervention, the primary aim of COH is to glean the divergent diplomatic pathways to success and failure, to breakthrough and stalemate, to war and peace in international politics. Understanding the factors that combine to lead to either missed opportunities or grand bargains between sovereign nations or between states and non-state actors offers significant insights about the role played by individual diplomats and those acting in non-official capacities in reaching those ends. Most importantly, then, the COH method, in addition to illuminating the historical record with new information about the imperfect rationale (and foreign policy decision-making, one learns, is *always* an imperfect and impoverished process) behind certain postures, decisions, and actions, focuses once again on the aims and foundations of diplomacy. It does so by asking the participants and the lay observer to reflect on what the fundamental purpose of diplomacy is in relations between estranged sovereigns and their peoples. What are the responsibilities of diplomats to this purpose, and how could they have gone about aligning their nations' interests with the moral imperative to understand and coexist on the basis of mutual respect? What obstacles stand in the way of exercising such responsibilities? What role do career considerations and institutional structures play in inhibiting reflective thought and understanding? What do retrospective investigations of collapses in diplomatic talks or of moments of crises reveal to us about how diplomatic agents could or should have behaved?

Reflexivity in diplomacy requires genuine, thoughtful responses to these questions (which are but a sampling of the kinds of questions that former officials are asked to reflect on). But such reflection can only be prompted by scholars and outside observers with deeper knowledge of the moral underpinnings as well as the political functions of diplomacy in international society. As the fruits of COH workshops have demonstrated time and again, even those diplomats who have reflected on their service in personal memoirs or interviews have nearly always done so without the necessary challenge of counterpoints or dialogues with their adversaries and allies. Reflecting on the promises and shortcomings of diplomacy entails the adoption of a multi-perspectival approach that seeks to interrogate the underlying assumptions, values, and preferences shaping both the development and the implementation of a given policy. Diplomats must be challenged to justify their (non)actions and characterizations in light of the documentary evidence, and not in reference to hypothetical scenarios or still-embargoed information.

Moreover, it is crucial to the task of reflection that all parties consent to the value of such an exercise in the first place. As agents of sovereign interests, values, and identities, diplomats have an all-too-convenient excuse (i.e. "I was merely doing my job") for their infractions and oversights if they are prompted to rethink their careers without an explanation of the ethical necessity to do so. A good case in point in this regard was the leak of a trove of United States diplomatic cables by the non-profit, transparency advocacy organization Wikileaks. Dubbed "Cablegate", the leaks shed light on behavior ranging from embarrassing to the potentially criminal. But rather than engender introspection among members of the Foreign Service, the knowledge gained from the leaked cables was deemed null on arrival. In fact, as of this writing all current and former employees of the United States government are forbidden from discussing the contents of the leaks in public, and indeed most genuinely regard the leaks as criminal acts of espionage.[8] The COH method, in contrast, is premised on the consensual and lawful admittance of diplomatic knowledge in the dialogue between diplomats. This does not mean that contentious issues of which there are very little in circulation by way of documentary evidence are not subject to self-examination and discussion. Rather, it means that the rules and limitations to which diplomats pledge genuine fealty must be accepted as a defining attribute of their role and imprint.

What I hope the preceding discussion has made clear, then, is the centrality of dialogue and third-party intervention to the enterprise of self-reflection concerning the discourse and practice of diplomacy. In the end, the aim of reflexivity in my conception is to narrow the gulf between the diplomat and the underlying moral reasons upon which the institution and practice of diplomacy are founded. Reflexivity in diplomacy, if it is to be prized as a necessary exercise, must demonstrate its instrumental as well as intrinsic values as regards the all-important burden of coexistence in a pluralistic international society. Reflection on opportunities lost or catastrophes averted can teach us important lessons about the utility and limits of certain actions, postures, and beliefs; more importantly, however, as the COH method demonstrates, it is a powerful reminder of the inherent value of diplomacy as a symbol for mutual respect and dialogue.

Conclusion

The practice of diplomacy is as varied as the modes of life it seeks to understand and reconcile. Yet, as this chapter has sought to demonstrate, diplomacy itself is a form of existence in international society. Those conceptions of diplomacy that assign to diplomacy circumscribed zones of activity—i.e. that of the sovereign state—do so at the expense of the moral principles of coexistence and mutual respect that lie at the foundation of diplomatic exchange. Understood as solely a tool of statecraft, therefore, diplomacy betrays a storied legacy of humanistic reflection and dialogue that accounts for its beginnings, evolution, and contemporary resonances.

I have argued that reflexivity is a necessary and natural extension of this moral conception of diplomacy; and yet I have also deliberately eschewed offering any specific criteria for how it might be effectively internalized as a hygienic exercise. The most obvious reason for not doing so is a practical one: there are simply far too many domains, too many modes of life in which diplomacy figures as a prominent institution. More importantly, however, I have limited my discussion to a series of theoretical considerations because I believe the normative core of a reflexive approach—as laid out in the moral conception—to be applicable to the practice of diplomacy regardless of the context in which it is exercised. To this end, I hope the preceding reflection on the practice of diplomacy is itself regarded as a reflexive intervention in the study of diplomacy.

Notes

1 By reflexivity I mean the practice of self-examination and of collective reflection. This refers to the constellation of standpoints, critiques, and practices to which the editors of this volume, Jack L. Amoureux and Brent J. Steele, refer in the Introduction.
2 Kennan's is simply a restatement of one of political realism's core tenets expounded first in Thucydides' *History of the Peloponnesian War* (432 BC [1954]): while it is perfectly fine for morality to inform politics in the personal and domestic realms of life, it has (and certainly ought to have) no bearing on interstate relations since the latter are dominated by entities that represent the interests of their members in the aggregate.
3 There simply are far too many reflections by diplomats on the primacy of national interests in diplomatic considerations to account for here; but among the most notable are statements by Machiavelli 1998a [1532]; de Callières 2000 [1716]; Nicolson 1961; Kennan 2012 [1985]; and Kissinger 1994.
4 I employ Avishai Margalit's (2010, p. 2) definition of morality in this article: "Morality is about how human relations should be in virtue of our being human and in virtue of nothing else." He distinguishes this definition from the concept of "ethics", which "in contrast, is about what relations we *should* have with other people in virtue of some special relationships we *have* with them, such as family relations or friendships" (2010, p. 3).
5 A wide range of positivist and post-positivist (i.e. liberal, constructivist, English School, critical, feminist, and post-modern/structural) theories of IR have compellingly demonstrated the complex relationship between, and the mutual constitution of, politics and morality in both the study and practice of world politics. The most notable of these include: Bull 1977; Walzer 1977; Doyle 1983; Onuf 1989; Tickner 1992; Nardin and Mapel 1993; Walker 1993; Beitz 1999; Linklater 1999; Jackson 2000.
6 A point of clarification regarding Constantinou's entirely convincing and insightful arguments, which nevertheless differ in an important sense from mine, is in order here. In his article, Constantinou offers a wonderfully rich account of reflexive possibilities in diplomatic practice, especially if the latter is to be understood as first and foremost a humanist tradition. This view is somewhat different from my conception of the moral basis of diplomacy in that it seeks to reframe diplomacy as a

wholly "subjective" practice in international affairs. While I share the premise of this argument as regards *diplomatic knowledge* (i.e. knowledge produced, utilized, and reproduced by diplomats), I hesitate to endorse the notion that diplomacy constitutes a subjective practice *all the way down*. While the aims and purposes of diplomacy may indeed be subjective, its *raison d'être*, indeed, what necessitates diplomacy in the first place, I would like to suggest, is the objective recognition of sovereign standing in international society—however thin or implied such a recognition might be. At any rate, Constantinou's contribution on the humanistic basis of diplomatic knowledge could hardly be improved upon, and indeed I refer the reader to it for a more complete understanding of reflexive possibilities in diplomatic practice and knowledge.

7 The results of the first workshop in US–Iran relations during the Iran–Iraq war were published in *Becoming Enemies: U.S.-Iran Relations and the Iran-Iraq War, 1979–1988* (Blight et al. 2012).

8 At any rate, as Neumann has noted, the leaks actually amounted to a very incomplete and inaccurate body of diplomatic knowledge: "Most commentators, and presumably most readers, seem to have taken these documents as representative of ministerial output. That is simply wrong. Such dispatches are the closest thing within a foreign ministry to the 'I' genre. Their main function is to serve as one out of many inputs into the production of authoritative documents. The individual diplomat reporting on what she experiences is one of the beginnings of the diplomatic knowledge production. She is never the end thereof" (Neumann 2012, p. 89).

References

Beitz, C.R., 1999. *Political Theory and International Relations.* Princeton, NJ: Princeton University Press.

Berridge, G.R., 2001. Machiavelli: Human Nature, Good Faith, and Diplomacy. *Review of International Studies*, 27(4), 539–556.

Bjola, C., 2013. Understanding Enmity and Friendship in World Politics: The Case for a Diplomatic Approach. *The Hague Journal of Diplomacy*, 8(1), 1–20.

Blight, J.G., Allyn, B.J. and Welch, D.A., 1993. *Cuba on the Brink: Castro, the Missile Crisis and the Soviet Collapse.* New York: Pantheon/Random House.

Blight, J.G. and Lang, J.M., 2012. *The Armageddon Letters: Kennedy, Khrushchev, Castro in the Cuban Missile Crisis.* Lanham, MD: Rowman & Littlefield Publishers.

Blight, J.G., Lang, J.M. and Welch, D.A., 2009. *Virtual JFK: Vietnam If Kennedy Had Lived.* Lanham, MD: Rowman & Littlefield Publishers.

Blight, J.G., Lang, J.M., Banai, H., Byrne, M. and Tirman, J., 2012. *Becoming Enemies: U.S.-Iran Relations and the Iran-Iraq War, 1979–1988.* Lanham, MD: Rowman & Littlefield Publishers.

Blight, J.G., Welch, D.A. and Bundy, M., 1989. *On the Brink: Americans and the Soviets Reexamine the Cuban Missile Crisis.* New York: Hill & Wang Publications.

Bull, H., 1977. *The Anarchical Society: A Study of Order in World Politics.* Basingstoke: Palgrave.

Butterfield, H., 1966. The New Diplomacy and Historical Diplomacy. In: H. Butterfield and M. Wight, eds, *Diplomatic Investigations: Essays in the Theory of International Politics.* Cambridge, MA: Harvard University Press, pp. 181–192.

Constantinou, C., 1996. *On the Way to Diplomacy.* Minneapolis: University of Minnesota Press.

Constantinou, C., 2013. Between Statecraft and Humanism: Diplomacy and Its Forms of Knowledge. *International Studies Review*, 15(2), 141–162.

Constantinou, C. and Der Derian, J., eds, 2010. *Sustainable Diplomacies*. New York: Palgrave Macmillan.

de Callières, F., 2000. *On the Manner of Negotiating with Princes*. New York: Houghton Mifflin Harcourt.

Der Derian, J., 1987. *On Diplomacy: A Genealogy of Western Estrangement*. Oxford: Oxford University Press.

Der Derian, J., 1996. Hedley Bull and the Idea of Diplomatic Culture. In: R. Fawn and J. Larkins, eds, *International Society After the Cold War: Anarchy and Order Reconsidered*. Basingstoke: Macmillan Press Ltd., pp. 84–100.

Doyle, M.W., 1983. Kant, Liberal Legacies, and Foreign Affairs, Parts 1&2. *Philosophy and Public Affairs*, 12(3&4), 205–235 and 323–353.

Hampshire, S., 1984. *Morality and Conflict*. Cambridge, MA: Harvard University Press.

Jackson, R., 2000. *The Global Covenant: Human Conduct in a World of States*. Oxford: Oxford University Press.

Jönsson, C. and Langhorne, R., 2004. *Diplomacy* (Vols I–III). London: Sage Publications.

Keck, M.E. and Sikkink, K., 1998. *Activists Beyond Borders: Advocacy Networks in International Politics*. Cambridge: Cambridge University Press.

Kennan, G.F., 1985. Morality and Foreign Policy. *Foreign Affairs*, 64(2): 205–218.

Kennan, G.F., 2012. *American Diplomacy: Sixtieth Anniversary Expanded Edition (Walgreen Foundation Lectures)*. Chicago, IL: University of Chicago Press.

Kennedy, R.F., 1999. *Thirteen Days: A Memoir of the Cuban Missile Crisis*. New York: W.W. Norton & Company.

Kissinger, H., 1994. *Diplomacy*. New York: Simon and Schuster.

Krasner, S.D., 1999. *Sovereignty: Organized Hypocrisy*. Princeton, NJ: Princeton University Press.

Larmore, C., 2008. *The Autonomy of Morality*. Cambridge: Cambridge University Press.

Linklater, A., 1999. *The Transformation of Political Community: Ethical Foundations of the Post-Westphalian Era*. Columbia, SC: University of South Carolina Press.

Machiavelli, N., 1998a [1532]. *The Prince*, 2nd edn. Translated by H.C. Mansfield. Chicago, IL: University of Chicago Press.

Machiavelli, N., 1998b [1531]. *Discourses on Livy*. Translated by H.C. Mansfield and N. Tarcov. Chicago, IL: University of Chicago Press.

Margalit, A., 2010. *On Compromise and Rotten Compromises*. Princeton, NJ: Princeton University Press.

Mattingly, G., 1955. *Renaissance Diplomacy*. London: Jonathan Cape.

Nardin, T. and Mapel, D.R., eds, 1993. *Traditions of International Ethics*. Cambridge: Cambridge University Press.

Neumann, I.B., 2005. To Be a Diplomat. *International Studies Perspectives*, 6(1), 72–93.

Neumann, I.B., 2012. *At Home with the Diplomats: Inside a European Foreign Ministry*. Ithaca, NY: Cornell University Press.

Nicolson, H., 1939. *Diplomacy: a Basic Guide to the Conduct of Contemporary Foreign Affairs*. New York: Harcourt Brace.

Nicolson, H., 1960. *Diplomacy*. Oxford: Oxford University Press.

Nicolson, H., 1961. Diplomacy: Then and Now. *Foreign Affairs*, 40(1), 39–49.

Onuf, N.J., 1989. *World of Our Making: Rules and Rule in Social Theory and International Relations*. Columbia, SC: University of South Carolina Press.

Rawls, J., 1996. *Political Liberalism* (revised edn.). New York: Columbia University Press.

Reinsch, P.S., 1922. *Secret Diplomacy: How Far Can It Be Eliminated?* New York: Harcourt, Brace and Company.

Risse-Kappen, T., Ropp, S.C., and Sikkink, K., 1999. *The Power of Human Rights: International Norms and Domestic Change*. Cambridge: Cambridge University Press.

Said, E.W., 2004. *Humanism and Democratic Criticism*. New York: Columbia University Press.

Satow, E., 1957. *A Guide to Diplomatic Practice*. London: Longmans.

Satow, E., 1979 [1917]. *Guide to Diplomatic Practice*, 2 vols. London: Longman.

Sharp, P., 1999. For Diplomacy: Representation and the Study of International Relations. *International Studies Review*, 1(1), 33–57.

Sharp, P., 2009. *Diplomatic Theory of International Relations*. Cambridge: Cambridge University Press.

Thucydides, 1954. *History of the Peloponnesian War*. Translated by R. Warner and edited by M.I. Finley. New York: Penguin Classics.

Tickner, J.A., 1992. *Gender in International Relations*. New York: Columbia University Press.

The Vienna Convention on Diplomatic Relations and Optional Protocols. Done at Vienna on April 18, 1961. Entered into force on April 24, 1964. United Nations, Treaty Series, vol. 500.

Walker, R.B.J., 1993. *International Relations as Political Theory*. Cambridge: Cambridge University Press.

Walzer, M., 1977. *Just and Unjust Wars: A Moral Argument with Historical Illustrations*. New York: Basic Books.

Watson, A., 1983. *Diplomacy: The Dialogue Between States*. New York: New Press.

12 When the fix *isn't* in

Toward a reflexive pragmatism

Wesley Widmaier

Over recent decades, scholars and policymakers spanning an array of theoretical perspectives have stressed the scope for constructing beliefs and "fixing" expectations, in ways that can see shared ideas acquire the reflexive weight of self-fulfilling prophecies. In International Relations Theory debates, scholars argued that the "strategic social construction" of ideas and norms might in turn acquire the force of self-reinforcing "taken for granted" beliefs.[1] For example, the broad notion of a "democratic peace" was heralded as enabling a self-reinforcing limitation on conflict among liberal states. Similarly, a Neoliberal "Washington Consensus" stressed the merit of free market economic policies as the foundation for what was seen as a self-reinforcing economic "Great Moderation"—until the onset of the Global Financial Crisis in late 2008. In this way, despite the substantive variation across issue areas, there existed a broad consensus on the scope for entrepreneurial efforts at the reconstruction of shared beliefs that might assume a reflexive momentum in reshaping policy reality.[2]

To be sure, such insights may have merit—particularly, in terms of the language employed in this volume—as they highlight the reflexivity of theoretical *critique* in the initial construction of orders as it feeds back on policy *practices*. Engaging these debates in this chapter, I acknowledge that such claims for ideational planning might prove viable for a time. Yet, I also suggest that planning encounters paradoxical limits as the very stability that it engenders can fuel a destabilizing convergence of expectations that enables renewed instability. Put differently, while it may appear for a time that the intersubjective "fix is in", efforts at sustaining stability nevertheless face a key limit as stability can paradoxically give rise to new, unanticipated expectations that undermine ostensibly self-sustaining orders. Developing social psychological insights, I suggest that such outcomes reflect Hyman Minsky's enduring insight regarding the paradoxical ways in which economic stability and policy success can fuel crises, as "stability causes instability" (Minsky 1986, 1992). To be sure, Minsky's analysis exists outside any formal discussion of ideas and institutions, pertaining instead to broad shifts in market attitudes regarding risk. Formalizing these insights, I build in the first section of this chapter on recent Constructivist and Institutionalist analyses of the interplay of stability and instability, suggesting that ideas which may initially reduce uncertainty and stabilize expectations may over time fuel a misplaced certainty, over-confidence and renewed instability.[3] Shifting to an empirical focus in the second section, I offer an illustrative discussion of the implications for the construction and conversion of the Neoliberal order over the 1980s and 1990s, through to the onset of the Global Financial Crisis. In terms of questions raised in this broader volume, such dynamics have implications for Brent Steele's questions regarding the potential emergence of subsequent "outcomes planned, unplanned, seen, and unforeseen".

In the third section, I draw together the implications of the different types of reflexivity identified in this volume in ways that speak to broader debates over the scope for refined planning or a more pragmatic recognition of the limits to knowledge. Put differently, this analysis suggests that the reflexivity of theoretical *critique* can feed back in unexpected ways by generating unexpected real-world destabilizing *practices*. This potential set of limits to reflexivity would therefore raise what might be termed the question of "What's a scholar to do?" Here I finally engage the volume's premise of a third notion of reflexivity, highlighting the need for scholarly self-awareness of the reflexive *positionality* of scholars themselves. Given these varying types of reflexivity, even as no Archimedean point can be established at which scholars can advance "intersubjective planning", the limits to formal blueprints still admit a pragmatic space for efforts to reconcile enduring *ethical* principles with varying institutional and coordinative means to these ends. From this vantage point, even where efforts at intellectualizing or formalizing policy models may ironically impede "intersubjective planning"—a degree of ethical engagement may imbue scholarly efforts with a more enduring shelf life. To highlight such dynamics, I address the work of John Kenneth Galbraith, whose ethical distinction between the scope for public and private interests has imbued his work with an enduring relevance—even where his issue-specific concerns for the wage-price spiral have been bypassed by institutional changes in the structure of the economy (Best 2005). In the conclusion, I pull back to address the implications for the contending relevance of critical and pragmatic approaches to theorizing, suggesting that key differences between them are less theoretical than substantive—as is implicit in Beattie's account in this volume—dispositional and affective, and so "beyond theory".

From the strategic construction to institutionalization of reflexive expectations

The reflexive construction of self-reinforcing expectations can be explained in Constructivist and Historical Institutionalist terms as reflexive dynamics can stem from *critiques* embodied in shared norms, or standards of behavior, that assume a self-reinforcing momentum with respect to the *practices* of state and societal agents (Finnemore and Sikkink 1998; Pierson 2000, 2004). From such perspectives ideational and institutional agents may be seen as capable of efficiently fixing material or social incentives, providing self-reinforcing bases of prolonged stability. Yet, such analyses may also be limited where they overrate the ability of policymakers and publics to efficiently stabilize incentives or internalize norms, underrating the ways in which intersubjective stability can feed a convergence of expectations and new sources of instability. In this section, I suggest that such pathological possibilities are better appreciated by adopting what Vivien Schmidt casts as Discursive Institutionalist insights regarding the scope for variation in the types and forms of ideas, in ways that highlight a wider array of potential pathological possibilities. In terms of historical processes, this suggests that the beginning stages of a policy order may be marked by stability as critiques assume a self-perpetuating force, but that such stasis may erode as risky practices culminate in crisis.

From Constructivism to Historical Institutionalisms: the limits to self-reinforcing stability

In highlighting the reflexive effects of ideas on expectations—and so moving beyond realist or liberal approaches which assume that material structures "speak for themselves" in shaping policy choices—Constructivist and Institutionalist approaches admit a potentially wider array of influences. Regarding the former, Constructivist perspectives highlight the ideas that shape state and societal interests—as Alexander Wendt (1999, p. 13) argues that ideas *are* interests, defined as "beliefs about how to meet needs". From this perspective, for example, the international distribution of power or coalitional preferences cannot be treated as self-evident. Instead, state and societal agents must always interpret their interests in some intersubjective context. Given the emergence of such varied ideas, Constructivists further highlight their potentially self-reinforcing nature, as they can acquire "lives of their own" and reduce uncertainty in ways that enable a self-reinforcing stability.[4] Characterizing the construction of economic orders, Mark Blyth argues that ideas reduce a "Knightian" deep uncertainty which emerges during economic crises and leads to the construction of institutions and conventions which stabilize expectations over the long term.[5] Similarly, Martha Finnemore and Kathryn Sikkink (1998, p. 895) describe a "norm life cycle" in which norm entrepreneurs persuade norm leaders of the merit of ideas justifying new standards of behavior. Where leaders succeed in convincing broader audiences of the merit of their views, this can set off "norm cascades" whose internalization gives norms or ideas a "taken-for-granted quality" in which they are "no longer a matter of broad public debate". Such norm entrepreneurs can be seen as harnessing the reflexive potential inherent in ideas, as they shape beliefs in ways that assume a prolonged, self-reinforcing momentum.

In this light, Constructivist analyses have a key advantage in highlighting socially constructed sources of a wider array of social possibilities and potentially prolonged stability. Yet, they also remain limited to the extent that they also obscure the ways in which ideas that initially reduce uncertainty can later contribute to a misplaced certainty, instability and crisis. Put differently, where constructivists argue that ideas limit uncertainty, this obscures the ways in which these same ideas can over time "harden" and generate a misplaced certainty, overconfidence and crises. For example, as Jacqueline Best (2005, pp. 28–29) argues, efforts to stabilize shared expectations can over time lead agents to define their expectations more narrowly, converging in ways that can fuel policy or market "manias" that are then vulnerable to collapse. Constructivists further underrate possibilities for instability where they advance views of the social distribution of knowledge which minimize the role of rhetorical leaders and overrate the efficiency of "norm entrepreneurs" who may be particularly prone to intellectualize debate in ways that fuel policy overconfidence (Finnemore and Sikkink 1998). For example, while the Keynesian values of the 1930s initially reduced uncertainty, their intellectualization in the Neoclassical Synthesis of the 1960s saw fiscal policymakers increasingly overrate their scope for control. In this light, efforts to *reduce* uncertainty by refining ideas can give rise to instability that *causes* renewed uncertainty.

In turn, having suggested that ideational stability causes instability, it remains necessary to identify the conditions under which either tendency becomes more likely—and so can either stabilize or destabilize orders across political time. In this light, while still treating exogenous shocks as the sources of change, Historical Institutionalists like Paul Pierson stress the role of critical junctures that "lock in" institutional arrangements. Such shocks act as critical junctures which "place institutional arrangements on paths or trajectories, which are then very difficult to alter" (Pierson 2004, pp. 135, 254). In this way, critical junctures are characterized by openings for change which may not be optimal, but which may nevertheless generate increasing returns as they acquire the self-reinforcing status of social facts. To be sure, more recently, Historical Institutionalists have resisted tendencies to treat ensuing orders as static, most prominently as James Mahoney and Kathleen Thelen (2010) highlight the overlooked scope for incremental change. Beginning with a stress on exogenous shocks to the "power distributional" bases of institutional orders, they advance a view of institutions as arbiters of societal resources or as "*distributional instruments* laden with power implications". Given these foundations, they note that institutional orders remain ambiguous by virtue of being "subject to interpretation, debate, and contestation". In this light, there can exist a degree of slack for interpreting institutional rules and procedures, in ways that permit a scope for flexibility in the ongoing implementation of policies. To capture such dynamics, Mahoney and Thelen posit an array of mechanisms of incremental change, as institutional orders are adjusted over time. For example the "conversion" and "displacement" of ideas and institutions can enable the adjustment of institutional orders, in ways that sustain efficiencies over time (Mahoney and Thelen 2010, pp. 7–9). More formally, while conversion occurs as beliefs are "interpreted and enacted in new ways" and given new meaning by agents, displacement is marked by developments which see existing rules or ideas "replaced by new ones" in policy struggles that play out over time (Mahoney and Thelen 2010, pp. 16–18).

Such analyses offer important contributions, correcting for tendencies to overrate a dichotomy between exogenous shocks and the stability of "taken for granted" orders. Yet, they also have limits where they underrate the need for agents to interpret incentives as well as the ways in which mechanisms like conversion can exacerbate instability—and so these power distributional Historical Institutionalist analyses obscure the ways in which incremental inefficiencies and dysfunctions might fuel the onset of punctuated shocks and crises. In recent years, however, such limits have been offset by Discursive Institutionalist analyses, as these highlight the paradoxical ways in which stability can contribute to instability (Skowronek 1993, 2011).

Reflexivity, planned and unplanned—from stable ideas to destabilizing choices

Historical Institutionalist emphases on power-distributional dynamics offer useful insights into the nature of transformative change and incremental adjustment. However, to the extent that they overlook the ambiguity of power-distributional dynamics and underrate the scope for ideational inefficiencies, they remain incomplete as truly general theories, capable of making sense of the interplay of stability, crisis and change. To redress these oversights, recent Discursive Institutionalist insights have directed attention to not only the ambiguity of "power-distributional" structures—and the ways in which they must not only be interpreted—but also the potential for such interpretations to engender pathological outcomes. To highlight this broader scope for tension and turmoil, I build on the notion of a distribution of ideas across what Schmidt distinguishes as normative and cognitive beliefs, tracing the reflexive construction of normative *critiques* as bases of cognitive stability and self-reinforcing *practices*, their displacement in ways that fuel risk taking and instability, and tensions between them that can fuel a similarly self-reinforcing collapse.

In terms of intersubjective structures, Schmidt (2008) disaggregates ideas into two broad types, encompassing normative beliefs regarding "what's right" and causal beliefs regarding "what works".[6] On the one hand, cognitive ideas "provide the recipes, guidelines, and maps for political action and serve to justify policies and programs by speaking to their interest-based logic and necessity". In this way, they provide utilitarian guides that "elucidate 'what is and what to do'" (Schmidt 2008, pp. 306–308). On the other hand, normative ideas speak to "what one ought to do" as they "attach values to political action and serve to legitimate the policies in a program through reference to their appropriateness" (Schmidt 2008, pp. 306–307). To be sure, normative ideas are not simply after-the-fact legitimating factors that make causal models more appealing. They are "social facts" that must be taken into account *in* causal models, as ideas about "what's right" have reflexive, self-fulfilling implications for "what works". For example, if consumers expect increases in the money supply will lead to inflation, they may take measures—seeking wage increases—that translate money supply increases into inflationary pressures. Conversely, where they lack such views, even an increase in the money supply need have no effect on wages or prices, as the velocity of money in circulation may fall in ways that keep the price level constant. In this way, normative beliefs prefigure cognitive paradigms and policy ideas. Taken as a whole, the stability of intersubjective structures derives from a balance between cognitive precision and normative engagement.

Given these distinctions, one can posit how these different types of ideational critique exercise different degrees of influence at different points in political time, in ways that can stabilize or destabilize broader orders and practices. Three such mechanisms are particularly important over time. First, in the *construction* of policy orders, rhetorical leaders advance principled critiques that reduce uncertainty and reshape institutional and societal practices. Secondly, however, the very stability that such principled foundations enable may in turn lead to the *intellectual conversion* of ideas, as policy and intellectual agents reduce principled beliefs to causal models which guide utilitarian practices. Finally, such intellectualization may ironically give rise to the sorts of misplaced certainty that threatens renewed instability, fueling policy and market overconfidence, as expectations converge in ways that fuel risk taking, instability and *crises*.

The construction, conversion and reflexive collapse of the Neoliberal order

To highlight these dynamics, I offer a plausibility probe pertaining to economic policy and the rise and fall of the Neoliberal economic order of recent decades. The construction of the Neoliberal order was rooted in policy critiques that stressed the self-reinforcing nature of inflation expectations, and argued for efforts to reset them in ways that would restore prolonged wage-price stability. For example, in addressing the problem of inflation in the 1970s at an early Federal Reserve meeting, Volcker highlighted the embedded nature of inflationary expectations in a self-reinforcing psychology, and cast the challenge of monetary policymaking as that of stabilizing new expectations. First, characterizing the runaway inflation of the 1970s, Volcker argued that:

> When I look at the past year or two I am impressed myself by an intangible: the degree to which inflationary psychology has really changed. It's not that we didn't have it before, but I think people are acting on that expectation [of continued high inflation] much more firmly than they used to. That's important to us because it does produce, potentially and actually, paradoxical reactions to policy.
>
> (Federal Open Market Committee 1979)

The operational means by which Volcker would engineer this shift would be through a change in Federal Reserve operating procedures, to target the money supply rather than interest rates—an approach which would hold for roughly three years. Advancing the case for this change, he would suggest to his colleagues at the Federal Reserve that "the traditional method of making small moves has in some sense, though not completely, run out of psychological gas" (Federal Open Market Committee 1979). To try to overcome the need for discrete, point-by-point votes on interest rates—given that "[s]ome board members were reluctant to take overt moves to raise interest rates", Volcker came to see a Milton Friedman-styled shift to targeting the money supply as an operational "way to get more unanimity" (Solomon 1995, p. 139). He hoped that once the Federal Reserve had changed its operating techniques, it "would find it difficult to back off even if our decisions led to painfully high interest rates". This shift further provided a means to reshape public expectations, Volcker argued, on the grounds that markets would always "seize upon markers of one kind or another", giving the Federal Reserve the opportunity to establish "some rule or indicator to supply discipline" (Solomon 1995, p. 140).

Over the next decade and a half, as reinforced by Ronald Reagan's dismissal of striking workers at the Federal Reserve, expectations would be accordingly reset. However, the resulting Neoliberal order would be undermined by operational and policy overconfidence. First, in procedural terms, was the Federal Reserve's integration of New Keynesian technocratic frameworks like the "Taylor rule"—which posited a trade-off between real growth and monetary volatility—with an increasing willingness to employ official discretion—in what Greenspan (2004) termed "risk management". This procedural overconfidence would be reinforced by a theoretical and policy certitude regarding the role of deregulation and monetary fine tuning in enabling the strong economic performance of recent decades. Characterizing these dynamics, Federal Reserve Board member Ben Bernanke (2004) would claim that a Great Moderation encompassing a "remarkable decline in the variability of both output and inflation" had emerged, in which recessions had become "less frequent and less severe". From Bernanke's perspective, while the poor state of economic knowledge had contributed to the economic disarray of the 1970s, the New Keynesian refinement of intervening decades—e.g., as given expression in the Taylor rule—had made possible this improvement. Lauding the trend to "deregulation in many industries" for having "increased macroeconomic flexibility and stability", Bernanke (2004) argued that monetary policy "played a large part in stabilizing inflation" and "helped moderate the variability of output as well". In this way deregulation and monetary fine tuning comprised key ingredients of a Great Moderation.

In taking the reins at the Federal Reserve, Bernanke initially maintained broad continuity with Greenspan. However, even in the context of these shared views, Bernanke would also manifest key differences that exacerbated market risk taking. More formally, Bernanke built on late-Greenspan-era trends in more clearly defining inflation targets and using "forward guidance" in public communications. While Greenspan had moved in this direction since the 1990s, he had never completely abandoned a preference for what he termed a "constructive ambiguity" as a means to keeping markets more competitive. Greenspan (2007, p. 151) had argued that "markets uncertain as to the direction of interest rates would create a desired large buffer of both bids and offers". Speaking to the implications for the subprime housing bubble, former Federal Reserve staffer Stephen Axilrod (2011, pp. 146–147) critiqued "the virtual guarantee ... probably encouraged market participants to take on more risk". In sum, policy and market confidence could together fuel excessive risk taking—as the economy would soon collapse as the subprime bubble was punctured and the Global Financial Crisis initiated instability and market collapse.

From reflexive critique and practice to a reflexive positional pragmatism

This analysis feeds back on some of the key themes advanced in this volume as it highlights the limits to efforts to attain theoretical clarity or precision in a way that applies across the range of the materialist-constructivist debate itself. Consider that Kenneth Waltz (1979, p. 6) famously argued for a view of theory that would enable efforts at explanation, prediction and control. From the perspective of this effort, the reflexive effect of theoretical critique on practices renders sustained prediction and control unlikely, as such efforts will—if they are accepted—lead agents to develop new patterns of behavior that may undo past relations, and so their own relevance as critiques. To paraphrase Charles Goodhart, when a theoretical critique becomes accepted, it can lose its relevance as a guide to future behavior. This insight also applies to the work of Alexander Wendt (1999), whose stress on intersubjective planning is similarly vulnerable to the extent that intersubjective critique and design are self-limiting—and so successful efforts at correcting past excesses can unwittingly fuel future pathologies.

This raises the question of what are the options for scholars interested in reflexive practice—with a key answer coming in the context of the third type of reflexivity referenced by Steele and Amoureux in the Introduction to this volume, pertaining to the *position* of scholars in debate, and the need for self-awareness regarding our relationships, as scholars, with those whom we study. Building on this insight, I suggest that reflexivity-as-positionality pertains not only to power relations, but also to ethical positions in broader principled debates that shape what policymakers consider in a "primary", ethical sense to count as "good reasons". These primary, principled concerns in turn shape the ensuing "secondary" structures of incentives that shape wider behaviors which occupy much of scholarship today—and often have a limited half-life. To the extent that scholars ignore their reflexive positionality vis-à-vis ethical debates and overrate the importance of secondary, causal relations, their work will likely also have a short shelf life.

However, to the extent that scholars focus primarily on ethical concerns, recognizing that the "mechanics" of policy relations are always contingent, theoretical claims may have a more enduring relevance. Consider in this light the work of John Kenneth Galbraith. In one sense, a key focus of much of Galbraith's past scholarly work has lost relevance over the decades. For example, where Galbraith focused on the role of wage and price guidelines over the 1950s and 1960s as means to blunt the social sources of market power driving the wage-price spiral, his work has lost relevance. Indeed, the defeat of unions in the 1980s eliminated inflation itself as a pressing threat. Perhaps more importantly, a shift to viewing inflation as a macroeconomic rather than institutional phenomenon has seen the economics profession abandon what might be termed a Galbraithian stress on institutional forces as causes of macroeconomic trends.

Yet, in another sense, Galbraith's work remains highly relevant, and shapes contemporary debates in often unconscious ways. First, in a secondary sense, Galbraith's analyses retain a technical applicability to spheres of the economy where market power still exists (e.g., with respect to "too big to fail" financial institutions). Secondly, and in a deeper sense, his work has remained relevant where it has focused on a larger concern for "social balance" between the public and private interests. As expressed in his 1958 effort *The Affluent Society*, Galbraith urged that "the useful economist" engage in ethical debates, and lamented economists' tendencies toward causal analyses at the expense of a concern for social purpose. Galbraith lamented that among academics, "considerable store is set by the device of putting an old truth in a new form" warning that when "accepted ideas become increasingly elaborate", defenders of prevailing academic orthodoxies might argue that "the challengers of the conventional wisdom have not mastered their intricacies". In such settings, mainstream scholars might succeed in limiting debate by insisting that key controversies could "be appreciated only by a stable, orthodox and patient man—in brief, by someone who closely resembles the man of conventional wisdom" (Galbraith 1958, p. 9). However, Galbraith favored a greater dialogue between academics and the public, and sought to encourage wider reflection not simply on the merits of wage and price guidelines, but also the more ethically fundamental balance that might be struck between public and private interests.

Indeed, *The Affluent Society* represented the clearest development of the Galbraithian vision—one that paralleled a Deweyan stress on the importance of "common understandings" and bringing economic debates into the public realm. In *The Affluent Society*, one might argue that Galbraith anticipated, by virtue of his expanded view of the public interest, the rise of the field of environmental economics itself. In one key passage in *The Affluent Society*, Galbraith drew into relief the imbalance between private and public wants in a specifically environmental setting:

> The family which takes its mauve and cerise, air conditioned, power-steered and power-braked automobile out for a tour passes through cities that are badly paved, made hideous by litter, blighted buildings,

billboards and posts for wires that should have long since been put underground. They pass on into a countryside that has been rendered largely invisible by commercial art ... They picnic on exquisitely packaged food from a portable icebox by a polluted stream and go on to spend the night at a park which is a menace to public health and morals. Just before dozing off on an air mattress, beneath a nylon tent, amid the stench of decaying refuse, they may reflect vaguely on the curious unevenness of their blessings. Is this, indeed, the American genius?

(Galbraith 1958, pp. 199–200)

In the macroeconomic realm, *The Affluent Society* would more broadly pull back to critique the ethical positions of "Social Darwinists and the utilitarian philosophers" in identifying "vitality and liberty with the free market" in order to ensure that "controls will be regarded as an even more far-reaching menace" (Galbraith 1958, p. 194).

In this light, I suggest that theorists and policymakers alike face a challenge of maintaining a sense of their reflexive ethical positionality in seeking to maintain a theoretical relevance. Put differently, while not denying the need for causal clarity, this analysis suggests that too much specificity can generate "diminishing returns" where it obscures the ambiguous ethical beliefs that help in enabling consensus, flexibility and scholarly relevance.[7]

Conclusion: reflexivity between extremes: control, power and hope

Over this chapter, having highlighted the limits to causal refinement—as theoretical critiques can reshape behavior in ways that gradually feed back and undermine theoretical relevance—I have stressed the importance of ethical positionality to sustained scholarly relevance. Yet, this analysis might still be countered on grounds that the scope for an expanded sense of social purpose is limited by the existence of Foucauldian-styled domination by Power/ Knowledge. Here I would engage with another essay, Chapter 8 in this volume—by Beattie on the traumas that can weaken scholarly hope regarding such possibilities. In her effort, Beattie highlights what might be considered a further kind of reflexivity, of an emotional or affective sort. To the extent that emotional or affective predispositions condition agents toward a pessimism with respect to social purpose, I would advance on Beattie's work by arguing that such affective "resonance" may assume a collective standing.

In this light, debates between Foucauldian critical scholars and Deweyan or Galbraithian-styled pragmatists may best be seen as affectively grounded and so "beyond theory", pertaining not to epistemological or ontological priors so much as purposeful predispositions. Characterizing this divide, Richard Rorty (1987, p. 253) posits how Deweyan pragmatism highlights "the moral importance of the social sciences—their role in widening and deepening our sense of community and of the possibilities open to this community". In contrast, from a more Foucauldian perspective, Rorty argues that scholars seek to emphasize "the way in which the social sciences have served as instruments of 'the disciplinary society'". While this debate is of enduring import, the analysis offered in this chapter suggests that it cannot be reduced to theoretical priors. In broader terms, as Rorty puts it, the debate between Galbraith and Dewey on one hand and Foucault on the other may be seen as pertaining not to "a theoretical issue, but [rather] ... what we [as scholars] may hope". In this light, to the extent that such emotional predispositions exert a reflexive effect on theoretical debates, this opens the door to a wider range of pragmatic, reflexive practices—as theorists might engage as actors, and theory might prove a factor, across a range of everyday settings.

Notes

1 For insightful comments, I owe debts of gratitude to Jack Amoureux, Martin Carstensen, Luke Glanville, Renee Jeffery, Zim Nwokora, Susan Park, Haig Patapan, Leonard Seabrooke, Vivien Schmidt, Jason Sharman, Brent Steele, Eleni Tsingou, and Patrick Weller. I would also like to acknowledge the support of the Australian Research Council in the form of an ARC Future Fellowship (FT100100833) and Discovery Grant (DP130104088).The usual disclaimers apply. On strategic social construction, see Finnemore and Sikkink (1998). On the "end of history", see Fukuyama (1991). For a parallel concept—embraced during a similar period of intellectual overconfidence, see Daniel Bell (1960) on an "end of ideology".
2 On the democratic peace, see Russett (1993) and Ray (1995). On the Washington Consensus, see Williamson (1993). On the Great Moderation, see Bernanke (2004).
3 On Constructivism, see Wendt (1999) and Blyth (2002). On Historical Institutionalism, see Pierson (2000, 2004), Mahoney and Thelen (2010) and Fioretos (2011). On Discursive Institutionalism, see Schmidt (2008, 2010).
4 On rationalist foundations, see Finnemore and Sikkink (1998), Fearon and Wendt (2002). Some constructivists have highlighted the scope for inefficiency: For example, Barnett and Finnemore (1999, 2004) stress the pathologies that produce institutional instability—but in abstraction from models of stability, crisis and change.
5 To be sure, foreshadowing Discursive Institutionalist insights as addressed below, Blyth (2002, p. 39) also distinguishes broad conventions from ideas.
6 This recognition of normative foundations—and their affective foundations—has been more recently stressed in IR debates by scholars like Andrew Ross (2006, pp. 199–200), who casts shared values as "inspired and absorbed before being chosen" and as shaping "our intellectual beliefs".
7 This fits with Jacqueline Best's (2005) view that successful governance does not necessarily entail encouraging convergent expectations. Best suggests that "[g]iven the self-fulfilling nature of market confidence"—i.e., its reflexive nature—"if expectations converge too tightly—expecting a very narrow set of economic outcomes from an inherently uncertain world—they are almost certain to be unmet, producing the all-too-familiar cycle of mania, panic and crash".

References

Axilrod, S., 2011. *Inside the Fed: Monetary Policy and Its Management, Martin through Greenspan to Bernanke*. Cambridge, MA: MIT Press.
Barnett, M. and Finnemore, M., 1999. The Politics, Power, and Pathologies of International Organizations. *International Organization*, 53(4), 699–732.

Barnett, M. and Finnemore, M., 2004. *Rules for the World*. Ithaca, NY: Cornell University Press.

Bernanke, B., 2004. The Great Moderation. Remarks at the Meetings of the Eastern Economic Association, Washington, DC, February 20. Available from: www.federa lreserve.gov/BOARDDOCS/SPEECHES/2004/20040220/default.htm.

Bell, D., 1960. *The End of Ideology: On the Exhaustion of Political Ideas in the Fifties*. Cambridge, MA: Harvard University Press.

Best, J., 2005. *The Limits of Transparency: Ambiguity and the History of International Finance*. Ithaca, NY: Cornell University Press.

Blyth, M., 2002. *Great Transformations: Economic Ideas and Institutional Change in the Twentieth Century*. Cambridge: Cambridge University Press.

Fearon, J. and Wendt, A., 2002. Rationalism v. Constructivism: A Skeptical View. In: W. Carsnaes, T. Risse and B.A. Simmons, eds, *Handbook of International Relations*. London: Sage Publications, 52–73.

Federal Open Market Committee, 1979. Meeting. August 14. Available from: www.federalreserve.gov/monetarypolicy/files/FOMC19790814meeting.pdf.

Finnemore, M. and Sikkink, K., 1998. International Norm Dynamics and Political Change. *International Organization*, 52, 887–917.

Fioretos, O., 2011. Historical Institutionalism in International Relations. *International Organization*, 65(2), 367–399.

Fukuyama, F., 1991. *The End of History and the Last Man*. New York: Free Press, 1991.

Galbraith, J.K., 1958. *The Affluent Society*. Boston, MA: Houghton-Mifflin.

Greenspan, A., 2004. Risk and Uncertainty in Monetary Policy. Remarks at the Meetings of the American Economic Association, San Diego, California, January 3. Available from: www.federalreserve.gov/boarddocs/speeches/2004/20040103/default. htm.

Greenspan, A., 2007. *The Age of Turbulence*. New York: Penguin.

Mahoney, J. and Thelen, K., 2010. *Explaining Institutional Change: Ambiguity, Agency and Power*. Cambridge: Cambridge University Press.

Minsky, H.P., 1986. *Stabilizing an Unstable Economy*. New Haven, CT: Yale University Press.

Minsky, H.P., 1992. The Financial Instability Hypothesis. The Jerome Levy Economics Institute Working Paper No. 74, May. Available from: www.levy.org/pubs/wp74.pdf.

Pierson, P., 2000. Increasing Returns, Path Dependence, and the Study of Politics. *American Political Science Review*, 94(2), 251–267.

Pierson, P., 2004. *Politics in Time: History, Institutions and Social Analysis*. Princeton, NJ: Princeton University Press.

Ray, J.L., 1995. *Democracy and International Conflict*. Columbia: University of South Carolina Press.

Rorty, R., 1987. Method, Social Science, and Social Hope. In: M.T. Gibbons, ed., *Interpreting Politics*. New York: New York University Press, pp. 241–259.

Ross, A.G., 2006. Coming in from the Cold: Constructivism and Emotions. *European Journal of International Relations*, 12(2), 197–222.

Russett, B., 1993. *Grasping the Democratic Peace*. Princeton, NJ: Princeton University Press.

Schmidt, V.A., 2008. Discursive Institutionalism: The Explanatory Power of Ideas and Discourse. *Annual Review of Political Science*, 11, 303–326.

Schmidt, V.A., 2010. Taking Ideas and Discourse Seriously: Explaining Change through Discursive Institutionalism as the Fourth "New Institutionalism". *European Political Science Review*, 2(1).

Skowronek, S., 1993. *The Politics Presidents Make.* Cambridge, MA: Harvard University Press.

Skowronek, S., 2011. *Presidential Leadership in Political Time: Reprise and Reappraisal.* Lawrence: University Press of Kansas.

Solomon, A., 1995. *The Confidence Game.* New York: Simon and Schuster.

Waltz, K., 1979. *Theory of International Politics.* New York: McGraw-Hill.

Wendt, A., 1999. *Social Theory of International Politics.* Cambridge: Cambridge University Press.

Williamson, J., 1993. Development and the "Washington Consensus". *World Development*, 21, 1239–1336.

13 A reflexive practice of prudence

Harry Gould

From Aristotle onward, we have been taught to think of prudence as an attribute either of the character or of the mind, but consistently as a virtue of the intellect (*aretai dianoetikai*).[1] Although in all understandings it is concerned with deliberate human action and practice, the tradition has always insisted that it is not just a skill. It had (at least until Hobbes) been understood to be something of a higher order than a (mere) skill (Hobbes 1996 [1651], I.V.VII–IX, I.VIII.IV–V, IV.XL.VI.II). I find the proposition that prudence is a virtue that can be possessed to be unsatisfactory; I propose rather that prudence is more fruitfully conceptualized as a practice, a much broader notion. To be prudent, or to act prudently is best captured not in Aristotelian or Stoic psychology, but as a practice informed by Wittgenstein's notion of "knowing how to go on". This points toward an understanding of prudence as a reflexive, rule-governed practice, as a "form of life" that involves thinking both about how we act and how we ought to act. As I will develop later, this is rather at odds with the predominant understanding of practice in the field, which by stripping deliberation from its understanding of practice, by making the relevant forms of knowledge wholly inarticulable and tacit, and by treating rules as enacted but never considered, strips all reflexivity from practice.

To get at the traditional understandings of prudence from which I begin, it will be useful to start with the respective treatments of the *composition* of prudence of several of the authors/traditions that have provided our core vocabulary and semantics of prudence. Aristotle gave us a list of five component sub-virtues (to which he subsequently added two more), the Stoics six, Cicero three faculties, Aquinas eight, and Kant three (see Table 13.1)

Surveying these sets of attributes points immediately to a conception of prudence as *cognitive* in character; in most of these treatments, the attributes identified are either mental *operations* or cognitive *capacities*. The very word "*phronesis*" derives from the verb "*phroneo*", to think. To use Kantian language, the components of prudence in these renderings are *faculties* (Kant 1998 [1781/1787], A95–115; 2000 [1791], 20: 206–208, 20: 245–247; Rorty 1979). This is admittedly less clearly the case with Aquinas' docility, caution, circumspection, and patience, however; they are difficult to

Table 13.1 The parts of prudence

Aristotle	Stoa	Cicero	Aquinas	Kant
Deliberation	Deliberation	Memory	Memory	Understanding
Judgment	Skill in conjecture	Intelligence	Understanding	Wit
Discernment	Quickness of mind	Foresight	Docility	Judgment
Practical intuition	Calculation of value		Shrewdness	
Cleverness	Knowledge of the good		Foresight	
(Skill in conjecture)	Resourcefulness		Circumspec-tion	
(Quickness of mind)			Caution	
			Patience	

characterize in purely cognitive terms, and seem more related to the *temperament* than to cognition. For this reason they are perhaps better thought of as *dispositions* than faculties, but like faculties, they are amenable to training and improvement.

Whether cognitive or dispositional, all of these constituents of prudence share a focus. In Aristotle, *phronesis* is related to the part of the intellect that is concerned with *action*. In Aristotle's schema, one deliberates, judges, intuits, discerns, and exercises cleverness to *guide action* toward a pre-given, but always subject-to-reflexive-reevaluation, aim. For Cicero, the memory, the operations of the intelligence and of foresight all function to *guide action*:

> *Prudentia* is the knowledge of things, which are good, or bad, or neither good nor bad. Its parts are memory, intelligence, and foresight. Memory is that faculty by which the mind recovers the knowledge of things, which have been. Intelligence is that by which it perceives what exists at present. Foresight is that by which anything is seen to be about to happen, before it does happen.
>
> (Cicero 1949, II.53)

Prudentia is doing "the right thing at the right time"; it is "the art of conduct" (Cicero 1913, I.142–143; 1931, V.16, 18). This understanding plainly held as well in Stoic accounts of *phronesis*, in which it consists "in the first instance [in] considering and doing what must be done, and, in the second instance, considering what one should distribute and what one should choose, and what one should endure" (Stobaeus 2008, II.VII.5b5). The focus on guiding action was central as well in the Thomistic and Kantian accounts of prudence; admittedly, however, in Kant's case, prudence was a guide to action that was inferior to moral deliberation (Kant 2011 [1785]). Prudence may be a mental state or a concatenation of mental states, an assemblage of mental operations, a form of knowledge or of reason, but it is always about *actions* and human *practices*. It is always about purposive human conduct.

Knowing how to go on

All of the conceptions of prudence we have surveyed share a great deal of common ground; the only significant divergence appears to be with regard to the question of whether action has to be in accordance with some external moral-evaluative standard to count as (truly) prudent. That distinction is hardly negligible, but it is overshadowed by the common elements summed up in Machiavelli's formula of prudence as "knowing how to assess the dangers, and to choose the least bad course of action as being the one to follow" or Cicero's "knowledge of things that one should pursue and avoid" (Machiavelli 2005 [1532], ch. XXI; Cicero 1913, I.153). They all share in common a concern with *action* with *doing*, and antecedently, with knowing how to act appropriate to ever changing circumstances. In other words, they are all concerned with "knowing how to go on".

I take my cue here from Wittgenstein's discussion of rule following in *Philosophical Investigations*; to understand a rule (his example is a mathematical progression) and to follow that rule enables one to say (within that context), "Now I can go on". At the risk of oversimplification, prudence is about knowing how to go on in all of the varied circumstances in which one might find oneself, or, at similar risk of reification, all of the varied circumstances in which a state might find itself (Levine 2012). Knowing how to go on is situation dependent and rule dependent. As Wittgenstein emphasized, it logically entails understanding the rule(s) at hand:

150. The grammar of the word 'knows' is evidently closely related to that of 'can', 'is able to'. But also closely related to that of 'understands'. ('Mastery of a technique')

151. But there is also *this* use of the word 'to know': we say 'Now I know!' – and similarly 'Now I can do it!' and 'Now I understand!'
   Let us imagine the following example: A writes a series of numbers down; B watches him and tries to find a law for the sequence of numbers. If he succeeds he exclaims: 'Now I can go on!' ...

179. ... It is clear that *we should not say B had the right to say the words 'Now I know how to go on', just because he thought of the formula – unless experience showed that there was a connection between thinking of the formula ... and actually continuing the series* ... The words 'Now I know how to go on' were correctly used when he thought of the formula ... but that does not mean that his statement is only short for a description of all

the circumstances which constitute the scene for our language-game. Think of how we learn to use the expressions 'Now I know how to go on', 'Now I can go on' and others; in what family of language games we learn their use.

(Wittgenstein 1958, §150, 151, 179, spelling modernized; emphasis in original)

Prudence is not the understanding of *a* rule, but the understanding of entire congeries of rules. There is no one rule of prudence any more than there is a specific, fixed set of rules that encompass prudence. It is a rule-governed practice, but as Dobel notes, it is more than simply a set of algorithms (Dobel 1998). History, *memoria*—our ability to usefully recall it—provide precedents and exemplars, but precedents and exemplars do not ever provide us with a simple if-then calculus or practical syllogism (*Nicomachean Ethics*, VI.7.1141b17–22). No two situations are ever identical. Hence the role of *intellegentia*; it serves *inter alia* to clarify the extent to which the present resembles the precedents of the past; it tells us the extent to which apparent exemplars are relevant, and enables us to reason by analogy accounting for those similarities and differences. Perhaps this idea of prudence as knowing how to go on is best captured in Cicero's linkage to *providentia*; knowing how to go on is about projecting patterns into the future; it is about extrapolation of trends and taking reasonable account of and making reasonable preparation for contingencies. It is not foreknowledge in the literal sense, but rather anticipation and preparation, the demonstration and application of foresight.[2]

So far, this reads little different than what we have seen so far minus the contested stipulation that ends must be moral for action to be prudent; that is precisely where this approach becomes relevant. The end that one is trying to achieve might have its basis in a traditional moral system, or it might have its basis in something selfish, or perhaps in *raison d'état* (which *is* after all, a moral system); ultimately this does not bear on the question of whether or not one knows how to go on in any given setting. Strictly speaking, that fact (the basis of the end being sought) is only one aspect of the situation; it is background information (Dewey 1991 [1938]). External observers might find your end laudable or condemnable, but whether you know *how* to achieve it is an empirical issue. The immediate response that this engenders is to assert that *contra* the insistence of Aristotle and particularly Aquinas, this makes prudence strictly instrumental; it reduces prudence from an exalted virtue to the mere cleverness or cunning from which Aquinas was at such pains to differentiate it and Kant so inclined to equate it. That distinction, however, does not bear scrutiny. Prudence is about practice, and while practice itself is always *normative,* it need not always have *moral* content *sensu stricto*. It is caution when caution is called for; audacity when audacity is called for; magnanimity when it is called for and cruelty when it is called for; violence when violence is necessary, and accommodation or flight when necessary. It is all of the things Machiavelli subsumed under "the path of wrongdoing" when they are necessary, and it is the Classical and Christian virtues when they are appropriate—no less a moralist than Kant understood this. Prudence is about determining *when* behaviors are appropriate—but in more than the March and Olsen (1998, 2006) "logics of appropriateness" sense—and it is always about *acting* upon that knowledge. This set of behaviors (and the related extrapolable rules an observer might tease out) constitutes a practice. Prudence is not only *about* practice; it *is* itself a practice, one that relies upon reflection and introspection prior to acting.

Practice without and with reflection

This gets us into the terrain of International Relations' "practice turn". In order to substantiate my assertion that beyond being a mental operation, prudence is a practice, I need to delve into ongoing debates in International Relations concerning what constitutes a practice. In IR, the understanding developed by Pierre Bourdieu holds sway. I find much of use in this approach, although I cannot accept it *tout court*, because it is in fundamental ways anti-reflexive; for that reason, I will return to Wittgenstein and the rule-based approach to practice he inspired to complete my account of prudence as a reflexive practice.

As Vincent Pouliot, International Relations' main expositor of Bourdieu's understanding of practices, distills them, "practices are the result of inarticulate, practical knowledge that makes what is to be done appear 'self-evident' or commonsensical" (Pouliot 2008, p. 258). In several places, Pouliot emphasizes that practice is, by its nature, unreflexive, as are the forms of knowledge and the dispositions upon which it relies. Key to this understanding of practice is that one thinks neither about *what* one is doing, nor *why* one is doing it.[3]

Pouliot asserts that practice rests upon "background knowledge", what Michael Polanyi called "tacit knowledge", or what James Scott calls *metis*, "a rudimentary kind of knowledge that can be acquired only by practice and that all but *defies being communicated* in written or oral form apart from actual practice" (Pouliot 2008, p. 207, emphasis added). This is a somewhat distinct conception of *metis* from that found in classical thought. *Metis*, here, is a kind of knowledge; in the classical tradition from which Scott adopted it, *metis* was a form of reason analogous, in fact, to *phronesis*, but lacking the latter's (contested) moral aspect (Hesiod 2007, lines 355, 885–890, 924; Brown 1952; Detienne and Vernant 1978; Holmberg 1997).

The practical knowledge that informs Pouliot's practices is "extremely difficult to convey … so implicit and automatic that its bearer is at a loss to explain it … [it is] tacit, inarticulate, and automatic … [and] appears self-evident to its bearer" (Pouliot 2008, in Scott 1999, p. 315).[4] Without reverting to Aristotelian vocabulary, Pouliot and Adler liken practical knowledge to *techne*/ skill rather than *episteme*, the sort of knowledge that can be represented (Adler and Pouliot 2011, p. 8). This is a false dichotomy; it ignores *phronesis*, the type of action-guiding knowledge concerned not with *making* like *techne*, but with *doing*, with conduct, with practice. Going back to Aristotle, we see that his conception of *phronesis* is much closer to Adler and Pouliot's concept of practical knowledge than his conception of *techne* was. *Techne* is concerned with making (*poiesis*), with the arts and artisanry; it is skill in a particular craft or knowledge of a craft's methods (*Nicomachean Ethics*, VI.4.1140a1–22). *Phronesis* guides action (*praxis*). *Praxis* referred more narrowly to "what results from deliberation (*bouleusis*) and deliberate choice (*prohairesis*)" (Reeve 2012, p. 140). "[M]aking is different from doing ... Hence, the rational quality concerned with doing is different from the rational quality concerned with making. Nor is one of them a part of the other, for doing is not a form of making, nor making a form of doing" (*Nicomachean Ethics*, VI.4.1140a1–5). *Poiesis* is about the making of *things*, of objects. Without a particular material product as its end, practice is done for its own sake; the performance *is* the purpose. More precisely, *excellent* performance is the purpose:

> with action (*praxis*) ... there is nothing by which to judge the case as an instance of doing well (*eupraxia*) apart from the action itself. We judge the producer by his producing, and this in turn by his product, so therefore the producer (indirectly) by something other than his activity. But we judge the practical agent simply by his doing and not in turn by anything external by which the doing is judged.
>
> (Broadie 1991, p. 208)

Returning to Pouliot, we see that there are three operative parts to the Bourdieuean understanding of practice, Habitus, Field, and Practical Sense. Habitus is a "system of durable, transposable dispositions, which integrates past experiences and functions at every moment as a matrix of perception, appreciation, and action making possible the accomplishment of infinitely differentiated tasks" (Pouliot 2008, p. 272). Habitus has an historical dimension inasmuch as human conduct tends to be significantly determined by previous experiences and through socialization and imitation. Practical knowledge of the sort referred to above is central to habitus; a practice is: "learned by doing; from direct experience in and on the world ... *Without reflection or deliberation*, habitus tends to generate 'reasonable, commonsense behaviors' which agents may be at pains explaining" (Pouliot 2008, p. 273, emphasis added).

The next element of practice is Field; "a field is a social configuration structured along three main dimensions: relations of power, objects of struggle, and taken-for-granted rules". The final aspect is the most important from present purposes: fields are "structured by taken-for-granted rules" (Pouliot 2008, p. 275). While practice retains a role for rules, it is one in which the latter operate only pre-cognitively; they "are not thought but simply enacted" (Pouliot 2008, pp. 270–271).

Bourdieu's third element of practice, Practical Sense, entails "a socially constituted sense of the game" that makes "certain practices appear ... 'informed by common sense'" (Pouliot 2008, p. 275). Pouliot explains, "It is through the actualization of the past in the present that agents know what is to be done in the future, *often without conscious reflection or reference to explicit and codified knowledge*" (Pouliot 2008, pp. 275–276, emphasis added). It is, in other words, what enables people to comport themselves in a situation without conscious reflection.

There is much of use here; there are a number of tantalizing analogues between aspects of this understanding of practice and prudence. Prudence is a practice that seems particularly to rest upon possession of tacit knowledge. Like tacit knowledge, most understandings of prudence do not convey any sense that it is amenable to *formal* instruction.[5] It appears to be "learnt experientially, in and through practice"; however, this can only be pushed so far or it runs the risk of neglecting the role of instruction, emulation, and example found in all of the treatments. Although not *formal* modes of education, the heuristic roles of exempla and maxims must be accounted a form of instruction. Perhaps Aristotle's treatment of the role of the *phronimos* comes closest to capturing the role of training or instruction in learning the practice of prudence. Although Aristotle's focus in discussing the *phronimos* was on the development of the virtues of the character, the point is that the conduct and reasoning of the *phronimos* provided a model for emulation. Some of this is captured in the historical dimension of habitus; its emphasis on imitation and socialization shows that even if instruction is not formal, the process of learning to be prudent, or more specifically, the process of cultivating the faculties and dispositions that are taken to sum to prudence is at the very least dialogic.

Another signal difference between prudence and the Bourdieuean notion of practice is the way in which the latter enacts a separation between its underlying form of knowledge (Practical Sense) and all others. Practical Sense is understood to operate prior to instrumental reason, norm compliance or communicative action (Pouliot 2008, p. 276). Rather than challenge the accuracy of this characterization, I will only say that as a form of practice, prudence does not comport with it. There is always an instrumental character to prudential reasoning, and there is always an instrumental character to the *practice* of prudence, to conducting oneself prudently. That is not something that is determined separately from the practice of *being* prudent; it is *intrinsic to* it. Prudence is about end-driven human conduct, and conduct is deliberate— that is what distinguishes it from behavior. Prudence is instrumental in the most basic sense of the term; prudence is knowing how to act to achieve some aim. One response to this might be to suggest that reasoning prudentially is merely another name for reasoning instrumentally, and is thus posterior to practical sense which tells us when to employ this type of reason. I do not believe that claim can be sustained, because prudence exceeds the category of modes of reasoning because it is always simultaneously a way of *acting*.

To supplement the Bourdieuean account of practice, and create one that captures the sense of prudence as reflexive practice, I turn to Richard Flathman's Wittgenstein-inspired account, an account that bears several similarities to Constructivism in its rule-oriented form. Practice here, relates to "actions that people take *intentionally, knowingly, for reasons*" (Flathman 1977, p. 12, emphasis added). It entails "sets of actions that recur over time and that are thought to be interrelated or to cohere together ... practices represent distinct, recognizable modes of activity marked by recurrent and interconnected characteristics" (Flathman 1977, p. 12). Rather than a specific defining type of action that marks one practice off from another, there tends instead to be a "configuration or pattern of actions that is characteristic of the practice and by which it is in fact identified" (Flathman 1977, p. 13).

Metis might at some level underlie actions, but there is *always* a deliberative, reflexive component to the practice of prudence. Practice involves "rules and rule-guided conduct ... practices can be best ... understood in terms of the acceptance by participants in the practice of rules according to which it is right ... that they act in certain ways and refrain from certain other actions" (Flathman 1977, p. 14). As Flathman notes, however, this "ought" may only imply a sort of "if-then" reasoning. "As ordered, regular, patterned as it often is, rule-governed conduct involves human *action*; it involves reflection, intention and decision on the part of the agents in question. Above all it involves having reasons for what one does" (Flathman 1977, pp. 14–15, emphasis in original). This differs starkly from Bourdieu; here practice is emphatically neither infra-conscious nor automatic. Reasons and reasoning play central roles; one reasons not just about the fit of ends to means, but about *why* one has the ends she has.

Flathman draws a parallel between this understanding of practice and Wittgenstein's notions of language-games and forms of life, "notions that refer to clusters, nodes or foci of meaningful activity that form more or less distinct aspects of the life". In drawing this parallel, Flathman returns to the centrality of rules:

> A key element in this mode of analyzing such clusters of meaningfulness is the notion of *rule* and *rule-governed* conduct ... the investigator who seeks to give an account of meaningful discourse in a particular aspect of human affairs will seek to identify the rules and conventions that are operative in communication that takes place in that discourse.
>
> (Flathman 1977, p. 18, emphasis in original)

Language-games and forms of life signify clusters of *meaningful, deliberate* actions by which we intentionally mark one part of the social world off from another, and by which we *make* some part of the world meaningful:

> The intimate relationship between meaning ... and the things we do and the contexts in which we typically do them ... is at the heart of Wittgenstein's

notion of language-games ... A social practice ... consists of a distinguishable and more or less internally cohesive cluster or set of rule-guided, purposive actions ... The shared ideas, values, and rules that figure in such a set, the concepts in which those ideas, values and rules are embodied and through the use of which they are expressed and otherwise acted upon, *supply participants with their way of making sense of the world* ... their way of understanding, organizing, and giving ... expression to those understandings.

(Flathman 1977, p. 123, emphasis added)

Conclusion

It is only by taking elements from both accounts that we can see how prudence constitutes a reflexive practice. Per the Bourdieuean account, prudence utilizes *metis*/Practical Sense. Prudence, like *metis*, comes—in part—from practice and defies being straightforwardly communicated; it is taught by example and emulation, by aphorism, apothegm, and maxim. Like Habitus, prudence is historical; this relates to the issue of the pedagogy of prudence; socialization—which is a form of education—is key.

Prudence may be difficult to explain; why a particular course of action is chosen or determined to be the prudent course may be difficult to explain. However, for present purposes, IR's dominant account goes too far in stripping reflection from practice altogether. Likewise, it goes too far in removing any meaningful notion of rules from practice. Yes, rules may often be taken for granted, but to claim that they are simply pre-cognitively enacted *qua* rules is insupportable in the specific case of the practice of prudence.

The actions comprising practice of prudence are *taken for reasons*. Perhaps Bourdieu is correct, and there is little deliberation *about* the reasons, but that does not mean that the specific practice of prudence operates consistently bereft of reflection. Flathman's emphasis on practice as a cluster of meaning-given activities ties prudence back to traditional understandings in one respect, but also emphasizes—as the traditional conceptualizations also did—that prudence is more than reasoning in a certain way; one does not simply *think* prudently, one either *acts* prudently—the purpose of prudence being to command the will—or one is not *being* prudent. In this regard we may rightly speak of prudence as a Wittgensteinian form of life.

As a practice/form of life, prudence allows us to make sense of some part of the world, *and* understand how to carry on in it. Prudence tells us whether and how to act, and retains a place for thinking about *why*. It guides our actions *and* gives reasons for and meaning to those actions. Prudence is a practice *par excellence* in which intention is central. All of the classically delineated mental operations (as well as the dispositions) that sum to prudence and prudent conduct are driven by anterior intentions—intentions albeit that may be inscrutable to observers.

Notes

1 Aristotle divided the virtues between those of the Intellect (*aretai dianoetikai*), and those of the Character (*aretai ethike*) (Aristotle, *Nicomachean Ethics*, VI.3.1139b23–32).
2 Aristotle's account was even more heavily built around sensory—especially visual—metaphors.
3 Pouliot later equivocally backed away somewhat from this position (Adler and Pouliot 2011).
4 Pouliot draws a comparison with §217 of Wittgenstein's *Investigations*, but ignores that passage's context within a discussion of rule following, which serves to undermine the comparison.
5 Kant's "Pedagogy of Prudence" is an exception (Kant 2007 [1803], 9:445, 450, 455, 486).

References

Adler, E. and Pouliot, V., 2011. *International Practices*. Cambridge: Cambridge University Press.

Aristotle, 1926. *Nicomachean Ethics*, translated by H. Rackham. Cambridge, MA: Loeb/Harvard University Press.

Aristotle, 2000. *Nicomachean Ethics*, translated by R. Crisp. Cambridge: Cambridge University Press.

Aristotle, 2009. *Nicomachean Ethics*, translated by W.D. Ross and L. Brown. Oxford: Oxford University Press.

Broadie, S., 1991. *Ethics with Aristotle*. Oxford: Oxford University Press.

Brown, N.O., 1952. The Birth of Athena. *Transactions and Proceedings of the American Philological Association*, 83, 130–143.

Cicero, M., 1913. *De Officiis*, translated by W. Miller. Cambridge, MA: Loeb/Harvard University Press.

Cicero, M., 1931. *De Finibus Bonorum et Malorum*, translated by H. Rackham. Cambridge, MA: Loeb/Harvard University Press.

Cicero, M., 1949. *De Inventione*. In: H.M. Hubbell, trans, *On Invention. The Best Kind of Orator. Topics*. Cambridge, MA: Loeb/Harvard University Press.

Detienne, M. and Vernant, J.-P., 1978. *Cunning Intelligence in Greek Culture and Society*, translated by J. Lloyd. Atlantic Highlands, NJ: Humanities Press.

Dewey, J., 1991 [1938]. *Logic: The Theory of Inquiry: John Dewey, The Later Works v. 12.*, J.A. Boydston, ed., Carbondale, IL: Southern Illinois University Press.

Dobel, P., 1998. Political Prudence and the Ethics of Leadership. *Public Administration Review*, 58(1), 74–81.

Flathman, R., 1977. *The Practice of Rights*. Cambridge: Cambridge University Press.

Hesiod, 2007. *Theogony*. In: G. Most, trans. *Theogony, Works and Days, Testimonia*. Cambridge, MA: Loeb/Harvard University Press.

Hobbes, T., 1996 [1651]. *Leviathan*. R. Tuck, ed., Cambridge: Cambridge University Press

Holmberg, I., 1997. The Sign of Μῆτις. *Arethusa*, 30(1), 1–33.

Kant, I., 1998 [1781, A edition; 1787, B edition]. Critique of Pure Reason. In: P. Guyer and A. Wood, eds, *The Cambridge Edition of the Works of Immanuel Kant: Critique of Pure Reason*. Cambridge: Cambridge University Press.

Kant, I., 2000 [1791]. Critique of the Power of Judgment. In: P. Guyer, ed., *The Cambridge Edition of the Works of Immanuel Kant: Critique of the Power of Judgment*. Cambridge: Cambridge University Press.

Kant, I., 2007 [1803]. Lectures on Pedagogy. In: G. Zöller and R.B. Loude, eds, *The Cambridge Edition of the Works of Immanuel Kant: Anthropology, History, and Education*. Cambridge: Cambridge University Press.

Kant, I., 2011 [1785]. Groundwork of the Metaphysics of Morals. In: M. Gregor and J. Timmerman, eds, *Immanuel Kant: Groundwork of the Metaphysics of Morals: A German–English Edition*. Cambridge: Cambridge University Press.

Levine, D., 2012. *Recovering International Relations: The Promise of a Sustainable Critique*. Oxford: Oxford University Press.

Machiavelli, N., 2005 [1532]. *The Prince*. In: P. Bondanella, ed., *Niccolò Machiavelli: The Prince*. Oxford: Oxford University Press.

March, J.G. and Olsen, J.P., 1998. The Institutional Dynamics of International Political Orders. *International Organization*, 52(4), 943–969.

March, J.G. and Olsen, J.P., 2006. The Logic of Appropriateness. *ARENA Working Papers*, April 9.

Pouliot, V., 2008. The Logic of Practicality: A Theory of Practice of Security Communities. *International Organization*, 62(2), 257–288.

Reeve, C.D.C., 2012. *Action, Contemplation, and Happiness*. Cambridge, MA: Harvard University Press.

Rorty, R., 1979. *Philosophy and the Mirror of Nature*. Princeton, NJ: Princeton University Press.

Scott, J.C., 1999. *Seeing Like a State: How Certain Schemes to Improve the Human Condition Have Failed*. New Haven, CT: Yale University Press.

Stobaeus, 2008. Anthology, In: B. Inwood and L.P. Gerson, eds, *The Stoics Reader: Selected Writings and Testimonia*. Indianapolis, IN: Hackett Pub. Co.

Wittgenstein, L., 1958. *Philosophical Investigations*, 3rd edn. G.E.M. Anscombe, ed., New York: Macmillan.

14 Reflexivity beyond subjectivism

From Descartes to Dewey

Mark E. Button

Reflexive (adjective): capable of turning or bending back.

Reflexivity (noun): The property in language, text, etc., of self-consciously referring to itself or its production.

What is the problem to which reflexivity is offered as a possible answer? If by reflexivity we mean the capacity of agents to reflect critically upon themselves as epistemic, political, and ethical agents, then a whole host of things stand before us as challenges to and problems for reflexivity: heteronomy, determinism, historicism, reification, willful blindness, naïve realism, introspective illusions, self-confirming biases, national chauvinism, transcendental exceptionalism, self-delusion, etc. For international relations theory with a critical edge, there is something initially enticing about a concept that promises to periodically trouble these forces as they operate in and through us as socially constituted beings. Owing to our ineluctable dependence on a wide variety of social institutions for our sense of moral and epistemic truth, reflexivity holds out the promise of a check on the social forces that constitute us as moral and epistemic subjects. In this sense, reflexivity makes after-thoughts, second-thoughts, and third-thoughts intellectual and practical virtues for moral agents, so long as these after-thoughts are able to reliably correct for incomplete, erroneous, or biased beliefs and judgments. Assuming (for now) that this latter condition holds, reflexivity might still be the type of practice that—like the owl of Minerva—will always arrive too late to be a useful guide to practical judgment and action. Nonetheless, at a deeper level, we might say that freedom of the mind and freedom of the will necessarily presuppose the ability of a subject to take itself as an object of inquiry, and therewith, to think and do otherwise than habit, custom, and institutions instruct (Frankfurt 1971).

In our role as political scientists, or at least as students of politics, reflexivity should be of interest to us insofar as it enables us to interrogate the diverse operations and effects of power—particularly in regard to the way in which dominant expressions of social and political power interpolate us within its means and ends. In this sense, reflexivity might come to the aid of what Weber called an "ethics of responsibility" because an ethics of responsibility (in contrast to an "ethics of ultimate ends") commits us to giving an account of ourselves and our actions as moral and political beings (Weber 1946, pp. 120–121; see also Ish-Shalom, Chapter 4 in this volume). But my critical, Nietzschean-inspired question for the contributors to this volume is whether reflexivity amounts to a false promise or a delusive ideal. Recall that the first line of Nietzsche's *Genealogy of Morals* reads: "We are unknown to ourselves, we men of knowledge—and with good reason. We have never sought ourselves—how could it ever happen that we should ever *find* ourselves" (1969, p. 1). Nietzsche goes on to argue that we are beings who have to misunderstand ourselves. A great deal of contemporary social and cognitive psychology provides abundant empirical confirmation for this essential Nietzschean insight. As I detail further below, social psychology reveals the significant and disturbing limits of our reflective capacities: we are naïve realists, prone to introspective illusions that we are not systematically biased in all kinds of ways, and each of these elements help to sustain the self-confirming belief that we are veritistic observers capable of sound judgment about the social world around us. The central argument of this chapter is that unless and until the defenders of reflexivity attend to these psychological and philosophical challenges, reflexivity is bound to be an article of unreconstructed Cartesian faith, rather than a pragmatic public process that might increase the scope and reliability of our knowledge claims.

***

Drawing upon the influential work of Anthony Giddens, it has been a commonplace in this volume to think of reflexivity as "a capacity [that] allows us to potentially reflect upon why we do what we do, and even modify our thoughts and actions" (Amoureux, Chapter 1 in this volume). This emphasis on an individual capacity for reflexivity spurs the additional (Kantian) thought that reflexivity is itself a certain kind of ethical practice (Amoureux, Chapter 1) or "style" (Levine, Chapter 5): a way for a self to possess a relationship to the self—and the broader cultural and institutional sources giving shape to the self—in a manner that is more self-aware and morally responsible than would be the case without the periodic exercise of reflexivity. Steele (Chapter 3) and Ish-Shalom each acknowledge important limitations in relation to the practice of reflexivity, but they still emphasize "the responsibilities and obligation of self-reflexivity" (Ish-Shalom, Chapter 4). This way of conceiving reflexivity—as a first-person perspective of monitoring the sources and credentials of one's beliefs and conduct—is something that Descartes and Kant would each recognize as fundamental to a normative model of epistemic agency (see also Korsgaard 1996; Sosa 2009). For Descartes, the mind reflecting upon itself—and thus detaching itself from the senses—is the necessary starting point for the pursuit of certainty in any and all philosophical and scientific inquiries (Descartes 1969, pp. 165–166). For all of his acute sensitivity to the role of history in the formation of human consciousness, Hans-Georg Gadamer shared in this basic Cartesian orientation to the mind by arguing that "the structure of reflexivity is fundamentally given with all consciousness" (1994, p. 341). For Gadamer this meant that an historically effected consciousness could always rise above that of which it is conscious.

Despite the hold that this image of the willfully self-transparent mind still has on scholars today, an extensive amount of recent work in social psychology and moral philosophy suggests that we should be a good deal more skeptical about the intellectual feasibility and ethical merits of this traditional, subject-centered construal of reflexivity. In what immediately follows I raise some critical questions about the way in which reflexivity has been conceived in many of the chapters of this volume. I develop these points not with the aim of undermining the coherence of reflexivity as an idea or an intellectual value, but with the goal of providing some initial suggestions about how scholars in international relations and within other fields of the social sciences might begin to realistically address these challenges. Ultimately I wish to call for less Descartes and more Dewey (or just more pragmatism) in our understanding of and approach to processes of reflexivity. In light of the intrinsic limits and biases to which first-person practices of self-reflection are prone, this chapter calls at once for less subjectivism and intellectual rationalism and for more pluralism and public-political scrutiny in our efforts to motivate and institutionalize the practice of a genuinely *social reflexivity*.

Limits of subjective reflexivity

Subjecting our beliefs to reflective scrutiny seems like a commonsensical way to try to ensure (or increase) the veracity of those beliefs. The motivation to engage in the reflective monitoring of our beliefs and knowledge claims would seem to be provided by the basic desire to hold true beliefs and by the equally basic desire to minimize the possession of false beliefs. In most cases of everyday human conduct, our ability to be effective agents pursuing whatever ends we set ourselves hinges on maximizing true beliefs and minimizing false beliefs. In this sense, reflexivity seems like a core requirement not only for an epistemically responsible agent, but for any kind of rational human agent at all. Likewise, in the Kantian tradition, the very possibility of a form of morality consistent with free human agency presupposes the reflective capacity of the mind to take its reason (and not its senses or desires) as the author of its principles or maxims (Kant 1959, pp. 66–67).

Yet without offering an account for how reflexivity can actually improve the epistemic reliability of our beliefs and knowledge claims we do not possess a sufficient defense of the epistemic value of reflexivity, nor do we have a convincing account of its connection to a normative model of ethical agency. As Hilary Kornblith has argued, "The mere fact that we have applied some additional check on our first-order beliefs tells us nothing about the reliability of the checking procedure" (2012, p. 17). For the field of International

Relations, as with the rest of the social sciences, the value of reflexivity for satisfying a model of responsible epistemic agency hinges on the quality and practical effects of reflective practices themselves. Thus, one of the first questions we must ask is: How good are we at scrutinizing the sources and evidentiary bases of our beliefs and judgments?

The answer that social psychologists and philosophers have been giving to this question for years is: not very good at all. First-person introspection on beliefs, judgments, and actions is extremely limited and prone to a variety of cognitive biases. The limits of our reflective capacities are bound-up with an assortment of features of human mental processes that fundamentally disrupt the phenomenology of reflexivity, including: sub-personal processes affecting judgments (including stereotypes), the unconscious influence of priming and other external cues on belief formation, and well-known self-confirming and belief-preserving biases, to name just a few (Tversky and Kahneman 1974; Nisbett and Wilson 1977; Kunda 1999). Given the prevalence of psychological propensities like the "bias blind spot"—wherein individuals identify the operation of bias in human judgment, except when it is their own—first-person subjective reflexivity faces a number of significant challenges. The first is motivational: the bias blind spot in human judgment not only obviates the impetus behind a principle of reflexivity since most people are overconfident in their freedom from bias, but this mistaken belief in the asymmetric distribution of bias is further underscored by the illusion that reflecting on one's judgments can correct for bias and systematic errors in judgment (Pronin, Lin, and Ross 2002; Pronin and Kugler 2007; Ahlstrom-Vij 2013). Because the processes that give rise to various forms of bias operate on a sub-personal level and do not leave any "phenomenological trace", first-person reflective scans for bias reliably produce a comforting (and false) null hypothesis. This last point introduces a second and even more difficult problem for the principle of reflexivity. When individuals are actively primed to consider the sources and influences that might have shaped their own judgments (like social group or ethnic attachments), these forms of influence and partiality are consistently viewed as uniquely valuable and enlightening, whereas memberships in complementary but opposing groups are viewed as distorting and biasing influences on others' ability to reason clearly about a shared problem (Ehrlinger, Gilovich, and Ross 2005).[1] In practice first-person reflexivity is often another word for retrospective belief consolidation or, more simply, rationalization (Kornblith 2012, pp. 23–26). In light of these widespread psychological constraints, recommendations for provoking reflexivity in others (Steele, Chapter 3) and exercising it as an ethical responsibility of individual scholarship (Amoureux, Chapter 1; Steele, Chapter 3; Ish-Shalom, Chapter 4) will need greater elaboration and, above all, more psychological and social refinement to serve as a meaningful form of epistemic improvement for beings like us.

If the multiple reports from social psychology are correct, reflexivity cannot pass a basic test of pragmatism: the experimental and practical application of the concept appears to have no relationship to the ostensible meaning of the term. Put even more strongly: if second-order beliefs—i.e., the products of reflective self-scrutiny—push veritistic self-knowledge further away from us while simultaneously generating the false idea that we are engaging in a process that makes those beliefs more reliable, then there is something essentially incoherent in the very demand for and expectation of reflexivity that still needs to be worked out. The idea of reflexivity generates the impression that the self is not only autonomous in relation to belief and opinion formation, but sovereign in regard to those beliefs because the agent can, in principle, revise or reject them in virtue of their executive reflective powers. As we have seen, however, this picture is largely an illusion: it is false about our access to and control over our mental states, and this mistaken belief facilitates the unfortunate condition in which the very thing—reflexivity—that we suppose will bring us closer to a critical knowledge of ourselves, pushes that end further away from us. If, therefore, a commitment to reflexivity in international relations is to avoid the problem of self-deception (and delusive self-congratulation) in regard to the epistemic reliability of self-scrutiny, it will need to draw on a more complete understanding of human psychology as it develops the theory and practice of reflexivity.

One way of construing the basic point of the preceding line of argument is that the products of reflexivity are no more self-legitimating than an act of political sovereignty—even under democratic conditions (Rosanvalon 2011 comes to a similar conclusion, without drawing on experimental psychology). This means that the practices of reflexivity need to be scrutinized in their own right and these practices will need their own additional checks and balances in order to bear the normative burdens that they are asked to carry within the conduct of the social sciences. In this respect, I agree with those scholars who have convincingly argued that we cannot rely on ourselves—as willful cognitive agents—for epistemic improvement (Frantz and Janoff-Bulman 2000; Ahlstrom-Vij 2013; Kenyon 2014). As Nietzsche put it, "We cannot look around our own corner" (1974, p. 336).

Empowering reflexivity: toward a pragmatist model

How, then, might the latent ethical and epistemic promise of reflexivity find motivation and exercise in such a way as to avoid creating another complex layer of self-deception and self-validation? Against the individualist epistemology that undergirds a subjectivist conception of reflexivity, I want to point to the value of a pragmatist model of reflexivity grounded in a social epistemology. The formation of true belief, as with the formation of false belief and willful ignorance, is something that is carried out on pathways that are fundamentally social (Goldman 1999); maximizing the former (true belief) and reducing the latter (false belief/willful ignorance) will depend—in part—on an appropriately social and political conception of reflexivity.

I can only provide a general outline of what this might look like, but I think reflexivity needs to be conceived as the organized force of plural political actors who question the fundamental terms by which political self-identity is constituted and defended, and who sustain cultural openings within which the terms of political identity and loyalty can be re-negotiated without resentment. In other words, we need to take reflexivity out of the domain of the self-referential and auto-ethnographic, where reflexivity refers to the capacities and agency of individual actors (Amoureux and Steele, Introduction; Dauphinee, Chapter 2), and instead see it as a public power made practical by various forms of political resistance and cultural challenge. To my mind, organized political dissent—whether in Ferguson, Missouri or in the streets of Hong Kong—is among the most important and consequential forms of reflexivity available to citizens today. In a democracy, organized political dissent will always be a vital way in which to make good on the latent epistemic powers that exist within a diverse and disaggregated public. Ultimately, then, socio-political reflexivity exercised through the organization and communication of latent forms of dispersed knowledge is one part of an answer to fulfilling the conditions of political and epistemic responsibility because we are limited and partial creatures who are invested in forgetting and denying these constitutive facts about ourselves. And subjective introspection alone is far from sufficient—indeed, it is part of the problem.

In this context I want to note a difference with Jack Amoureux. Reflexivity in Arendt can certainly be characterized as the two-in-one of solitary thought; but a less self-referential version comes out of Arendt's appreciation for Kantian publicity which indicates how thought depends on the presence of others to be possible at all. Kant argues that since we always think in community with others with whom we communicate, to be deprived of the freedom of speech and writing is also to have *the freedom of thought* removed (Kant 1991, p. 247; Arendt, 1982, pp. 40–41). Reflexivity in this alternative Kantian mode not only unites intellectual freedom and civil freedom, but ties the conditions for the full respect for human dignity to the gradual acceptance of this reciprocal relationship on the part of governments as well. This suggests that a research program dedicated to the political and cultural extension of reflexivity will need to be committed to highlighting and defending those organized political movements (like Occupy Wall Street) and cultural practices (like Greek tragedy) that help a group of people to resist and overcome the collective delusions that it always feeds itself.

The writings of John Dewey are especially suggestive here because he aligned the endurance of democracy to the spread of a scientific attitude in relation to practical political problems (Dewey 1993; see also Anderson 2006). For Dewey, neither legitimate democratic institutions nor the preservation of an experimentalist scientific attitude on their own were sufficient for sustaining a democratic culture capable of responding effectively to social and political problems. The aim for Dewey was to infuse democratic practices of pluralistic public discussion and opinion formation with a spirit of scientific experimentalism and to open the practices of science to the spirit of democratic accountability. A model of reflexivity that takes its philosophical and practical cues from Dewey would seek to institutionalize fallibilism and a spirit of open experimentalism by emphasizing the epistemic and political significance of intellectual and cultural pluralism, extensive public communication across multiple forms of diversity, and frequent critical feedback on, and accountability for, the production of knowledge claims. A pragmatist model of reflexivity thus calls for scholars to enrich and support the epistemic powers of democracy both within and outside the academy as a primary condition for their own intellectual development. Translated into a more critical-analytic framework this model of reflexivity would direct scholars to examine the degree to which institutions and customary social scientific practices either facilitate or impede those features (like intellectual pluralism, free and open communication, and frequent feedback) that are among the necessary conditions for a genuinely *social mode of reflexivity.*

If we applied this test to the field of international relations—and to the chapters in this volume in particular—we might discern a set of countervailing trends. On the one hand, the fact that a volume like this exists is an important development in its own right. All of the chapters in this volume bear testimony to the vital commitment—necessary for any empirically progressing research program (Lakatos 1970)—to improve our understanding of international relations through a critical confrontation with the theories, methods, and concepts that ineluctably enable and constrain the study of world politics. On the other hand, I have argued that the predominant model of reflexivity at work in this volume has been overwhelmingly and unduly Cartesian in its embrace of reflexivity as an intellectual and ethical capacity of individual epistemic agents. In this sense, my contribution to this volume has been an attempt to apply the principle and practice of reflexivity to itself. I have done so out of the Nietzschean-inspired worry that the scholars assembled here (including this one) have not yet sought themselves. Like the subjects in a psychology experiment, we human beings preternaturally think that we can account for and correct our own cognitive biases, including our faith in the self-redemptive features of reflexivity. Nonetheless, the fact that a political theorist has been invited to offer this critique to a group of international relations scholars suggests that the kind of intellectual pluralism, open communicative exchange, and critical feedback that I have argued are constitutive of a genuinely social model of reflexivity is a message this is not without some (limited) purchase today.

Note

1 I discuss these findings and their meaning for political ethics at greater length in Button (2015).

References

Ahlstrom-Vij, K., 2013. Why We Cannot Rely on Ourselves for Epistemic Improvement. *Philosophical Issues*, 23, 276–296.

Anderson, E., 2006. The Epistemology of Democracy. *Episteme*, 3, 8–22.

Arendt, H., 1982. *Lectures on Kant's Political Philosophy*, R. Beiner, ed., Chicago, IL: University of Chicago Press.

Button, M.E., 2015. *Political Vices*. New York: Oxford University Press.

Descartes, R., 1969. *Meditations on First Philosophy*. In: M.D. Wilson, ed., *The Essential Descartes*. New York: Meridian.

Dewey, J., 1993. *The Political Writings*, D. Morris and I. Shapiro, eds, Indianapolis, IN: Hackett Publishing.

Ehrlinger, J., Gilovich, T., and Ross, L., 2005. Peering into the Bias Blind Spot: People's Assessments of Bias in Themselves and Others. *Personality and Social Psychology Bulletin*, 31, 680–692.

Frankfurt, H.G., 1971. Freedom of the Will and the Concept of a Person. *The Journal of Philosophy*, 68, 5–20.

Frantz, C.M. and Janoff-Bulman, R., 2000. Considering Both Sides: The Limits of Perspective Taking. *Basic and Applied Social Psychology*, 22, 31–42.

Gadamer, H.G., 1994. *Truth and Method*, translated by J. Weinsheimer and D.G. Marshall. New York: Continuum.

Goldman, A., 1999. *Knowledge in a Social World*. New York: Oxford University Press.

Kant, I., 1959. *Foundations of the Metaphysics of Morals*, translated by L.W. Beck. Indianapolis, IN: Bobbs-Merrill.

Kant, I., 1991. *Political Writings*, H. Reiss, ed., Cambridge: Cambridge University Press.

Kenyon, T., 2014. False Polarization: Debiasing as Applied Social Epistemology. *Synthese*, 191, 2529–2547.

Kornblith, H., 2012. *On Reflection*. Oxford: Oxford University Press.

Korsgaard, C.M., 1996. *The Sources of Normativity*. Cambridge: Cambridge University Press.

Kunda, Z., 1999. *Social Cognition: Making Sense of People*. Cambridge, MA: MIT Press.

Lakatos, I., 1970. Falsification and the Methodology of Scientific Research Programmes. In: I. Lakatos and A. Musgrave, eds, *Criticism and the Growth of Knowledge*. Cambridge: Cambridge University Press.

Nietzsche, F., 1969. *On the Genealogy of Morals*, translated by W. Kaufmann. New York: Vintage Books.

Nietzsche, F., 1974. *The Gay Science*, translated by W. Kaufmann. New York: Vintage Books.

Nisbett, R.E. and Wilson, T.D.C., 1977. Telling More than We Can Know: Verbal Reports on Mental Processes. *Psychological Review*, 84, 231–259.

Pronin, E. and Kugler, M.B., 2007. Valuing Thoughts, Ignoring Behavior: The Introspection Illusion as a Source of the Bias Blind Spot. *Journal of Experimental Social Psychology*, 43, 565–578.

Pronin, E., Lin, D.Y., and Ross, L., 2002. The Bias Blind Spot: Perceptions of Bias in Self Versus Others. *Personality and Social Psychology Bulletin*, 28, 369–381.

Rosanvalon, P., 2011. *Democratic Legitimacy: Impartiality, Reflexivity, Proximity*, translated by A. Goldhammer. Princeton, NJ: Princeton University Press.

Sosa, E., 2009. *Reflective Knowledge: Apt Belief and Reflective Knowledge*, Volume II. Oxford: Oxford University Press.

Tversky, A. and Kahneman, D., 1974. Judgment under Uncertainty: Heuristics and Biases. *Science*, 185, 1124–1131.

Weber, M., 1946. Politics as a Vocation. In: H.H. Gerth and C.W. Mills, trans. *From Max Weber: Essays in Sociology*. New York: Oxford University Press.

Conclusion

Iver B. Neumann

LONDON SCHOOL OF ECONOMICS AND THE NORWEGIAN INSTITUTE
OF INTERNATIONAL AFFAIRS.

In 1995, the annual gathering of the different study circles at select universities that made up The Nordic Summer University took place in Iceland. One of our guests, Slavoj Zizek, opened his first lecture by noting how, in the days of Freud, psychoanalysts would be busy interpreting dreams about slashing one's way through roses and ivy in order to enter closely guarded castles. These days, on the other hand, they will pop up and tell the psychoanalyst about dreams of moats and castles and ask "Doctor, why am I having these banal Freudian dreams?" The people we study seem, on average, to be increasingly reflexive. Of course social analysis should be interested.

The introduction lays out three different meanings of the term. These are a) thought: self-situatedness, where scholars themselves reflect on what they are doing, why they are doing it and what effects that may accrue; b) action: as a being-in-the-world, and c) writing: as an intersubjective practice of critique of the work of scholarly writings, be that one's own or those of others. Hannah Arendt, who is a major source of inspiration for this volume, thought that the *via activa* and the *via contemplativa* were two different ways of being in the world. I think otherwise. Politics may use anything, even the most obscure scholarly writing, as a lesser language. Given the knowledge/power nexus, there is no place where contemplation can take place independently of politics. No thinking is above reproach. To take but one example, during the run-up to the Second World War, Danish sociologist Svend Ranulf (1939) charged Durkheimian thinking on collective consciousness with being a forerunner of fascism. Marcel Mauss, always the reflexivist, answered the reproach by stating that it had been a "true tragedy" for Durkheimians that they had not thought through how their thinking dovetailed nicely with Nazi celebrations of the collective, and gave as his reason that they simply had not foreseen how humans in complex societies would be as entranced by propaganda "as are the Australians by their dances" (quoted in Ranulf 1939, p. 32). As Arendt's own life amply demonstrates, there is no necessary difference between contemplation and action. If we think of scholarly writing as a kind of action, and I do, then we may conflate b) and c). Indeed, in Chapter 1, Amoureux himself does so when he notes how IR has primarily been interested in reflexive thought processes accompanying research (a above), rather than in the lived reflexivity, or lack thereof, of the practitioner (b above) *and* the scholar (c above).

The volume's main message seems to me to be that we have given rather too much attention to reflexiveness as self-situatedness, and too little to reflexiveness as practice. I concur, and kudos to the authors for beginning to rectify that situation. I must also add, however, that I think we should see both these two types of reflexiveness as relevant, and also as complementary. We need self-situating thought not only for ethical reasons, but also to produce better data (Neumann and Neumann 2015). In Chapter 14, Mark Button took his cue from Nietzsche to point out that we may reflect as much as we want, but we will never "find ourselves". Only a Cartesian would be so naïve. Well, yes, in a philosophical sense, we are doomed to be unknown to, and hence stranger to, ourselves (Kristeva 1991). The incoming evidence from neurosciences to this effect is also convincing, as is the evolutionary idea of parochial altruism and, to hark back a bit, a psychological need for cognitive consistency. This volume, however, is not a volume of philosophy (although philosophy does play its appropriate role as a supporting discipline), but rather a volume of social analysis. A more appropriate measuring stick than Nietzsche himself may, therefore, be a Nietzschean who did theoretically informed social analysis, namely Foucault, who once noted that the main problem that he saw was not that people do not think about what they do, or not even why they do it, but that so few people gave any thought to what that which they do, does. Button is right to highlight the limits of autobiography, but he does, I think, overlook how the psychological and the social are intertwined and complement one another. Yes, it is very hard to become aware of, let alone overcome, one's biases by cognitive work alone. The social usually has to intrude. Without cognitive work, however, one is neither primed for taking in social corrections to what one does, and neither is one able to translate social corrections into new ways of thinking. The two kinds of reflexivity in play here complement, even presuppose, one another. A number of the chapters on practitioner reflexivity bear this out empirically.

Two particularly interesting practices in this regard are prudence and parrhesia—fearless, truth-telling speech. Gould's exposition of prudence as a reflexive practice is a fine contribution to practice work in IR that succeeds in theorizing what practitioner reflexivity is supposed to mean. It could have been used more extensively by the contributors who look at that phenomenon. Ilieva's and Steele's chapters on parrhesia speak directly to the ever-present power dimension of knowledge, and they remind us that thought reflexivity at some point will have to give way to action reflexivity in order to be politically effective. The moment of decision may, *pace* Kierkegaard, be madness, but there is, as the earthy American idiom has it, a time to shit or get off the pot and try truth-telling. When one does, courage is hardly enough. When historian David Irving questions the existence of the holocaust, it is certainly courageous, given that he challenges not only his colleagues but also the world, but is it parrhesia? No. The truth-claim comes up

against so many immediately obvious problems (material, visual and documentary evidence, thousands of often mutually independent eyewitness
reports etc.) that it is very hard to see this as truth-telling at all. If parrhesia is
one person's truth, the onus is on the parrhesiast to live down alternative, and
by definition more dominating, truths. As social scientists, we should therefore expect a number of seemingly parrhesiastic interventions not to be such,
most of the rest to be non-starters, and most of the remaining ones to fail.
That is no argument against trying—the obligation loses none of its power for
being a hard one to handle—but it means that a parrhesiast who is surprised
when parrhesia does not work and the danger that is invariably involved
becomes real has not really been thinking things through. There is a lack of
reflexivity involved if one thinks there is no price to pay for parrhesia.

Ilieva concludes her reading of the academic debate over the Human Terrain System, where anthropologists were used by the American military to
garner information about the enemy's social organization, by stating that
those who went for outright rejection and condemnation of this program
simply went for a withdrawal from the political. Perhaps it is no coincidence
that this debate is finally coming to the fore in the year of 2015, as the fist-
pumping baby boomer high modernists reach the traditional goodbye-age of
70. It is certainly no coincidence that the one person who is most often
involved in this volume as a model parrhesiast is Edward Said, who was neither a fist-pumper, nor a high modernist, nor a baby-boomer. He showed
where he stood, he spoke clearly, and—and this is, I think, the crucial part—
he left room for the criticized party to answer. A scholar who leaves no room
for answering, is by definition part of the discourse police. Pointing out cases
of this, as does Steele in regard to scholars who served as propagandists for
George W. Bush, is indeed an important reflexive job. By the same token, if
such interventions leave no room for the accused to answer, they fail as
intellectual interventions and become exclusively political. I think the discipline has much to learn in this regard, and the conversation on reflexivity
that this volume has certainly propelled forward is a particularly promising
one within which this may happen.

References

Kristeva, J., 1991. *Strangers to Ourselves*. New York: Columbia University Press.
Neumann, C.B. and Neumann, I.B., 2015. Uses of the Self: Two Ways of Thinking
    about Scholarly Situatedness and Method. *Millennium*, 43(3).
Ranulf, S., 1939. Scholarly Forerunners of Fascism. *Ethics*, 50(1), 16–34.

Index

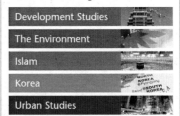